A GARLAND SERIES

THE RISE OF URBAN BRITAIN

A Collection of
Thirty-five Important Titles
Documenting This Major Transformation
and the Responses to It

Edited by
LYNN HOLLEN LEES
University of Pennsylvania
and
ANDREW LEES
Rutgers University

Municipal Life and Government in Germany

William Harbutt Dawson

Garland Publishing, Inc.
New York & London
1985

For a complete list of the titles in this series
see the final pages of this volume.

This facsimile has been made from a copy in
the Library of Congress.

Library of Congress Cataloging-in-Publication Data

Dawson, William Harbutt, 1860–1948.
Municipal life and government in Germany.

(The Rise of urban Britain)
Reprint. Originally published:
London ; New York : Longmans, Green, 1914.
Includes bibliographical references and index.
1. Municipal government—Germany.   2. Municipal
finance—Germany.   3. Cities and towns—Germany.
I. Title.   II. Series.
JS5431.D28   1985   352'.0072'0943   84-48286
ISBN 0-8240-6288-4 (alk. paper)

The volumes in this series are printed on
acid-free, 250-year-life paper.

Printed in the United States of America

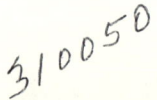

JS
5431
.D28
1985

MUNICIPAL LIFE AND GOVERNMENT IN GERMANY

MUNICIPAL LIFE AND GOVERNMENT IN GERMANY

BY

WILLIAM HARBUTT DAWSON

AUTHOR OF "THE EVOLUTION OF MODERN GERMANY," "GERMANY AND THE GERMANS," "SOCIAL INSURANCE IN GERMANY," ETC. ETC.

WITH APPENDICES

LONGMANS, GREEN AND CO.
39 PATERNOSTER ROW, LONDON
FOURTH AVENUE & 30TH STREET, NEW YORK
BOMBAY, CALCUTTA, AND MADRAS
1914

PREFACE

THE completion of this book realises a long-cherished wish and intention the fulfilment of which, owing to many reasons, has repeatedly been deferred. In various writings on German life and institutions, now covering a period of just twenty-five years, I have touched upon isolated aspects of the subject of municipal government. Now, for the first time, I have the satisfaction of dealing with the subject systematically, and so of giving to it, as I trust, a treatment worthier of its importance. The actual work of writing has been spread over four years.

The book, as its title explains, is concerned solely with questions of urban administration, yet without the limitation which the use of the word "municipal" might seem to suggest. The larger German cities and towns correspond for all practical purposes to the municipalities of the United Kingdom, as the smaller German towns correspond to our urban districts; hence it has appeared to me justifiable to consider convenience rather than strict historical and technical accuracy in the use of the terms "municipality" and "municipal," and to follow common wont in applying these terms to urban organisations, institutions, and activities generally, irrespective of the question of incorporation as understood in this country.

On the subject of sources, a special remark needs to be made. This is not a book written from books, though German literature has, of course, been freely used. A picture of German self-government derived merely from the study of laws and commentaries would be not only inadequate but misleading. A true picture must be drawn from the life, and whatever value this book may possess is due to the fact that it shows German municipal authorities as they actually are, and engaged in the practical day-to-day tasks of local administration.

Several facts should emerge definitely and clearly from this story of the life and government of German towns if it has been told successfully.

One is the far wider range of administrative powers which the German towns possess and exercise as compared with the towns—even the large incorporated cities—of the United Kingdom. This fact is illustrated by almost every chapter, and need not be enlarged upon in this place, but municipal workers will find the fact itself, and still more its explanation, deserving of more than passing thought. If it be true that the average English citizen has little idea of the degree to which the authorities which govern him are bound fast in legal fetters, it must also be confessed that these authorities themselves show a strange disposition to accept their fate as natural and inevitable. In the development of its system of urban government Germany followed principles so elastic and so accommodating that its municipalities have been able to cope with their growing responsibilities with surprising ease and facility. Impressed by the larger autonomy enjoyed by German towns, I have even dared to ask the question, whether in this country—the proverbial home of free institutions—we yet really understand what true self-government means? The reader must answer that question for himself after weighing the evidence offered for his guidance.

Stress has also been laid on the important and almost dominant position occupied in German local government by the permanent official and expert. In emphasising its respect for systematic training and special knowledge in that domain, however, Germany is merely carrying out a principle which rules in every other department of its national life. I am duly conscious of the fact that the setter forth of strange gods, that belong not to the national pantheon, is guilty of the worst kind of sacrilege. Yet I do not forget that an investigation which leads to no clear conclusions is like an uncompleted syllogism; it may affirm interesting propositions, but its main purpose is not fulfilled. Hence the candid avowal of my conviction that, while German municipalities can teach us little or nothing worth learning in regard to the electoral basis of local government or the constitution of the town councils, their institutions of the professional and salaried mayor and aldermen represent the highest and most efficient development of municipal organisation reached in any country.

Most Englishmen at heart prefer the worst of amateurs to the best of experts, and would rather be wrong with the one than right with the other. They will long persist in that preference, and will long cling to the honest belief that the country's greatness is based upon it. Frankly recognising, therefore, the impossibility of carrying all my readers with me on this question, I shall be satisfied if what is said in these pages should serve to secure for the German system of administration by trained officials greater consideration than it has yet received.

It would assuredly be unwise, even if it were possible, to imitate the German system in any indiscriminate and wholesale fashion. Nevertheless, many of those readers whose opposition to that system is rooted in a stubborn prejudice against what is vaguely called "bureaucracy" may be reassured if they remember that "bureaucracy" means different things in different countries, and that bureaucratic abuses seldom threaten and can never prevail where there exist a wholesome public opinion and a vigorous public spirit.

CONTENTS

CHAPTER I
THE TRADITION OF SELF-GOVERNMENT

Rise of the towns in mediæval times—Decay of the towns in the era of absolutism—Stein's municipal reforms in Prussia—The revisions of Stein's Municipal Ordinance—Municipal constitutions of the other States . 1

CHAPTER II
ADMINISTRATIVE POWERS

The status and connotation of towns—Principles of local administration—Range of obligatory and permissive functions—Powers reserved by the State: the Police authority—State control over education—General scope of State supervision 29

CHAPTER III
CONSTITUTION OF TOWN COUNCILS

The franchise and mode of election—The "Three-class" system of election and plural voting—Eligibility of electors and the privilege of houseowners—Procedure at elections—Working-men on municipal authorities . 58

CHAPTER IV
DISTRIBUTION OF ADMINISTRATIVE POWERS—TOWN COUNCIL, EXECUTIVE AND MAYOR

Position of the town councils—Organisation and constitution of the executive—Functions of the executive—The mayor and his functions—The "magisterial" and "mayoral" executive systems compared—Devolution of administrative duties: Deputations, Commissions, etc.—Honorary service in communal administration—The administrative staffs—Schools for communal government—Municipal congresses and leagues—Joint administrative boards for common purposes—State supervision and control 81

CHAPTER V
LAND POLICIES

Extent of land owned by the towns—Communal estate as a source of revenue—Influence of land policies upon municipal development—Sale of public land for housing schemes 123

CONTENTS

CHAPTER VI

THE PLANNING OF TOWNS

The modern town plan—Alignment plans and building permits—Special taxation of building sites and betterment contributions—Power to expropriate landowners and to pool properties—Protecting the streets against disfigurement—Administrative area of German towns—The modern incorporation movement 141

CHAPTER VII

HOUSING POLICIES

Character of the housing problem in German towns—The evil of land and house speculation—Remedial measures adopted by the communes—The reaction in favour of small houses—Miscellaneous administrative measures—Erection of houses by local authorities—Public assistance to building societies—Municipal inspection of dwellings—Municipal house registries—Building regulations 161

CHAPTER VIII

PUBLIC HEALTH

Public health authorities—The public hospital system—Inspection of foods and drinks—Sewerage, drainage, and scavenging—Public swimming baths—Parks, gardens, and recreation and sports grounds—Municipal cemeteries and crematoria 189

CHAPTER IX

TRADING ENTERPRISES

The old German tradition—The modern revival of municipal trading—The system of concessions combined with royalties—Scope of modern municipal enterprise—Revenue and profits from trading enterprises—Gas supply—Electric light and power works—Water supply—Tramways and transport—Docks and quays—Furtherance of trade and industry—Public abattoirs, market halls, and food supply—Municipal savings banks—Mortgage and rent-charge banks—Insurance enterprises—Miscellaneous trading enterprises—The execution of public works: *régie* versus contract—Municipal workpeople: conditions of employment . . . 208

CHAPTER X

RELIEF OF THE POOR

Characteristics of the German poor relief system—Organisation of the poor relief authority—The Elberfeld system of poor relief—Character of assistance given—Assistance in return for work—Forced labour houses for workshies and loafers—Cost of poor relief in German towns . . 260

CONTENTS

CHAPTER XI
SOCIAL WELFARE WORK

Scope and purpose of social welfare policy—The crusade against infant mortality—Municipal guardianship of illegitimate children—School doctors—School dentists—Feeding of necessitous children—Children's care centres—The crusade against tuberculosis—Convalescent homes—Municipal lodging-houses for single men—Municipal labour registries—Assisted unemployment insurance funds—Public works for the unemployed—The poor man's lawyer—Municipal pawnshops—Miscellaneous welfare work . 279

CHAPTER XII
INTELLECTUAL LIFE

Public libraries and reading-rooms—Primary schools—Secondary schools—Continuation and technical schools—Municipal expenditure on education—The drama and music 311

CHAPTER XIII
MUNICIPAL FINANCE

Sources of municipal revenue—The budget—Borrowing powers and loans—Extent of communal indebtedness—Improvement of municipal credit facilities—Balance sheets of municipal authorities . . . 337

CHAPTER XIV
MUNICIPAL TAXATION. I.—THE LOCAL INCOME TAX

Local autonomy in taxation—Variety and incidence of local taxes—Individual basis of taxation—Communal taxation in Prussia—Principles governing the choice of taxes—The local income tax—Relief to small incomes—Local income taxes in the other States 362

CHAPTER XV
MUNICIPAL TAXATION (*continued*). II.—THE REAL ESTATE TAXES

The land and building taxes—Property transfer tax—Unearned increment tax—"Betterment" taxes or special assessments . . . 386

CHAPTER XVI
MUNICIPAL TAXATION (*continued*). III.—TRADE, CONSUMPTION, AMUSEMENT, AND OTHER TAXES

The trade tax—Tax on large stores—Consumption taxes (entrance dues and excise duties)—Amusement taxes—Miscellaneous local taxes—Church taxes 403

CONTENTS

CHAPTER XVII

MUNICIPAL TAXATION (*continued*). IV.—CORRELATION AND YIELD OF LOCAL TAXES

Disparity in local taxation—Relative yield of local taxes—Taxation of real estate in Prussia—Relative local taxation in Germany and England . 419

CHAPTER XVIII

SURVEY AND COMPARISON

Modern reform movements—Constitution of local authorities—Derivation of duties and powers—Scope of administration—Systems of local taxation—External supervision and control—Concluding remarks . . . 435

APPENDICES

I.—Organisation for purposes of local government in Germany 461

II.—Regulations of municipal land funds . . . 468

III.—By-laws relating to betterment contributions . . 473

IV.—Town planning and expropriation legislation of Germany 476

V.—Agreement for the erection and sale of working-class dwellings by the municipality of Jena . . . 484

VI.—Rules of the municipal legal advice office at Nuremberg 489

VII.—Municipal theatre regulations of Halle (the subsidy system) 491

VIII.—Municipal reform programmes 496

Index 501

MUNICIPAL LIFE AND GOVERNMENT IN GERMANY

CHAPTER I

THE TRADITION OF SELF-GOVERNMENT

Rise of the towns in mediæval times—Decay of the towns in the era of Absolutism—Stein's municipal reforms in Prussia—The revisions of Stein's Municipal Ordinance—Municipal Constitutions of the other States.

IT is the purpose of this book to explain the organisation and scope of municipal government in Germany, and to follow its actual workings in the life of the communities of to-day. Often, however, the present is only understood by the past, and to its problems the past sometimes holds the key. This is pre-eminently the case with the government of German towns, and hence a brief historical survey of the subject seems essential. Such a survey must at least bring into prominence the early tradition of self-government, must trace the vicissitudes through which the towns passed, from their rise to independence in the middle ages to their fall during the period of absolute sovereignty, and must show the profound significance of the great municipal reform—the charter of rights of modern German towns—which was introduced in Prussia by Stein at the beginning of the nineteenth century, and which set all Germany on a new path of municipal development.

For the purpose of a review confined within limits so narrow, three periods in the history of German towns may be fixed. The first may be held to cover the second half of the middle ages, down to the Reformation, during which period the towns gradually gained a position of unexampled freedom and autonomy. The second period covers the two centuries which witnessed the ascendency of the doctrine of absolute sovereignty and the decadence of the towns, culminating in their lowest degradation at the time of Germany's subjugation by Napoleon. The third period dates from the municipal and agrarian reforms of Stein, and embraces not only the political regeneration of Germany, but the rebirth of the towns, which have won back much of their olden independence, and have gained more than their olden prestige and prosperity.

The current of municipal history did not, of course, continue unbroken in any one of the periods indicated; the towns experienced many oscillations of fortune; within each period times of progress alternated, locally if not generally, with times of reaction; yet the foregoing epochs synchronise with certain broad streams of tendency and they may serve our purpose.

RISE OF THE TOWNS IN MEDIÆVAL TIMES.—A history of German municipal life would carry us back to the early centuries, when many of the Roman camps and colonies on the Rhine and other rivers formed the nuclei of towns. For the most part these towns were destroyed by the German tribes who contested the Roman occupation, though they were rebuilt at a later date and still remain, the most ancient survivals of urban organisation. A more definite point of departure would be the tenth century, to which fell the reign of the Saxon Emperor Henry I. (919 to 936), known distinctively in German history as the " town builder," because as a measure of protection against the Hungarians and Slavs he promoted the settlement of towns and freely conferred upon them important privileges.

For the halcyon days of municipal life and government, however, it is necessary to advance still farther in mediæval times. Never before or later did the towns on the whole enjoy so large a measure of autonomy as in the twelfth and thirteenth centuries. Of these centuries Dr. H. Preuss writes that " they formed one of the most brilliant and fruitful periods for the internal development of Germany, a period of great progress in intellectual and material culture, of great increase in national wealth, and in population. The two hostile forces whose contest dominated the internal history of the centuries immediately following, the towns and the princes, laid in the same epoch the foundations of their power."[1]

Long periods of preoccupation with political affairs indisposed the rulers, imperial and territorial, to give serious heed to questions of local government, or to be jealous of the growing powers and assumptions of the towns, while their continual want of money led them to barter away privilege after privilege, the acquisition of which proportionately strengthened the towns in their endeavours after independence. Often the emperors found the towns useful auxiliaries in their warfare with the bishops and feudal princes, and for friendly services thus performed they were willing to pay a good price in the bestowal of civil rights and franchises.

At that early period it was the fixed ambition not only of the large but of the smaller towns to be self-governed, self-contained and self-sufficient. To that end they sought to acquire from their rulers and overlords, often at great sacrifice, the suzerain rights which connoted a condition of dependence, —market rights, rights to levy tolls and dues, coinage rights, legal jurisdiction, and the like. Often these struggles for freedom were crowned with complete success, and many mediæval German towns became for all practical purposes States within the State. As a rule the towns determined their own forms of government, and the result was that in the thirteenth century no two towns had the same constitution; each had some feature peculiar to itself in regard either to organisation, powers, mode of appointing councils, or names and titles.[2]

Burghership[3] of one of the autonomous German cities of the middle ages often ranked higher in local estimation than State citizenship; the civic tie was stronger, the civic sense

[1] " Die Entwickelung des deutschen Städtewesens," Vol. I, pp. 30, 31.
[2] F. W. Barthold, " Geschichte der deutschen Städte," Vol. III, p. 3.
[3] The word " Burg," meaning originally a fortified place or castle, which occurs in so many combinations, and which appears in English in the old town-name " burg " and the later " borough," was the earliest German term for town. The citizens became " Bürger " (burghers or burgesses), and the head of the community " Bürgermeister " (burgomaster, or mayor).

of community more personal, the civic feeling of independence more real, than the political, in countries which were rent by feud and in which the spirit of nationality was weak and undeveloped. And so an old German rhyme ran :—

> "No man's lord and no man's wight,
> That is the freeborn burgher's right."[1]

There is no clear evidence to determine the time at which the towns became formally governed by councils and senators. Preuss writes : " The same historical obscurity and the same conflict of learned opinion prevail as to where, how, and when a council (*Rat*) was established in German towns as a civil form of government, as on the question of the origin of the town itself whose corporate constitution found characteristic expression in this institution." This writer, however, concludes that the institution of the local council was common by the middle of the twelfth century.[2] The council did not proceed at first from the citizens as a whole, but was formed by the more influential families and was composed of members of these on a self-applied principle of social precedence.

In some parts of the country thriving cities and towns combined in federations and leagues for mutual defence against predatory knights and the feudal nobility, for the preservation of peace, and for the furtherance of the common interest of trade and commerce. The most powerful of the purely defensive leagues was that of the Rhenish towns, formed in the middle of the thirteenth century under the leadership of Mayence and Worms and embracing a hundred towns, with many territorial overlords. In the following century the Swabian League similarly united all the towns of South Germany. These and other federations, in Bavaria, Westphalia, and elsewhere, were formed primarily for political purposes.

More important from the economic side of the life of the towns, and more lasting in its influence, was the great federation of the northern trading centres. Small local guilds of

---

[1] " Niemands Herr und Niemands Knecht,
Das ist des Bürgerstandes Recht."
[2] " Die Entwickelung des deutschen Städtewesens," Vol. I. pp. 28, 29.

traders—known by the Low German name of "Hansen"—had existed before, but it was not until the thirteenth century that the historic "Hansa," known later as the Hanseatic League, was formed for the systematic conquest of foreign markets. When the Hanseatic League was at the height of its power, in the second half of the fourteenth century, it contained nearly ninety seaport and inland towns in Germany, Sweden, the Netherlands, and Russia, had depots in many foreign trading centres, in London, Bergen, Bruges, Novgorod, and elsewhere, and even maintained its own fleet. From the sixteenth century onward the Hansa dwindled until before the Thirty Years' War it embraced only fourteen towns, a number later reduced to three, Hamburg, Bremen, and Lübeck, the only free cities of Germany that remain.

In spite of these alliances, however, the towns clung tenaciously to their individual independence as much in economic as in administrative matters, and jealousy for their own special trades and handicrafts led them to surround themselves with customs barriers as formidable as the walls by which they were protected against unfriendly neighbours.

But the time was at hand when the vigorous energy which had wrested independence from needy rulers was to be undermined and paralysed by internal rivalries and dissensions. From the beginning of the fourteenth century the power of the local aristocracies was seriously challenged by new forces which had risen up in all the larger towns. Already the merchants and handicraftsmen had formed themselves into corporations and guilds, and as the strength and prosperity of their orders increased they sought to obtain a corresponding influence in local administration. The struggle was especially keen in those towns in which the dominant families and factions had used their power for their own purposes. In many of these the franchise was restricted to a small privileged class; office was appropriated by usurpers without right to speak or act for the community; and often the very formality of election was abolished and the clique in power governed as arbitrarily as the overlords in the past. Life appointments and an abusive use of the power of co-optation paved the way for a sort of dynastic succession in local government. Membership of the councils ran in families, and no one without patrimonial influence had a chance of serving the commonwealth. Now the trade and handicraft guilds contested the claim of the patricians to rule, and in some towns the struggles between the rival forces were marked by great bitterness and even by violence.

For a long time the fortunes of war were uncertain, for the families fought hard for their privileges. In the fourteenth century the corporation of the rich citizens of Cologne prevented the introduction of a representative council by assuming the functions of the council itself and appointing its own members to the mayoralty and other offices. At Nuremberg also the patricians obtained complete power and long maintained it. In that town a score of patrician families claimed to fill the town council and to hold all offices. On the other hand, at Ratisbon (Regensburg) and elsewhere they were entirely superseded or were required, to their disgust, to join the guilds. At Augsburg and Speyer, the patricians and guilds came to terms and divided the local council between them. In some towns the old patrician council survived in the form of a " small " or " inner " (*engerer*) council, as distinct from the " great " or " general " (*grosser*) council formed by the guilds and able to impose its will upon the selecter body in all important matters. This two-chamber system of government is perpetuated in different forms in modern municipal constitutions. In the middle of the fourteenth century there were in Augsburg fifty-one " families " and seventeen guilds. The small council consisted of fifteen members of the " families " and twenty-nine delegates of the guilds, with two mayors, one nominated by each constituent body; while the great council represented only the seventeen guilds, each of which nominated twelve members. In most places the ultimate result of this class contest was that the guilds first gained an entrance into the local councils and then step by step controlled them.

DECAY OF THE TOWNS IN THE ERA OF ABSOLUTISM.—The acquisition of office by craft and guile inevitably led to abuses of many kinds—to self-enrichment, nepotism, and wholesale corruption; and these evils created others even more disastrous in their ultimate effects. For the citizens, cut off from intimate association with the corporate life of their towns, lost in civic pride and attachment, and their very spirit of independence became weakened. A social structure, civil or political, is only stable in proportion as it is stayed on broad and secure foundations. This condition of strength was lacking to the later mediæval town oligarchies, and their weakness became the opportunity of the princes, now eager to reassert their old suzerain rights and to regain the old position of domination.

Just as aforetime the towns had become powerful and their autonomy had been strengthened in proportion as authority at the centre became weak, so from the sixteenth to the end of the eighteenth century the process was reversed; the rulers reasserted their power and revived and extended their early prerogatives, while the towns settled more and more into the position of governed rather than self-governing communities.

Sometimes the citizens themselves called in outside help, and the princes had then a stronger pretext for active interference. For a time they made no deliberate attempt to abolish the systems of local government which had grown up during the time of their lethargy, but contented themselves with the exercise of large powers of direction and supervision. As absolutism gained ground, however, the State more and more invaded the sphere of purely local administration. Step by step the governing power was wrested entirely from the hands of the citizens and the delegated councils, and was exercised, down to the minutest details, by the central authority in the name of the ruler.

This recovery of renounced prerogatives was not, however, in all cases a mere parade of force, but sometimes followed almost inevitably from predisposing causes. The Thirty Years' War (1618–1648) had left the whole country poor, exhausted, and demoralised, its industry and trade ruined, its population decimated. Towns which had grown prosperous by successful industry or by bold trading adventure both at home and abroad were thrown back centuries in numbers and in wealth. Thus before the war began there were in Berlin and Kölln (old Berlin) 1236 inhabited dwellings, but in 1651 (three years after the peace) 1052; in Brandenburg the number fell from 1144 to 554, in Frankfort-on-the-Oder from 1029 to 523, in Potsdam from 191 to 101, in Rathenow from 299 to 153, and in Mittenwalde from 245 to *nil*. It was the same in the South. Augsburg in 1618 had a population of 45,000; in 1645 the number had fallen to 21,000. Many towns suffered still more; in some the population was reduced by more than three-quarters, while their trade was wiped out altogether.

German historians have pictured the devastation wrought upon the towns at that period by siege and sack, by sword, fire, and plunder. " For every town," writes Gustav Freytag, " there were intervals of comparative tranquillity, lasting for years, and places—no large number—which were destroyed but once during the war were able to recover. But the most terrible thing was the second, third, fourth repetition of the old misery. Leipzig was besieged five times, Magdeburg six times, and most of the smaller towns were still oftener occupied by foreign soldiers, so large and small towns equally were ruined. . . . By this war Germany was thrown back two hundred years as compared with its more fortunate neighbours, the Dutch and English."[1]

The renewal of prosperity within the sorely afflicted States was a work altogether beyond the power of local effort. Sagacious princes, like the Great Elector in Prussia, devoted themselves unweariyingly to the task of building up the lost fortunes of their lands, their peoples and towns. But with the succour which they brought to the towns went hand in hand, almost inevitably, a growing usurpation of the privileges which the towns had possessed, and now held within a wavering grasp. Liberty weighs but lightly against poverty and distress in the scale of human values, and under the prevailing circumstances the princes were able to regain without great difficulty all and more than all the power they had lost.

Absolutism conquered all along the line; and even the Governments of the City Republics reflected the prevailing

[1] " Bilder aus der deutschen Vergangenheit," Vol. III, pp. 198, 199, 235.

spirit. Just as the prince spoke of "his" subjects, so the oligarchic council of Hamburg spoke of "its" citizens, and admonished them in the best manner of the autocratic overlord. So we find that council issuing a proclamation in 1602 affirming the principle of absolutism in its purest form. "If a Government should be godless, tyrannical and covetous, the subjects have still no right to resist; they should rather regard such a condition as a punishment of the Almighty visited upon them for their sins."

The reaction reached its flood mark in the middle of the eighteenth century, by which time urban autonomy had virtually ceased to exist in most of the German territories. If local government bodies were allowed to continue, they were deprived of power, were reduced to a condition of absolute subordination, and were treated simply as committees for executing the orders of the sovereigns. More often these, through their agents, governed the towns at will, imposed and collected the taxes they thought best, and from the proceeds at once defrayed the costs of local administration and reinforced the State exchequers, yet without deigning to render an account.

Nowhere was this autocratic system carried to greater extremes than in Prussia—raised to a kingdom in 1701— under Frederick I., Frederick William I., and Frederick II. (the Great), who incorporated as no other German sovereigns the revived spirit of autocracy. The Hohenzollerns had never favoured the excessive independence of the towns. Before they became electors of Brandenburg the towns within this territory had enjoyed the utmost freedom, but with the new dynasty a reaction at once set in. Hitherto the towns had adopted their own constitutions, and the forms they chose were such as best suited their needs. The Elector Joachim I. deemed that the interests of the State would be served better by uniformity. Hence, after travelling through his lands and visiting the towns in turn, he drew up a general ordinance (1525) providing for the creation everywhere of town councils similar in character and number of members. Experience soon proved the impossibility of imposing upon the towns any such uniform system of local government, but the first step had been taken towards depriving them of the old autonomy.[1]

The later Prussian monarchy was built up by the jealous and persistent enforcement of the principle that no internal power might contest the will of the Crown and State in any department of national life. Hence, the more the monarchy was consolidated, the more were the rights and independence of the towns restricted, until by the middle of the eighteenth century the towns were reduced to the position of vassal communities.

The spirit of absolutism was never more frankly avowed than in a document of the year 1736 in which one of the War and Domain Chambers[2] of Frederick William I. laid down the relationship of that sovereign towards the government of Berlin, the capital of his young kingdom.

" That the president of the town," said this declaration of royal right, " should be nominated and appointed by his Royal Majesty is self-evident; . . . but that the *consules*,[3] syndici, and senators should be appointed entirely by the Council and then merely be confirmed by his Majesty is contrary to the maxims and constitutions hitherto governing the Rathaus system. ' Principia republicana ' bring the ' publico ' more harm than good and have long ago been purposely suppressed and abolished and in consequence cannot be reintroduced without infraction of the royal authority. His Royal Majesty and his High Councils know better than the magistracy how the Rathaus should be formed, the town governed, and the common weal be best served."

[1] Ludwig vom Rönne and Heinrich Simon, " Die preussischen Städteordnungen vom 19 November, 1808, und vom 17 März, 1831," pp. 18, 19.

[2] The principal concerns of the early Kings of Prussia were the " army " and the " domains," which formed the main sources of their revenues. In the latter part of the Great Elector's reign there were two Finance Ministers, one for each of these departments. " Under Frederick William I. the two departments were united, and a General Supreme Financial War and Domains Directory was established, while in every district the representative of the Government was the War and Domains Chamber." These chambers interfered in every department of local government, which they virtually annexed. (J. R. Seeley, " Life and Times of Stein," Vol. I, p. 48.)

[3] The members of the council or *Rat* appear to have been described in Latin documents as " consules " from the first quarter of the twelfth century forward. (Barthold, " Geschichte der deutschen Städte," Vol. I, p. 257.)

When such sentiments could be avowed so frankly there was clearly no possibility of disputing them. Frederick William I. openly declared that it was his policy in local government to appoint mayors who should be his " creatures." " In that way," he added, " I shall remain master. Otherwise I must be dependent upon my subjects, and that is not to my mind."[1]

The King even sold the positions of magistrates or senators to the highest bidders, and filled public offices with retired soldiers for whom a livelihood could not otherwise be found. Side by side with—or over—the municipal mayors he appointed military governors, who had jurisdiction over most matters of local government, e.g., building, market regulation, street lighting, cleaning, and paving, and poor relief, while the Crown directed the entire system of local taxation and finance. The theory was even set up that municipal property was State property, and certainly it often passed under the control of State officials.

All sorts of privileges and immunities were arbitrarily conferred by the Crown. The officials of the Court, State officials, and the military were excluded from the jurisdiction of the local authorities, and the King exempted from local taxation whom he would; even the court purveyors went free. Dr. Hugo Preuss estimates that early in the eighteenth century one-tenth of all the properties in Berlin were " free houses," the occupants of which were exempt from the local property tax payable by the ordinary citizens. Every community over which the ruler set his agents was thus divided into rival camps—Crown and town—with conflicting loyalties and antagonistic interests. In Berlin at the close of the century one-half of the population was exempted from the jurisdiction of the civil government.

[1] The words suggest comparison with the speech on the constitution question made by Frederick William IV. to the United Diet in April, 1847. " I feel bound," he said, " to make the solemn declaration that no power on earth shall move me to convert the natural relationship between sovereign and people—with us especially so powerful because of its inner truth—into a conventional, constitutional relationship, and that I will neither now nor ever allow a written paper to interpose like a second providence between our Lord God in Heaven and this land, in order by its paragraphs to govern us and to replace the sacred fidelity of old."

How complete was the triumph of absolutism was shown when the Prussian Common Law (*Landrecht*) came to be promulgated in 1794; for while this document confirmed the nobility and the feudal proprietors in all their privileges, including independence in administration, it declared all the powers and rights of the towns to be subject to royal grant. Thus the Crown formally set its seal upon its claim that the towns possessed no life and individuality of their own.

At the opening of the nineteenth century the form of government under which Berlin, the capital, lived was that of a semi-military autocracy. There were both a mayor and an executive of sorts, but they were not chosen by the citizens, and when members of the executive died or retired, new ones were co-opted by the remaining body. The powers exercised by the executive were unimportant—the management of public buildings and other property, the oversight of the guilds, presentation to certain of the churches, and a limited responsibility for the care of the poor. The general administration of the city—the maintenance and lighting of the streets, the provision of schools, the care of public health, public poor relief, and the rest—was in other hands, and chiefly in those of authorities or individuals appointed by the Crown and responsible to it alone.

Not only in Berlin, however, but everywhere local initiative and responsibility had been reduced to a shadow.

"The spirit of distrust which prevails throughout the Prussian system of State administration," wrote the Königsberg Police Director Frey, " has heaped control upon control, and has led to the affairs of the communes being brought under the same system. Everything, however trivial it may be, must be examined by the authority above, everything must be there decided, everything be there ordered."

It was the custom of Napoleon when he found German towns without a representative government promptly to call one into existence, and set it in the place of the agents of the Crown. Accordingly when, after the battle of Jena (October, 1806), which completed the collapse of Prussia, Napoleon entered Berlin, he abolished the military and Crown government of the city and created a civil authority called the *comité administratif*, which was elected by a constituent body of sixty delegates chosen by 2000 of the most substantial citizens. The sixty hoped that they were intended to act as a deliberative assembly, but such was not Napoleon's intention; having chosen his committee they were not called together again. On the other hand, the *comité administratif* remained in office for two years. In some other towns Napoleon introduced the French system of municipal government by mayor and council, under which the former, nominated by the Crown, was made responsible for the entire management of local affairs.

STEIN'S MUNICIPAL REFORM IN PRUSSIA.—For the next half century the history of municipal reform in Germany is virtually the history of the system of local administration introduced in 1808 by the Minister Baron vom Stein, and copied, in its main principles, with modifications, by the other important States.

The German principalities succumbed before Napoleon and the armies magnetised by his genius for the same reason that the town governments had fallen three centuries before,—because of the narrowness of their foundations. Absolute rule, rooted in militarism, had been tried and had failed as a basis either of political or civil government, and in its abolition lay the only hope of national renewal. " The State," writes Seeley of Prussia, " seemed to have fallen in pieces because it had no principle of cohesion, and was only held together by an artificial bureaucracy. It had been created by the energy of its Government and the efficiency of its soldiers, and now it appeared to come to an end because its Government had ceased to be energetic and its soldiers to be efficient."[1] " The absolute monarchy, with all its unlimited power," says a German writer, "proved incapable of either creating or replacing a State or national fellowship."[2]

Absolutism continued so long as the sovereigns were strong enough to be supreme in their own territories, and when it fell there was nothing left to take its place. The collapse of the absolute monarchy in France saw the rise of a new nation

---

[1] " Life and Times of Stein," Vol. I, p. 261.
[2] Preuss, Vol. I, p. 197.

upon its ruins. In Germany nationality was only a name. In degrading the status of local citizenship the rulers had destroyed the citizen's attachment to town and State at once.

Hence it was that when Prussia's hour of supreme trial came in 1806 the people were at first too crushed and apathetic to respond. " In reducing the communes to a condition of enfeeblement," writes Dahlmann, " the nation as a whole had been deprived of power and courage ; for having been disqualified from discharging the duties of everyday life it was incapacitated from meeting larger responsibilities."[1] " Then it became evident," writes Rönne, " how many civic virtues had been extinguished, that the towns were without public spirit, that all desire to bring sacrifice for the common weal, all zeal and all love for public affairs had been lost, and that thus the surest foundation of true patriotism was lacking."[2]

So completely had the German peoples been dragooned by their multiplicity of petty autocrats, so well had they learned the lesson that the first and only duty of the citizen is to obey the ruling power, that when Napoleon entered the country they accepted the new suzerainty almost as a matter of course, and when the usurper approached their towns it happened that not only patricians and populace, but State officials and military officers, received him at the gates. So lightly may the sentiment of loyalty hold a compelled and over-disciplined people.[3]

[1] F. C. Dahlmann, " Die Politik," 1ster Band, p. 216.
[2] Ludwig von Rönne and Heinrich Simon, " Die preussischen Städteordnungen vom 19 November, 1808, und vom 17 März, 1831," p. 25.
[3] Writing of the disintegration of the Empire as formally ratified by the Peace of Luneville in 1801, Treitschke says, " The German nation bore the overwhelming blow with incredible indifference. Scarcely a cry of patriotic anger arose when Mayence and Cologne, Aix-la-Chapelle and Treves, the spacious, beautiful lands which were the cradle of our earliest history, passed over to the stranger. . . . The great majority of people regarded what had happened as an inevitable necessity, and even across the right bank of the Rhine everyone believed that Germany's western frontier had now been settled for all time." Treitschke, however, laid the whole blame for this strange national apathy to the influence of the Roman Catholic Church—to " crozier government." (" Deutsche Geschichte im neunzehnten Jahrhunderte," 1ster Theil, pp. 172, 173, 175 ; see also p. 251 for the reception of Napoleon in Prussia after the battle of Jena.)

All this story of the temporary eclipse of patriotic fervour only adds greater glory to the sequel. If this were a political history, it would be necessary to tell of the noble uprising of the German peoples, first of the north and then of the south, during the years 1807 to 1815, culminating in Napoleon's overthrow and in the birth of modern Prussia and Germany.

In the disaster which overwhelmed Germany during the years of Napoleon's domination, 1806 to 1812, the greatest losses, territorial, financial, and moral, fell on Prussia, because it had most to lose. With the battle of Jena Prussia's power was completely destroyed, and by the succeeding Peace of Tilsit (July 7, 1807) it lost all its territories west of the Elbe, with part of its eastern provinces, and its population was reduced from ten to five millions.

When Prussia's fortunes were at the lowest ebb, and its very extinction as an independent State seemed imminent, Stein succeeded in convincing the King (Frederick William III.) that the only hope of national renaissance lay in the abolition of the feudal system and the emancipation of the peasantry, combined with a fundamental reform of local government, leading up to the institution of a national parliament. Here we have to do only with Stein's administrative reforms, though, like them, the land reforms associated with his name, and in a less degree with that of Hardenberg, his colleague in the Ministry until January, 1807, were inspired by the conviction that Prussia's greatest misfortune was deprivation of liberty, and that its only hope lay in its restoration.[1]

Stein aimed at the creation of free towns in a free State. It was his belief that Prussia could only be recreated by its own forces and energies. If a new State was to rise upon the ruins of the old it must be by the co-operation of the whole nation. To him the most natural field for the exercise of such co-operation was the commune. Hence, his first task was to strengthen whatever remained of the old tradition of free, self-governing communities, to adapt the old communal system to new conditions, and to modernise the administrative organisation of the provinces. But there he did not intend to stop. Above a reformed system of local and provincial government, broad based upon it, he desired to construct a system of national government, regulated by a free constitution. Thus the nation was to be fitted for political duties

[1] The Land Edict was dated October 9, 1807, and its purpose was described as to facilitate ownership and the free use of landed property and to determine the personal position of the agrarian population. " After Martinmas, 1810," it ran, " there shall only be free men."

and rights by being first trained in the duties and rights of citizenship in town and village, in district and province.

The idea which underlay all Stein's plans was a large decentralisation of State authority, which was to add weight and importance to civic life without organically weakening the central power. So long as absolute sovereignty lasted, the hand of the State controlled all local affairs, and as these were claimed as part of the State's sphere the local authorities themselves came to be regarded as State agents. Stein wished to readjust this unnatural relationship, to rehabilitate the civil authority in local self-government, to assign to it a wide province of action, and within that province to make it virtually supreme.

The debased condition of municipal government in Prussia at that time, and with it the vastness of the change contemplated, are well reflected in a letter written by Stein to his colleague Hardenberg. "I regard it as important," he said, "to break the fetters by which the bureaucracy obstructs all human movement, to destroy the spirit of avarice and pernicious self-interest, and the attachment to mechanical forms which dominate this form of government. The nation must be enabled to manage its own affairs and to emerge from the condition of tutelage in which an ever restless and vigilant Government seeks to keep it."

While Stein was contemplating his great reform an event occurred which might have changed the whole course of Prussia's internal history. In a strong and almost violent letter of reproach, the King, on January 3, 1807, charged Stein with being a "contumelious, defiant, obstinate, and disobedient servant of the State," and warned him that unless he became more tractable he would be deprived of office.[1] The next day Stein handed in his resignation, which the King accepted in silence. The double affront was soon to be avenged. In July came the Peace of Tilsit, and in the hour of that crushing humiliation all eyes turned to the dismissed states-

[1] If the word "Crown" had been substituted for "State," the hard words might have described Stein not unfaithfully. A German writer speaks of the "divine bluntness" (*Grobheit*) and "scathing sarcasm" which brought him into frequent collision with the King. For Stein was one of the few men who dared to tell the King the truth—the things he ought to know, instead of those he wished to know.

man. Yielding to the wishes of his people and his Queen, and to the advice of Napoleon himself, the King urgently invited Stein to return. Stein magnanimously obeyed the summons, and took over office on his own terms. During the succeeding fourteen months he was at the head of the Government, until on November 24, 1808, he received dismissal again and finally left the Prussian service, the victim of royal weakness and fickleness and of the animosities and conspiracies of petty and incapable rivals. Napoleon immediately followed his dismissal with a decree of banishment from Prussian territory, but the odium of his exile was not Napoleon's, but the King's.

During his brief retirement in 1807 Stein had occupied himself with the question of local government, and his reflections were set down in an essay " On the proper Form of the Central and Provincial Councils of Finance and Police in the Prussian Monarchy." In this document he proposed a municipal reform by which the military bureaucracy was to give place to self-government by the citizens. Directly he returned to office Stein told the King that one of the first things to be done must be to reform local administration, and the King agreed. Nor need it be doubted that Frederick William was perfectly sincere in his acceptance of his Minister's proposals as right and necessary for the time, little though the prospect of popular government even for the towns can have appealed to his political instincts.

The first-fruits of the reforming spirit was the Municipal Ordinance of November 19, 1808, applying to all the towns of the kingdom, as reduced by Napoleon. It is a much-debated question how far this reform, in its final form, was the work of Stein. Stein is described by his equivocal friend and captious critic, Theodor Schön, as lacking in constructive statesmanship, yet quick to detect worth in the ideas of others and to give practical effect to convictions clearly formed. In this case Stein was clearly a borrower. Of the necessity of municipal reform he had been convinced, not only by the fact of Prussia's fall, but by the study of English local government and political institutions, which he held in great admiration ; that he used the advice, suggestions, and even the plans of

c

others when the time came for practical measures is no derogation of his genius as an original thinker and an epoch-making statesman. More than the Emperor Henry I. he deserves to be regarded as Germany's pre-eminent "town builder."

Seldom has a great measure of social reform fructified so rapidly as that enacted in the famous municipal edict bearing Frederick William III.'s signature but Stein's name. The first crude suggestion may be traced to a scheme for the reform of the local government of Königsberg, devised in 1807 by a judicial official of that town, by name Brand, and submitted by him to Stein, then Minister, and afterwards, on Stein's advice, to the King. Even more, however, Stein appears to have been influenced by another Königsberg jurist, the Police Director Frey, a man who had come under the personal influence of Kant—whose personality had dominated the intellectual life of that "city of pure reason" up to 1804—and who in public spirit and political sagacity was far in advance of his time. German authorities all agree that next to Stein himself Frey deserves the principal credit for this great reform.

A recent writer, Dr. Clauswitz, points out that the literature of the time to which Stein's Municipal Ordinance fell "contains no indications that there was then any active desire on the part of the citizens of our towns for a more effective share in the management of their affairs, and up to the present no evidence to this effect has been produced from the archives of the towns and the Governments."[1] Not only so, but no endeavour appears to have been made to sound the towns beforehand as to their wishes in the matter. When the suggestion was made even Frey himself opposed it as purposeless, believing that in the existing conditions of municipal life there would be "few people able to pass a mature judgment upon the most suitable organisation of town government; better show the dependent communes the way by which they may attain independence, without asking them whether they are disposed to follow it."

Emphatically the reform was given to the nation "from

[1] "Die Städteordnung von 1808 und die Stadt Berlin," p. iii.

above." In truth, Stein wished to create an effective system of self-government as much for the sake of the State as in the interest of the people, who were henceforth to manage their own affairs. By it the State was to gain some relief of duty and responsibility, and the people a new training in civic virtue.

The purpose of the Municipal Ordinance was formally defined in the preamble as follows: " To give to the towns a more independent and efficient constitution, to create for them in the civil parish a firm point of union, to give to them active influence upon the government of the community, and by such participation in local government to stimulate and preserve public spirit." In a word, the State was once more to stand aside and to give to the corporate life of the towns room to move and expand. As we shall see, the reform created also a strong local bureaucracy, but this bureaucracy was intended to keep in close touch with the citizens, deriving from them its authority and responsible to them for its actions.

For the beginning of the nineteenth century, and for a country whose civic life was just emerging from the occultation of absolutism, the first Municipal Ordinance was, with all its limitations, a singularly enlightened measure; even tried by modern ideas, it must be held to rank as a fine piece of constructive statesmanship, and the proof of this claim is furnished by the fact that it has proved adaptable to all the changed conditions incidental to a century of growth, and that under the revised forms in operation to-day the German towns are exercising in some directions wider powers of self-government than any other towns in the world possess.

It is worthy of note that greatly as both Stein and Frey admired English political institutions and were influenced by English political thought, the Municipal Ordinance of 1808 bears no direct trace of English influence. In all his reforms and projects of reform, Stein constantly referred to the example of this country, but it was the free spirit of English public life and institutions rather than the institutions themselves that he sought to transplant into Germany. So in the case of municipal reform, it was the free play of public opinion and the free expression of personality as he observed them in England, that he wished to cultivate; for the forms in which they should be embodied he went to the history and genius of his own nation. On the other hand, the Ordinance contained obvious traces of the municipal reforms introduced in France at the Revolution, and several of its clauses were taken bodily from the Municipal Decree of December, 1789.

Any detailed examination of the provisions of the original Ordinance would be superfluous in a book which is concerned rather with present conditions than the beginnings from which these conditions have emerged, yet a brief summary of some of the principal administrative clauses will enable the reader, as he follows the later chapters, to observe for himself how far Stein's reforms have determined the course of municipal government down to our own day.

First, the representative principle was frankly recognised. The government of the towns was to be by mayor, magistracy or executive, and popular assembly, and all were to issue directly or indirectly from the free choice of the citizens. The assembly was to be elected on a franchise which for the time was liberal; and it was to appoint in turn the executive body and the head of the community.

The old and arbitrary method of election by guilds and corporations was abolished, and the popular assembly was made eligible by the entire body of enfranchised citizens. For this purpose the inhabitants of a town were divided into (a) burgesses (burghers), or freemen, in full possession of civil rights, including the right to hold property and follow trades in the commune, and to exercise both the "active" and "passive" franchise, i.e., to elect and be elected to public office; and (b) the denizens or residents (*Schutzverwandte*), who were to be entitled to the full use of all communal institutions, but not to elect or be elected; while both classes of citizens were liable to pay local taxes on equal terms.

For the purpose of fixing qualifications for the possession of the franchise, the towns were divided into three classes on the basis of civil population, viz., "large" towns, containing over 10,000 inhabitants, "medium" towns, containing from 3500 to 10,000 inhabitants, and "small" towns with a population below 3500.[1] The right to vote was conferred upon property owners and all males, otherwise qualified, in receipt of income of at least 200 thalers (£30) in large towns and 150 thalers (£22 10s.) elsewhere, and it was stipulated that two-thirds of the members of a town council were to be house-owners. Election was for three years, one-third of the members retiring annually. Further, voting was to be secret and votes were to be of equal value.

With a view to ensuring the utmost independence for the assemblies elected, the Ordinance stated—in words taken in part almost literally from a French law of the Revolution time—" The communal deputies do not require a special instruction or authority from the citizens, nor are they obliged to account to the latter for their decisions. The law and their election are their authority, their conviction and their view of what is best for the commonweal of the towns are their instruction, and their conscience the authority to which they have to give account." The first portion of this proviso is still in force.

Municipal office was to be honorary unless a man gave his whole time to the work. Not only so, but acceptance of office was to be obligatory, and refusal to act when required was to be punished by deprivation of civil rights and higher taxation. But, again following French example, no judges or judicial officers were to be eligible to sit upon municipal bodies. Mayors and members of executives were to be appointed for six years at a time, with the proviso that if salaried officers other than the mayor and the treasurer were not reappointed they should be pensioned; later these appointments were made for twelve years, and the pension proviso was extended to the mayor and treasurer.

It is characteristic of the first Municipal Ordinance, as compared with later revisions, that it concentrated power in the hands of the representative authority. "The town councillors as a whole," it said, " control the entire administration of the municipality in all its branches." The executive

[1] In the whole province of Brandenburg there were at the beginning of the nineteenth century only three " large " towns in this sense: Berlin, Potsdam, and Frankfort-on-Oder.

was not only to be elected by the town council, but was to be entirely subordinate to it. The questions entrusted to the local authorities comprised finance, taxation, and loans, the care of the poor, of schools, and of public health, and the right to acquire and hold real estate, but all judicial jurisdiction was withheld from them. Here the municipal edict did not go as far as Stein wished. In particular no police functions were conferred upon the local authorities. Upon this point Stein and Schön were in conflict, and for the sake of peace and of seeing something done speedily, Stein gave way, accepting as a compromise the provision that the State might devolve police functions—not on the commune, as the French Municipal Decree provided—but on the municipal executive.

While thus endeavouring to rehabilitate the towns, Stein had no desire to deplete the power of the central executive unduly. Hence, a general right of supervision was retained by the State, "lest (in his words) a number of small republics should be created." Stein's memorandum, accompanying the law, stated : "The citizens are charged with the undivided administration of their communal affairs. The influence of the State is entirely restricted to supervision, with a view to seeing that nothing is done contrary to the purpose of the State and that the existing laws are observed." It was required that appointments of "magistrates" or aldermen should be confirmed by the provincial authorities, while the chief mayors of the large towns were to be nominated by the Crown from lists presented by the towns.

The Ordinance was introduced first in the provinces of East and West Prussia, in Königsberg and Elbing respectively, at the beginning of 1809. A little later it was introduced in Berlin, in the province of Brandenburg, and during the next two years it came into force throughout the whole of the diminished kingdom. Five days after the promulgation of the Ordinance, Stein had been dismissed from office. On the whole it does not appear that the electors used their new liberties rashly. The prevalent depression and hopelessness of the nation were alone sufficient to deter them from venturing upon radical changes. Often the old mayors were returned again to office, and some towns even appointed military officers

THE TRADITION OF SELF-GOVERNMENT

to important positions in the local government. The Vienna Congress of 1814 restored to Prussia the provinces since known as Posen, Rhineland, and Westphalia, part of Pomerania, and Saxony, but the King was not in a mind to make further concessions to popular movements, and the Ordinance was not at once introduced into the regained territories.

While in the eastern part of the monarchy municipal government was reorganised under Stein's Ordinance, and reflected to some extent the spirit of the French Municipal Decree of the Revolution, in the western provinces of Prussia, and in the west and south of Germany, Napoleon's municipal legislation had great influence. Napoleon had modified local government in France in the direction of centralisation ; not only were the mayors appointed by the State from lists submitted by the local councils and constituted for all purposes State agents, but the councils were neither so independent nor entrusted with such wide powers as in East Prussia. This system had been introduced in the Rhine province and in Bavaria, created a kingdom by Napoleon's grace, before the issue of Stein's Ordinance, but it was amended a little later. In Würtemberg, another of Napoleon's kingdoms, municipal reform on very democratic principles was introduced at the same time. There a departure from Prussian principles was made in that town council and executive were both made eligible, on a liberal franchise, by the citizens, who also selected three candidates for the mayoralty, from whom the Crown made choice. Town council and executive consisted of the same number of members, and all important decisions required the assent of both, but provision was made for joint sittings. In this State, too, the police authority was vested in the communes.

THE REVISIONS OF STEIN'S MUNICIPAL ORDINANCE.—The revisions of the various systems of town government which gave to them the existing forms need not detain us long, as their interest is for the most part only historical. The most critical was that to which Stein's reform was subjected, while the cause of Prussian liberty was under the shadow of the July Revolution of 1830. All the portents were unfavourable, but if the towns had enemies they had also friends, and one of the staunchest of these was Wilhelm von Humboldt. From the first Humboldt fought resolutely against the reactionary spirit which had gained the upper hand; he was jealous for Stein's noble handiwork, and resented the idea of its being despoiled by violent hands. "The Municipal Ordinance," he wrote in an address to the Crown Prince in 1831, "has for twenty-two years proved itself a beneficent law, and has become precious to the citizens. The visible evidence of its wholesome influence may be seen in the prosperity of the urban populations, in a higher civic sense, an increased participation in municipal affairs, and a greater readiness to introduce praiseworthy reforms." He apprehended, after reading the draft, that the Government proposed to restrict the independence of the communes in a way Stein never contemplated, and he warned it in particular against disturbing the relationship between town councils and executives.

Humboldt's fears for the independence of the town councils were in part realised. Hitherto the executive had been subject to the council and had been bound to carry out its wishes; under the revised Ordinance of March 17, 1831, it became the predominant partner. There was a reapportionment of administrative functions. Some were reserved for the town council alone, some for the executive, and some for joint action; but in regard to the first the executive was empowered to object, while as to the last there was always the possibility of conflict, in which case the Government would be able to intervene. The State claimed the right to appoint a commissary in the event of delay in appointing an officer needing its approval, and also to dissolve any town council which "continually neglected its duty or fell into disorder or partisanship"—a characteristically vague proviso, capable of arbitrary interpretation.

As to the constitution of the town councils, the franchise was raised, for the acquisition of citizenship carrying the power to vote was now made dependent upon the ownership of real estate of a value of from 300 to 2000 thalers (£45 to £300), according to the size of the town, or an income from a fixed trade of from 200 to 600 thalers (£30 to £90), or, subject to two years' residence, of an income from other sources of from 400 to 1200 thalers (£60 to £180), though persons not so qualified who had shown themselves " worthy of exceptional confidence " might be enfranchised by the vote of the town council and the municipal executive. Election by guilds and corporations was again permitted. On the other hand, the towns were given more latitude in regard to the number of councillors and members of the executive eligible, and the proportion of house-owners upon the councils was reduced from two-thirds to one-half, as it still remains. Salaried members of the executive were henceforth to be appointed for twelve years and unsalaried members for six years, but life appointments were allowed. While thus there were gains as well as losses, the general effect of the revision was reactionary, and when the Government tried to apply the new Ordinance to the old provinces the resistance offered was so great that the attempt was abandoned. It was, however, introduced in other parts of the monarchy, including the province of Westphalia and several Rhenish towns.

In Saxony, where a constitution was introduced in 1831, a reformed municipal ordinance, based on the Prussian and Bavarian laws, was passed in the following year. In 1831 also, Baden abandoned the Napoleonic system and adopted a municipal organisation more suited to the liberal spirit of its people, and approximating to that of Würtemberg. The Crown still claimed the right to confirm appointments to the mayoralty, but if a town chose the same man thrice its veto lapsed. The law of Bavaria was revised in 1834.

The next revision was that of May 3, 1853, which gave to the Prussian Municipal Ordinance for the eastern provinces its present form. The object of this further revision was to adjust the constitutions of the towns to the altered political conditions. But the new conditions were those of a time, not of growth and expansion in political life, but of unrest and reaction, and some of the alterations reflected the anti-democratic spirit then dominant in Government circles throughout Germany. Inspired by the French Revolution of 1848, the German peoples had similarly tried conclusions with their rulers, and had failed. No time could have been less opportune for the reconsideration of the question of self-government. Three years before (March 11, 1850) a local-government law applying to all communes, both urban and rural, had been passed, and, reflecting the liberal spirit prevalent for the moment, it introduced a number of improvements, but a short trial proved the impossibility of bringing town and country under one system, and it was repealed.

The Ordinance of 1853 applied only to the towns. The distinction between burgesses and denizens was abolished, but so also was Stein's principle of equal and secret voting, which gave place to the three-class system of election;[1] the representative body was still further subordinated to the executive; and the State reasserted much of the influence and control in local government which it surrendered half a century before. A detailed consideration of this Ordinance and of the laws which, with it, govern the administration of Prussian towns to-day must, however, be reserved for separate chapters. The new Ordinance disappointed the popular parties everywhere, and when the first elections took place under it in Berlin in 1854 so indifferent were the electors that not one in five took the trouble to vote.

In general principles the systems of municipal government at present in force in the western provinces of Prussia follow that applying to the eastern provinces, though most of them were modified in some respects by general laws of July 30 and August 1, 1883. The towns of the province of Westphalia are governed under a constitution dating from March 19, 1856; those of the Rhine province under a constitution of May 15, 1856; those of the province (and former kingdom) of Hanover, annexed by Prussia in 1866, under its old constitution of June 24, 1858; and those of the province of Hesse-Nassau, formed out of territories similarly annexed in 1866, under a constitution dated August 4, 1897. Frankfort-on-Main, until 1866 a free city, is governed under a separate constitution of March 25, 1867; the province of Schleswig-Holstein, annexed in 1864, under a constitution of April 14, 1869; and the territory of Hohenzollern under one of July 7, 1900.

[1] For an explanation of this system of voting, see pp. 64, 65.

MUNICIPAL CONSTITUTIONS OF THE OTHER STATES.—In the rest of the Empire municipal government in general follows the Prussian system, the East Prussian organisation of the executive being in force in some States and the West Prussian or French organisation in others. The towns and other communes of Bavaria are governed under laws of April 29, 1869 (the territories right of the Rhine), and July 1, 1869 (the Palatinate) ; the towns of Saxony, except Dresden, Leipzig, and Chemnitz, which have separate constitutions, under two laws (for large and for medium and small towns respectively) of April 24, 1873 ; the towns and other communes of Würtemberg under a law of July 28, 1906, since revised ; the towns and other communes of Baden under laws of November 19, 1906 (for towns with over 3000 inhabitants), and September 26, 1910 (for small towns and rural communes). In the Saxon duchies of Central Germany, urban government is not regulated by uniform ordinances, but by special local laws and decrees. Peculiarities presented by these various laws, where of sufficient importance, will be noted in the proper place.

The entire subject of local self-government is regulated by each State for itself. The diversity of political and communal life is so great, particularist traditions are so strong and so characteristic, in the various States, that the idea of imperial municipal legislation on the lines, for example, of the English Municipal Corporations Acts of 1835 and 1882 or the Local Government Act of 1894 has never been seriously proposed. The premature imperial constitution which was drafted by the Frankfort Diet of 1849 did, indeed, include in its generous survey of German affairs the " fundamental rights of the communes," but with wiser restraint the authors of the constitution of 1869-1871 left the federal States to manage their own internal affairs, even, in the case of Bavaria, to the extent of retaining a poor-relief administration at variance with the practice of the rest of the Empire. Altogether it is estimated that there are in operation in Germany at least thirty municipal ordinances, to which must be added a number of special ordinances regulating the government of the rural communes. All the main principles of local organisation and government are laid down in these statutes, but the towns are left to decide many matters of detail by local by-laws, subject in some cases to approval by the State supervisory authority.

In a country divided into so many independent political territories and jurisdictions, this separate legislation creates serious administrative difficulties, particularly in the border districts. The most confused systems of local administration are found in the duodecimo States of Thuringia, where State boundaries often meet in the middle of towns and villages. There are in that part of Germany over forty communes, large and small, in which this division exists, the two portions of the commune being subject to different administrative laws, e.g., of Prussia and Weimar, of Weimar and Gotha, of Altenburg and Saxony, of Reuss and Bavaria, of Meiningen and Weimar, etc. In some places urban properties and even single dwelling-houses fall in two States, with the result that a higher rate of taxation is paid in one part of the town than in another. Or the anomaly may take the form of a double provision of churches or schools in small villages.[1] During recent years, however, an attempt has been made to remove anomalies of the kind by exchanges of territory where the areas of conflict were of small extent.

[1] This conflict of administrative authority at times has a humorous side. In a small Thuringian village there was a few years ago (and may be to-day) a public-house situated in two States with different closing hours, so that when the earlier hour struck, the guests adjourned to a room in another part of the building and there continued their libations in due legal form.

CHAPTER II

ADMINISTRATIVE POWERS

The status and connotation of Towns—Principles of local administration—Range of obligatory and permissive functions—Powers reserved by the State: the Police authority—State control over education—General scope of State supervision.

FOR the purpose of this book only such towns as come under the special laws on the subject of urban government (*Städteordnungen* or Municipal Ordinances) enacted in the various States have been considered. Nevertheless, as the object throughout has been to offer points of contact and comparison with English municipal boroughs and urban districts, particular reference is made to the larger towns, a course attended by the great advantage that statistical and other data relating to the government of these towns exist in great abundance.

THE STATUS AND CONNOTATION OF TOWNS.—No very definite meaning is attached to the term "town" in Germany. For it must be remembered that Stein's Municipal Ordinance did not create towns or even prescribe the conditions upon which the status of town might be acquired; it only laid down the manner in which towns then existing or to be created should be organised for the purpose of self-government.[1]

There is plenty of documentary evidence of the granting of charters to new communities, emerging from a rural to an urban character, from the eleventh and twelfth centuries

---

[1] Dr. O. Most writes (" Die deutsche Stadt und ihre Verwaltung," Vol I, p. 5): " A civil parish (*Ortsgemeinde*) is a town in an administrative sense if its constitution and government is ' urban '; in other words, if it has possessed a municipal constitution always or has received it in the course of its history."

forward. But, says a studious writer, "of the origin of this particular municipal charter right (*Stadtrecht*), when, how, and where the actual conditions became crystallised in a special law and a special social structure, we know nothing at all."[1] The mediæval town, however, stood for a definite social conception—that of a more or less autonomous community possessed of certain charter rights, depending in the main upon trade and industry, and often surrounded by fortifications. Some of the old characteristics of urban organisation no longer apply; yet two, at least, are clearly marked. One is the greater independence of the towns for purposes of local government and the higher development of their civic life, and the other is the predominance in the towns of commerce and industry in various forms. As to the latter, however, just as there are in Germany towns with a population almost exclusively agricultural, so there are "rural" villages which are entirely dependent on industry.

In the past, population had little significance in determining urban organisation, so that to-day German "towns" differ far more in number of inhabitants than do the boroughs of England or the burghs of Scotland. In one province of Prussia (Brandenburg) there is a town with a population below 500, while in another province (Rhineland) a commune with 101,700 inhabitants ranked until 1910 as a village. At the last census (December, 1910) Prussia had 1276 towns, of which only 282 had a population exceeding 10,000, while 229 had from 5000 to 10,000 inhabitants, 477 had from 2000 to 5000 inhabitants, and 288 had under 2000 inhabitants. On the other hand, 106 rural communes had a population in excess of 10,000, and five of them one of over 50,000. In Baden there is a town with less than 200 inhabitants.

The International Statistical Congress regards as towns all places with a population in excess of 2000, and this definition, though arbitrary, is commonly accepted by German municipal statisticians. Above this limit of 2000, differentiation in nomenclature begins. Towns with less than 5000 inhabitants are regarded as "rural" towns, those with under 20,000 inhabitants as "small" towns, those with from 20,000 to

[1] Preuss, "Die Entwickelung des deutschen Städtewesens," Vol. I, p. 13.

100,000 as " medium " towns, and those with over 100,000 inhabitants as ." large " towns ; while of late years a new class of " million " or " world " towns, to comprise those with a population exceeding a million, a class at present containing the imperial capital only, though Hamburg will soon join it, has been recognised.

The status of a " town " is now usually acquired in virtue of population—the number varying in different States—by the grant of what would in this country be called a charter of incorporation in the case of a borough. In Prussia and Bavaria towns are given this status in virtue of separate Royal Orders, in Saxony by resolution of the Minister of the Interior, followed by royal sanction. Nowadays the status of town is not given readily in Prussia. Of 119 Prussian towns with over 25,000 inhabitants in 1910 only thirteen were created during the past sixty years. One reason for the reluctance to create towns is the objection of the circle authorities to see their jurisdiction narrowed.

PRINCIPLES OF LOCAL ADMINISTRATION.—The government of a German town answering to the description given is composed of three co-ordinate factors : the town council, the executive (differently named), and the mayor. In explaining the position which each of these factors occupies in the administrative system, attention will be concentrated upon the practice of the four kingdoms, and particularly the various provinces of Prussia. Before that is done, however, it is necessary to make clear wherein German local government consists. The characteristics of German municipal government which must chiefly impress the outside observer are the wide power exercised by the local authorities and the facility with which these powers are from time to time extended and adjusted to changing conditions.

Perhaps the first question that would most naturally occur to an English student wishful to know the range of these powers would be—in what law or laws are they specified ? Our inquirer would ask for such laws in vain, however, for the administrative powers of German towns are not specifically laid down in statutes and therein formally delegated by the

State. Reading through what are known as the "constitutions" of the towns of Prussia—the so-called Town or Municipal Ordinances—one is struck by the fact that their authors were not concerned to define precisely the duties which the towns might discharge and the powers which they might exercise. All that these documents do is to charge the local authorities with the general administration of communal affairs, so that whatever became at any time a "communal affair" fell *ipso facto* within the sphere of the municipal government. As though they had foreseen a vast development of municipal life, they refrained from handicapping the future by undue limitations. Hence it was that when the great era of town extension opened in Germany, over forty years ago, the local governments were at once both ready and able to meet their new responsibilities without any such fundamental administrative reforms as were called for in the case of the boroughs of this country twice within half a century.

It will be necessary to recur repeatedly in the course of later chapters to this unique characteristic of German municipal government—its flexibility and adaptability to new conditions. The local authorities have to govern their communes, but it is not said in what government consists, where power to govern begins and where it ends. They are authorised by general laws to raise revenue by taxation, yet these laws do not enumerate all the taxes at their command; certain traditional taxes are named, and these may be levied or not at will in the future as in past, yet if they prove insufficient the right is given to introduce or invent others, for it is one of the fundamental principles of German local government that the communes shall be able within limits to choose such taxes as they like. So, too, the authority has to administer the town's property, but no limit whatever is set to the kind or amount of property which it may acquire and hold.

The law is similarly silent upon the important question of trading enterprise; this wide realm of activity a town is left to enter and possess at will, with none to say it nay. The corporation of a great town like Manchester is compelled to defend in the highest courts in the land its claim to carry parcels by its tramways, and the power is denied it. German municipal tramways carry parcels, coals, and even (at night) coffins—anything which it is expedient to handle.[1] The corporation of Sheffield similarly goes to the High Court for decision of the question whether it can sell gas stoves, and it learns that it does not possess this dangerous power. German towns can traffic in any article by the sale of which they can promote the convenience of the community, without leave of Parliament, Ministry, or law court. In a word, where in this country the powers and duties of local authorities are set forth in statutes of the realm, and local Acts having the same force, which may be neither enlarged nor diminished, every German commune is its own law draughtsman and, within certain limits, its own legislature.

Let the town clerk of an English municipal borough be asked what powers his council can exercise, and he will point to volumes of laws and heaps of textbooks and answer that he is trying to learn but does not yet know for certain. And the greater his experience the greater will be his incertitude. For not only are the warrants for these powers scattered about in countless statutes and orders and by-laws, but nothing can be done for which there is not express legal sanction; the powers granted are often subject to a variety of interpretation, and no one can be sure what the plainest of laws means until it has been rewritten by the courts, while the bogey of *ultra vires* confronts the local authority at every turn. It is probable that almost every town clerk in the country sooner or later climbs the stairs that lead to the chambers of some noted parliamentary lawyer in London in order to ask if this thing may be done and if that must be left undone, and what is the inner meaning of terms and phrases apparently so simple, yet, in fact, beset with endless pitfalls for the unwary.

On the other hand, let the mayor of a German town be similarly questioned and he will at once answer that there is practically no limit to the administrative powers which he and his colleagues may exercise; they can do everything, in fact, that the good government of the town may seem to require. A German town, likewise, is governed by laws, by-

---

[1] In 1911 the tramways of Germany carried over 1¾ million tons of goods of all kinds.

laws, and orders of various kinds, but for the most part, they are of its own making, and together they form the " communal law" of the town.

A form of government devised on these autonomous and elastic principles enables the German States to dispense with any Ministry corresponding to the Local Government Boards of the three British kingdoms. Control is, of course, exercised in various directions, in major questions by the Ministries to which the matters at issue naturally belong, and in minor by the State commissaries who have the oversight of local government; but there is no room or necessity for State departments charged with the special function of keeping the local authorities in order, lest they should by a hair's breadth exceed the law in one direction or fall short of it in another, and incidentally of doing much of their work over again. The questions of competence and the disputes between communes and the supervisory authority which inevitably arise do not involve long protracted and expensive legal proceedings, but are determined by special Administrative Courts with jurisdiction over all matters of local government.

The difference between the German and English systems may be illustrated by the administration of the Poor Law. Remembering how in this country local administrative action upon this question is directed in every detail, from the building of a workhouse to the ingredients of the inmates' soup, by the central authority in London, let the reader contrast the position of an important English Board of Guardians with that of the poor relief board of a German municipality, which is simply a part of the general local administration, working autonomously, devising its own policy and executing it, without dictation or even advice from outside, and as free from State interference as the committee that manages the gas works or pays the salaries of the official staff.

Or the difference may be illustrated in another way. Special laws have recently been passed in this country to enable local authorities to introduce the system of school doctors, to feed necessitous children, and to plan their towns rationally. All these things were done long before in Germany as a matter of course, in every case without special legislation, and simply on the voluntary initiative of the communes themselves. Again, there are scores of English towns which would like to make known their attractions as residential places or health resorts. They have medicinal baths and springs, for example, but cannot make them known as they would. The reason is that without special powers, obtainable only by costly Acts of Parliament, they cannot expend any money on advertising these advantages. One reason why English people crowd to German baths is that the municipal authorities in these places have so persistently advertised the special goods they have to offer as to create the idea that the same goods cannot be obtained elsewhere, which is not always the case. The medicinal virtues of these places may be all that is claimed for them, but without advertising they would not attract as they do. In thus advertising themselves, German towns need no special powers or permission. They can spend what they like on what they like, and they do it.

There is the same facility of action in so important a matter as the incorporation of suburbs. Except in the rare case of two towns amalgamating legislative procedure is unnecessary, and there is not even an inquiry answering to the Local Government Board inquiries in this country. All that is needful is that the communes which desire to come together shall embody the conditions of amalgamation in a formal agreement, and directly this has been sanctioned by the Government or its agents the transaction is complete. Incorporation is, in effect, marriage before the registrar, whose only function is to witness the contract and wish the new partners for life a happy and prosperous union. The necessary costs involved would be hardly more onerous on either side were it not that communes whose absorption is desired by their larger neighbours often stipulate for a substantial payment down by way of solatium, or for partial exemption from certain taxes during a prescribed period.

So the principle runs throughout the entire administration of German towns ; except where the State has reserved special powers of intervention, the towns are as free from control from above as a German principality is free in its internal affairs from the control of the Imperial Legislature. To use a homely simile: while the German town, grown to man's estate, exercises the freedom and independence of manhood, the English town is still protected and chaperoned by its ever present and often fussy nurse, the " Board above." Realising the incomparably greater elasticity of the German system and the almost unlimited scope which it offers for any extension of functions or powers which changing circumstances may show to be needful or expedient, one is at times inclined to ask if in our own country, the vaunted home of free institutions, we really understand at all what self-government means.

The far-reaching powers of German local authorities are so little recognised or understood in this country that it seems desirable to emphasise them, and the theory underlying them, at the outset. Repeated decisions of the Prussian Supreme Administrative Court on the subject hold good in principle for all the States. " No Prussian law," runs a decision of that Court of March 10, 1886, " sets definite limits to the activity of the communes as such. The communes have a general right to promote the moral and economic interests of their members in so far as special laws may not prescribe definite exceptions. In the absence of such laws the boundary between the province of the communes and that of the State, as the higher commonwealth, is determined solely by ' local ' considerations, i.e., by the consideration that communal duties shall be of a local character. Whatever communes may do within their own province and with their own resources for the advancement of those interests, unless it is on principle forbidden, may be regarded as a communal affair." A decision of the same court of September 21, 1886, bears out this view: " The urban commune, using its own resources, may claim as falling within its sphere everything that promotes the welfare of the whole community and the material interests and intellectual advancement of the individual members. It can of its own accord establish any institutions and arrangements for the public good which serve this end. It has a general right to promote the moral and economic interests of its members, and to use the resources available for the purpose, though always—and herein is the limit the transgression of which would constitute an infraction of the law—subject to the condition that it and its organs restrict themselves to the care and representation of local interests."

It is worth while to quote the comment upon these rulings of a careful German writer on municipal government. " It is the object of urban administration," says H. Kappelmann, " to maintain the local commonwealth in a vigorous condition, to strengthen and increase its vitality, and to equip it for the fulfilment of all the duties required by a progressive age and the demands of civilisation. It is not sufficient merely to meet the necessities of the moment, but the needs of the future must be anticipated. The administration must not be carried on too one-sidedly from the standpoint of finance, but must comprehend the entire being of the communal organisation, must develop its latent powers and use them for the common good."[1]

One of the most practical advantages of the German system of local government is its unity. The whole work of administration (excepting certain functions reserved to the police) is concentrated in the hands of one authority, which, in spite of the devolution of powers to subordinate bodies, exerts complete control. For example, though the taxes levied in a German town are many, falling upon the citizens in varying number and with varying weight, there is only one taxing authority—the local council and its executive; and all taxes pass into a common fund from which the needs of the various spending departments are supplied. The same authority administers education and poor relief; it is responsible for the planning of the town, for the roads, and for sanitary arrangements, and in addition to discharging all the other multifarious duties which the widest idea of local government would convey to the English mind, it directs the social welfare activities of the community, and promotes the interests of art and learning, music and the drama, not within the limits of a penny or any other rate, but exactly in the degree of its appreciation of the importance of culture, for in regard to none of the matters specified are its spending powers restricted.

[1] "Verfassung und Verwaltungsorganisation der Städte," 1ster Band (Prussia), p. 55 (Verein für Sozialpolitik).

The effect of this unity of government and powers is that the citizen in all civic matters has to do with one authority only, and the arrangement makes as much for his convenience as for efficiency and economy in administration.[1]

RANGE OF OBLIGATORY AND PERMISSIVE FUNCTIONS.—In course of time a wide range of activities has become the common possession of all towns. Of these some are obligatory, others voluntary, and it rests with each local authority to narrow and widen its voluntary activities at will. To the obligatory functions of municipal government belong the general work of administration, including sanitation and other measures for protecting public health, the laying out of streets, the provision of elementary schools, and the care of the necessitous poor. Further duties not immediately connected with self-government are assigned to the local authorities by special laws either of the Empire or the States, e.g., the establishment and conduct of industrial and commercial courts of arbitration, the keeping of the civil registry, and certain duties in connection with the administration of the social insurance laws, the enrolment of recruits, the preparation of jury lists, the assessment and collection of certain State taxes, etc. The State also delegates to the mayors or executives a number of duties, generally of a minor order, with a view to lightening the work of the central authority in matters of local interest.

Many powers exercised by the communes are permissive, and are acquired in virtue of local statutes or by-laws—a clear survival of the larger autonomy of the distant past. For example, the Municipal Ordinance for the eastern provinces of Prussia provides for the adoption of by-laws (*Ortsstatute*) concerning " those affairs of the commune and the rights and duties of its members " in regard to which the Ordinance allows of diversity of practice or contains no special stipulations, also concerning special local conditions and institutions,

[1] In contrast to this unity of administration the case of the Yorkshire township of Wilsden—mentioned in the newspapers while this chapter is being written as " a curiosity in local government "—may be cited : " Wilsden pays rates in one urban district, is in two other administrative districts for hospital and poor law purposes, buys its gas from one town and its water from another, and finally votes for parliamentary purposes in a different area altogether."

such as the introduction of new or the modification of existing local taxes. No. definite limit is set to the directions in which this important right to acquire additional powers by by-laws may be exercised; except that the by-laws may not contravene Imperial or State laws.

Where the adoption of by-laws is proposed, the municipal executive first makes its recommendations to the town council, and before the latter comes to a decision upon them the matter is left open for the expression of public opinion. A town council may at times decide before the public has been consulted, but it does so in disregard of the strict letter of its obligation. The two branches of the local authority having assented, the sanction of the supervisory authority is necessary. Not only, therefore, can by-law powers be obtained expeditiously, but no expense is entailed. Upon this subject the deputy-mayor of one the largest towns in Prussia writes: "There are no costs incidental to the obtaining of local by-law powers. By-laws simply require the sanction of the District Committee in order to become at once operative. The time necessary to the granting of this sanction varies according to the simplicity or otherwise of the legal questions involved. Many local by-laws are sanctioned within a fortnight of their having been adopted by the town council."[1]

Far more of the permissive powers now exercised by the communes in virtue of by-laws are authorised by imperial and State laws as passed from time to time, and naturally the number of these constantly increases. Thus in virtue of such by-laws towns may establish continuation schools where the law does not make this act obligatory; they may assign

[1] Compare with this statement the fact that during the seventeen years 1897 to 1913 the Corporation of Leeds was compelled to obtain nine special Acts of Parliament in order that it might administer its area efficiently, and that the cost incurred in so doing was £64,795. Further, a House of Commons return of December 17, 1906, of the expenditure incurred by the twenty-eight metropolitan borough councils during the years 1901 to 1906 in promoting and opposing Bills in Parliament showed that the sum of £9844 was expended by twelve councils (more than one-half by a single council) in promoting Bills and the sum of £62,089 by all councils (£26,954 by four councils only) in opposing Bills. The total expenditure incurred in both these ways was £71,933. A return of the same date relating to the London County Council shows that during the years 1903 to 1906 that council expended £67,967 in promoting and £33,066 in opposing Bills in Parliament, a total expenditure of £100,973.

dangerous and noxious trades to prescribed portions of the administrative district ; they may restrict the hours of labour of assistants, apprentices, and workpeople engaged in business undertakings on the church festivals and Sundays beyond the limits laid down by the Industrial Code ; they may fix the intervals at which wages must be paid to workpeople coming under that statute and may require employers to pay the wages of minors to their parents or guardians ; they may adopt measures to protect the public streets and squares from disfigurement ; they may introduce systems of house inspection ; and towns with a population of 15,000 and upwards may adopt by-laws requiring that licences for pawnshops, inns, and restaurants shall be granted only on proof of public need. The issue of early closing regulations for shops rests with the higher administrative authorities, but the local authority must be consulted before they are enforced. Similarly, the communes must be heard before premises are licensed for the sale of alcoholic beverages where such licences are granted by a State authority.

A very wide range of functions commonly discharged by the municipal authorities are quite voluntary in character. Such are the provision which they make for higher education, since this is regarded as primarily a State affair, the various measures known under the collective term " school hygiene," including the appointment of school doctors and dentists and the feeding of the children of the poor, measures for the advancement of science, art, and culture generally, such as the establishment or support of libraries, museums, art galleries, theatres, concerts, and the like, the provision of public baths, market halls, abattoirs, certain arrangements for disinfection, hospitals of certain kinds, institutions for advice to mothers and the care of infants, dispensaries for consumptives and dipsomaniacs, and a host of other institutions and agencies of the kind embraced in the term " social welfare."

Most of the larger towns carry on savings banks and pawnshops, finance building societies, and conduct mortgage banks for the purpose of advancing to landowners and builders money wherewith to develop their property in the commune ;

they act as legal guardians of Poor Law children and children of illegitimate birth ; while house registries, labour registries, legal advice and information agencies, house building, unemployment insurance schemes, fire insurance, and trading enterprise on a wide scale belong to the normal work of progressive communes. Such a programme of duties and functions carries the conception of town government far beyond the narrow view still prevalent in our own country. " Old in history, yet young in their energetic advance," said a recent German writer with truth and pardonable pride, " the German towns are to-day the standard-bearers in intellectual, economic, and social progress."[1]

In one direction the competence of the local authorities, in Prussia, at least, is specifically and effectively restricted ; they may not in their discussions stray from the domain of local affairs into other paths ; in other words, they may not mix in politics. For a vague and ambiguous prohibition of the Municipal Ordinances, capable of wide application, is in practice interpreted in this one sense, with the result that if ever a town council should be so daring as to make representations to the Government on political questions they are flatly ignored. The prohibition, dating as it does from a remote and transitional period in Prussia's constitutional history, is felt to be an unnecessary restriction of the right of self-government. In the life of modern communities it is often impossible to draw a clear dividing line between political and economic or social questions, but the Government overcomes the difficulty by extending the ban to all matters of party controversy. For example, it is notorious that the large towns of Prussia suffer from a quite indefensible under-representation in the State Diet, though by far the greater part of the proceeds of the State income-tax is derived from the urban populations. Nevertheless, the Supreme Administrative Court has decided that a communal authority is not competent to petition Parliament for the reform of the franchise and an increase in the representation of the towns, and if petitions in this sense are sent, as they occasionally are, they are invariably rejected as unconstitutional.

[1] Dr. Most, "Die deutsche Stadt und ihre Verwaltung," Vol. I, p. 51.

In the Southern States there is not this fear of political discussion. Thus in Bavaria party political matters may not properly be brought into the council-chamber, but far from objecting to the discussion of legislative questions, whether they border on politics or not, the Government encourages the local authorities to make their views thereupon known in this way.

Not only are the latitude and power of initiative which German municipal governments exercise—and exercise, as we have seen, by prescriptive right rather than by formal legal permission—so extensive as to be without theoretical limits, but the urban communes are on the whole free from vexatious control and restriction at every turn by slow-moving and often captious Ministries of State. The "Board above" is not the terror which it is in some countries. It is possible for German communes to enlarge their spheres of activity and enterprise in entirely novel ways, and even to adopt and impose new taxes, without going to Parliament for special powers. Authority may, it is true, have been obtained in matters of this kind, but to obtain it is almost a formality; and in no case does it involve elaborate and procrastinating procedure. Even in the case of a new local tax, all that is necessary is to convince the supervisory authority of its wisdom and urgency and then, without appeal to the Legislature and costly struggles in parliamentary committee-rooms, sanction is obtained, and the tax becomes at once operative.

A particular illustration will best serve to show the facility and expedition with which important reforms in local taxation can be introduced in Germany, and conversely the almost insuperable obstacles which stand in the way of similar reforms with us. Everybody knows the controversy which in this country has raged over the vexed proposal to tax urban land values for local purposes. Resolutions and Bills have been debated in the House of Commons, and to at least one Bill a second reading has been given; the municipal authorities of the United Kingdom have held conferences on the subject; and the London County Council tried to persuade Parliament to confer upon it particular powers for dealing with the question in connection with public improvement schemes by its "betterment" taxation proposal. In spite, however, of many years of persistent agitation it has proved impossible as yet to secure legislation to enable municipal bodies to raise revenue by special taxes upon the land within their administrative boundaries, and the taxation of "unearned increment" has only been introduced as a State measure.

Germany is supposed to be a country peculiarly conservative in traditions and habits of thought, and certainly the legitimate rights of property are not less carefully guarded there than here. Nevertheless, the very principles of real estate taxation which some prominent English statesmen have professed to regard as impossible and others as dishonest have for years been in actual operation in all the large German towns, having been adopted on the proposal of the local authorities, endorsed by the State supervisory officials. There are in Germany five municipal real estate taxes, working smoothly and yielding large revenues, that are as yet unknown in this country—(1) the land and (2) building taxes, which have from the first been one of the main foundations of local taxation, and which differ from our nearest approximation in that they fall not on the occupier but directly on the owner; (3) a tax on all sales and exchanges of real estate; (4) unearned increment taxation; and (5) "betterment" taxes on property the value of which is increased by public expenditure. The last three taxes have been introduced by a local option as complete and as easy to exercise as the option to acquire gas and water works or to build a swimming-bath. These with the other customary local taxes will be duly considered in later chapters.

POWERS RESERVED BY THE STATE : THE POLICE AUTHORITY. —Nevertheless, there are certain restrictions of the powers of self-government, more indeed in the nature of direction and supervision than of absolute curtailment; and behind all State powers of control lies in reserve an *ultima ratio* more summary and powerful than the English *mandamus.* For in Prussia a town council may in extreme circumstances be dissolved by royal decree on the proposition of the Government, in which event a re-election must take place within six months from the date of the decree, and in the meantime the business of the municipality be discharged by special authorities or officials. This drastic power is seldom used.

The very wide powers of supervision and control exercised by the central executive over local authorities in England have their principal justification in the large grants made by the State towards the cost of certain branches of local government. In Germany such control is justified solely on the theory that all local government is a devolution of State function and authority. The State has renounced certain powers, but subject to the condition that it may still claim to satisfy itself that these powers are properly exercised by the authorities to which they have been transferred.

The sphere in which this devolution or decentralisation of powers has been least complete is that of police functions.

By the old common law of Prussia " it is the office of the police to provide the measures (*Anstalten*) necessary to maintain public peace, security, and order, and to avert danger threatening the public or individuals." This definition of police function, of course, goes far beyond the conception held in this country. Under it, for example, the police authority in some States claims competence in such matters as the issue of building regulations and the control of building, the regulation of public traffic, the administration of the laws and regulations affecting the sale of food, the inspection of dwellings, and the regulation of lodging-houses.

In early times the towns exercised both independent police and judicial functions. This right they lost in course of time, and Stein's municipal reform of 1808 simply set its seal upon the arrangement then existing in Prussia. "The State reserves the power to establish its own police directions in the towns, or to transfer the exercise of police functions to the magistracy, which will then exercise the same in commission. In this capacity the magistracies shall be regarded as State authorities." So ran Section 166 of the first Municipal Ordinance, and in Prussia this provision remains still in force. Under the influence of the Liberal ideas which flowered prematurely in 1848, only to be nipped by the cold winds of reaction, the first draft constitution for Prussia (December 5, 1848), as drawn up by the National Assembly, included "local police functions" amongst the larger powers to be granted to the communal authorities, but the constitution as promulgated a year later (January 1, 1850) was without this provision, and instead it asserted the unconditional right of the Crown to control the police in every department and to depute its administration to communal officers at will, always "in the name of the King."

The powers reserved to the State police authority inevitably lead to certain anomalies and to a conflict of authority which, though it may not be attended by serious practical disadvantages, is deplored by municipal reformers.[1] Thus it may happen that a local authority may build a street, yet be unable to open the street to traffic or to close it when once opened; it may build a dock or a canal, but be unable to say how they shall be used; it may build a market hall, but the regulation of business therein may be determined by another body altogether. In some of the large towns the fire brigade arrangements are in the hands of the police, though the towns bear the whole expense.

The case of Berlin and the adjacent royal residence towns of Charlottenburg and Potsdam is perhaps abnormal, but it well illustrates the practical effects of this division of authority. The Prussian Alignment Law of July 2, 1875, makes the laying down of all street building-lines in these places "and their immediate surroundings" dependent upon royal sanction, which in most cases (though by no means universally) is given or withheld by the Government and not by the Crown. On the strength of this provision, the Government claims on behalf of its royal master the right to say whether and where public monuments of all kinds shall be erected in the streets of Greater Berlin—a claim which the

[1] I have thought it right to represent the anomaly of the police system as it appears to German municipal authorities themselves. To an outsider it might appear that the grievance is more theoretical than practical. For in a majority of towns the mayor is the State commissary for police purposes, so that the functions of police administration, though reserved by the State, may be said in a sense to come back to the town through its chief citizen. Nevertheless, this view of the question does not take account of the strong sentimental objection to the existing arrangement, and of the value and importance of sentiment in such a matter a foreigner is not in a position to judge fairly.

municipality of Berlin resists, yet without power to make its resistance effective. The Government has also the power—and has on several occasions exercised it—to grant or prolong the concessions of tramway companies, or otherwise to sanction large street works, without consulting the local authority; not long ago a tramway concession was thus prolonged in spite of the fact that the undertaking was about to fall to the town in virtue of a legal contract.

In asserting the theory of State responsibility for police action on this wide basis, a Government may adopt one of three courses: it may either place the entire police arrangements of a town in the hands of its own independent staff of officers, who are in Prussia known as the royal police; or it may transfer the police authority to the municipal government, while placing at the head a Crown official; or, finally, it may confer this authority personally upon the mayor or another member of the municipal executive, who is for police purposes regarded as a State commissary. If a member of the executive other than the mayor is entrusted with the superintendence of the police, he is in that capacity quite independent of the mayor, and is answerable for his acts only to the Government. In towns which form part of rural circles the supervision of the police administration is exercised by the Landrat. At the same time all regulations issued in towns by the local police authority need the assent of the municipal executive unless they refer to measures of public security, but if this assent is refused appeal may be made to the District Committee, which has power to quash such refusal. With the assent of this Committee a District President may also annul police regulations so issued.

The theory of police control of public health and sanitation is a mechanical deduction from the fact that the efficacy of such control rests ultimately on prohibition and if necessary on compulsion, the exercise of which depends in the last resort upon appeal to *force majeure*. It is, however, contended that it is irrational to entrust to the police the purely negative function of forbidding and punishing acts prejudicial to the common welfare without at the same time arming it with power to promote public health by positive and preventive measures. The advocates of municipal unity concede that positive and preventive measures are the corollary of penalties and prohibitions, yet they maintain that such measures belong in a special manner to the province of local government and not to that of the police.

The anomaly of the existing dualism is increased rather than diminished by the fact that, while the State persists in retaining so many of the old police functions, it usually exercises them vicariously through the mayor of the commune, who must act as the State's deputy if required. The mayor in consequence occupies an invidious position; on the one hand he is the official head of the town, chosen by and responsible to the representative assembly; on the other hand he is the State's agent, so embodying in his person and discharging democratic and autocratic functions simultaneously.

Nearly all German towns with over 200,000 inhabitants have a State police organisation, and it is significant that of the seven exceptions only three are in Prussia. In the towns with from 100,000 and 200,000 inhabitants the organisation is about equally State and municipal, while in towns with a smaller population the police authority is almost invariably municipal; but the term "municipal" implies in Prussia that the local mayor acts as the State's deputy.

In those Prussian communes in which the police administration is wholly or in part in the hands of Crown officers the State is liable for two-thirds of the cost, while the communes pay the remaining third and also about one-sixth of the cost of pensions. Where the police administration is in local hands the communes bear the whole costs. In the other important States the costs of police administration where exercised by the State—as it is in the large towns—fall primarily upon the towns concerned, and the State either bears a fixed percentage of the total sum or makes a capitation grant on population.

The police question is one of the few outstanding causes of discord between large municipalities and the Government in Prussia. Try as they will to enlarge their jurisdiction in this direction the local authorities have so far failed completely. When several years ago a bill came before the Prussian Diet imposing additional police charges to the aggregate amount of a quarter of a million pounds upon the twenty-five "large towns" of the kingdom, the representatives of Berlin, Breslau, Danzig, and Posen vigorously protested and demanded that the entire police administration should be transferred to the municipalities, which would then, they said, "be glad to bear all the necessary expense." The Minister of Finance brusquely replied that they "had to bear all the necessary expense already, on which account the Government was under no obligation to bargain with them."

In South Germany the police system is, as a rule, a recognised part of local government, and is administered, like any other branch of local government, by the mayors and executives in their capacity as municipal officers, though subject to the usual oversight. In Bavarian towns police matters are referred to a special police senate of the executive, charged with independent powers. Only in the larger towns does the State exercise police functions direct. In Saxony the Prussian system prevails.

STATE CONTROL OVER EDUCATION.—Another sphere in which the local authorities are subject to unlimited financial liabilities without possessing complete administrative powers is that of elementary education. Here Government interference is at least as far-going as in this country, yet with the less justification, according to English ideas, since the greater part of the cost of primary education falls upon the local authorities. The Prussian Supreme Administrative Court in 1914 gave a decision which was intended to make clear the position of the State and the local authority in relation to education. "In determining the question whether the Government was justified in intervening in a school question it is necessary to distinguish between questions of internal and those of external school administration. The administration of internal school affairs is the business of the State. Within that province the State does not simply exercise supervision over an outside administration; the State itself manages all internal school matters. It may naturally delegate its powers to others, as to school deputations, but when the State itself acts it alone exercises authority."

To say that the State jealously guards its powers is to put the matter mildly. As the use of school buildings is regarded as an internal matter, the Government claims to decide both how these shall be used and how not be used, although it may have made no contribution whatever to the cost of providing them. The commonest conflict between the Government and the local authorities on the subject arises out of the desire of the latter in many towns to treat the Socialists as citizens rather than outlaws. The Municipal Ordinance of 1853, still in force, states that " institutions belonging to the town shall be accessible to all citizens without distinction." The intention of the statute is plain enough, but there are ways of evading it, for before parliamentary legislation came absolutism ruled and its prerogatives, though restricted in 1850, were not abolished.

The following is a common illustration of how both the letter and spirit of the local constitution are overridden. A town council offers schoolrooms to a Socialist organisation for gymnastic exercises. The supervisory authority advances the plea that gymnastic exercises are part of education and to this plea it attaches the reminder that in virtue of a Ministerial decree of 1839 no one can teach without a certificate duly issued with State sanction; such a certificate cannot be given to a Socialist body: hence the permission to use the schoolrooms must be revoked, and revoked it is. The logic of this reasoning may be admirable, but its ingenious authors forget that in the government of men and women too much logic can be a dangerous thing.

Here, again, it is in Prussia only that the State bureaucracy shows this unyielding distrust of popular movements. As in every department of government, national as well as local, a more accommodating spirit prevails in the South.

Because of the firm hand which the Government still maintains upon the schools, the two officially recognised churches, the State Protestant and the Roman Catholic, are allowed in some States far more direct influence in the form of inspection than the laity in general would be disposed to concede.

GENERAL SCOPE OF STATE SUPERVISION.—In addition to the influence which it exerts upon local administration owing to the reservation of powers, as already explained, the State exercises a general control over certain acts and proceedings of local authorities by requiring these to be submitted to its agents for sanction. In Prussia the primary responsibility for this control rests with the Ministry for the Interior, corresponding to our Home Office, but in special matters oversight is exercised by, and sanction must (where necessary) be obtained from, the Ministry of Finance (taxation, loans, etc.), the Ministry of Ecclesiastical, Educational, and Medicinal Affairs (education and also, with exceptions, public health), the Ministry of Public Works (railways and tramways), the Ministry of Commerce (docks, harbours, and navigation), and the Ministry of Agriculture (forestry, fishery, veterinary police, etc.). These Ministries do not as a rule communicate directly with the local administrations, as do the Local Government Board, the Board of Trade, the Board of Education, and the Home Office in this country, but through provincial officials and authorities, to whom their supervisory powers in most matters are for this purpose delegated.

The sanction of the supervisory authority is usually needed alike in Prussia and the other States in the case of alterations of the communal area (including the incorporation of suburbs), the appointment of mayors and other members of the executive, the making, alteration, and repeal of local by-laws, the sale of communal estate, the issue of loans, the imposition of fees and dues of certain kinds, to the special assessment of property to "betterment contributions," the introduction of new taxes, the alteration of existing ones, and to the increase of certain taxes beyond the rates specified in the law sanctioning them. The Municipal Ordinance for the eastern provinces of Prussia also specifies the sale or material alteration of objects of special scientific, historical, or artistic value, and particularly of archives, and changes in the common use of town properties, e.g., forest, meadow, pasture, turbary, etc. The State is able to make its oversight in these matters effectual in virtue of its right to require reports, to inspect documents, and to call for oral information.

ADMINISTRATIVE POWERS

It will be seen that nearly all the matters in regard to which the State asserts a right of veto—which in effect generally means no more than a right to be consulted—are either (*a*) matters in regard to which the State and the local authority are equally concerned (e.g., the appointment of members of the executive, in view of the State functions which they may have to exercise, and finance and taxation, in view of the inter-relation of national and local taxation, as will be explained later); (*b*) matters in which two or more local government bodies are concerned (e.g., incorporation proposals), or (*c*) they involve interests extending beyond the present, and in regard to which an outside and impartial judgment may be advantageous (e.g., the alienation of public property).

The right of the State to supervise the action of local authorities is exercised through officials and bodies differing alike according to the State, the special local authority concerned, and the importance of the measure requiring State approval. To enumerate the various "instances" through which the State acts, even in the case of the four kingdoms, would confuse rather than assist the reader without a detailed explanation of the organisation of local government in each of these States. It will be sufficient to say that supervision is exercised in the case of Prussian towns through the Chief Presidents of Provinces, the Government or District Presidents, and the District Committees, except in the case of Berlin, where sanction is given by the Chief President of the Province or the Government. In most cases appeal is allowed to the State official or authority next in administrative rank, and the special Minister of State to whose department the matter in dispute belongs is the final instance.

There are several ways of enforcing decisions. In the event of a mayor and executive refusing to obey an order of the supervisory authority to discharge duties incumbent on them, the authority may impose a fine not exceeding £15, with imprisonment not exceeding four weeks in default of payment, or may institute disciplinary proceedings. A fine can be repeated until the order of the supervisory authority has been obeyed. Under certain circumstances works can be executed by the supervisory authority at the cost of a commune. Finally, as we have seen, if a town council prove refractory, it may be dissolved and the election of a new council may be ordered, the Government, meantime, carrying on the administration by commission.

The extent of this delegated State interference depends largely on the degree of sympathy and the spirit of accommodation shown by the supervisory authorities and the communes in their relationships one with the other. When the State commissary and the head of the commune are on good working terms everything goes smoothly; there is a minimum of obstruction, and irksome vetoes are rare. Often, however, the attitude of a Government or its agents is obviously dictated by political considerations. Thus police powers are delegated to the authorities of some towns which are refused to Berlin, since Berlin stubbornly persists in being governed by a council which is not merely under Liberal influence, but contains a strong and an increasing representation of Social Democracy. Where Socialism in any way enters into a case of reference, the local authority may confidently count in advance on the exercise of the official veto. Hence, in Prussia appointments of Socialist town councillors to education committees are invariably vetoed, however suitable these men may be owing to education and experience, and though eligible to sit on any other municipal committees. In some cases the town councils enter silent protest against this form of interference by leaving vacant the positions which cannot be filled according to their judgment.

In some parts of Germany it might seem that the necessity for State interference in local government would cease altogether but for this perpetual fear of Socialism. The town council of Gera, two-thirds of whose members are Socialists, decided in 1911 to publish public advertisements in the widely circulated local Socialist newspaper as well as in the burgher Press. The Government stepped in and prohibited the proceeding on the ground that " the communes are part of the body politic, and for that reason must scrupulously avoid any business connection with a party which seeks the subversion of the existing social order." The curious thing is that it never occurs to the most timorous of Governments or State commissaries to refuse to allow the local authorities to collect the tainted money of the Socialist citizen in the form of taxes.

Occasionally a town resists Government attempts to thwart its will, and wins. Not long ago an interesting dispute between the municipality of Nuremberg and the Bavarian Government had this result. An extension of cemetery accommodation being necessary, the town council proposed to make provision in the new burial ground for a crematorium. Prejudice against cremation at that time was nowhere so violent as in Bavaria, and the Government on hearing of the proposal warned the executive beforehand that the expenditure of public money on such an object would not be allowed. The project seemed doomed, until it occurred to the municipal executive to ask the Government to produce any law forbidding a project of the kind or expenditure upon it in the next budget, or, conversely, requiring the Government's consent in the matter. The Government was unable, and the town set aside the necessary sum for building. This item the District Committee, in the exercise of its supervisory functions, disallowed, whereupon the executive appealed to the Courts against its action as an infraction of the right of self-government and won its case. The same disallowance by the District Committee was repeated when the town council in its budget provided the sum needed for working the crematorium. Appeal again followed with the same success. The Government thereupon acknowledged itself beaten, and when the crematorium was completed issued regulations for its use.

Perhaps the most irritating feature of this species of interference, however, is that it is exercised for the most part in relation to petty matters; and often the only apparent purpose is to remind the local authority that the power to amend and reject certain measures remains intact. At a recent municipal congress a speaker of high authority in municipal politics, alluding to the interferences of many supervisory officials, said that were they to cease, German towns " would have more self-government than England, which would have reason to envy us." Yet when the worst has been said the fact remains that irksome State control is not inherent in the law. There is no necessity for it; it is simply exercised in virtue of an abstract right, and is due to a wrong-headed belief that because rights exist it is essential that they should be used. The remedy, therefore, requires no amendment of the law, but simply the cultivation by the supervisory authorities of broader and suaver views, and above all of a greater faith in the desire of the local authorities to do well than in their proneness to make mistakes.

At the same time there are certain departments of local administration in which the warmest friends of self-government would not desire that every town should enjoy complete autonomy. So long as the preponderant representation on the councils of property owners continues[1] it is perhaps safer that buildings regulations, for example, should be issued from above, and that local taxing powers should to some extent be subject to the sanction of an independent outside authority. Writing in a German Socialist review, a well-known authority on municipal government contended that the fact that building regulations were issued by the State police authorities had "preserved the population from unrestricted exploitation by the 'house agrarians,' and that the State bureaucracy was far more free from the direct influence of the urban landed interest than were the communal authorities."[2] He applied the same principle to local taxation (as to which the Governments of most German States give a prominent place to taxes on real estate), and came to the conclusion that "unlimited local self-government would mean the abrogation of a large part of the State control and supervision that is necessary under existing social and economic conditions, to the special injury of the working classes."

While, therefore, some measure of State oversight is universally regarded as necessary and useful, it is complained that the supervision shown is often far too inelastic, mechanical and formal, and has the effect of obstructing free movement and of delaying necessary decisions. The towns can and do exercise wide powers—powers wider, perhaps, than belong to local authorities anywhere else—but they wish to exercise

---

[1] See Chapter III, pp. 71–73.
[2] Dr. Hugo Lindemann, in "Sozialistische Monatshefte," No. 21, 1910.

these powers with more facility and expedition, and, above all, to be freer from purposeless restraint in small, unimportant matters. It must be confessed that there seems little prospect of any immediate change in this direction. The Governments speak continually of the " need for greater decentralisation," but to them and the local authorities these words mean different things ; the Governments understand by decentralisation merely the delegation of duties from a higher to a lower State authority, the Government having still the last word, and reform on those lines can bring little relief to the town councils and their executives.

When the worst has been said on the subject of State supervision, however, it is necessary to warn the reader against rash conclusions and unwarranted prejudices. It may be granted that, according to all the laws of probability, municipal governments so formed and so hemmed around by possibilities of obstruction should be futile and inefficient, doomed by their very constitution to a mechanical and unfruitful existence. The fact that the contrary is the case shows how unsafe it is to judge social institutions, whose vitality and vigour depend less upon formal legal sanctions than upon the force of human personality within and behind them, by the mere letter of the statutes by which they are created and regulated.

Anyone who makes a careful study of German systems of municipal government will sooner or later arrive at a point at which two sets of impressions confront him, and seem to contend for direction upon his judgment. Rising from the study of laws and commentaries he finds, perhaps, that the picture left in his mind is that of local authorities subordinated to a rigid bureaucratic system. He is impressed by the devices which seem to have been specially created for the purpose of subordinating these authorities to the central executive, of ensuring that their activities shall in no respect conflict with the general policy of the Government, and that the old idea of the town as a sort of local republic shall not again assert itself. If his inquiries went no further he might be inclined to conclude that whatever else such authorities might be and do, they had little relationship with genuine self-government.

Turning, however, from the study of the theory of his subject to administration in practice, he sees the town governments pulsing with life and energy, bold in enterprise, executing on their own initiative policies of far-going public importance, and claiming as a right wide spheres of administrative activity which are entered either little or not at all by the corresponding bodies in this country. He sees powers being exercised from day to day and from hour to hour for which there is no specific legal sanction. He knows that the State's rights of control of which he is aware might, if applied arbitrarily, make self-government in any true sense of the words impossible, yet that wide self-government is the secret of the splendid administration of these towns.

The antinomy created by the apparent conflict of theory and practice will hardly perplex the student who has followed the evolution of German communal government sufficiently far into the past, for such a search will show that, except during the period of absolutism, when the State claimed to direct every department of the national life, the powers exercised by the towns have never been subject to hard and fast limitations, that the local government laws do not, indeed, recognise any such limitations, and that at all times the local administrations have resolutely striven to enlarge their independence, and as far as possible to take the place of the central executive in the corporate life of their communities.

"It is the object of every German town," says a recent German writer, "to become a State." This ambition, as we have seen, was often realised in the middle ages; it was rudely dispelled during the period of absolutism; yet though Stein, when he gave to the Prussian towns a new constitution and a new life at the beginning of the nineteenth century, sought to guard against a revival of the old local sovereignties, the ancient spirit and aspiration still persist under modern conditions.

Unquestionably the law offers scope for unnecessary and even vexatious interference by the State and its authorities, but defects of this kind must not be allowed to conceal or minimise the essential fact that self-government in practice

ADMINISTRATIVE POWERS

is broad and generous, because the principles upon which it is based permit of indefinite development and expansion. " Like the absolute State of old," says a recent German writer, " the modern towns are conscious of the will and the power to advance and to direct the entire social life of their citizens. Once again they are endeavouring as in the golden age of municipal life to associate economic power with the promotion of social activities, to become nursery grounds for the sciences and the arts, and centres of culture. It is in the nature of every vigorous community that it should desire to become a ' State ' and to be everything to its members."[1]

[1] Dr. Phillipp Stein, " Das Verhältniss der freiwilligen und zwangsgemeinschaftlichen Körperschaften in der Wohlfahrtspflege," in " Gemeinde-Betriebe," p. 432 (vol. of " Verein für Sozialpolitik," 1ster Band).

CHAPTER III

CONSTITUTION OF TOWN COUNCILS

The franchise and mode of election—The " Three-class " system of election and plural voting—Elegibility of electors and the privilege of house-owners—Procedure at elections—Working-men on municipal authorities.

THE representative assembly is differently named in different States, e.g., communal council, town deputies' assembly, citizens' committee, college of representatives, etc. It will be convenient to adhere to the term adopted in incorporated towns in this country, and speak of town councils. In most States the number of members of a town council is proportionate to the population of the commune. In Prussia it varies from four to 144; in Bavaria, 18 to 60; in Saxony, three to 84; in Würtemberg, five to 43; in Baden, 40 to 115; in Hesse, 12 to 42; and in Alsace-Lorraine, ten to 36. The Municipal Ordinance for the eastern provinces of Prussia fixed the number of councillors at 18 in communes with from 2500 to 5000 inhabitants, at 24 in those with from 5001 to 10,000 inhabitants, 30 for 10,001 to 20,000 inhabitants, 36 for 20,001 to 30,000 inhabitants, 42 for 30,001 to 50,000 inhabitants, 48 for 50,001 to 70,000 inhabitants, 54 for 70,001 to 90,000 inhabitants, and 60 for 90,001 to 120,000, with 6 more for every 50,000 additional inhabitants. This ratio was fixed at a time when large towns were few, and if applied to many of the populous centres to-day councils of unmanageable size would sometimes be the result. Thus Berlin might have a council of 300 members instead of 144, and Charlottenburg one of 120 instead of 72. Hence it is seldom that large towns elect to have councils of the full number allowed by law.

The Municipal Ordinance for the Rhine Province fixes a lower ratio; the number of councillors is 12 in communes

CONSTITUTION OF TOWN COUNCILS

with not more than 2500 inhabitants, 18 in those with from 2501 to 10,000 inhabitants, 24 in those with from 10,001 to 30,000, and 30 in those with over 30,000 inhabitants ; but the statutory maximum may be increased by local by-law. In the province of Hanover the number may not be less than four nor more than 24; in the province of Schleswig-Holstein not less than six nor more than 30.

The councils of some of the larger towns of Prussia are composed as follows (the populations in 1910 are given in parenthesis) :—Berlin (2,071,200), 144 ; Königsberg (246,000), 117 ; Breslau (512,100), 102 ; Charlottenburg (306,000), 72 ; Magdeburg (279,700), 72 ; Neukölln (237,300), 72 ; Stettin (236,100), 72 ; Frankfort-on-Main (414,600), 71 ; Halle (180,800), 66 ; Essen (294,700), 62 ; Cassel (153,200), 54 ; Danzig (170,300), 63 ; Cologne (516,500), 45 ; Düsseldorf (358,700) 58 ; Aix-la-Chapelle (156,100), 39 ; and Hanover (302,400), 36. Most of these councils are below the full permissible size.

In some of the other States a rather lower ratio of representation is adopted, though in them likewise the communes are grouped according to population, and the number of councillors is uniform for each group, subject in some States to the right of the communes to modify the normal ratio by by-laws. The town councils of important towns in the minor States contain members as follows :—Leipzig (589,900), 72 ; Chemnitz (287,800), 57 ; Munich (596,500), 60 ; Nuremberg (333,100), 60 ; Stuttgart (286,200), 32 ; Mannheim (193,900), 96 ; Karlsruhe (134,300), 98 ; Strassburg (178,900), 36.[1]

THE FRANCHISE AND MODE OF ELECTION.—The modern municipal constitution marks, in most States, a complete departure from the time-honoured tradition of the " burgher " or freeman, who alone was admitted to civil rights and privileges in the old German towns. Until the beginning of the nineteenth century, indeed, the unit of urban self-govern-

[1] The membership of town councils in towns of the same size in Great Britain may be illustrated by the following figures, which in every case include the mayor and aldermen : Birmingham, 120 ; Bolton, 96 ; Bradford, 84 ; Bristol, 92 ; Cardiff, 40 ; Dundee, 28 ; Glasgow, 113 ; Huddersfield, 60 ; Leeds, 68 ; Leicester, 64 ; Manchester, 140 ; Newcastle-on-Tyne, 76 ; Salford, 64 ; Sheffield, 64.

ment, where it existed in an effective form, was the *Bürgergemeinde*, or community of such fully enfranchised inhabitants. They alone possessed the right to take part in the town's government, the right to use the common lands, the right to share in the benefits of the town's charities, foundations, and other institutions, and the right to maintenance at the common charge in the event of poverty. The rest of the inhabitants were outside the pale of this complete citizenship and were simply denizens; they were known as *Beisitzer* or *Schutzverwandte*, that is, they had a claim to shelter and protection, but not to the privileges enjoyed by the freemen. The same distinction between freeman and denizen is still drawn in some parts of Germany, where the enjoyment of certain civic privileges is reserved to the "burghers"—who there form an oligarchy within the local republic—and is not extended to the residents generally, even though in possession of legal settlement.

Often the freemen in this restricted sense formed of old a very small section of the inhabitants. Thus in 1805, before the first Municipal Ordinance was introduced in Prussia, Berlin had only 12,860 freemen in a population of 155,700. The status, and with it the rights, of full citizenship were generally acquired by descent, and only in rare cases by gift or purchase; but with the growth of the towns the existence of the two orders of citizens, living side by side, became increasingly anomalous. Often it happened that the prosperity of a town was entirely due to an influx of enterprising men, who brought with them capital, industry, and intelligence, and bore most of the taxation; yet all the rights and privileges of citizenship were monopolised by an insignificant minority of men, for the most part without education, substance, or public spirit, while the only privilege granted to the newcomers was that of paying taxes.

The reform of local government introduced by Stein in Prussia placed citizenship upon a broader basis. The status of the freeman, carrying the right to take part in local elections and to undertake office in the communal government, continued in virtue of certain prescribed conditions, but it was not acquired exclusively by birth, gift, or purchase.

The Municipal Ordinance in operation in the eastern provinces to-day states that the franchise may be exercised by " independent " persons, subject to certain qualifications, and it defines as " independent " all males who are twenty-four years of age, have households, and have the free disposition of their goods. The occupation condition of the franchise has in general been abandoned, however, and with greater reason, inasmuch as all persons in receipt of a fixed minimum income are liable to local taxation. Thus lodgers so liable and otherwise qualified are held to be eligible to vote, even though they are the sons of the occupier or share rooms with others.

The right to vote is restricted to males and, as a rule, to residents, and the usual qualification in Prussia is the ownership of a dwelling-house in the commune, assessment to State income-tax, or the carrying on of an independent business or of a regular occupation for gain, all these conditions implying liability to pay local taxation. In most of the provinces of Prussia absentee owners of property taxed in the higher classes can also vote in local elections. A taxation qualification of some kind applies in all the other States. A term of residence is also prescribed, and this is usually one year, as in Prussia, though it is sometimes two years, as in Bavaria and Baden, or three years, as in Würtemberg, and the usual age qualification is twenty-four years, but in Bavaria twenty-five years, and in Baden twenty-six years. In most Prussian provinces the franchise is given only to persons of Prussian nationality, but in the provinces of Schleswig-Holstein, Hesse-Nassau, and Hohenzollern, and in some of the other States, it may be exercised by all Germans duly qualified. In some States women owning property may vote by proxy.

There are certain disqualifications, either permanent or temporary; the former include chiefly judicial conviction of certain offences, and the latter bankruptcy, refusal to undertake honorary civil office when required, non-payment of taxes due in respect of the preceding year, and the receipt during the twelve months preceding an election of poor relief in money, but such relief must be continuous or periodical in order to disqualify; relief on a single occasion, or even casually to meet passing need, does not count. Assistance given out of public funds other than those expressly assigned for the relief of the poor does not create a civil disqualification. Towns have often charitable funds at disposal, and help from these does not rank as poor relief.

As a rule the details of the franchise qualifications and disqualifications are determined by every town for itself, and are embodied in its electoral by-laws. Thus the qualifications of an elector in Berlin are that he shall be twenty-four years of age, be a Prussian subject, shall have lived in the commune for twelve months, be a householder or a lodger, have paid his current local taxes, and shall not have been in receipt of poor relief for twelve months. Sometimes a very lenient view is held on the subject of poor relief. The Schöneberg and Charlottenburg town councils have decided that the receipt of poor relief shall only disqualify for the exercise of the local franchise (a) when relief is continuous and in money, relief on account of children being here included ; (b) in the case of prolonged maintenance in an infirmary or similar institution ; and (c) in the case of temporary maintenance in hospital in place of relief of the first two kinds. Single doles of money, school materials for children, and casual assistance to meet pressing distress do not disfranchise.

The franchise provisions of the Prussian municipal constitutions have in the main been adopted in Baden, Oldenburg, Hesse, and the Bavarian Palatinate, but Bavaria right of the Rhine, Würtemberg, and several smaller States retain a restricted definition of citizenship, while Saxony and the province of Hanover combine the Prussian and South German principles, and Alsace-Lorraine still adheres to the general principles of the French communal system.

Burgess fees are still collected in many parts of the country. In Prussia they are common in the eastern provinces, where the fee varies from a few shillings to £2 or more. In some cases the fee is graduated according to income, and where the amount is high the burgess may be allowed to purchase his citizenship on the instalment principle. In the province of Hanover fees are almost general, and range from £3 to £9. In Bavaria the freemanship fee varies with the size of the commune. In towns with over 20,000 inhabi-

CONSTITUTION OF TOWN COUNCILS

tants it may be as high as £8 10s., in towns with from 5000 to 20,000 inhabitants, £6 8s.; in towns with from 1500 to 5000 inhabitants, £4 5s.; and in smaller communes, £2 2s. The communes are not compelled to levy fees, but nearly all do, as much for the sake of revenue as from jealousy of the stranger. Thus Nuremberg receives more than £6000 a year from this source. There the fees charged are from £2 10s. to £8 10s. for persons with a settlement in the town, from £5 to £8 10s. for German subjects without a settlement, and from £10 to £17 for foreigners. There are, however, certain exemptions, as, for example, domestic servants, shop assistants, factory operatives, and other wage-earners who have a settlement and have followed an occupation for fifteen years since coming of age with the same employer. In Würtemberg communes may charge new residents admitted to the franchise from 5s. to 10s., but this does not supersede the condition of three years' residence. In Baden persons who acquire freedom by birth may be required to pay from 6s. to 16s. according to local circumstances, and in the case of others the fee is from 5 to 10 per cent. of the sum of taxed capital of the commune divided by the number of its inhabitants, all freemen excluded.

Where the vote is restricted to freemen it often happens that the majority of the adult inhabitants are disfranchised. While in nearly all the provinces of Prussia, with their wider local franchises, from 15 to 18 per cent. of the inhabitants are qualified to vote, in Bavaria the proportion ranges from three to six per cent. The proportion in Berlin is about 19 per cent., but in the town of Hanover it is less than four per cent. The latter town had in 1911 a population of 360,000, and 60,000 of its inhabitants paid local taxes, but only 12,000 persons, mostly house-owners, were enfranchised citizens. This small body elects the town council, and the town council in turn elects the aldermen. In all the towns of the province of Hanover there were only 23,000 voters out of a total of 263,000 taxpayers—a ratio of one in eleven as against one in five in the town of Hanover—and in many of these towns local government is entirely in the hands of the house-owners and the officials, the latter possessing the franchise in virtue of their position.

Occasionally the freemanship of a town is conferred on residents and others who have distinguished themselves by local enterprise or public work, but the honour does not appear to carry the weight attached to it in this country. The same compliment is still more rarely paid to noted women, yet with less grace, since, owing to the sex disabilities suffered by women in civic affairs, they cannot exercise the rights which citizenship carries with it.

There is wide diversity in the method of electing the town councils. Most State laws simply prescribe the general principles of election and leave the towns to adopt by-laws determining not only the qualification for the franchise but the manner of its exercise. Almost the only point of agreement is the disqualification of women both for election and for the vote.

Two principal methods of voting are practised, an equal franchise for all persons entitled to elect, as in Bavaria, Würtemberg, and Alsace-Lorraine, and the " three-class " system of voting, or a modification of it, as adopted in most of the Prussian provinces—though not in the provinces of Schleswig-Holstein and Hanover, nor yet in the former free city of Frankfort, which are all governed under separate Municipal Ordinances—in Baden, Brunswick, and some parts of Saxony. Some Saxon communes are allowed to vary the " three-class " grouping by classing the voters in broad occupational groups.

THE " THREE-CLASS " SYSTEM OF ELECTION AND PLURAL VOTING.—What is known as the " three-class " system of election is so general in Prussia and withal so unique that a brief description is desirable. Under this system the burgesses of a commune are divided into three classes according either to the amount of their incomes or more usually of the direct State and local taxes they pay. The classification is made in the following manner:—First, the aggregate sum of the income of the electors or the aggregate sum of the taxation payable by them, as the case may be, is ascertained. Then the names of the electors are recorded in a list according to the amount of their income or of the taxes they pay, and they are divided into three groups, the first containing so many as are necessary to make up exactly one-third of the total income or taxation, the second containing so many of the next following names as make up another third, and the third containing the remainder. Persons who are not assessed to any State tax owing to exemption fall always into the third class. Provisions exist to meet the case of persons of equal income or taxation falling into different classes. Each of these three groups elects one-third of the councillors. If the number to be elected should not be divisible by three, the second division claims the first member who is left over, though if two are over one falls to the first division and the other to the third. This is the same system of voting that was prescribed by the Prussian constitution of 1850 for the choice of the primary electors in the election of the Lower House, and it was embodied in a revision of the Prussian Municipal Ordinance for the eastern provinces which took place in 1853.

A variation of the "three-class" division of the electorate was introduced by a Prussian law of June 30, 1900, applying to communes with more than 10,000 inhabitants. Under this law the electors are first divided into three groups on the normal principle, and all who pay more than the average amount of taxation, calculated on the aggregate sum, are put in the second or the first class. For the purpose of determining in which of these classes they will vote the total taxation now represented by the two classes is halved, and there vote in the first class so many of the highest taxed electors as are necessary to make a moiety, while the rest go into the second class. The effect of this arrangement is to increase the first two classes of voters—and especially the second—and proportionately to diminish the third, which more than ever becomes a working-class group. The same law empowers communes, by adopting a by-law, to divide the electors, on the same principle of average taxation, into twelfths and to assign them to the three classes in the ratio of five, four, and three, as determined by the sum of taxation payable.

The effect of the "three-class" method of apportioning voting power is that in towns with a considerable section of well-to-do or wealthy taxpayers these form the select first and second classes, while the vast majority of working-people vote together in the third class. Only in towns where social extremes are absent are the three classes at all fairly proportioned in number, and these towns are rare. As a rule, from one to four per cent. of the electors are in the first class, from ten to 15 per cent. in the second, and from 85 to 90 per cent. in the third. In 1912 the citizens of Berlin qualified to vote in communal elections numbered 386,736. Of this number, 353,704, or 91·5 per cent., were in the third class; 32,096, or 8·3 per cent., in the second class; and 936, or 0·2 per cent., in the first class. Yet each set of voters had the right to elect one-third of the councillors. In other words, a taxpayer in the first class had more than thirty times as much voting power as one in the second class and nearly 400 times as much as one in the third class.

Much the same ratio of voters exists in the neighbouring town of Charlottenburg, where in 1909 1·5 per cent. of the whole fell to the first class, 12·5 per cent. to the second, and 86 per cent. to the third. Charlottenburg, however, is a town of rich people, and a man must there pay at least £140 in taxation in order to vote in the first class. Of 48,800 electors in Neukölln, near Berlin, in 1912, 618 or 1·3 per cent. formed the first class, 11,100, or 22·7 per cent., the second class; and 37,100, or 76 per cent., the third class. The average taxation in these classes was £126, £7, and £2 2s. respectively. In Cologne in 1913 the proportions were one per cent. in the first class, nine per cent. in the second, and 90 per cent. in the third. A recent classification of the electors of 114 Prussian towns showed that 8600, or 1·3 per cent., fell in the first class; 48,950, or 7 per cent., in the second; and 629,360, or 91·7 per cent., in the third. In some towns it happens that a single voter forms the first class for himself. The disappearance of a single rich inhabitant may entirely change the balance of voting power. At Essen so long as the last member of the Krupp family lived the first class of electors consisted of four individuals; on the death of Herr Krupp the number at once increased to six hundred, and there was a large transference from the third to the second class.

The effects in actual electoral results are equally anomalous.

Thus in a recent election to the Berlin city council, in the smallest electoral district into which the voters of the first class were divided sixteen electors returned three members, while in the district with most voters of this class three members were returned for 110 electors. In the third class the number of electors per member ranged from 6500 to 8900.

The skilful use of this curious system of electing members of the local councils enables the mining companies in the colliery districts of Westphalia to secure predominant influence on these bodies in small places, and so to regulate taxation. In one commune several years ago there was only one taxpayer in the first class—a colliery company, which elected two of its officials; in the second class there was also one taxpayer—another company, which likewise sent two of its officials into the council; while in the third were the colliers, who chose a colliery manager and a contractor acceptable to the company. It happened in a small industrial commune in 1913 that the director of the manufactory which employed most of the inhabitants voted alone on its behalf in the first class and elected one councillor, then voted alone on his own account in the second class and elected himself.

Baden has also a modification of the "three-class" system of election, but in 1910 it was amended; for while formerly the electors were allotted to the three groups by twelfths, viz., one-twelfth to the first class, two-twelfths to the second, and nine-twelfths to the third, they are now divided into six, and assigned in the ratio of one, two, and three, and in addition the proportional principle has been introduced in the elections both to the town councils and the executives.

In Saxony, while the normal basis of election is equality of franchise, the law gives communes the right to adopt by-laws dividing the electors into classes, as in Prussia, and allotting a certain proportion of the seats to each of these classes or to distinct districts. Some years ago Leipzig introduced the Prussian system and its example has been followed by other towns, as the only way of preventing the capture of the councils by the working classes. Chemnitz has gone further and introduced a system of representation of estates. Here the electors are divided into five classes. The first or general class contains all who do not belong to the other four classes and has subdivisions composed of persons who are assessed to the State income tax to the amount of £90 10s., and those who pay from £90 10s. to £125. The second class comprises the wage-earners; the third the learned professions, including officials, teachers, clergy, lawyers, doctors, etc., paying State income tax on incomes in excess of £125; the fourth the industrial class with a like taxable income and the heads of the trade guilds, and the fifth the tradespeople with the same income, and directors of public companies. The town council consists of fifty-seven members, one-third of whom are re-elected every two years in the proportion of three or four to each class of voters.

Dresden has adopted a social or occupational grouping of the voters independently of amount of income or taxation. There are five classes, viz. : (*a*) those who follow no calling, as *rentiers*, pensioners, etc.; (*b*) work-people and others corresponding to them in social position ; (*c*) officials, teachers, clergymen, lawyers, doctors, and artists; (*d*) independent tradesmen in so far as they do not fall in the next class ; and (*e*) persons who are liable to pay contributions towards the costs of the Chamber of Commerce. Each of these classes is again divided into two sections, viz., citizens who have been in possession of freedom longer than ten years, and those who have had it for a shorter period, and the 84 seats in the town council are allotted to the electors of these sub-classes in the following proportions :—Classes (*a*) and (*b*), 6 in each sub-class, total 12 ; classes (*c*) and (*d*), 6 in the first sub-class and 18 in the second, total 24 ; class (*e*), 6 in each sub-class, total 12.

Like several other devices in the political constitution of Prussia, from which it was taken, intended to serve as a breakwater against popular pressure, the three-class system of election is almost generally condemned, yet the parties whose influence it preserves find it very convenient in practice. The system is, of course, a thorn in the flesh to the Labour party, which under it fails to secure representation proportionate to its numbers. Even the Liberals readily admit that it is an awkward and obsolete arrangement which would have little chance of adoption in modern legislation, yet théy are not

CONSTITUTION OF TOWN COUNCILS

eager to abolish it, for while they accept the principle of a universal and equal suffrage in political government they are not prepared to apply it in local affairs.

That the system is undemocratic is not, of course, an argument against it in an undemocratic country; but putting political theories on one side it may be claimed for this unequal distribution of voting power that it broadly asserts the principle of proportional representation according to liability to taxation, and as in Germany local taxation falls with far greater weight upon the rich than the poor the system is perhaps less anomalous in practice than it appears in theory. It should be remembered that while, owing to the operation of this system of voting, the mass of small taxpayers are unable to commit a town to large enterprises the cost of which would fall with enormous preponderance upon others, should such a power be exercised by a combination of the larger taxpayers they would have to bear the brunt of the burden.

The province of Hanover still retains its old plural system of voting, the number of votes—up to a maximum—being proportionate to the amount of taxation paid. So lately as 1910 a town council in the province was refused permission to reform its system of voting on the ground that the new franchise would have restricted the electoral privileges of the large taxpayers. In some towns one vote may be claimed for every 5s. of taxes paid, with the result that a handful of electors may appoint the local council and hence control its policy.

A plural franchise exists also in several of the small Thuringian States. Thus in the Duchy of Saxe-Meiningen it may be exercised to a maximum of ten votes in the towns, the ratio being one vote in respect of local taxation up to 15s., two votes for taxation from 15s. to £1 10s., three votes for £1 10s. to £2 10s., four votes for £2 10s. to £3 15s., five votes for £3 15s. to £6, and one vote more for every additional £5 of taxes paid to the maximum stated.

At the present time there is in some States a strong movement in favour of proportional representation in the election of municipal bodies, and in several States the system has already been introduced, either generally or partially. The motives which influence the friends of proportional representation differ in various towns. Where the three-class system of voting prevails it is the Social Democratic party that seeks a change, since it is unable otherwise to obtain representation corresponding to its electoral strength, or even to secure representation at all. On the other hand, where election is direct and the taxpayers do not vote in classes, the Labour party sometimes obtains a representation which threatens middle-class preponderance, and in such cases the call for the adoption of the proportionate principle comes from the parties still in power. Proportional representation in local elections has been introduced in Bavaria (where it applies to all communes with over 4000 inhabitants), in Würtemberg (where it applies to towns with over 10,000 inhabitants, and to elections to town councils and executive alike), in Baden (where it likewise applies to the election of the executive bodies), in Oldenburg, and elsewhere, but in some cases its adoption is optional.

ELIGIBILITY OF ELECTORS AND THE PRIVILEGES OF HOUSE-OWNERS.—In order to be eligible for membership of a municipal council a person must be a qualified voter and be in the enjoyment of full civil rights. Various persons are, however, disqualified by their position, e.g., in Prussia, officials and members of the authorities by which the State exercises oversight over the communes, members of the local executive, and all paid officers of the commune, clergymen, certain servants of the Church, such as organists, cantors, ushers, and even grave-diggers, elementary school teachers, judicial officers of certain classes, and police officials. The same disqualifications apply more or less in the other States; Saxony extends the ban even to clerks and night-watchmen in the town's service, but exempts teachers in public schools. Again, father and son or two brothers may not simultaneously be members of a council, and if elected the elder is admitted to membership. There is no rule disqualifying persons who have business dealings with a local authority from sitting on that authority. Some Municipal Ordinances contain the provision that town councillors may not take part in discussions or negotiations relating to matters in which they are pecuniarily interested, but as a rule both councillors and unpaid members of the executives are permitted to contract with the authority of which they are members, though the practice is much criticised. Not long ago a Social Democratic member of a Central German town council brought forward a motion intended to prevent colleagues from concluding contracts with that body. The proposal was resented by the rest of the councillors as superfluous and offensive, yet it was referred to committee for examination. The result was the discovery that nearly one-half of all the members were regularly doing business with the council.

In general, it may be said, the government of German towns is undoubtedly clean and wholesome. Instances occasionally come to light of land speculation by town councillors at the public expense, of bribery of minor officials, and the like, but they are the exceptions that prove the rule, and the severity with which public opinion visits irregularities of the kind bears testimony to the existence of a healthy sentiment on the subject.

An antiquated provision contained in the Municipal Ordinances of many parts of the country is that requiring that a fixed proportion of the councillors shall be resident house-owners.[1] In the earliest Prussian Ordinance of 1808, the proportion was two-thirds. The Ordinance of 1831, while increasing the income qualification for the vote, reduced the representation of the house-owners to at least one-half of the total, and this ratio still continues both in Prussia and Saxony. The revised Municipal Ordinance issued for Saxony in 1873, indeed, empowers towns to adopt by-laws giving to house-owners representation beyond one-half, and some towns have fixed the proportion at two-thirds. In practice the ratio invariably exceeds that required or allowed by law; often it is as high as 70 and 80 per cent., and sometimes it exceeds 90 per cent. The number of house-owners in the councils of some of the larger Prussian towns in a recent year was as

[1] The Prussian Municipal Ordinance of 1853 for the eastern provinces, as now in force, amplifies the term as follows: " Owners, usufructuaries, and such persons as have an inherited right of ownership."

follows :—Berlin 92 out of 144 councillors, Charlottenburg 37 out of 72, Königsberg 53 out of 102, Coblence 25 out of 30, Breslau 52 out of 102, Danzig 45 out of 63, Aix-la-Chapelle 38 out of 39, Barmen 29 out of 36, Bielefeld 35 out of 45, Cassel 47 out of 60, Düsseldorf and Hanover 31 out of 36, Crefeld 33 out of 36, and Bonn 38 out of 39.

The house-owners' privilege is a source of much controversy. There was no doubt a practical justification for it at the time of its introduction, and even much later—so long, indeed, as the systems of plural ownership, house speculation, and house farming had not set in. It has been estimated that even up to the middle of last century half the voters in the first and second classes in many towns were actually house-owners. In the larger towns to-day, however, houses are largely bought to sell again and not to live in; a large proportion of the houses in towns of rapid development change hands almost with the frequency of popular stocks and shares, and the direct interest of the owner in his building is often quite impersonal and fugitive. The old house-owners formed a settled element in the population; they were men of substance, who had a large stake in their town's welfare. The real house-owners are now the mortgage and land banks, which finance the nominal proprietors, and the fact that in large towns a modern " house " connotes not one dwelling but several or many, owing to the practice of barrack building, restricts the house-owning class still more. An analysis of all the citizens of Schöneberg, near Berlin, brought to light the fact that the total number of house-owners qualified to be elected to the town council in 1908 was only 900, or about 3 per cent. of a total of 28,000 persons so qualified. In Berlin it was found that there were only 9000 house-owners eligible for election, yet the total number of electors exceeded 350,000. The privilege is doubly inequitable in towns where the basis of taxation is predominantly income and not real estate.

Further, it is becoming more and more recognised that the limited choice of representation which this system imposes is incompatible with the great tasks which modern municipalities have to discharge, such as the carrying out of enlightened land, housing and sanitation schemes, and the like, and thus is contrary to the welfare of the general body of citizens. It may be admitted that the " house agrarians "— as the urban property owners are commonly called—have not in general flagrantly abused their great powers, and that in many cases their domination has proved compatible with the pursuance of a steady, if not a heroic, policy of progress, yet it is unquestionable that the strong property influence upon the town councils would nearly everywhere have been used with far less discretion and moderation did not the German system of municipal government place at the head of local affairs a permanent mayor and executive, virtually independent of the representative assembly, and required both by law and tradition to keep free from all outside interests and influences.

In a Bill for the amendment of the Municipal Ordinance, which was introduced in 1876, the Prussian Government proposed to abolish the house-owners' privilege, since (said the *exposé des motifs*) " the need and even the utility of such a provision singling out for privilege a particular class of the inhabitants have been much called in question, and apparently not without reason." The Bill was not passed, and the Government has not again proposed this reform.

PROCEDURE AT ELECTIONS.—The period of election is various; in Prussia (except in the province of Hanover), Baden, and Alsace-Lorraine it is six years, in Bavaria and Hesse nine years, but in Saxony as a rule only three. One-third of the members retire every two years in Prussia, and in Bavaria every three years. Elections take place in November in Prussia, and voting lists are published in the preceding July for inspection. Towns are divided into districts or wards for electoral purposes; the Prussian Municipal Ordinances provide that if any class of voters (on the " three-class " system of grouping) contains more than 500 persons, two or more electoral districts may be formed, but modifications of this provision are allowable. Where the electors vote by wards, the candidates may be chosen from amongst the general body of qualified citizens. Thus the area of Berlin is divided for voting purposes into forty-eight wards, and the number of voters in the various districts ranges from about 4000 to 7000. The polling is conducted by committees appointed by the mayor and town council. A fortnight before the date fixed for the election the voters must be invited by individual or public notice to attend at a time and place stated to record their votes. The period during which voters may exercise the franchise is fixed by the council of every town for itself; in large towns the votes of the electors in the numerous third class are sometimes taken on several days. In recent years there has been a growing tendency, especially in Saxon towns, to hold the elections on Sunday. The municipal authorities of Berlin and several of the adjacent large towns, of Mannheim and other places, recently decided to allow the electors in the third class to vote on Sunday.

Some of the laws and ordinances on municipal government are without provisions as to the publicity or otherwise of elections, and leave the towns to decide for themselves by by-laws whether they prefer secret or open voting. Secret voting is the rule in Bavaria, Würtemberg, and Alsace-Lorraine, but open voting by oral declaration is usual in most parts of Prussia and in some other States.

Voting is everywhere direct; that is, the method, followed in the Prussian parliamentary elections, of choosing primary electors who make the definitive selections does not here apply. Election is either by absolute majority of votes cast (with second ballots between the candidates who fail to obtain an absolute majority), as in Prussia, Bavaria, and Alsace-Lorraine; or by simple or "relative" majority, as in Saxony.

Membership of a town council is almost invariably an honorary office. Some Municipal Ordinances expressly prohibit the payment of salary or remuneration for services rendered, but allow the refund of out-of-pocket expenses. It has been decided that such a return of bare expenses precludes the payment of any fixed sum, but the latter practice is nevertheless followed. In many towns, councillors have free tramway tickets, but this privilege has been discontinued in some Prussian towns owing to a recent decision of the Supreme Administrative Court declaring it to be an infraction of the spirit of the law. Würtemberg is an exception to the rule of honorary service, for there payment is allowable at the rate of 5s. a day in small communes, 10s. in communes of medium size, and 15s. in large towns.

In some parts of the country—e.g., the Rhineland province of Prussia, the Bavarian Palatinate, and Alsace-Lorraine—the mayor is *ex officio* chairman of the town council. In the eastern provinces of Prussia and elsewhere, however, the chairman is a member of the council, chosen by it, and occupying the position of the President or Speaker of a German legislature, while the permanent mayor corresponds to the head of the Government. An elected chairman is usually appointed for one, two, or three years.

The Municipal Ordinances as a rule fix no special times of meeting, but provide only that the councils shall "meet as often as business requires," yet shall be convened at the discretion of the chairman, or on the requisition of one-fourth of the members. Monthly ordinary meetings are common. As a rule one-half of the members form a quorum. Sittings are public—in Bavaria this applies also to meetings of the executive—but in certain circumstances a council may deliberate behind closed doors. Questions are, as a rule, decided by a bare majority of votes, and in the case of a tie the chairman has a casting vote. In Prussia, however, certain decisions can only be adopted by a two-thirds majority, as, for example, the introduction, alteration, or repeal of by-laws. Power is reserved by the Government to dissolve a town council by royal order in extreme cases, and to take over its duties until a new body has been elected.

Nowadays, elections in the towns are largely fought on political lines, though not as understood in this country. In the Protestant parts of the country the struggle is mainly between the Liberal, Conservative, and Socialist parties, but in the Roman Catholic districts the Centre or Ultramontane party joins issue, with the usual success. The Conservatives, however, do not enjoy in Prussia, under the Municipal Ordinances, the privileged position secured to them by the parliamentary system, with its unequal distribution of seats, for, not being specially a plutocratic party, the "three-class" method of voting does not help them in the towns. Hence they are often content to allow the Liberals of different complexion to contest supremacy with the Socialists, though there are towns in which Conservatism is a very active factor in local government. Except in times of special political excitement, or when religious or confessional issues are involved, as is often the case in the large Rhenish towns, the electorate does not exercise its privilege in any large measure. In recent elections to the Berlin City Council less than 50 per cent. of the qualified electors on the average exercised the franchise, and in some wards the proportion was as low as 30 per cent., while the highest proportion was 60 per cent. in wards completely under Socialist domination. In the adjoining town of Charlottenburg barely one-third of the qualified electors took the trouble to go to the poll.

WORKING-MEN ON MUNICIPAL AUTHORITIES.—In composition German town councils are not unlike English, except that Labour has on the whole less representation. Thus, of 39 members of the Aix-la-Chapelle town council as constituted in 1912, two were doctors, two lawyers, three architects, four officials, two agriculturists, three were *rentiers*, eight were business men, 13 were manufacturers and directors of works, one was an engineer, and one an apothecary. Of the 59 members of the Chemnitz town council in that year, two were doctors, two lawyers, eight officials, 23 business men, four manufacturers, nine handicraftsmen, two *rentiers*, two engineers, two architects, and there were also one apothecary, one editor, and one working-man.

The attitude adopted towards municipal service by the working classes, or, to give them their corporate description, the Labour party, calls for special reference owing to the intimate relation between Labour and Socialism in Germany. The Labour party is in effect the party of Social Democracy, for hardly in any other capacity are the working classes represented in local politics. The part played in municipal life by the Social Democratic party during the past twenty years has been very conspicuous, and its influence upon the action of the local authorities has been fruitful in many directions. During this period the attitude of the Socialists towards municipal work has undergone a complete change. A party resolution of the year 1888 declared that " the expenditure of intellectual and material force involved in participation in local elections is quite disproportionate to the possible advantages to be secured, and, further, the gain of a few seats in the communal councils has in nowise promoted the development of the Labour party."

This negative declaration of policy is not the only one which the Socialists of Germany have found it expedient to revise and reject during recent years. Experience proved that abstention from local elections and refusal to participate in local government placed the party at a great tactical disadvantage, and deprived its leaders in town and village of many opportunities of advancing the social and material interests of the working classes. The old position of aloofness was abandoned, and for some years the Socialists have made strenuous efforts to assert for themselves upon local government bodies as strong a position as that which they have obtained in the Imperial legislature and the Diets of some of the Southern States. Berlin is a noteworthy example of the advance of Socialist influence in municipal government. In 1884 the Socialists held only five seats in the council of 144 ; ten years later they held 16, and their number is now 45, all elected as representatives of the third class of voters. Upon the councils of some of the smaller towns they have a permanent majority. They have played the part, it is true, of the proverbial " pike in the carp pond," for they have invariably carried sword and not peace into the council-room, yet the severest of their critics has never denied that their influence on the whole has been on the side of efficient and progressive, if expensive, government.

It is notorious also that no party more ardently and unwearyingly insists on clean and straightforward dealings in local administration, or more relentlessly makes war against corruption than the Socialists, whose only defect in this matter is a too ready inclination to believe that all men save themselves are liars, and to suspect dishonesty and double-dealing where they do not exist. It must also be said to the credit of the Socialists that they do not act upon the comforting faith that "where God gives office He gives brains," but take great pains to qualify themselves for public life. To this end the party organises courses of study in the theory and practice of municipal government, and holds national and local conferences for the exchange of views and experiences. Many municipal assemblies would breathe a serener atmosphere if the Socialists would revert to their old self-denying ordinance and keep out of municipal politics altogether, yet no one will deny that they have raised the standard of administrative efficiency and have greatly accelerated the pace of municipal advance.

Sometimes they set a pace which the rest of the community finds too rapid, and occasionally their very ardour proves their undoing, for success at one election is followed by rout at the next. Mülhausen, in Alsace, is one of the towns which for a time passed under Socialist influence, and the history of the few feverish years of Socialist domination (1902 to 1906) illustrates the zeal and temper of the party. During that period the wages of municipal workpeople were increased, and their hours reduced, and minimum rates in the one case and maximum hours in the other were fixed; all these workers were given holidays—six days after one year's service, and 12 days a year after three years' service; full right of coalition was given to them, and the strike clause was abolished from public contracts. A free labour registry was established, assistance was given to workers and their families during labour disputes, works for the unemployed were made a part of municipal policy, contracts were given only to firms which paid standard rates of wages, coal was supplied at cost price to the inhabitants during the winter months; and the outdoor relief granted under the Poor Law was raised to what was called an "existence minimum." The salaries of elementary teachers were increased until the school staff of Mülhausen was the best paid in the province. Model dwellings were built for workpeople and families with small means. Fine new schools were provided, school fees were abolished, teaching materials were freed, a dental clinic was opened for scholars, school baths were provided, sickly children were sent to "cure" baths and "holiday colony" schools, continuation schools were introduced and attendance thereat was made compulsory, and a forest school was established. The entrance duties (octroi) on necessaries of life were abolished. Large purchases of land were made ; the streets were asphalted, electrical tramways were introduced, the theatre was taken over and worked by the town, cheap performances being arranged for scholars and for working-people; an efficient sewerage system was carried out, and finally a debt of a million pounds was contracted. Less owing to dissatisfaction with their policy than its cost the middle-class parties combined and swept away the precipitous reformers, and with them the mayor and the too energetic members of the executive.

The Socialists have found it a more difficult task to penetrate into the executive bodies; for there ratification from above is usually necessary, and few Governments allow Socialists to occupy offices election to which is subject to official veto. In Prussia this rule applies not only to appointments to the mayoral office and to the executive, but also to appointments to such subordinate bodies as education committees, since education falls within the province of State supervision. Although the constitution declares that "all Prussians are equal before the law," there were Royal and Ministerial Decrees before the constitution was granted, and one of these, dated 1701, requires members of education committees to see that the children under their care are " trained to be loyal, moral, and religious members of society." On the strength of this hoary document Socialist educationists, however eminent and however competent in every other department of local administration, are refused a place on these committees. In the South a more tolerant spirit prevails; and in Baden and Würtemberg there are both Socialist senators and mayors.

According to a report made to the party congress held at Jena in September, 1913, the Social Democrats are now represented on the local government authorities of 509 towns and 2973 rural communes, their representatives on the town councils numbering 2753, and on the rural councils 8928.

Further, they had representatives upon the executives of 133 towns, and upon the executives of 120 rural communes. Most of the Social Democratic members of municipal executives (93 per cent. of the whole) were found in Bavaria, Würtemberg, and Baden ; only two in Prussia (in Frankfort-on-Main, where confirmation by the Crown is not needed), and two in Saxony.

CHAPTER IV

DISTRIBUTION OF ADMINISTRATIVE POWERS—TOWN COUNCIL, EXECUTIVE AND MAYOR

Position of the town councils—Organisation and constitution of the executive—Functions of the executive—The mayor and his functions—The "magisterial" and "mayoral" executive systems compared—Devolution of administrative duties: Deputations, Commissions, etc.—Honorary service in communal administration—The administrative staffs—Schools for communal government—Municipal congresses and leagues—Joint administrative boards for common purposes—State supervision and control.

THE German town council, as we have seen, is constituted of much the same material as the English borough or urban council, but the German mayor and executive have no equivalent in the local government system of this country. For, wide as are the powers of self-government possessed by German towns, these powers are exercised, not directly by the representative assemblies, but by executive bodies as a rule chosen by them and for the most part consisting of what would be regarded in this country as permanent officials. Herein lies the most noteworthy feature of the German system. Perhaps the most convenient name by which to describe the members of these bodies is "aldermen," a term the more allowable since the unsalaried members of a municipal executive correspond with sufficient closeness to the aldermen of English corporations. In the province of Hanover and the Free Cities of Hamburg, Bremen, and Lübeck the term "senators" is used; but in the governments of these city States the college of senators discharges legislative as well as executive functions.

POSITION OF THE TOWN COUNCILS.—In the mediæval town governments of Germany the executive powers were usually divided between the "*weiterer*" and the "*engerer*" *Rat*—a more or less representative council chosen by the freemen and an inner and smaller council which acted as a sort of second chamber. The old tradition has its counterpart in the bi-cameral system which was introduced by the Municipal Ordinances of last century. Under that system it is the right and duty of a town council to exercise general oversight over the government of its area—in the words of the Municipal Ordinance of 1853 for the eastern provinces of Prussia, to "control the administration"; but while it is theoretically responsible for the decisions adopted to this end and has unlimited power of initiative, all administrative functions are delegated to a "magistracy" (*Magistrat*) or executive, of which the mayor is the president or chairman. "The 'Magistracy,'" says this document, "is the supreme authority of the town and administers the communal affairs of the town."

Neither in Prussia nor any other State was the representative assembly intended to be the predominant partner in the local administration. The terms in which Stein explained the purpose of his Municipal Ordinance of 1808 made this clear. Its object was said to be "to form by law a firm point of union for the citizens, *to afford them influence upon the administration of the community*, and by this means to stimulate their public spirit." Local government was still, however, to be controlled by executive officers: all that the citizens as a body might do was to create the machinery of government and to give to this machinery impulse and direction.

Most of the Prussian Municipal Ordinances now in force date from the reactionary period which followed the revolutionary movements of 1848, and they bear strong traces of the heavy hand of autocracy, which after having been rudely shaken had once more recovered confidence. Throughout, their provisions betray a somewhat grudging assent to the principle of popular government as understood in this country. The State—or rather the Crown—is shown as ceding part of its power unwillingly and with a fixed determination not to allow that ceded power to travel too far away from its grasp. Hence while representative assemblies were created they were hemmed round by limitations; in no department of municipal life were they to have a perfectly free hand; and frank recognition of a right of popular supremacy in local affairs in the English sense finds no expression in these documents.

True, the electorate was no longer narrowed down to a select body of freemen as of old, yet it was limited by property and income franchises, and an endeavour was made to dissociate from the citizens the assembly elected by and from them and to make it independent of popular influence, for the town councillors were told that they were "not bound by any instructions or directions of the electors or electoral districts." The jurisdiction of these bodies was also carefully and jealously defined. They were, indeed, entitled to decide all communal affairs which were not assigned to the executive, yet so wide did the competence of the latter go that in no other sphere than finance could the town councils claim to hold the balance of power.

Their very powers of deliberation were restricted, for it was provided that "the town councillors may only discuss matters other than communal matters if these have been referred to them by special laws or, in individual cases, by the supervisory authorities." And finally, as if uncertain whether constitutional checks would prove effective to curb popular assumption and avert disaster, the local constitution-makers of that day invoked the good offices of the church and of Providence, for the Municipal Ordinance for the eastern provinces of Prussia contains the direction that at the principal service on the Sunday preceding the election of town councils all clergymen should call attention to "the importance of this proceeding."

More important was the entire divorce of the executive from the legislative side of government. Although local councils might not now be taken away, it was conceived that they might be effectively checkmated by the creation of senates holding a quasi-State status and representing still to some extent the tradition of government from above. Hence each council was to choose a college of executive officers who when once elected were to be more or less independent of the constituent body. Even these executives themselves were only half trusted, however; hence in order to ensure their acceptability to the Government the confirmation of each individual member by the Crown or its agents was required.

The confirmation provisions of the Municipal Ordinance of 1853 faithfully reflected the spirit of distrust in which this enactment was conceived. " In the confirmation of magistrates," ran the Instructions to the Ordinance, "the greatest conscientiousness must be exercised. The right to cancel election and in consequence to order administration by commission must be dutifully exercised in all cases in which the interests of the communes or the State require it, without regard to the consideration whether temporary discontent may as a consequence be occasioned."

Throughout Germany, indeed, the system of municipal administration repeats still on a small scale the system of political government. In it are found all the well-known constitutional provisions for limiting the direct authority of the electorate, all the checks and safeguards against precipitous action, all the devices for placing executive functions and powers beyond the control of the popular assembly. Just as the Imperial and State Parliaments lack legislative independence, genuine executive authority, and effective control over the bureaucracy which really rules the country, so the town councils are subsidiary or at most auxiliary bodies; their jurisdiction is limited at every turn; first by the limitation of their deliberative powers, then by the institution of the permanent mayors and executives, and finally by the supremacy of the State authorities in certain matters.

So, too, the doctrine of " Ministerial responsibility," which is affirmed by the political constitutions of most States, yet is without reality in any of them, has its counterpart in local government in virtue of the fact that in some parts of the country the mayors, once chosen, are not only independent of the town councils, but are practically irremovable, even when provision is not definitely made—as is the case in some States—for their appointment for life. Just as in relation to the national legislature the Ministers stand outside the body to which they are nominally responsible, so in some parts of Prussia the salaried aldermen are not members of the local councils and have no right to vote in their proceedings. Ministers and aldermen are alike, however, in the fact that they can claim to attend all meetings and to speak—or to be heard through a deputy—at any time upon any subject belonging to their jurisdiction, just as legislature and council respectively can require their attendance for the purpose of information.

There is one sphere in which, in municipal as in national government, the popular assembly is almost supreme. This is the sphere of finance. Herein lie the principal check of the town council upon the executive power and the effective safeguard of its ultimate responsibility, and, in the event of serious conflict, of its ultimate power to assert its will. For no tax can be adopted or collected without the town council's sanction ; the council decides how the moneys of the town shall be employed ; and it votes the budget, which may be fixed for one or three years at a time. In regard to the budget, indeed, the citizens in general have to be considered in Prussia, for it must be published for a week for their information, and must simultaneously be presented to the supervisory authority. It follows also that the council has a right to require a full account of the use of public funds. In the words of the Prussian Municipal Ordinance of 1853, just as the council " controls the administration," so it is " therefore entitled to be satisfied . . . as to the employment of all communal revenue. For this purpose it can require the magistrates to produce all documents and appoint committees, to which the mayor is empowered to delegate a member of the executive (magistracy)."

Other questions belonging specially to the town council's province are the use and disposal of public property, the validity of elections, the election of mayor and aldermen, the contracting of loans, and the adoption of by-laws, decisions as to some of which require confirmation by the supervisory authority.

In the South more power is, on the whole, reserved to the town councils, and in Baden—as, indeed, in the Prussian provinces of Schleswig-Holstein and Hanover also—the councils and executives act together; but most German forms of urban government repeat with greater or less fidelity the leading features of the Prussian bicameral system as in operation in the eastern provinces. The supremacy of the professional executive conflicts altogether with the practice of local government in this country, where a bad amateur is usually more acceptable than the best of experts; but there can be little doubt that the German system represents both a higher and a more efficient form of municipal organisation than our own. To deny that would be to imply that the modern Parliament, with its corollaries of a paid Ministry and a body of permanent officers known as the civil service, represents a decline from the old national folkmote.

ORGANISATION AND CONSTITUTION OF THE EXECUTIVE.—It is the purpose of the representative assembly to represent the entire community and to voice its opinions and wishes, but the execution of resolutions adopted by the assembly rests with the mayor and a certain number of magistrates or aldermen who form the executive. The organisation of the executive takes two principal forms.

The form introduced by most Prussian Municipal Ordinances is commonly known as the " magisterial constitution," under which the executive power is vested in a body which acts collectively and of which the mayor is *ex officio* the head. This body is known as the magistracy (*Magistrat*) in East Prussia and Bavaria right of the Rhine, and elsewhere senate or council. The magistracy is a replica of the Ministry of State, each of whose members administers his department independently, though when matters have to be decided jointly decision follows the vote of the majority. Under this system the mayor does not act as chairman of the communal assembly.

The other form, which is peculiar to the Prussian province of Rhineland, to Hesse, the Bavarian Palatinate, and Alsace-Lorraine, and owes its existence largely to French influence, is known as the " mayoral constitution," and under it the conduct of communal affairs is vested in one officer, the mayor, who is simultaneously the chairman of the town council. In the work of administration he is similarly assisted by colleagues, known as *Beigeordnete*, corresponding to the French *adjoints*—who together may likewise be known as the magistracy—but his authority is larger than that of the mayor under the magisterial system.

Some of the Municipal Ordinances of the western districts of Germany allow choice to be made between the two systems, but it would appear that towns under the "mayoral" constitution seldom or never go over to the "magisterial" system. In towns with no more than 2500 civil inhabitants in some parts of Prussia the mayor may discharge executive functions alone, in which event he also acts as chairman of the council.

The general rule is that both the mayor and the members of the executive, whether salaried or not, are elected by the town council. In Würtemberg and the Prussian province of Schleswig-Holstein, they are chosen by the burgesses in the same manner as the town councillors; while in Westphalia the mayor and salaried aldermen are elected by the town council, and the unsalaried aldermen by the town council and executive in joint sitting.

There is great diversity in the size of the executive in different States. The Municipal Ordinance for the eastern provinces of Prussia lays down the following ratio of aldermen to population : in communes with less than 2500 inhabitants, two ; in communes with from 2500 to 10,000 inhabitants, four ; from 10,000 to 30,000, six ; from 30,000 to 60,000, eight ; from 60,000 to 100,000, ten ; and in communes with a population over 100,000, two more for every 50,000 additional inhabitants. In Westphalia the ratio is two for towns with less than 2500 inhabitants, four for towns with from 2500 to 10,000 inhabitants, six for those with from 10,000 to 30,000 inhabitants, and two more for every additional 20,000 inhabitants. In Rhineland the ratio is two for towns with less than 10,000 inhabitants, four for towns with from 10,000 to 20,000 inhabitants, and six for towns with over 20,000 inhabitants. As a rule the normal membership of the executive may be modified by local by-laws.

In Bavaria the executive consists of the mayors (of whom

there may be two in communes with a population over 10,000 and three in those with a population over 50,000), legal members, civil members (varying from six to twenty according to the size of the town), and technical experts, the last-named voting only on matters affecting them. In many towns the ratio of town councillors to aldermen is three to one. In Baden the executive numbers from fifteen to thirty-one.

It was originally intended that the unsalaried members of the executive should predominate and that professional members should be the exception. With the multiplication of municipal business and the extension of trading enterprise to provinces never contemplated when the existing laws were enacted, the number and influence of the salaried aldermen have constantly increased. It is regarded as essential that the heads of all the great departments of municipal work should enjoy the highest administrative rank as members of the executive; hence in the large towns that body comprises not only jurists, but experts on education, Poor Law, medicine, and public health, as well as technical experts of various kinds, though a certain number of honorary members are also elected, these occupying virtually the position of English borough aldermen, and, like them, often elected term after term.

The Prussian Municipal Ordinances provide specifically for the appointment of paid aldermen to the offices of syndic, chamberlain or treasurer, secretary for education (*Schulrat*), commissioner of public works (*Baurat*), corresponding broadly to the Roman ædile, and administrator of forests (*Forstrat*). It is the chief business of the syndic to see that the executive in any of its measures or resolutions does not act contrary to the law, to put in legal order all actions at law or other proceedings of a legal character in which the town may be involved, and in general to watch the legal side of municipal work in every direction. This official must have had a proper legal training, and have passed the State legal examinations. The chamberlain or treasurer superintends all financial business, prepares the budgets, controls revenue and expenditure, investments, loans, etc. The secretary for education is at the head of the educational system of the municipality, and serves on the school committee. The commissioner of public works is responsible for the order and security of the municipal real estate, including all buildings and land belonging to the town, and he also advises on all new erections and prepares plans for the same. He is, however, an official distinct from the usual town surveyors, architects, and building inspectors. Other technical experts are nowadays appointed according to need, and the number is never final.

The appointment of unpaid aldermen is almost universal, and their presence on the executive is regarded as of great advantage. Their duty is to see that the opinions of the popular assembly receive due consideration, and in general they serve as a useful counterbalance to the influence of the permanent officials, who may incline towards mechanical and strictly formal views on questions of policy. As a rule, honorary aldermanship is the reward of long years of public life. In the executives of most large towns are usually found men of ripe experience, sound business training, shrewd practical judgment, and often of ample leisure, who bring to official deliberations and decisions the quick judgment and free play of the unofficial mind. In the province of Hanover some of the unpaid aldermen or "senators" must belong or have belonged to the trading class.

Sometimes unpaid aldermen are given full responsibility for important departments of work and even for trading enterprises, but their proper function is deliberative.

Although the spirit of the Municipal Ordinances requires that the salaried and honorary members of the executive should be well balanced, with a leaning to an excess of the honorary element, so as to secure to lay influence proper weight, there is no definite rule as to the ratio of the two sections of the executive. They are often elected in equal numbers, but while in some towns there is a strong preponderance of unpaid members, in others there are no honorary senators at all.

The following figures, showing for a recent year the ratio of salaried to unsalaried members of the executives in some of the larger towns of Prussia, illustrate the prevailing diversity of practice (the salaried members include one or more mayors) :—

	Salaried Members.	Unsalaried Members.	Total.
Aix-la-Chapelle	6	2	8
Barmen	6	4	10
Berlin	17	17	34
Bielefeld	4	7	11
Breslau	14	15	29
Cassel	7	17	24
Charlottenburg	10	15	25
Cologne	13	—	13
Danzig	13	12	25
Düsseldorf	12	—	12
Elberfeld	8	3	11
Essen	9	1	10
Frankfort-on-Main	11	13	24
Hanover	11	10	21
Königsberg	10	14	24
Magdeburg	12	15	27
Posen	9	12	21
Stettin	11	13	24

The executives of large towns in other States are formed as follows :—

	Salaried Members.	Unsalaried Members.	Total.
Augsburg	11	14	25
Chemnitz	12	18	30
Dresden	17	22	39
Karlsruhe	4	23	27
Leipzig	14	17	31
Mannheim	4	23	27
Munich	17	20	37
Nuremberg	13	20	33
Stuttgart	5	28	33
Strassburg	7	—	7

There is a danger always of the number of aldermen exceeding that at which executive work can be transacted with a maximum of efficiency and expedition and a minimum of inconvenience, while experience has shown that the larger the executive becomes the more the danger of cliques and parties increases. Hence additional aldermen are appointed sparingly, and often only when the multiplication of municipal enterprises requires some reinforcement of the responsible expert chiefs.

Berlin has for sixty years had an executive of thirty-four members, one-half salaried and the rest honorary. When new officials of the first rank have been needed the executive has on several occasions averted addition to its ranks by appointing responsible heads of departments, without seats in the executive, with the name " magisterial directors." The town council dislikes this arrangement, however, inasmuch as while it possesses the sole right to appoint the executive, the right to appoint staff officials rests with that body alone, and it is unwilling to forgo control over appointments to the more important offices. This attitude in 1913 led to a departure from the tradition which fixed the number of senators at thirty-four, for in that year an alderman was elected to take charge of the department of public health.

As in the case of membership of town councils, father and son, father-in-law and son-in-law, brothers and brothers-in-law may not be simultaneously members of an executive in Prussia, and should such couples be elected the elder of the two is chosen. Nor may such relatives be chosen simultaneously as members of the executive and the town council. Other persons disqualified from being members of the executive are officials and members of authorities through whom the State exercises oversight over the communes, town councillors, and certain minor communal officials, clergymen, church ushers, and teachers in public schools, judicial officers, with the exception of technical members of the commercial, industrial and similar courts, officers attached to the State Attorney-General's office, and police officials.

The executives in the Southern States have peculiarities of their own. In Bavaria a modification of the East Prussian executive, called also by the same name, viz. " magistracy," is in operation. In Nuremberg the executive not only administers the civil affairs of the town, but acts as the police authority. The executive is composed of the chief or first and a second mayor, both jurists, seven " councillors " with legal training, two technical experts (for the departments of buildings and schools), and twenty civil (burgher) councillors, the maximum allowed by law. The first mayor is elected for life, the second mayor for six years at a time, though in his capacity as a member of the senate his is also a life appointment; the legal and technical members of the executive are appointed for varying periods, and the civil members for six years. The civil members are chosen from amongst the enfranchised citizens. Both the legal and civil members of the executive have a right to vote upon all questions, but the technical members vote only upon questions affecting their special duties.

The arrangements in the towns of Baden correspond rather closely to those in English boroughs, for the town council and a body of aldermen act together both for deliberative and executive purposes. The various departments of public work and enterprise are managed by technical officials, who enjoy wide powers and considerable independence. These officials are members of the committees which deal with the matters in their care, and vote at meetings, but they are not represented in the senate, where the mayor alone represents their opinions and expounds their proposals. The principal drawback of the Baden system is that it throws upon the mayor responsibility for an immense amount of detail and to that extent curtails the time available for more important duties. Hence there is a strong movement in favour of the addition to the senate of permanent officials on the analogy of the " magisterial " or " mayoral " *régimes* of Prussia, but no one wishes to see the honorary members outnumbered.

The term of election of the aldermen or *adjoints* is different according as they are unpaid or paid. The Prussian Ordinances usually fix six years for the unpaid members and twelve years, as in the case of mayors, for the paid, though both mayors and salaried aldermen may be appointed for life. In Würtemberg, where the town council and the executive are equal in number, the aldermen are elected for six years ; in Baden the salaried aldermen are elected for nine and the honorary for six years. In the Prussian province of Hanover life appointment is required by law from the first and in the kingdom of Saxony in the case of re-elections.

Although municipal bodies, the executives are regarded as mediate State authorities in distinction to the immediate authorities appointed directly by the Government in the name of the Crown. The Municipal Ordinance for the province of Hanover says expressly : " The magistracy is the administrator of communal affairs, *and at the same time the State authority.*" On this theory of their office is based the right of the Crown or Government in most States to confirm the appointment of members to these bodies, and to remove them from office if found guilty of conduct contrary to the supposed interests of the State, a right exercised as a rule through the subordinate supervisory authority.[1] Thus in the eastern provinces of Prussia all appointments of aldermen, salaried or honorary, require to be confirmed by the District President, who can only object if the District Committee agrees with him ; should the Committee disagree, the District President may appeal to the Minister of the Interior to decide, and the same right of appeal is allowed to the municipal executive or assembly in the event of an appointment being quashed. In Berlin appointments to the executive are confirmed by the Chief President of the province of Brandenburg (who is also the Chief President of Berlin), without the District Committee being consulted. Where sanction is withheld it is not necessary to give reasons. In Bavaria only the legal members of the executive need to be confirmed.

Refusal to confirm is comparatively rare, except when persons known to belong to the Social Democratic party are chosen, yet even then it occurs only in Prussia and the other States in which the acceptance of Socialistic views is held in official circles to incapacitate a man from serving the community faithfully. The right of veto proves at times a useful political weapon in the hands of the Prussian Government in its crusade against Polish and Danish influence.

The custom as to qualifications for the position of salaried or professional aldermen is various. In Prussia, where the authors of the existing Municipal Ordinances were more concerned that these officials should be acceptable to the Crown and Government as loyal and pliant individuals than experi-

[1] Dr. Hugo Preuss says : " In Prussia there is no delegation of State functions to the mayors of towns, even of large towns, and indeed least of all of such towns. And yet all Prussian Municipal Ordinances require that the mayors shall be confirmed by the Government. This provision is nothing less than a survival of the direct Government appointment of State officials." Nevertheless, the transference to the mayors of certain police functions reserved by the State, as already explained, must be regarded as in conflict with the early part of this statement.

enced in the arts and sciences of town government, appointment is still not legally dependent upon the possession of special qualifications, except in the case of the syndic and the public works commissioner, and the same thing applies in Würtemberg, Baden, and Hesse. Special training is prescribed, however, by the laws of some of the other States. Thus the law of Bavaria requires that paid members of the executive, except those occupying technical positions, shall be jurists ; and the law of Saxony requires that at least one member of the executive shall be so qualified.

This is a question, however, which custom has decided in a way not contemplated by law. The development of municipal government, the extension of its powers and functions, and, above all, the widening of the scope of public economic enterprise have everywhere compelled German towns to turn more and more from the rule of the amateur to that of the expert, and the modern administrator is expected to combine special fitness for his particular department of work with personal qualities of the highest order.

FUNCTIONS OF THE EXECUTIVE.—The duties of the executive are multifarious, and belong to the most important pertaining to local government. The executive is first of all responsible for the due execution of all Imperial and State laws and regulations incumbent on a commune, in which relationship it is quite independent of the town council. Further, it has to execute the resolutions passed by the representative assembly, for though the latter possesses full right to initiate measures and proposals it is the business of the executive to put these in proper form, and when they have been adopted to apply or enforce them, though it is not legally justified in doing this unless it has convinced itself that they are legitimate, unobjectionable, and in nowise contrary to the law or the public welfare. The Municipal Ordinance for the eastern provinces of Prussia specially mentions the following matters as falling to the province of the executive :—

(1) To execute all laws and decrees as well as the orders of the authorities to which it is subject ;

(2) to formulate the resolutions of the communal assembly

DISTRIBUTION OF ADMINISTRATIVE POWERS

and give effect to them " in so far as it agrees with the same " ;

(3) to administer the communal institutions and to superintend the institutions for which special administrations are appointed ;

(4) to administer the revenues of the commune ;

(5) to administer the property of the commune and to protect its rights ;

(6) to appoint communal officers after hearing the communal assembly thereupon and to supervise the same ;

(7) to have custody of the documents and archives of the commune ;

(8) to represent the town in external matters and to negotiate with authorities and private persons in its name, to carry on correspondence and to execute communal documents; and

(9) to apportion communal contributions and services (taxes) according to the laws and resolutions amongst those liable and to collect the same.

The Ordinance states generally, however, that it is the duty of the executive to enforce the decisions of the town council " in so far as it is in agreement therewith." The reservation is one of the utmost significance, for it gives to the executive a position of great independence. Should the executive refuse to enforce any resolution of the council on the ground that it exceeds the latter's competence or is contrary to the public interest, it must duly report to the council its reasons for such refusal. Should the council hold to its decision and the executive still decline to give way, appeal may be made to the District Committee to decide between the conflicting opinions. Naturally local authorities are slow to call in the aid of the supervisory body, and internal disputes are usually settled by compromise.

A large number of the duties of the mayor and executive lie quite outside the sphere of communal government, as, for example, those relating to the elections to the Diets, to the Imperial Parliament, the assessment and collection of certain State taxes and contributions, certain military matters, the preparation and publication of jury lists and the election of arbitrators, the supervision of the trade guilds and the regulation of various matters within the sphere of the Industrial Code, the decision of disputes of certain kinds where there is no Industrial Court, and the institution and management of industrial, commercial, and trade guild courts, and courts of arbitration, together with the many duties imposed upon them by the social insurance legislation. In addition, the chief mayors of some of the large towns are called to the upper chamber of the Diet.

It is, however, in its capacity as a body of permanent heads of departments that the executive does its most important work. It is responsible (under the mayor) for the administration of all municipal institutions and enterprises, such as schools, hospitals, savings banks, parks, markets, Poor Law agencies, houses of correction, sanitation, sewerage, and water works, and the various works connected with transport, lighting, etc. Other duties are the administration of the town's property and finances, and the regulation of local taxation (subject to control by the town council), the collection of the taxes, the guarding of the town's rights in all directions, the appointment and the supervision of officials, the care of the public archives, and the representation of the municipality in its corporate capacity, though here the person of the mayor comes into special prominence. Most important of all, while it is the business of the executive to work out and put into operation the schemes of the representative assembly, its own power of initiative is unrestricted, subject to endorsement by that assembly.

The executive with its head, the mayor, may be regarded as at once the brain and the hands of the communal assembly. It is a standing committee, watching day by day the interests of the town, ever on the look out for new opportunities of useful action, exercising direct control over every one of the town's manifold activities, and bringing to the discharge of all its functions the skill, resource, knowledge, and experience that may be expected from a body of trained experts. The work of the executive goes on all through the year, and from year to year. The town council may meet often or rarely, but the executive never suspends either energy or vigilance. It is the sleepless eye of the municipality, that looks behind and before, and keeps continual guard upon the interests of the community.

Perhaps in no department of affairs has the German faith in the value of science and training been more justified than in local government, for the institution of the permanent executive places at the service of every town a body of skilled experts, each equipped for his work by special knowledge and preparation. It is a commonplace observation that German municipal enterprise years ago extended to some directions which are only now being touched in this country. Yet this fact need not excite surprise when it is remembered how long and how well Germany has been served by these special corps of trained men, whose business it is not merely to wait on public opinion, which is as a rule so little informed as to a community's real needs and truest interests, but to anticipate those needs and to safeguard those interests by the exercise of intelligent foresight, ever influenced in its action not by fugitive exigencies, but by considerations of future and permanent utility and advantage. If it be conceded that the institution of the standing executive possesses these great merits, it must be admitted that a rare degree of insight and prescience characterised the statesmen who created this institution generations ago, when communal government was in its infancy, and when its scope and responsibilities were insignificant in comparison with the requirements of the present day.

In some of the large towns of Prussia constant increase of municipal work has led to the appointment of a certain number of paid adjuncts to the magistracy with the name " assessors " (*Magistratsassessoren*), who after a certain term of service become " councillors " (*Magistratsräte*). They are assigned to the various committees, and sometimes are entrusted with the direction of minor departments of administration. Some of these officials are elected for six years at once, and later they may be appointed for life.

The executive decides at will the frequency of its meetings. As a rule, it meets once a week on a fixed day in the larger towns, but in the smaller towns it may meet only when required.

THE MAYOR AND HIS FUNCTIONS.—Although considered last, the mayor is the most important member of the municipal government. He is the crown of the structure, perfecting but also adorning it and binding it together. The representative authority, in the words of the Prussian Municipal Ordinance for the eastern provinces, " controls the administration," the magistracy or executive is " the supreme authority of the town and manages its communal affairs," but the mayor " directs and superintends the entire business of the urban administration." In the larger towns the Crown often confers upon the mayor proper the title of first or chief mayor, and where in such cases a deputy is appointed he is known as second mayor or only as mayor; except in Saxony and Bavaria, the title of chief mayor is honorary and not statutory, and is held by favour of the Crown. Berlin, Cassel, Charlottenburg, and Frankfort-on-Main have each a chief mayor and one mayor; Munich and Mannheim have a chief mayor and three mayors; and many large towns only a chief mayor or mayor.

Whatever their rank, mayors are, as a rule, chosen for twelve years, and on re-election they may be appointed for life. The new Municipal Ordinance for Würtemberg, however, abolished life mayoralties in the case of new appointments and fixed the tenure at ten years, but gave existing life mayors the right to submit themselves for re-election if they were so disposed. In that State the mayors are chosen by the general body of enfranchised citizens, and only the aldermen are chosen by the town council.

Appointments to the office of mayor unconditionally require confirmation by the Government in Prussia and Bavaria; conditional confirmation only is necessary in Würtemberg, i.e., if a nominee has received two-thirds of all votes given by the electors (in this case the qualified citizens) he needs confirmation only on a declaration of unfitness made by a Disciplinary Court; in Baden confirmation is not necessary. In Frankfort-on-Main, which is under a separate constitution, the chief mayor is nominated by the Crown, and the second mayor needs confirmation. The mayors are also chosen by the Crown in the communes of Neu-Vorpommern and Rügen. In the eastern provinces of Prussia the Crown confirms appointments both of mayors and deputy mayors in towns with more than 10,000 inhabitants; while in smaller towns these appointments are confirmed by the District President, who may only refuse assent if the District Committee supports him, but the District President may appeal to the Ministry of the Interior when his decision is not endorsed.

The provisions applying in Prussia in the event of non-confirmation of appointments are the same in the case of mayors and members of the executive generally. If confirmation is withheld in due form the town council or the executive may appeal to the Ministry of the Interior, who may reverse the refusal. When an appointment is not confirmed it is the duty of the town council to present another nomination, and in the event of this not being acceptable, or of the same candidate being presented, or of refusal to present at all, the District President may appoint a commissary to act at the town's expense until the town council makes an acceptable appointment.

The German mayor stands in the forefront of municipal life and government in a way that the English mayor and the Scottish provost do not. An English mayor has no administrative power beyond that which is conferred upon him by the town council, every one of whose members is his equal in matters of jurisdiction. The German mayor has the same status and authority in the domain of local administration as that which belongs in Germany to the head of a Government. To add to his dignity, if he happens to be the head of one of the larger Prussian towns he is invariably called to the House of Lords as a member for life. The presidency of the executive is his first function. He directs its proceedings, allots to the members their several *ressorts* or departments of work, and requires of them a periodical account of their stewardship, for to him directly they are in the first instance responsible. There is not a functionary in the service of the municipality who does not owe him perfect obedience and undivided fidelity, and over whose actions he has not a controlling voice. Just as the executive may refuse to permit the town council to do actions which it believes to be illegal or improper, so it is the right and the duty of the mayor to control the action of his own colleagues, whether they form with himself a college or not ; if they in turn are about to commit themselves to a questionable course of procedure he may intervene with a definitive prohibition, and their hand is at once stayed.

In all his relations with his colleagues, indeed, whether they be fellow-members of a "magistracy," as in the eastern parts of Prussia, or *adjoints*, as in the west of the kingdom, the mayor occupies a dominant position. So far does his power go that, in the event of laxity on the part either of municipal officials or of members of the executive, it is the mayor who finds fault, admonishes, warns, and, if need be, resorts to severer measures. So, too, he grants leave of absence, or refuses it at will. The "right to reprove" the mayor may exercise very sparingly, yet he asserts it very jealously as against any pretensions of the town council to use it in his place. Not long ago, during a sitting of the Berlin City Council, a remark made by a member of the executive led the chairman to reprove that official. The chief mayor promptly rose in protest. "Reproof," he said, "is a disciplinary measure, and the chairman of this assembly possesses no right of reproof in respect of any member of the executive ; that right belongs to me alone." The right is, indeed, formally secured to him by the Municipal Ordinance under which the towns of the eastern provinces of Prussia are governed.

It has even been decided by Court of Appeal that a mayor has a right to reprove an unsalaried member of the executive in the event of abuse of office. This right to control and judge the official conduct of his colleagues on the executive extends also to the subaltern officials, and here again the mayor will suffer no interference. The Charlottenburg chief mayor recently issued an order forbidding the drinking of beer during office hours. This infraction of a treasured privilege excited protest, and the town council wished to debate the obnoxious order. In the exercise of his right to determine the agenda the chief mayor refused to allow his authority even to be criticised. There is only one exception to this personal supremacy of the mayor ; it is the case of the member of the executive who represents the police authority in its relationship to the municipality where the mayor himself is not chosen to do so, as he usually is.

Even under the "magisterial" system the mayor can in certain eventualities act entirely on his own responsibility. Such are the cases in which a prior resolution by the executive would occasion a harmful loss of time; the mayor must then decide alone, yet report to the next meeting of the executive for the purpose of having his action ratified or reversed. Further, in respect to functions which the State transfers to him the mayor is perfectly independent and is under no obligation to consult his colleagues or the town council. In passing, there are certain notable disqualifications for the office of mayor, as there are for that of the magistracy; persons interested in the retail sale of intoxicating drinks, agents of fire and hail insurance companies, and collectors of State income tax are all excluded.

The mayor is a salaried official, and his position is a professional one, requiring in the occupant special training. This office has been compared to that of the English or Scottish town clerk, but the analogy is very slight. The German mayor does, indeed, discharge personally or by deputy many of the functions which belong to the town clerk, but his power goes very much further, and his influence and official dignity are greater. He is, in truth, a microcosm of the entire administrative life and activity of the town. Nothing can be done without him; he is elected by the municipal body, but in many ways is independent of and superior to it. He directs policy, initiates measures, and helps forward or discourages the measures of others according to his wisdom. He represents the town in all public capacities and official relationships. He is its Prime Minister, its Home Secretary, and its Foreign Secretary all in one. To take a homelier illustration, he is both the mainspring of the municipal clock and the clock face; he keeps the machinery going, and he tells the time. His colleagues on the executive are the wheels, and indispensable though they are, they would be useless without the motive force which propels them; and just as there are clocks which go without wheels, so a German municipality might dispense with an executive, and still more a town council, but without its mayor it would be the mere shadow of a reality.[1] Such a man and such an office carry great weight in Germany. The mayor of a large provincial town is an enviable person who, having arrived at this goal of ambition, is usually content to remain where he is for life. For the fine flower of the municipal service, however, fate sometimes has richer rewards in store. For just as every professional alderman is the potential mayor of some commune or other, larger or smaller, so the first citizen of one of the great towns has ever before him the possibility of becoming one day a Minister of State.

The law of Prussia prescribes no specific qualifications for the position of mayor, yet the fact that it is a professional and, nowadays, a highly paid position, carrying great influence and an enviable social position, has widened the area of choice and attracted to the office men of the highest attainments. Alike in large and smaller towns the great majority of mayors and many of the salaried members of the executives are men of legal training. Of 329 salaried officials belonging to these ranks in 33 large towns of Germany in 1911, 235 were jurists, 54 technical experts, 22 philologists, three doctors, three political economists, and 12 other men with some other special training. Side by side with them were experts who had the management of special departments of municipal work, e.g., doctors, architects, educationists, experts in forestry, etc. Less importance is attached nowadays to a purely legal training and preparation. This may be useful, but it is felt that for an official who has to administer finance, commercial enterprise, education, poor relief, social reform, and above all

[1] As an illustration of the way in which the fortunes of German towns are made by able mayoral administrators, whose business it is to devote all their thought to this end, the following public tribute to the retiring chief mayor of Duisburg-on-the-Rhine may be quoted from a Berlin newspaper of February 12, 1914:—

" The chief mayor of Duisburg is about to seek well-earned rest after thirty-four years of work. When in 1880 he took over the direction of the town's affairs Duisburg had 34,000 inhabitants. To-day Duisburg, with the amalgamated Ruhrort and Meiderich, has a population of 244,000. This remarkable development is specially due to the far-sighted municipal policy pursued by the chief mayor, who made it his endeavour to attract new industries to the town. His greatest triumphs were the formation of the partnership with the State for the creation of the docks—as the result of which Duisburg is the largest inland port in the world—and the incorporation of Ruhrort and Meiderich in 1905."

to manage men, other qualifications are more necessary, such as a thorough grasp of economic science, great business aptitude, practical sense and *savoir faire*, and a considerable knowledge of the world and men. Recently there has been a disposition in some towns to seek mayors outside the ranks of those trained in municipal service, for the belief is growing that for this office and the responsibility which it carries " the best is only good enough."

Not many years ago no body of public servants were paid so poorly relatively to their responsibilities and rank as the mayors and permanent aldermen of German towns. Of late there has been a great improvement, and the salaries of these officials are still on the up-grade, thanks to the keen competition of the larger towns for good men. Berlin pays its chief mayor a salary of £2,000, Frankfort-on-Main pays £1800, and the salaries in other towns are: Düsseldorf, £1650; Charlottenburg, £1525; Breslau and Cologne, £1500; Nuremberg, £1360; Essen, £1350; Leipzig, Magdeburg, and Altona, £1250; Hanover, £1200; Stettin and Aix-la-Chapelle, £1150; Königsberg, Schöneberg, and Elberfeld, £1100; Barmen and Wilmersdorf, £1075; Dortmund and Freiburg, £1050; and Dresden, Chemnitz, Crefeld, Duisburg, Mannheim, Strassburg, Posen, Stuttgart, and Wiesbaden, £1000. Many other large towns pay their chief mayors between £800 and £1000, while the salaries paid in smaller towns are proportionately lower. " Second mayors " receive as a rule from £800 to £1000, but the latter sum only in exceptional cases. Sometimes a mayoral residence or a grant on account of residence is added to the chief mayor's salary. In some cases representation money is also paid, though all costs of the kind are usually discharged by the town direct. In towns with from 5000 to 10,000 inhabitants the mayor's salary commonly ranges from £250 to £400.

The conditions of retirement are liberal. Thus the Municipal Ordinance for the eastern provinces of Prussia provides that both mayors and paid members of the executive shall in the event of incapacity, or of their not being re-elected at the expiration of any period of appointment, receive as pension one-quarter of their salary after six years of service, one-half after twelve years, and seven-tenths after twenty-four years.

Service in one communal administration counts for pension in another; hence when a pensioned officer enters State or communal service elsewhere his pension is either forfeited or suspended to the extent that his pension and his new salary together may exceed his earlier income. Statutory provision is also made for widows and for orphans up to a certain age.

The "Magisterial" and "Mayoral" Executive Systems Compared.—Reference has been made already to the two principal forms in which the executive is found in Prussia and other parts of Germany—the "magisterial," as in the eastern districts, and the "mayoral," as in the west—and several peculiarities of the two forms may be noted here. Under the "magisterial" system the executive acts as a body and its decisions are determined by the vote of the majority. The mayor as its chairman can give a casting vote in the event of a tie, but otherwise as a member of the executive he is simply *primus inter pares*, and he is bound by the decision of a majority of his colleagues except in the exercise of powers transferred to him personally by law or the Government. Some Municipal Ordinances give the mayor the right to object to resolutions of the executive, in which case its only remedy is to appeal to Government or to the Administrative Court. It would lead us into details too technical in character to explain the course of procedure laid down for the meetings and deliberations of the "magistracy"—to instance the questions which can only be determined in plenary sitting, those less important matters which can be transacted without severe formality, the order of business which must be followed, the system of reports and references, and the like. While in parts of Bavaria meetings are open to the public, in Prussia secrecy as to all proceedings is usually prescribed by law, and neither verbal nor written communication may be made by a member of the executive as to any business that has been transacted, on pain in certain eventualities of dismissal from office. Should a member be in any way personally interested in any matter of discussion he may not take part, but must withdraw from the sitting.

Under the "mayoral" *régime* the town councils withhold from the executive certain powers possessed by the "magistracy," but they lose them to the mayor. This official is both the administrative head of the town and the president of its representative assembly; he directs the entire work of the commune, and assigns to each of his *adjoints*, whether paid or unpaid, his special duties, while the *adjoints* are responsible to him personally. There is here no college of aldermen in which every question has to be decided by the majority, for the *adjoints* are in effect the mayor's assistants. Except in questions of prime importance, each *adjoint* is supposed to manage his department independently, and to bear responsibility for his own decisions, yet this independence is only theoretical, for the mayor has the last word always, and he can accept or reject at will any policy or measure proposed by his colleagues, so that in the event of disagreement the *adjoint* has to choose between compliance and resignation.

It is a much discussed question which of the two systems of executive government is the more efficient. The question is clearly one for the application of the dictum: "That system of government is best which works best," and the fact that towns which have organised their government upon one method seldom or never go over to the other suggests that there are advantages as well as possible defects on both sides. Hitherto the idea has been widely prevalent that the "mayoral" system was best suited to small towns or suited to them only; nowadays, owing to the greater expedition of business promoted by this system, it is regarded by many authorities as even more expedient in large towns than in small. On the other hand, under the "mayoral" system there is always a fear of the mayor becoming excessively bureaucratic. For though the chairman of the town council, like the English mayor, and controlled by that body, he is still the executive head of the town, and responsible for the direction of all its affairs. Such a position carries great responsibility and requires the exercise of wide powers, but it also conduces to a sort of informal dictatorship. The East German mayor is likewise the head of the executive, but he is subject, in theory at least, to the control of his colleagues, who act with him as a college; under the "mayoral" system this control is absent, while the control theoretically possible to the town council is in practice unreal and apparent.

Under the " magisterial " system also the popular assembly is at a disadvantage in its relations with the executive. Not only do the individual magistrates or aldermen under this system possess far more power than is enjoyed by the *adjoints* under the " mayoral " system, but as between executive and town council the balance of power is overwhelmingly on the side of the permanent officials. Herein lies a source of frequent friction. Because they possess such large power, and because they are in a sense set apart from the town council, to which none the less they owe their existence, the " magistrates " in their corporate capacity are far more ready to assert their rights, and far more jealous of any invasion of them, than the *adjoints*. It is a common experience that the mayor and senators of a town under the " magisterial " *régime* do not invariably show the same spirit of accommodation and the same friendly co-operation which seem to characterise the general relationship of town council and executive under the rival system. When the interests of the town are threatened from the outside, whether by the State or private individuals, " magistracy " and town council work together with undivided will, but in internal matters the relationship between the two bodies is apt to be strained owing to suspicion on both sides, and here and there to partake even of the character of an armed peace. It is not that the men who form the " magistracy " in Eastern Prussia are different in character and temperament from the mayor and *adjoints* of the west, but that the conditions under which they work are not equally conducive to harmonious dealings.

Not long ago a thoughtful writer in the "Cologne Gazette" (June 3, 1911) called attention to this fact, and his observations will probably be endorsed by all impartial observers of the two systems in actual working. He wrote : " The meetings of the municipal bodies in Rhenish towns create always the impression that the mayor, *adjoints*, and town councillors regard each other as equal partners, co-operate willingly, and evince no natural antagonism. In Berlin, on the other hand, one has only to read the reports of the city council's meetings in order to be convinced that the 'magistracy' and the council regard each other as born enemies, each eager to invade the domain of the other and to resist invasion in return. Nor must it be supposed that the jealousy shown towards the municipal bureaucracy is confined to the Social Democrats, for it inspires all parties, which in this common prejudice forget their own antagonisms." A council can, of course, exercise the right to refuse to reappoint undesirable honorary senators when their time of office expires, yet even if changes are made it is with the knowledge that the new men will be sure, sooner or later, to assimilate the prevailing temper and tradition.

DEVOLUTION OF ADMINISTRATIVE DUTIES: DEPUTATIONS, COMMISSIONS, ETC.—Just as the English borough and urban district councils work through a series of committees, so under the German system of communal government subordinate bodies are formed for the management of various branches of municipal work and enterprise and for purely deliberative purposes. These bodies are constituted in any desired number by the executive, to which they are directly subordinate, and they have no direct contact with the representative assembly or any outside authorities. They are named differently in different towns, but the principles upon which duties are devolved upon them are everywhere the same. In Berlin and other Prussian towns these bodies are of two kinds—" Deputations" and " Commissions." Among the branches of administrative work which are most commonly entrusted to these bodies are finance, buildings, poor relief, public health, municipal estate, town planning, land purchase, abattoirs, gas and power works, tramways, sewerage, education, theatres, public parks, market halls, and scavenging.

The Deputations and Commissions may consist (1) of members of the executive only, (2) of these and members of the town council, or (3) to both elements a sprinkling of outside citizens may be added. In large towns the first constitution is usual, since greater unity and expedition of procedure is thus attained. The members of the executive who sit upon these bodies are elected thereto by the executive itself, while the town council elects its own body and co-opts the outsiders. The honorary members of all kinds are generally elected in proportion to the strength of parties represented in the town council. The mayor is *ex officio* the chairman, and in his absence the senior member of the executive present takes his place. In no way, however, is the authority of the mayor limited or weakened by the existence of these subordinate bodies, however formed. The Deputations and Commissions receive their orders from that officer and the executive, and within the limits of the work and authority entrusted to them they enjoy considerable independence, with the proviso that they are in the last resort subject to the control of the authority from which they proceed, and that they have no control over finance. The Deputations occupy a higher status than the Commissions, however, in that they possess administrative functions while the Commissions are deliberative bodies. At the same time even a Deputation cannot bring forward in the town council any proposal independently of the executive. If individual members do so it is only in their capacity as councillors.

Special rules apply in Prussia to the constitution of the School Deputation, which must consist (according to the size of the town) of one to three members of the executive, one to three members of the town council, an equal number of experts on educational questions, and when non-municipal schools are subject to the Deputation a representative of such schools must be added. As a rule this Deputation numbers nine (or ten) in the larger towns, six (or seven) in towns of medium size, and three (or four) in small towns. All the members of such a Deputation need to be confirmed in office by the Government, which claims this right in virtue of the contention that such a Deputation is a subsidiary part of the State education authority, while all other Deputations are merely auxiliary to the municipal executive. The consequence of this liability to confirmation is that persons politically objectionable to the Government can always be kept out of office.

As illustrating the close connection between State and Church in Prussia, it may be stated that in small towns the leading clergyman must be one of the experts on the School

DISTRIBUTION OF ADMINISTRATIVE POWERS 109

Deputation; and indeed the co-operation of the clergy in education is enjoined by law as of special importance.

The place which the Deputations occupy in the administration of a large city may be illustrated by the case of Berlin, which has separate Deputations for poor relief, the care of orphans, finance, schools, taxation, public libraries and reading-rooms, industry (including the supervision of the trade guilds), building plans, etc., means of communication (tramways, railways, steamboats, etc.), gymnastic halls and bathing-places, charitable foundations, municipal real estate, sewerage and the sewage farms, the artistic property of the city, the market halls, waterworks, gasworks, the labour house and shelters for the homeless, the care of the blind, technical and continuation schools, municipal fire insurance, higher schools, hospitals and public health, the care of imbeciles, parks and gardens, the provision of fuel, the provision of writing materials, chemical laboratory for hygienic and industrial purposes, the internal decoration of the town hall, and street cleaning. There is also a large group of Commissions.

Devolution to bodies smaller and of minor importance, known as curatories (*Curatorien*), is also usual in Berlin. These bodies have charge of the convalescent homes, the savings banks, the public cemeteries, the Frederick William Hospital and Invalids' Homes, and the cattle markets, abattoirs, and meat inspection.

To take a Prussian town of smaller size, the town council of Aix-la-Chapelle, in the Rhineland province of Prussia, has Deputations, Commissions, and Committees for fifty-nine different branches of municipal work or enterprise.

In illustration of the plan of devolution usual in South Germany the case of Nuremberg may be cited. There a warden or curator (*Pfleger*) is assigned to every municipal institution, property, and branch of public work, and it is his duty to exercise supervision over his trust in the name of the executive, and to see to the execution of all decisions of that body in relation to it. Special councils (*Räte*), of which the first mayor is chairman, exist for the administration of poor relief and of the schools, and for the care of orphans. Other departments of public work and enterprise for which special administrative or supervisory committees exist are the gasworks, electricity works, tramways, buildings, gardens, cattle market and abattoir, chemical laboratory (analysis of foodstuffs), hospitals, cemeteries, pawnshop, savings bank, insurance, labour registry, schools, library and archives, charitable endowments, statistical office, registry of birth, deaths, and marriages, finance, hospitals, etc.

Many of the larger towns keep in touch with public opinion by the issue of daily or weekly Official Gazettes (often called *Gemeindeblatt*). Primarily intended for municipal announcements, reports of town council meetings, and other official information, these journals sometimes devote attention to the affairs and news of the day—party politics excluded—and in several towns they compete for public favour with the ordinary newspapers.

In addition to publishing official bulletins, Berlin, Mannheim, Cologne, and several other large towns have municipal intelligence bureaux, for the purpose of supplying the Press and the citizens with information relating to administrative matters. Another and more important branch of the municipal intelligence service is the Statistical Office, an institution which has reached a high standard of efficiency in German towns, and is worthy of wider imitation in this and other countries. Forty-six German towns have organised special and permanent departments for statistics, directed by trained men of the highest capacity, and producing year by year reports and records which of their kind are rarely equalled in any other country. Some of these Statistical Offices date from half a century ago, and most of them can boast a distinguished record of honourable achievement in the service of local government.

It must be added that German towns appear to take great pride in the worthy housing of their local administrations. The new town halls of some of the great towns—Munich, Leipzig, and Berlin among the number—are noble and dignified structures that fitly typify the largeness of conception which characterises municipal life and enterprise in Germany. Often the ambition to own a stately town hall leads towns into extravagant outlay far beyond either their financial resources or their needs; debts of some such towns bear traces of the penalty of unjustifiable ostentation, but this is a matter in which German towns generally are disposed to prodigality, and their autonomy enables them to indulge in architectural luxury to any extent they please.

HONORARY SERVICE IN COMMUNAL ADMINISTRATION.—It will be seen from the plan of devolution described that although the German system of municipal government is based on the principle of rule by the expert it does not taboo honorary service. Rather it sets the professional officer and the voluntary worker in their right relationship; with the former at the front, always directing and controlling municipal policy. But devolution does not stop with the larger administrative committees, upon which the permanent officials predominate or otherwise exercise complete control, for room is found in other directions for a large variety of honorary service. In most States such service is an obligation not to be evaded save on ample grounds. The first Prussian Municipal Ordinance of 1808 went so far as to punish citizens who systematically neglected to exercise the vote by disentitling them either to vote or to take any part in the government of their commune. That provision no longer stands, yet all citizens eligible to vote in local elections are still liable to accept honorary office in the communal government if called upon so to do, and to hold such office for three years, unless exempted by reason of permanent illness, affairs which require their frequent or protracted absence from home, age (over sixty years), the holding of some other public position, practice as a physician or surgeon, or other special circumstances. The punishment for refusal to accept office is deprivation of rights as a citizen for a period of from three to six years, and taxation on a higher scale.

Apart from membership of the representative assembly, honorary service plays a prominent part in connection with the committees for poor relief, the care of orphans, housing, education, and the management of charitable foundations administered by the town.

The army of honorary workers may be divided into two

sections—a first reserve, composed of " burgher deputies " and district superintendents, and a second reserve, comprising the large body of miscellaneous citizens, both men and women, who are liable to serve on committees, or in such other ways as the mayor and executive may think best. The " burgher deputies," who are found both in North and South Germany, are co-opted citizens of character and substance, upon whom the mayor and executive are able to fall back when special work of an honorary kind has to be done. These "burgher deputies" do not sit on the council, but are prominent upon the more important committees, such as the assessment and taxation committees.

An important part in the public life of the town is also played by the district superintendents (*Bezirksvorsteher*), who are honorary officers appointed by wards or localities for the purpose of assisting the executive in various matters within their districts, e.g., the general oversight of the streets, bridges, watercourses, wells, etc., ambulance depots, and the hundred and one petty matters of order and decorum that mean little individually but together contribute so much to the amenity of public life. The district superintendent is also expected to acquaint himself with the social conditions of his fragment of the town, so that his knowledge and advice may be of value in the administration of poor relief and the " social welfare " agencies of the municipality.

More numerous are the workers who are called upon to co-operate on the various committees already enumerated. In the constitution of these committees a fair attempt is made to enlist the services of all sections of the community. For example, Berlin had in 1913 no fewer than 446 district poor relief committees, with 5650 members, of whom 2299 were described as tradesmen and handicraftsmen, 837 merchants, 351 manufacturers, 140 *restaurateurs*, 98 architects, surveyors, engineers, and chemists, 52 doctors, veterinary surgeons, and dentists, 265 schoolmasters and teachers, 13 clergymen, 351 State and municipal officials, 5 lawyers, 58 apothecaries, 46 bank officials, 22 church and cemetery officials, 548 *rentiers*, 91 overseers and journeymen, 7 unskilled labourers, and 134 followed miscellaneous occupations. When, in 1914, Berlin set

DISTRIBUTION OF ADMINISTRATIVE POWERS

up its new Housing Board it was formed of 20 paid officials and 743 honorary members, these being divided amongst 118 district committees, each with from four to 12 members.

In some of the spheres of work above mentioned women take an important part, though still prevented by the prejudice, conservatism, and shortsightedness of the sex in power from contributing all the effort and influence they would like to the common stock. In many towns they are admitted rather than welcomed to the education, housing, poor relief, and orphans' committees, yet sometimes on unequal terms, being permitted only to deliberate and not to vote. They are more readily nominated upon the less official committees which direct certain branches of the town's general " social welfare" work. It is estimated that a total of 18,000 women are engaged in communal work of various kinds in some 300 communes, and that about 450 occupy positions as salaried officials. The States in which on the whole the value of women's work in local administration has been most widely recognised are Baden, Bavaria, and Saxony, yet comparing individual towns there is still great disparity in the degree of recognition extended to women.

THE ADMINISTRATIVE STAFFS.—The general conditions of service of municipal officials, their rights and duties, their pension claims and the claims of their survivors are, as a rule, laid down in special laws in each State. The rules as to the appointment of mayors and salaried members of the executives have already been explained. The higher officials next under them are appointed either by the mayor or the executive or by the town council—for the practice differs in various States; but the officers of minor rank are invariably appointed by the mayor alone or in conjunction with his colleagues of the executive. In general, the higher appointments are, either legally or by prescription, life appointments. It has been estimated that over 40 per cent. of the officers engaged in the general administration and under 30 per cent. of those engaged in the technical departments of government are so appointed. As a rule, the aspirants for positions on the permanent staff are required to serve for several years either without salary or for a nominal payment, and, in view of this long time of probation and of the high educational qualifications required, the salaries paid, even to the occupants of the highest positions, cannot be described as excessive.

Nevertheless, the competition for admission to the municipal service is keen, and the administrations of large towns in particular have always long lists of aspirants-in-waiting, ready to take the place of the probationers directly these have been settled in permanent positions or otherwise disposed of. The supernumerary offices are filled subject to less onerous qualifications, though here, again, it is probably the fact of certain employment, the prospect of good retirement allowances, and the satisfaction supposed to be incidental to employment in the public service that attract to the ranks rather than liberality in present remuneration. In many towns the minor offices are systematically thrown open to young men who have passed through elementary schools and have carried further their education by private effort, while in some towns the municipal executive superintends the special training of the future officers of the lower grades. In most Prussian towns the salaries of officials on the establishment are paid quarterly, but in the larger towns of other States monthly, in advance.

The efficiency of the administrative staffs of German towns is best proved by the results of their work as seen in the exemplary government of these towns. The one fault found by German critics of the organisation of local government is that it has imbibed the spirit of the State bureaucracy too freely; resolutions are adopted with laudable promptness, but their execution is apt to be unduly delayed owing to the wearisome routine which has to be observed, not because routine is necessary, but because it has come to be regarded as part of the system. German municipal officials themselves often complain of the futile, tedious, time-wasting red-tapeism by which they are bound or bind themselves, and it is a fair conclusion that an average English mayor or town clerk would make short work of much of the needless circumlocution and formality which German municipal governments have unwisely borrowed from the State bureaucratic system.

SCHOOLS FOR COMMUNAL GOVERNMENT.—It would be strange if the land of schools failed to link up its seats of learning with its system of communal government. The science of local government—for Germany persists in so regarding local government—may be studied in a host of colleges and schools in all parts of the country. Düsseldorf and Cologne have special colleges for communal administration where future officials and town councillors are taken through the entire range of administrative questions. Other schools in Prussia are those of Hagen, Aschersleben, and Bochum, while in Berlin instruction is given in some of the continuation schools to young people desirous of entering the lower grades of the municipal service. In Saxony there are schools for communal officials at Cottbus and Nerchau (the latter with 145 pupils in training in 1911). The same purpose is served in Bavaria by the regular courses of lectures held in connection with the Munich Trade College. A school for communal officials exists at Eisenach for the Thuringian States, with a two years' course on such questions as local finance and taxation, education, poor relief, town planning, police functions, and social legislation. Other towns, like Ludwigshafen, have established schools for the training of police officials. The municipal authorities of some of the larger towns directly superintend the training of certain classes of minor officials. Accepting young men direct from school as probationers, they prescribe for them a suitable course of instruction in continuation classes, and, after three years, examinations are held upon the results of which depends the chance of permanent engagement.

MUNICIPAL CONGRESSES AND LEAGUES.—German municipal authorities unite in a large number of federations and congresses for mutual protection, assistance, advice, and the periodical discussion of questions of common interest. The most influential of these organisations is the Municipal Congress for the Empire (the *Deutscher Städtetag*), to which are affiliated all towns with a population exceeding 25,000 and ten municipal leagues. Its members represent more than one-fourth of the population of the Empire. The Congress exists to further the interests of the affiliated towns and their governments in every possible way, to afford opportunities, by conference and otherwise, for the exchange of ideas, and to place at the disposal of the affiliated authorities the collective knowledge and experience of the members. The Congress meets every three years in different parts of the country, and meetings of the executive are held as circumstances may require. When important questions of public policy or legislative proposals affecting the towns come to the front, the Congress or its executive presses its views upon the Government and is heard with respect, if not always with agreement. The Congress has in Berlin a central office (*Zentralstelle*) which, in addition to keeping a large library, serves as a clearing house for the collection and dissemination of information relating to any and every department of town government. Local authorities report to it their experiments and experiences, and it calls upon them for reports upon such special questions as may be submitted to it for investigation. Its journal is a treasure-house of useful and informing facts bearing on practical questions of local government. Separate municipal congresses exist for all the important States, and for some of the Prussian provinces. In addition there are many conferences of mayors.

JOINT ADMINISTRATIVE BOARDS FOR COMMON PURPOSES.—The opportunity of combining for special purposes, on the principle of the English joint board or committee, is offered to adjacent communes by special laws in Prussia, Saxony, and other States. " Communal unions " of this kind have long been common in Saxony, and a law of 1910 further facilitates their formation. The purposes usually served are tramway construction and regulation, road maintenance, and the supply of water, gas, and electricity, but in some cases communes have combined for the purpose of obtaining loans on more advantageous terms. The formation of an intercommunal union of the kind, and the regulations under which it works, are subject to the sanction of the Government or the higher administrative authorities. In the new law the Government reserves power to compel communes or manorial districts

DISTRIBUTION OF ADMINISTRATIVE POWERS

to combine when by remaining apart they would be unable to discharge certain of their duties satisfactorily.

Prussia first adopted legislation to facilitate such combination in the case of rural districts in the form of the Rural Commune Ordinance (*Landgemeindeordnung*) of July 3, 1891, applying to the seven eastern provinces of the kingdom. This permissive measure allowed combinations of adjacent rural parishes and manorial districts, and of these and towns; but towns might not combine amongst themselves. Nevertheless, experience showed that there were many cases in which joint action between adjacent towns was desirable and almost imperative—as, for instance, for the provision and regulation of transport arrangements, for town planning, building regulations, forest preservation, water supply, hospital provision, taxation, education, poor relief, sewerage, etc. In order to meet such cases a law was passed in 1911 not merely placing urban districts on the same level as rural in this respect, but providing for the compulsory combination of urban and rural districts under certain circumstances.

A separate law on the same lines was passed in the same year creating for the larger part of the area of Greater Berlin —including seven urban districts and two rural districts (circles), the latter comprising a number of populous communes of an urban character,—a joint board (*Zweckverband*) for the purpose of regulating the entire tramway systems of the district, of acquiring, building, and working tramways on the common account where necessary, for town planning, and the acquisition and maintenance of large areas of land to be kept out of the builders' hands and reserved as forest, parks, gardens, sport and recreation grounds, and the like. The joint board was an administrative necessity, called for by the omission of Berlin to incorporate the neighbouring areas years ago, when the Government was not only willing but wishful that Greater Berlin should form an administrative unit. A lethargic and short-sighted city government allowed the precious opportunity to pass unimproved and it has lamented its mistake ever since.

The consequence is that within this large area—to all intents and purposes a single community—administrative anarchy prevails, as illustrated by the absence of any uniform plan of town extension, street building, or traffic regulation, unequal taxation, conflicting practices in poor relief and educational policy, etc. For a distance of over twelve miles in various directions the boundary of Berlin consists of streets which are common to the city and the suburbs, so that it is only necessary to cross a street in order to enter another jurisdiction, while forty Berlin streets are continued in suburban communes without break of any kind. In a memorial on the subject addressed to the Government several years ago, the Chief Mayor stated : " The city of Berlin in the execution of traffic schemes has to encounter almost insuperable obstacles in consequence of the absence of organisation in Greater Berlin. Every individual commune carries out its own traffic policy without regard to the interests of the whole or even of its neighbour commune." Not only so, but the adjacent communes wilfully obstruct each other whenever there is the slightest conflict of interest. A few years ago the municipality of Berlin proposed to erect a hospital on a piece of land belonging to it in an adjacent township. This friendly neighbour not desiring the presence of the hospital, its council promptly prepared a building plan for the area to which Berlin's land belonged, and ran a street through the site, which, in consequence, became useless for the purpose intended.

The union with Berlin of all the adjacent communes is the logical solution of the problem, but as that is no longer possible some mitigation of existing difficulties is being sought by means of a joint board for the purposes named. Its members number 101, and comprise the chief mayor of Berlin (as chairman) and 100 representatives of the affiliated communes and districts, allotted in the ratio of population, and elected by the communal authorities (by town councils and executives together in the case of towns) and "circle" diets. There is a representative executive committee, but the practical work of the board is conducted by a permanent paid director, assisted by a staff of technical and other officers.

The joint board is a first step towards greater uniformity of action within an area which should never have been allowed to be subdivided into administrative fragments, and while

DISTRIBUTION OF ADMINISTRATIVE POWERS 119

there is no likelihood that it will pave the way for any large measure of incorporation, the extension of its present purposes and powers will inevitably be brought about by the mere force of circumstances.

ORGANS OF STATE SUPERVISION AND CONTROL.—The municipal administrations come into contact at many points with the higher local government authorities, inasmuch as these exercise supervision on behalf of the State. For that reason, and because these authorities will be mentioned repeatedly throughout the following chapters, it seems desirable to indicate at this stage the broad outlines of the Prussian system of "provincial," "district," and "circle" government, reserving a fuller exposition for the Appendix. The corresponding organisations in the other States differ more in name than in functions.

For administrative purposes the monarchy is divided into twelve provinces, thirty-seven "Government districts" (*Regierungsbezirke*), and further into rural and urban "circles" (*Kreise*), and rural and urban communes, and manorial districts. In 1910 the circles numbered 592 (of which 105 were urban), the town 1276, the rural communes 35,970, and there were 15,368 manors.

The "circles," exclusively of the towns within them, are also divided into sub-districts (*Amtsbezirke*) for the administration of various police functions in the German sense.[1]

The head of the province is the Chief President (an official created by Stein as part of his scheme of administrative reform), who is assisted by a Provincial Council; there is a representative assembly or diet, and the executive body is the Provincial Committee. For administrative purposes Berlin is detached from the province (Brandenburg) to which it belongs geographically, and is constituted a separate "Government district."

The "Government districts" are organised for purely State purposes, in contrast to the province and the "circle," both of

---

[1] The laws relating to local administration in Prussia will be found in "Organisationsgesetze der inneren Verwaltung," by Anschütz, and an exposition of them in Hue de Grais' "Handbuch der Verfassung und Verwaltung."

which have also corporate rights. The head of a "district" is the Government President, and the executive body is the District Committee, a majority of whose members are laymen nominated by the Provincial Committee.

At the head of the "circle" is the Landrat, whose office and title have existed in the Mark of Brandenburg for many centuries. He directs the executive, viz., the Circle Committee, which is elected by the representative body, the Circle Diet. In each of the foregoing administrative districts the general direction of affairs is exercised by the permanent heads, who are all State officials. The towns, as we have seen, are governed by a mayor, a magistracy or executive, and a town council.

In regard to the "circles" it should be stated further that towns with a civil population of at least 25,000, 30,000, or 40,000, according to the province, have a right to withdraw for administrative purposes from the "circle" to which they naturally belong, and to form independent urban "circles"; and towns with a smaller population may be given the same right in special cases.[1] Where a town forms a "circle" it has a "town committee," composed of the mayor or his deputy, as chairman, and four other members who, in a town governed by a magistracy, are chosen by that body out of its members, and in other towns are chosen by the town council. This "town committee" discharges the duties of an ordinary Circle Committee, one of which is to act as a court of administration in the case of certain disputes, and another to grant concessions or licences of certain kinds.

Graded though they are in rank in the bureaucratic system, the chief presidents, district presidents, and landrats are all supreme in their several jurisdictions; they "act

[1] In Bavaria the larger towns occupy a corresponding position and are known as "immediate" (*unmittelbar*), inasmuch as they do not belong to a minor but a major provincial division, as the large Prussian towns to a "district" and not to a "circle."
Similarly the English Local Government Act of 1888 recognises as "county boroughs" those boroughs which on June 1 of that year had a population in excess of 50,000. Under the same Act the Local Government Board may constitute any borough with the requisite population a "county borough." The effect of this status is that the boroughs are for certain purposes taken out of the county, so that they combine county with borough council powers, and in consequence are exempted from county taxation.

independently with full personal responsibility within their respective spheres of administration, except in matters regarding which joint action is prescribed by the law."[1] These officials have no counterpart in British local administration. The Prussian Provincial and Circle Diets and Committees may appear at first sight to have an analogy to our county and rural district councils, but directly the organisation, functions, and competence of the two groups of authorities are examined fundamental differences come to light which far out-balance the identity of certain of their duties.

The importance of the provincial, district, and circle authorities for the purposes of communal government lies in their supervisory functions, and in the case of the last two in their functions as lower administrative courts. Responsibility for the general oversight of local government rests with the Ministry of the Interior (Home Office), but while financial and educational questions are referred to the Ministries for these departments, decrees issued by the latter are signed also by the Minister of the Interior. Practical oversight, however, is delegated to the local administrative officials and bodies through whom the provincial, district, and circle administration is carried out.

Here we are concerned only with the towns. " State oversight of the administration of communal affairs in towns is exercised in the first instance by the Government President, and in higher and final instances by the Chief Presidents, in so far as the laws do not provide for the co-operation of the District Committee and Provincial Council."[2] (In the case of Berlin the Chief President takes the place of the Government President, and the Minister of the Interior that of the Chief President.) The District Committee is the lower supervisory authority in most important matters regarding which municipal action requires sanction. In the case of by-laws introducing new taxes or altering existing ones, however, the assent of the Government President and of the Minister of Finance is also necessary.

[1] Section 3 (2) of Gesetz über die allgemeine Landesverwaltung of July 30, 1883.
[2] Gesetz über die Zuständigkeit der Verwaltungs- und Verwaltungsgerichtsbehörden, August 1, 1883, Titel IV, sect. 7.

The Provincial Councils and the District and Circle Committees act in certain cases as courts of appeal, and the last two as administrative courts, subordinate to the Supreme Administrative Court, which is a purely judicial tribunal. The District Committee deals with disputes relating to boundaries, complaints against resolutions of a town council relating to the acquisition, possession, or loss of burgher rights, inclusion in voters' lists, elections to the council, the right to decline or resign office, etc., alleged transgression of powers by the mayor, members of the executive, or other municipal officers, complaints against the executive in matters of taxation, disputes as to claims for pensions, etc. Disputes between poor relief unions regarding liability for maintenance are also referred to the District Committee in the first instance, the Federal Settlement Board acting for Prussia as a final court of appeal.

CHAPTER V

LAND POLICIES

Extent of land owned by the towns—Communal estate as a source of revenue—Influence of land policies upon municipal development—Sale of public land for housing schemes.

THERE are few German towns that do not own a considerable proportion of the land within their administrative areas. Often this intra-urban estate is supplemented by far larger possessions outside the boundaries. One of the first things a modern town does on receiving the urban status is to buy as much land as possible for the purpose of meeting all conceivable public needs, present and future, of competing with private adventurers when the interests of the community seem to require it, and incidentally of securing to the town a share in the increasing value of land which experience shows will inevitably result from public and private enterprise and growth of population. Not only does a town thus largely buy land, but it endeavours to distribute its estate as equally as possible throughout its area, so that in all directions it may make its influence as a proprietor felt in the land and house market.

The ownership of land is, however, an old tradition of communal life in Germany, going back to a period far antecedent to the existing systems of local government. The practice cannot be attributed to legislation, nor is it followed by virtue of any special powers granted to the towns; for while the powers of English urban districts in relation to land ownership are severely restricted by law, German towns are free to buy real estate on any scale whatever without permission of any kind, unless, indeed, the contracting of a special loan should be necessary, in which event the assent of the State commissary is necessary. This assent, however, entails no local inquiry corresponding to the inquiries of the Local Government Board, simply because the German States have no Local Government Boards and no use for them; the proceeding is almost a formality, intended to remind the communes that the State, though it devolved upon them their wide powers of self-government, likes still to be consulted now and then, and it is arranged expeditiously through the post. For, strange as it may sound to English ears, the Governments of Germany, without exception, far from wishing to hamper the towns in their land investments, have often urged the towns to buy as much land as possible, and not to sell.

EXTENT OF LAND OWNED BY THE TOWNS.—The extent of land owned by German towns will probably surprise those who are unacquainted with the large views of communal enterprise held in Germany, where large towns are as ready to spend a quarter of a million pounds in buying land as an average English town of the same size is to spend ten pounds upon a watering-cart. For example, the following are the percentages of their entire administrative areas that were owned by the towns named in 1910 (roads, streets, railways, water, and fortifications are all excluded, but the property of charitable foundations under public management is regarded as town property) :—Freiburg in Baden, 77·7 per cent.; Fürth, 66·2 per cent.; Stettin, 62·5 per cent.; Heidelberg, 61·1 per cent.; Coblence, 59·5 per cent.; Brandenburg, 52·8 per cent.; Augsburg, 49·0 per cent.; Mannheim, 48·6 per cent.; and Frankfort-on-Main, 47·7 per cent. Cologne, Munich, Saarbrücken, Wiesbaden, Hildesheim, Karlsruhe, and Darmstadt own from 30 to 40 per cent. of their areas, eleven other towns about one-quarter, and five others about one-fifth.

Taking actual areas, the following was the extent of land (exclusive of roads) owned by some of the larger German towns in 1910 or 1911, with the ratio to population :—

EXTENT OF TOWN ESTATE AND RATIO TO POPULATION.

| Towns. | Population (1910). | Extent of town lands. ||| No. of acres per 1000 inhabitants. |
		Within administrative area.	Outside administrative area.	Total.	
		Acres.	Acres.	Acres.	
Berlin	2,071,300	5,452·8	46,899·6	52,352·4	25·3
Brandenburg	53,600	9,264·2	8,375·3	17,639·5	326·6
Breslau	512,100	2,667·4	14,127·7	16,795·1	32·8
Frankfort-on-Main	414,500	11,868·4	3,554·3	15,522·7	37·4
Frankfort-on-Oder	68,300	3,062·8	9,509·5	12,572·3	184·8
Freiburg-in-Baden	83,300	9,846·2	2,247·9	12,094·1	145·7
Fürth	66,600	3,670·2	8,813·5	12,483·7	186·3
Görlitz	85,800	758·3	76,944·9	77,703·2	903·5
Mannheim	193,900	7,339·6	160·5	7,501·1	38·6
Munich	596,500	5,724·7	7,068·2	12,792·9	21·4
Rostock	65,400	911·7	27,632·6	28,544·3	439·1
Strassburg	178,900	6,549·2	4,915·3	11,464·5	64·0
Stettin	216,100	8,810·5	7,162·0	15,972·5	73·9

These figures are exclusive of lands belonging to charitable foundations under municipal management or oversight, the extent of which sometimes exceeds that of the land which the towns own outright.

A return of the land owned in 1911 by 51 communes forming the heart of Greater Berlin, published by the Charlottenburg Statistical Office, shows that all these owned estates, varying in extent from 1 to 40 per cent. of their areas. But the total proportion of land in public ownership was far greater, for in many communes the municipal authorities of adjoining places, the State, and other public bodies had also large freeholds. Taking only the larger communes the ownership of their areas was divided as follows :—

Distribution of Communal Areas in Greater Berlin, in Percentages.

Communes.	Proportion of area owned by		
	(a) The Commune.	(b) Other communes, State, and other public bodies.	(c) Private individuals.
	%	%	%
Berlin	34·8	?	?
Charlottenburg	32·2	12·9	54·9
Friedenau	33·8	—	68·2
Grunewald	23·1	0·2	76·6
Johannisthal	1·3	75·6 (State)	23·1
Neukölln	17·4	26·8	55·8
Reinickendorf	9·5	8·5	82·0
Schöneberg	32·5	18·7	48·8
Spandau	39·9	17·7	?
Steglitz	12·1	2·8	85·1
Tempelhof	20·7	41·2	38·1
Treptow	13·3	65·5	21·2
Weissensee	19·6	12·5	67·9
Wilmersdorf	25·1	6·4	68·5

The largest estates were owned by the following towns :—

Towns	Population (1910).	Extent of town lands.			No. of acres per 1000 inhabitants.
		Within administrative area.	Outside administrative area.	Total.	
		Acres.	Acres.	Acres.	
Berlin	2,071,300	5,425·8	46,899·6	52,352·4	25·3
Charlottenburg	305,980	1,861·4	2,659·7	4,521·1	14·7
Neukölln	237,300	510·8	2,729·1	3,239·9	13·7
Schöneberg	172,800	759·3	1,886·1	2,645·4	15·3
Steglitz	62,950	172·2	1,311·6	1,483·7	23·6
Tempelhof	20,700	588·6	1,037·4	1,626·0	78·5
Weissensee	43,000	516·2	1,674·7	2,192·9	51·0

Berlin has an estate (principally acquired for irrigation purposes) more than three times greater than its administrative area, and Schöneberg, Steglitz, Neukölln, and Weissensee all have estates larger than their own areas.

As in Prussia so in the less progressive parts of the country. According to a return published by the Bavarian State

Statistical Office the landed estate of all the communes of Bavaria has an area of one and a half million acres, of which rather more than one-half is forest.

What the large and wealthy towns do on an imposing scale, the small towns do with equal enterprise, if in a more modest way. Of towns with a population between 50,000 and 60,000, Offenbach owns 2230 acres of land, Hildesheim 2770 acres, and Kaiserslautern 5785 acres. During the present year the little town of Kalbe on the Saale expended just £14 a head of its 12,000 inhabitants in buying for £168,000 a large estate for the purpose of creating a number of small holdings and labourers' allotments, as well as for disposing of sites for industrial works. One reads with astonishment also of the Rhenish town of Wermelskirchen, with a population of 15,000, which has during the past thirty years increased its estate from two to 1270 acres.

Long views and wide perspectives characterise the land policies of German towns. Their eyes are set not upon the needs of to-day—for these often were foreseen and provided for long ago—nor yet those of the near future, though " near future " in German official language connotes a period of 25 years, but upon the interests of coming generations. It is significant that a friendly critic of the energetic land purchase policy which Frankfort-on-Main pursued under the direction of its late Chief Mayor Adickes, remarked :—" Adickes worked less for the present generation or even the children of the present generation than for its grandchildren and great-grandchildren ; his work will bear fruit in distant generations." Even Görlitz with its 77,700 acres of land—an estate sixteen times the area of the town—is still unsatisfied. Quite recently the local House Occupiers' Associations, in petitioning the municipal executive, which initiates and controls land purchase there as everywhere, to add further to the town's estate, urged it in extending its land policy to " count not by years, but by centuries."

The steady and systematic manner in which land is purchased might be illustrated by the experience of almost any large town. Thus during the period 1880 to 1908 Breslau expended over a million and a half pounds in the purchase of land within the communal area, of which sum £1,199,000 was expended on land needed for public purposes, and £330,000 on land intended for re-sale. The land transactions of this town have throughout this period been on an increasing scale. During the first half of the period the purchases amounted to £420,000, during the second half to £1,094,000. In addition, land was purchased to the value of £308,000 outside the municipal area, £139,000 being expended in purchases in the immediate neighbourhood of the town. At the present time Breslau owns about one-quarter of the entire municipal area, and six times as much outside that area.

The town of Königsberg increased its estate as follows during the years 1890-1909 :—

Year.	Within the municipal boundaries.	Outside the municipal boundaries.	Total.
	Acres.	Acres.	Acres.
1890	390	756	1146
1905	1060	973	2033
1906	1186	973	2159
1907	1284	1462	2746
1908	1351	1499	2850
1909	1414	1586	3000

In addition, foundations belonging to the town and under municipal management owned 57 acres of land in 1909.

The estate of Munich increased as follows during the eighteen years 1891-1908 :—

Year.	Within the municipal boundaries.	Outside the municipal boundaries.	Total.
	Acres.	Acres.	Acres.
1891	2610	2318	4,928
1895	2931	2927	5,858
1900	3921	6782	10,703
1901	4025	6790	10,815
1902	4264	7030	11,294
1903	4395	7343	11,738
1904	4513	7669	12,182
1905	4662	7567	12,229
1906	5035	7780	12,815
1907	5331	8240	13,571
1908	5332	8439	13,771

The town now owns nearly one-third of the entire municipal area, and an area half as large as the whole commune outside. The steady growth of municipal estate is shown further by the following table setting forth the proportions of the administrative area owned by some of the larger German towns (exclusive of roads, streets, water, and fortifications) in 1910 as compared with 1906 and 1901–2 ; where a decrease is shown, it is usually attributable to the incorporation of new suburbs :—

PERCENTAGE OF MUNICIPAL AREA OWNED BY TOWNS AT DIFFERENT PERIODS.

	1901–2.	1906.	1910.
Augsburg	53·7	54·6	49·0
Barmen	2·1	11·3	20·0
Charlottenburg	4·2	10·0	23·9
Cologne	17·8	28·3	31·9
Crefeld	4·3	17·2	13·6
Darmstadt	—	33·1	33·3
Frankfort-on-Main	57·8	59·8	47·7
Halle	18·2	—	22·1
Hanover	44·0	43·8	24·9
Karlsruhe	13·7	19·8	38·7
Königsberg	—	12·7	18·6
Liegnitz	—	17·6	23·9
Mannheim	—	39·6	48·6
Munich	20·6	26·6	30·8
Nuremberg	8·3	9·6	15·4
Posen	6·1	8·9	10·4
Spandau	50·8	48·3	42·3
Strassburg	47·5	—	41·5

In 1910 alone 73 of the large towns of Germany bought land to the aggregate extent of 9584 acres, and to the aggregate value of over £4,000,000. The 51 communes in Greater Berlin purchased during the ten years 1901–11, 20,600 acres of land at a cost of £17,500,000. Half of this land was in their own areas, and the remainder in communes for the most part near at hand. Thus Berlin bought during this period 5460 acres, Charlottenburg 2560 acres, Weissensee 2080 acres, Schöneberg 2060 acres, Neukölln 1690 acres, Pankow 1500

K

acres, and so on. Charlottenburg now owns 2500 acres of land as yet not built upon, with a value of over a million and a quarter pounds, and the value of all its real estate is about four and a half millions sterling. In 1886 Freiburg-in-Baden owned 11,000 acres of land with a value of £925,000. In 1909 its estate was only 2000 acres larger, but its value was then £3,200,000.

Kiel has bought land so systematically during the past thirty years that it now owns a large part of the land on the periphery of the town, including most of the choicest forest and woodland. So long as the building land is not needed it is let as garden allotments, with the result that the town has now between 4000 and 5000 tenants, from whom it receives £2500 a year in rents.

Sometimes a town will make a great coup, and occasionally single land-purchase transactions running into a million pounds are carried out. The city of Berlin has of late made large additions to its estate and particularly its forest land. Several valuable estates lying north and north-west of the city, and containing some of the most favourite river and lake scenery of the province of Brandenburg, have been acquired to an aggregate extent of some 13,000 acres. Within the last few months Berlin has bought another estate of 15,000 acres (Lanke) at some distance from the city, at a cost of just under a million pounds; part of the land is to be sold on lease for the building of small houses, but the greater part will probably be converted into public park.

So, too, the municipality of Königsberg in 1909 bought from the Imperial War Department the fortresses with the moats there, comprising a total area of 755 acres, for the sum of £1,450,000, payable in twenty yearly instalments without interest. The cost of demolishing the buildings and walls, levelling the ground, and laying out streets and roads is estimated at about an equal sum. The town council of Halle in 1909 similarly voted over a million pounds, to be raised by loan, for the acquisition of land " in the interest of a progressive land policy."

As a rule, it will be found that, where forest and woodland surround a town, the municipal authority has taken care to secure as much as possible for the use of the inhabitants. Germany has immemorially protected its forests, and next to the States the largest owners of forest lands are the communes. Of a total area of 35 million acres of forest in 1900 the States owned 11,075,000 acres, and the communes 5,645,000 acres. The largest proportions of forest in communal ownership are in Baden and Alsace-Lorraine, viz. 45 per cent.; the proportion in Hesse is 36 per cent., in Würtemberg 29 per cent., in Prussia and Bavaria only 12 per cent. Of the larger towns, Frankfort-on-Oder owns 15,570 acres of forest, Brandenburg 11,220 acres, Stettin 10,570 acres, Frankfort-on-Main 8590 acres, Breslau 5140 acres, Wiesbaden 4750 acres, Coblence 5000 acres, and Aix-la-Chapelle 3230 acres. Many of the small communes of woody Würtemberg own tracts of forest larger than those of all but a few favoured towns; for example, Baiersbronn with 7200 acres, Freudenstadt with 6200 acres, Rottweil with 5600 acres, and Hall with 5000 acres.

Some of the larger towns of Prussia have of late years greatly increased their forest estates by purchases from the State, which is usually ready to sell to the communes on more or less favourable terms. The Government recently offered to the Joint Traffic and Town-Planning Board (*Zweck-Verband*) for Greater Berlin 25,000 acres of forest for the sum of £2,500,000, subject to the conditions that the forests shall be maintained and that if any portions are needed for State purposes they may be repurchased at the selling price, viz. 6d. per square metre, the State paying interest on the money and refunding outlay upon land so bought back. The idea is to make wide approaches to the forest from all the large railway stations, so that it may be easy of access from any part of Greater Berlin. Kiel, Düsseldorf, Hanover, and Cologne have also been able to buy forest land from the State on a price varying from 6d. to 2s. per square metre.

In the eastern provinces of Prussia the communes are required to cultivate their forests on systematic principles, and their plans of cultivation need to be submitted to the District Presidents for approval. The District Committees are also empowered to call upon the communes to afforest suitable areas, and on their recommendation State grants may be made for the purpose. In other provinces the State exercises oversight over communal and other forests by means of its technical officials.

COMMUNAL ESTATE AS A SOURCE OF REVENUE.—The ownership of land and forest by the communes often proves an important source of profit. Many of the small communes of Baden derive much of their revenue from forests ; in some cases the proceeds amount to 30s. and even 40s. a head of the population. The inhabitants of two little towns, Wellendingen and Oberwinden, are exempt from taxation owing to the yield of the public forests, and the Oberwinden folk are supplied with fuel free of charge. The village of Langenanbach with 780 inhabitants owns land and forest yielding in timber and limestone £2500 per annum, an amount which covers all local expenditure and the cost of water, and leaves a balance to be added to the credit of the commune yearly. The revenue of one small but favoured Würtemberg commune is increased by £12,000 a year by its forests and that of another by £8000. The little Prussian town of Goslar owns forests which yield £6500 a year in profit.

All such profits pall, however, before the gains which accrue to many large towns owing to their systematic trading in land. In the administrative year 1911-12, Düsseldorf made a profit of £21,400 on the turnover of its municipal land fund. Magdeburg bought land on the south side of the town at 10s. 9d. a square metre, to a total value of £300,000, and succeeded in selling two-thirds of it at £4 a square metre for £1,300,000, while it bought land on the north side of the town for 23s. a square metre, and sold it for 43s.

In 1912 Cologne owned land to the value of £2,900,000. Since a separate department was created thirty years ago for the administration of the town's estate, a profit of £625,000 has been made upon land transactions, and the department has paid its way always. During the ten years 1901-11 land purchases to the value of a million and a half pounds were made, and in addition the town acquired for extensions the site of the old fortifications and other State lands for about the same amount, while it sold land to the value of a million pounds. In 1911 the town of Ludwigsburg on the Rhine bought 48½ acres of land within its area for £13,940, and sold 14½ acres for the same sum. There was thus an addition to the public estate of 34 acres without cost.

One of the most interesting examples of successful land enterprise is furnished by the old Würtemberg town of Ulm, whose population is 56,000. Since 1891 Ulm, under the rule of a mayor convinced of the wisdom of a progressive land policy and strong enough to carry it out, has bought some 1280 acres of land at different times for £316,000, while it has sold 420 acres for £406,000, showing a cash profit of £90,000, apart from the addition of 860 acres to the town estate. As a result of Ulm's land policy its assets increased between 1891 and 1909 from £583,500 to £1,990,000, an increase of £1,407,000, equal to £25 a head of the population. Another result is that of the larger towns of Würtemberg only one has a lower taxation than Ulm. It is solely owing to its successful land policy that this enterprising town, without imposing heavy burdens on the general body of ratepayers, has been able to undertake a programme of social reforms which has created for it an honourable reputation throughout Germany.

The objection is sometimes raised that to the extent that the towns increase their proprietary share of the administrative area they proportionately diminish the revenue derivable from the land taxes, which are so important a source of local revenue in Germany, such as the land tax, the tax on the sale and transfer of real estate, and the unearned increment tax. This loss, however, is usually more than compensated for by the gain which rewards prudent trading, irrespective of the saving effected by acquiring betimes land necessary for public purposes at a later date.

Many towns follow this policy of land purchase so systematically and on so large a scale that they have found it necessary to create special administrative departments, under responsible and expert officials, to direct this branch of municipal activity. It is a common practice to float the Municipal Land Board with a large grant or loan, which may range from a quarter to a million pounds. In 1910, 50 of the 91 German towns with a population over 50,000 had established special land purchase funds.[1]

INFLUENCE OF LAND POLICIES UPON MUNICIPAL DEVELOPMENT.—But land buying and selling is not an end in itself. As a consequence of its land policy a German municipal authority generally has land of its own suitable for public works which it desires to take in hand ; it can determine within certain limits in what directions the town shall extend ; by the steady increase in the value of its estate it shares with private owners in the material gain caused by municipal growth and development; it is able to institute and assist important housing schemes ; and to some extent it can check private and professional land speculation. Instances might be given of municipal authorities which, owing to the large reserves of land in their ownership, have been able to give a new impetus to industrial development, and to renew the life of old and stagnant communities.

"In the modern development of towns a relatively large ownership of land is of fundamental importance for a commune," wrote the late chief mayor of Mannheim, whose land policy was marked by unique enterprise. "Such municipal property represents an asset of indispensable and continually increasing value, and therefore provides the surest basis for the financial policy and the credit of the commune. An extensive and favourably situated estate makes the municipality almost independent of private property in the discharge of its own duties in the matter of building, enables it to compete with private owners in the general land market, and places it in the position to check the worst evils of land speculation. The ownership of land, besides being so important for a town from a financial standpoint, places in the hands of the local administration a valuable instrument for regulating building enterprise and housing conditions, and a lever by means of which the commune may influence the development of industrial and commercial conditions." The case of Mannheim is of special interest, inasmuch as its modern land policy is merely the development of a tradition as old as the history of

[1] See Appendix II, "Regulations of Municipal Land Funds," pp. 468–472.

the town. When the town was formed out of the two villages of Mannheim and Dornheim over three centuries ago it was already rich in public lands, of which it owned 750 acres. On the demolition of the fortifications the commune took over the land thereby set free for residential and other public purposes. Other additions followed, and in 1890 the town owned 1375 acres of building land, in spite of large sales for industrial and residential purposes, the formation of parks, streets, etc. The town's land policy was placed on its present basis in 1888, when the town council, acting on the recommendation of its mayor and executive, decided to expend in future at least 10 per cent. of the proceeds of all sales of town land in the purchase of new property. From that time forward the town appeared in the market as a buyer whenever land was for sale, and no opportunity was lost of preventing eligible land from becoming the object of private speculation. Up to the end of 1904 a further 390 acres of land had been acquired for building and street purposes, 102 acres for the purpose of industrial undertakings, 284 acres for the construction of an industrial dock, and 929 acres for the purpose of rounding off existing properties. When the two communes of Käfertal and Neckarau were incorporated 3550 acres were added to the public lands, and at the end of 1905 the communal estate, after further sales and assignments of all kinds, had an area of 6080 acres, or more than a third of the entire area of the municipality.

The extent to which the town was interested in the estate market at that time may be seen from the fact that of 9800 transfers of real estate, representing a value of 18¼ million pounds, which occurred in Mannheim between the years 1892 and 1905, the municipal transactions (purchases and sales) numbered 1600 or 16 per cent. of the whole, with a value of a million and a half pounds, or 8½ per cent. of the whole. The foresight shown in assuring to the town the control of the outer districts, a matter so important for a large town alike from the standpoint of housing, transit facilities, and public health, may be seen from the following statement showing the proportions of land in municipal ownership in eight rings of a kilometre (⅝ mile) wide from the centre outwards in so far as this area belonged to Mannheim :—

1. First kilometre	13·26	per cent.
2. First to second kilometre,	27·52	,,
3. Second to third ,,	37·59	,,
4. Third to fourth ,,	24·36	,,
5. Fourth to fifth ,,	21·20	,,
6. Fifth to sixth ,,	23·09	,,
7. Sixth to seventh ,,	54·40	,,
8. Seventh to eighth ,,	73·41	,,

To-day Mannheim owns 7500 acres of land, all but 160 acres within its enlarged administrative area, the extent of which is 18,470 acres. Its estate averages over 38 acres per 1000 inhabitants. Not only has the town's modern industrial prosperity been built upon its land policy, but the municipal authority claims that this policy has had a steadying influence on land prices and has in no small degree discouraged land gambling by removing a large amount of the best land beyond the reach of the land and estate companies and other private speculators.

Equally interesting in its way, as an illustration of how the development of a modern town may be beneficially influenced on the social side owing to its land policy, is the case of Essen, the seat of the cannon industry. Before the great development of Essen began some thirty or forty years ago the town had owned considerable estate, but most of it had been sold by town councils who were unable to foresee the town's coming expansion and needs, in order to pay off debts incurred for public purposes. Later, when the steel age in the history of Essen opened, the enterprising men at the head of its government pursued a vigorous land-purchase policy. Several large estates within the municipal area were bought on favourable terms, and while much of the land was used for streets and cemeteries and open spaces, for churches, schools, and public buildings, other portions were set apart for residential purposes. Architects and town planners were called in, and the town built on its own land many blocks of working-class dwellings, artistic in design and healthy and convenient in arrangement. Private builders imitated the town's example, and handsome new quarters came into existence. In spite of the rapid increase of its population, the housing problem was never allowed to become acute, and a new and progressive movement was given to the development of the town.

SALE OF PUBLIC LAND FOR HOUSING SCHEMES.—Wherever German municipal authorities are most earnestly endeavouring to cope with the housing problem, made difficult and urgent owing to conditions met with only in a country of rapid industrial development, one of their most powerful auxiliaries is the ownership of an abundance of building land. In using this land for housing purposes a town usually follows one of three principal courses, viz. (a) it builds houses upon its own land ; (b) it sells land to co-operative and other building societies formed for providing working-class dwellings ; or (c) it combines these two methods by disposing of land on the leasehold principle. The Governments urge the communes to buy land freely, and to promote house building by leasing it to public utility building societies, but not to sell outright. In a circular letter addressed to the Government Presidents of the country, the Prussian Ministers of Trade and Commerce, Education, and the Interior of that State, said :—

" A judicious communal land policy is of far-reaching importance for the better adjustment of housing conditions. The existing evils have their chief source in unhealthy land speculation, which in part can only be combated by changes in legislation. A powerful means of checking this speculation is, however, available at present in the acquisition of as much landed estate as possible by those communes whose continuous growth converts the surrounding agricultural and garden land in ever increasing measure into building land. The manner in which the land so purchased, which as a rule should permanently remain in the hands of the commune, should be used for building—whether the commune itself, either directly or through contractors, should erect dwellings upon the land and either let or lease them, must be left for each commune to decide for itself. It is, however, specially consonant with a healthy land policy that the land in the possession of a town which is suitable for small dwellings should on principle not be sold, even though a temporary dearth of dwellings should exist. The sale of communal land for the purpose of combating the dearth of dwellings may, indeed, have the momentary effect of causing dwellings to be built and offered in larger number and at lower rents, but in the end it can only serve the ends of land speculation. The sale of communal land for the erection of small dwellings can only be judicious if the commune reserves a conditional right of pre-emption, or if other effective security is offered that the land shall not become the object of private speculation."

The Saxon Minister of the Interior has issued a similar admonition to the communes in that country to " increase their estates betimes to the extent of their power, yet to retain all land in their possession and only to sell where there is a guarantee that no speculation will take place."

All three methods are followed ; yet while in the past the towns have been ready to sell outright, the present tendency is to dispose of it only on the leasehold principle, with a view not merely to controlling the manner of its use, but of securing to the community the benefit of all increasing value. Land is so sold on a large scale by the municipalities of Mannheim, Leipzig, Charlottenburg, Neukölln, Breslau, Halle, Dortmund, Frankfort-on-Main, Aix-la-Chapelle, Düsseldorf, Duisburg, Elberfeld, Essen, Würzburg, Ulm, Karlsruhe, and Strassburg. This public land is usually sold subject to conditions intended, as far as possible, to prevent speculation in the houses built upon it. In some cases the town reserves a right of pre-emption, in others an unqualified right to buy back after a certain term of years. The term of lease varies from 60 to 100 years.

The plan of selling land on lease has been widely followed in Posen by the Government (the land being State property) and in Frankfort-on-Main, the land being sold alike to building societies, co-operative societies, and private individuals, chiefly for the erection of small dwellings. The usual term of the lease is from 60 to 70 years. In some cases the yearly payment is calculated per square metre of land leased; in others it is 2½ per cent. or, as in Posen, 3 per cent. of the sale value of the land.

Mannheim disposes of land on different methods, e.g., sale subject to a right to repurchase at the expiration of a fixed term, such repurchase applying both to the land and the buildings erected upon it, and leasehold tenure on the English system, under which both land and building revert to the town without any consideration on the determination of the lease.

Several years ago the municipality of Bremen bought a large area of land in the north-west of the municipal area with a view to offering at a reasonable price sites for industrial extension and new undertakings, and of providing for the future requirements of the town itself. This land has since been systematically planned, streets have been laid out, an area has been marked out and partially sold for industrial purposes, other land has been reserved for working-class dwellings, and tramway connections have been provided. Land is offered to working-men at a low price, which includes all costs of street-making and sewering, on condition that only buildings for one or two families may be erected, and money is lent at 4½ per cent. interest to the extent of 90 per cent. of the cost of land and buildings, this being advanced by the State Pension Board with municipal guarantee, while the final tenth part is either paid down or is guaranteed by the workman's employer. With a view to preventing speculation the town reserves the right to buy the house during a period of twenty-five years should the owner or his successors wish to sell, should the property be wilfully depreciated in value, or should the owner get into financial difficulties. In fixing the terms of repurchase all value due to unexhausted improvements approved by the town will be added to the original cost, and, on the other hand, depreciation will be deducted.

Many other towns give security for loans advanced to building societies by the statutory Pension Boards or by the Governments, and still more advance building money at 3½ or 4 per cent. to the extent of from 75 to 90 per cent. of the land and buildings together.

How towns are enabled by their land policies to counteract and even prevent speculation was explained by the mayor of Saarbrücken to a recent meeting of the Rhenish Association for the Building of Small Dwellings. Since 1885 the municipality of Saarbrücken has bought land systematically in all parts of the communal area, and has resold it at moderate prices on condition of its being built upon within two years. " In consequence," said the mayor, " systematic commercial land speculation has not been able to secure a footing in Saarbrücken. The acquisition of suitable land by the town is facilitated owing to the fact that the town from time to time notifies to the public only that part of its town plan which relates to the streets just about to be opened, and for the rest publishes only the general provisions relating to town extensions or indeed withholds information altogether. The carrying out of the town building plan has throughout been attended by no real difficulties, and the pooling and re-parcelling of private sites have been easy to carry out always, since those interested have ever the example and influence of the town before their eyes. Under these circumstances the rational opening up of the land has had the effect of keeping building enterprise in healthy lines, and housing conditions have been greatly improved." So, too, the chief mayor of Ulm stated at a meeting of the German Land Reformers' League held at Gotha on October 3, 1910 : " The town now owns four-fifths of the entire municipal area. With us an unearned increment tax has no purpose, since there can be no speculation."

CHAPTER VI

THE PLANNING OF TOWNS

The modern town plan—Alignment plans and building permits—Special taxation of building sites and betterment contributions—Power to expropriate landowners and to pool properties—Protecting the streets against disfigurement—Administrative area of German towns—The modern incorporation movement.

BUT a land purchase policy needs as its complement a policy of land and town development. All the enterprise shown by German towns in the increase and management of their land reserves would be futile and its financial success would be dearly bought, if it exerted no direct and beneficial influence upon the building of the town, its housing conditions, and its outward amenities generally. Here are seen the real purpose and the wisdom of the German system of town planning. One may often read in German newspapers that such-and-such a town has bought a large adjacent estate " with a view to the expansion of the town." The English idea is that towns should expand " naturally," without any attempt by the local authorities to regulate their growth. And our towns may so expand and do: it is only a question of how they expand—whether fortuitously or on rational and healthy lines.[1] The German regards his town as a living organism, whose development both deserves and needs to be controlled with the utmost thought and care. The official town plan in which this idea of town life finds expression is a

[1] The Housing and Town Planning Act of 1909 is, of course, a long stride forward—a stride made on sudden impulse, in our English way—but it remains to be seen how far public opinion, still so largely uninformed on this question, will provide the motive and impetus necessary to carry reform to practical issues. Hitherto both foresight and the instinct for order and system have been lacking, and these cannot be created by legislation; its business is rather to devise machinery and methods.

distinctly German conception, and is one of the most valuable contributions made by Germany to the science of civic government.

The spirit in which the governing authority of a large and progressive German town views this question is well shown by the following statement of the principles on which the land and housing policy of Mannheim is directed :—" Every town in course of development needs to its extension outwards a uniform and comprehensive building plan. If this plan is to offer a foundation for the art of town building it must be drawn up on large lines, must anticipate the needs of a distant future, and pay due regard to the requirements of traffic, hygiene, and taste. The fulfilment of this task constitutes a very important part of all social reform in our towns." Thus the modern industrial era of Mannheim may be said to have opened towards the end of the 'sixties of last century. Its movement forward had hardly begun before the municipal authority proposed a plan for the extension of the town in various directions, so that the growth of Mannheim during all the past forty years has followed lines deliberately laid down with a view to organic and systematic development.

THE MODERN TOWN PLAN.—The earlier town plans proceeded too exclusively from the standpoint of convenience of communication ; local authorities were apt to be satisfied if provision existed for wide—often too wide—thoroughfares, and everybody was given a fair chance of moving from place to place with ease. Housing considerations in particular were given a secondary place. Now a larger conception prevails, and in the drawing up of modern town plans regard is had to every factor in the life and development of the community—traffic, housing, trade and industry, recreation, access to the open country, and the like. Most towns in planning their areas adopt what is called the " zone " system. The so-called " zones " are not, however, concentric areas extending outward, but merely separate districts to which different building regulations apply, e.g., as to the amount of a building site to be left free, the height of buildings, and the width of streets, the general rule being followed that higher buildings may be erected and a larger proportion of the ground be covered in the inner district, and that building must be less dense and houses lower in the outer areas. Graduated building regulations of this character are in operation in many of the large towns in relation to new town extensions.

A still more important division of the town area is that into districts as determined by the purposes for which the land may be applied. Thus the newer town plans invariably set apart a special area for industry, and there the erection of factories and workshops is permitted. In many cases the location of this industrial district has been determined by nature or unalterable conditions, e.g., rivers, canals, or railway systems; but where a town is able to begin with a clean sheet industry is given the least delectable part of the municipal area, and regard is had to the prevailing winds, so that annoyance from smoke and noise may be reduced to a minimum. Another district is usually reserved for houses of a better class; others are intended for working-house dwellings, and sometimes there is a country-house area, in which only villas surrounded by gardens may be erected. Provision is also made for public gardens and other open spaces. The width of the streets varies according as they are main arteries, secondary thoroughfares not intended for heavy traffic, or are merely intended for local use. It is not unusual for new main streets in large towns to be divided into sections, each devoted to a distinct kind of traffic. For example, on each side of the street, divided in the middle by an avenue of trees, may be found in succession *trottoir*, carriage-way, tramlines, and footway or riding-way. In the laying out of new districts traffic is sometimes relieved by running auxiliary streets parallel with the main arteries.

Apart from the ordinary building alignment laws and the laws on the subject of expropriation, no special legislation has been needed in order to enable the local authorities to carry out even the largest of their town planning schemes. Such works fall within the general scope of communal government, and now as in the past the towns usually act on their own initiative and responsibility, though the Governments are not slow to bring pressure to bear upon backward authorities. The Prussian and Bavarian Governments have for years been specially insistent upon the importance of the early and systematic planning of urban areas subject to rapid increase of population. The larger towns, however, need no outside pressure of this kind. It is questionable whether a town of any importance can be named which has not taken up the question in the spirit of earnestness which it deserves, and the credit for what has been done in Germany in this domain belongs almost wholly to the local authorities. Help, advice, and suggestions are, of course, obtained from every source available. Thus the incorporation in 1910 by Leipzig of six suburbs, adding 5000 acres of largely undeveloped land to its administrative area (now 18,400 acres) and the necessity of making certain clearances and improvements in the centre of the town, have led the town council there to establish a special Town Extension Office for the working out of its town plan on a larger scale and on more systematic lines than before.

So, too, Düsseldorf, in view of its largely increased area (now 27,900 acres), due to repeated incorporations, in 1911 instituted a competition for plans for the laying out of the undeveloped districts by the town, and prizes of £4000 were awarded for the best schemes submitted. One of the most ambitious projects of the kind contemplates the planning on comprehensive lines of a large part of the industrial district of which Düsseldorf is the natural centre. The underlying idea is to earmark the entire area for the special purposes for which it is best suited. A large housing plan is proposed as an essential part of the scheme, portions of each urban and rural area being assigned exclusively for residential purposes. The industrial zones are to be marked out, the heavy iron and steel industry having its allotted sphere of influence, beyond which it is not to be allowed to go. Provision is to be made for adequate road systems and for efficient tramway communications through and within the district, and it is proposed that a large area shall be devoted to open spaces—forest, parks, gardens, recreation grounds, playgrounds for children, etc.

THE PLANNING OF TOWNS

In proof of the great interest taken in the future development of suburban Berlin on uniform lines it may be stated that the Association of Berlin Architects some time ago drew up a scheme for the systematic laying out of an extensive area, comprised within a radius of fifteen miles from the centre of Berlin, and including, at least, a hundred townships of all kinds. It is proposed that due provision shall be made for a network of streets and thoroughfares of width proportionate to their purpose, running into the outskirts, and intersecting these in various directions, with special ways for motorists, cyclists, and equestrians; for new railway communications joining those already existing; for tramways, canals, and wharves; for special residential and industrial districts, each with parks, gardens, lakes, children's playgrounds, and other open spaces; for recreation grounds for adults, race-courses, sports fields, allotment gardens, and the like; while sites are to be reserved for public buildings—churches, libraries, museums, schools, theatres, gymnastic, swimming and bathing establishments, hospitals. Since these proposals were made, a statutory Joint Traffic and Town Planning Board has been created by special law for Greater Berlin, and whatever scheme may eventually be carried out under the new conditions, the hope and aim is to secure that the future development of this immense area shall follow uniform lines and be part of a comprehensive plan.

Apart from the influence derived from the ownership of a large part of the administrative area, a local authority is able to make its town planning schemes effective in several ways, viz., (a) by the power to restrict the right to build to land lying on streets made by the authority or by it declared ready for use; (b) by the enforcement of building regulations (in some States with the approval of the supervisory authority) prescribing among other things the width of the streets, the maximum proportion of a building site that may be built upon, the minimum area of courtyards and gardens, the height of buildings, the ratio of cubic contents to number of inhabitants, etc.; (c) by the power to levy upon adjacent owners special contributions towards the cost of public improvements and other works increasing the value of their property; and (d) by powers of expropriation and in some communes power to pool the property of various owners and to re-apportion it in a different manner where otherwise areas are difficult of development. In the words of a well-known German authority upon the land and housing question: "The Building Alignment Law, the Building Regulations, and the Law of Expropriation are the fundamental conditions of modern town planning."

ALIGNMENT PLANS AND BUILDING PERMITS.—In Prussia the orderly planning of towns is made immeasurably easier owing to the right of local authorities to decide which land within the administrative area shall be eligible for building purposes. Owners of land are not able to build where and when they will. In order that a site may be built upon at all, however suitable it may seem in the eyes of its owner, it is essential that it shall be formally recognised on the building plan as ready for the purpose and shall lie upon a street duly planned by the local authority. Hence no land or estate company would dream of laying out its property without coming to a clear understanding with that authority. Such an understanding is more than a formality, for, while the local authority usually puts no needless obstacle in the way of town extensions promoted by private enterprise, it insists upon public interests being respected at every turn. A speculative land company may use unscrupulous methods in disposing of its land, but the fact that it sells land as "building land" does not make it such.

The legal aspect of the matter was recently stated by the Landrat of the Teltow Circle, near Berlin, in a formal warning to land purchasers. "In view of the increasing parcelling of estates in the vicinity of Berlin," he said, "it appears desirable to warn intending buyers. By means of favourable representations these are often led to believe that the plots of land which they propose to buy are building sites. As to that I would remark that only such land can be described as a building site which lies on a street provided for in a building plan, and prepared in accordance with the local by-laws for

THE PLANNING OF TOWNS

public traffic and for building. Buyers of land are, therefore, urgently advised to inform themselves on this point by application to the communal, police, or supervisory authorities before completing purchase."

On the other hand, the German official does not spare the land gamblers. If these people are found trying to dispose of land which has not been approved by the local authority for building purposes the public is frankly warned against them. Thus the president of a commune near Berlin (Zehlendorf) in 1910 published the following official notice :—

"No building plan has been proposed for the land lying in the south-east of Zehlendorf, and for that reason the laying out of streets in that district cannot be expected for years ; all applications for permission to build will, without exception, be refused. The commune has nothing whatever to do with the ground plan of this estate used by the Land Company concerned, and this plan has no prospect whatever of being sanctioned."

This power to regulate the opening up of new areas enables German local authorities to obtain from landowners concessions important for the planning of their towns. As in this country a local authority can claim from adjacent owners the land necessary for public streets as well as the whole costs of making such streets, and of providing drainage, paving, lighting plant, etc., which costs are, as a rule, payable as soon as building commences, but it can do much more. In Prussia the legal limit of the land that must be made over to the local authority for street making is $84\frac{1}{2}$ feet, or $42\frac{1}{4}$ feet for the adjacent owners on either side of the street. Often such a width is not needed, yet in large towns from 100 to 130 feet of road are not infrequently given free by owners anxious to get their land into the market. As the local authority has the final word in determining whether a new district shall be developed or not, it is seldom difficult to compel the owners to cede to the town all the land desired not only for wide streets and squares, but for schools and other public buildings that may sooner or later become necessary owing to growth of population. Valuable concessions of this kind are constantly obtained by the municipal authorities of Berlin and its suburbs in their dealings with the many land development companies there.

SPECIAL TAXATION OF BUILDING SITES AND BETTERMENT CONTRIBUTIONS.—But here the powers of the local authority over the owners of building land are not exhausted. German towns insist that when the community carries out extension and improvement schemes that bring profit to private persons the latter shall contribute fairly to the cost. In Prussia this is effected by two useful provisions of the Communal Taxation Law of 1893, one of which says that lands whose value is increased owing to the fact that building lines have been fixed in respect of them, may be taxed at a higher rate than other properties, the increase being proportionate to the greater value acquired, while the other and more important provision empowers communes to exact "betterment" contributions from the owners of property which benefits by public expenditure.[1] Communes are required, however, to levy such contributions when otherwise the costs—inclusive of the interest on capital and the redemption charges—would have to be raised by taxes. Before works of the kind are carried out a plan with estimate of cost has to be published and opportunity allowed for objections within a period of at least four weeks, and the sanction of the supervisory authority must also be obtained. The contributions may take the form of a single payment or of a yearly charge, the latter commutable on terms to be arranged.

The principal public works towards the cost of which adjacent owners may be required to pay special contributions include extensions of streets or portions of streets, clearances of old buildings, the new paving or repaving of streets, the construction or renewal of footways, the erection of bridges, overhead ways and subways, the laying out of open spaces and public parks, the connecting of houses with the main

[1] This provision is independent of the power given to communes by the law of July 2, 1875, relating to the planning and alteration of streets, to require adjacent owners to contribute towards the cost of such works.

drainage, and the opening up of new areas. The law of Bavaria does not recognise " contributions " in the Prussian sense, though here and there communes have been authorised to levy them under a different guise, and Bavarian municipal reformers strongly advocate the granting to the local authorities of the large powers possessed by Prussian communes.

The power to make these special assessments opens the way for " betterment " taxation on a wide scale and it is applied in many forms. For example, the municipality of Breslau used it in 1910 when it acquired and transformed into a garden and recreation ground for children an area of land at the junction of several streets which had hitherto served as a tipping place. The adjacent owners resisted the demand that they should bear part of the cost, yet although their objections were carried to the highest Court of Appeal the action of the municipality was supported. Again, in the same year, the town of Bautzen, at a cost of £14,000, completed the building of a bridge across a valley dividing the town from a district suitable for building purposes. Towards the cost of this bridge the town council made an assessment of from 7½d. to 1s. 3d. per linear yard of frontage on all sites adjacent to the streets laid out in the building plan for the district.

A more extended application of this principle of special assessments took place at Königsberg a short time ago. There the municipal executive had an offer from the State of the site of the old fortifications. The executive wished to buy, but they made the conclusion of the contract dependent upon the acceptance by an unwilling town council of an amendment to the existing Municipal Land Tax Ordinance providing for the special taxation of such land in private ownership as would become more valuable owing to the demolition of the fortifications and the opening up for building purposes of the adjacent area.[1] " The extraordinary increase in value," they asserted in a memorandum on the subject, " which is experienced by land adjacent to fortifications by the abolition of the radial restrictions on the use of the land suggests the thought and

[1] Where fortifications exist all building is prohibited within a prescribed area, and this area is generally used as field and garden.

the wish that the land so freed from restrictions shall make some compensatory return to the commune. This wish is the more justified, and becomes, indeed, an absolute demand of justice, when the commune pays for the demolition of the fortifications and the abolition of restrictions on the use of land, and to this end incurs far-going obligations and so large a risk, at the cost of the whole community, as is the case with our town." The executive proposed a tax of £4 and £8 per £1000 respectively (according to eligibility) of the sale value upon all land thus freed for building purposes, and on this being agreed to the project was carried through.[1]

POWER TO EXPROPRIATE LANDOWNERS AND TO POOL PROPERTIES.—Finally, in some of the States the towns, in the interest of public improvements and the systematic development and planning of their areas, have at command powers of expropriation of a kind unknown in this country.[2] No general law of expropriation applies to the Empire as a whole. The question of expropriation is, indeed, dealt with in the Imperial constitution, but only in relation to the construction of railways which may be deemed to be necessary for national defence or in the interest of the whole Empire, and even here expropriation must be legalised by special statute in each individual case. Most of the federal States have Expropriation Acts, however, some of them going back to the first half of the nineteenth century. Two methods of expropriation are followed, viz., (*a*) either the principle of expropriation for reasons of public interest is laid down in general terms, without enumerating the permissible objects of expropriation, or (*b*) the cases and the circumstances in which expropriation may be resorted to are specified. Laws of Saxony and Baden may be instanced in illustration of the first method, and laws of Prussia and Bavaria in illustration of the second. In general, expropriation in any given case is authorised by Royal Ordinance or Ministerial Decree, and no special or local statute is necessary to put the law in

[1] See Appendix III, " By-laws relating to Betterment Contributions," pp. 473-475.
[2] For a fuller statement of the German laws on the subject of expropriation, see Appendix IV, pp. 476-483.

operation. The State of Hamburg is, however, an exception to this rule.

In Prussia, owners of land can be expropriated under two laws : (a) for the purpose of street planning under the Building Alignment Law of July 2, 1875, relating to the " construction and alteration of streets and squares in urban and rural districts," and (b) for a wider range of purposes under the general law of June 11, 1874, relating to " the expropriation of landed property." Expropriation can be resorted to of right in the former case by any commune which has adopted an alignment plan to the execution of which land belonging to adjacent owners is necessary, while in the latter case a special Royal Order is necessary in every case. The general law of 1874 provides for expropriation " for reasons of public welfare in respect of undertakings to the execution of which the exercise of the right of expropriation is necessary," and it is occasionally applied when land is needed for the laying out of streets and squares and the construction of buildings and works of public interest, such as hospitals, poorhouses, abattoirs and stockyards, market halls, schools, tramways, water conduits, etc., and for the removal of blocks of insanitary houses. The cost of procedure is light, since it consists merely of the fees of experts and surveyors. As a rule, expropriation proceedings for the purpose of street works under the law of 1875 can be carried through in three or four months, while a year or more may be needed in the case of expropriation under the general law of 1874. The full, but not a speculative, value must be paid for land compulsorily taken, the value being fixed by a committee of experts appointed by the State supervisory authority.

In general no great regard is paid in Germany either by law or custom to the interests of speculators or the expectations of landowners who regard public need as their most valuable asset. The Prussian law of expropriation expressly says that in estimating the compensation to be paid no account shall be taken of " the increased value that may be acquired by the property in consequence of the new works." It is worth recalling here that when the Imperial War Department decided a few years ago to construct a great military road running from Berlin through Charlottenburg, across the river Havel, and on in a straight line for a total distance of twelve miles to the military camp at Döberitz, it expropriated the owners of the land needed, and in spite of the fact that speculation and frequent re-sale had driven up the former value ten and fifteen fold it paid compensation only on the valuation officially ascertained before the project was proposed.[1]

The modern German laws on town planning go beyond crude expropriation, however, for they provide for the compulsory "pooling" of entire areas of undeveloped urban land with a view to the re-distribution of this land amongst the various owners, in the old proportions either as to area or value, in such a way as will best promote the opening up of the district affected, the laying out of public streets, roads, and spaces, and the advantageous use of building plots (*Umlegung*). Baden has a general law on the subject, dating from 1896, and its powers have been used repeatedly by the town of Mannheim, though compulsion was not needed in all cases. The law of Saxony provides for the expropriation and pooling of urban properties by means of local by-laws which only need to be sanctioned by the Minister of the Interior. In Prussia similar powers have been conferred upon four large towns by special laws, but as yet there is no general statute on the subject.

Frankfort-on-Main first obtained a local Act in 1902, and it is significant that the mere possession of the power to compel unwilling owners to come into the pool made its application unnecessary. During the first ten years 14 areas with a total extent of 375 acres were pooled and re-distributed, with the assent of the owners. Originally consisting of 643 lots belonging to 149 different owners, the land was re-parcelled into 298 lots after a deduction ranging from 25 to 40 per cent. for street purposes, and the greater part of the land is now built upon. When the Frankfort-on-Main law (called—after its

[1] The Prussian Canal Law of April 1, 1905, providing for the construction of a canal from the Rhine to the Weser, empowers the State to expropriate the owners of land within one kilometre (five-eighths of a mile) of the canal, such power to be exercised in favour of the provinces of Westphalia, Rhineland, and Hanover, and the State of Bremen, with a view to securing to them the increased value which may be given to the land owing to the works carried out.

author, the chief mayor of the town—"*lex Adickes*") was under discussion an endeavour was made by a body of ardent municipal reformers to have it applied to Prussia generally, but without success. Posen, Cologne, and Wiesbaden have, however, since secured the same powers, and there is a strong movement in favour of legislation to enable all communes so disposed to acquire these powers by the simple device of adopting by-laws to that end. What the energetic governing authorities of the large Prussian towns in particular want is some more summary and more expeditious method of planning and developing the new areas which they are constantly absorbing than tedious and uncertain applications for Parliamentary powers or even the less circumstantial device of the royal decree, and it is hoped that the Government and Legislature will before long fall into line with Baden, Saxony, and other States.

PROTECTING THE STREETS AGAINST DISFIGUREMENT.—One other illustration of the concern of German local authorities for order and dignity in the appearance of their towns must be mentioned. This is the care taken to prevent the disfigurement of the streets and public places by hoardings or by buildings and other erections of an inartistic character, or even out of keeping with the general architectonic aspect of their surroundings. In so doing the authorities are assisted by general laws, police regulations, and the power to adopt special by-laws on the subject. Hoardings are tolerated in few towns, and so far does the German æsthetic sense rebel against public *réclame* that railway stations and tramcars are equally free from the meretricious allures that in this country greet the eye wherever it turns. The old common law of Prussia of 1794 contains the provision that buildings which spoil the appearance of a public place may be prohibited by the police authority charged with the regulation of buildings, and this authority can require the removal of any erection or street obstruction that is offensive to the eye.

A law of July 15, 1907, deals with the question on more general principles. Under this law the building authority is empowered to refuse sanction to the erection of any buildings or to alterations that would grossly disfigure important streets or public places either in town or country, or in general spoil the aspect of a locality. Power is given to communes to adopt by-laws for the protection of the architectural characteristics of important streets or places of special historical or artistic interest. These by-laws may make the use of signboards, inscriptions, or the like dependent upon police permission. Before the police as the building authority can either grant or refuse sanction to build, the opinion of experts and of the mayor or municipal executive must be taken, and the local authority is given a right of appeal against police decisions to the higher administrative authority.

A number of Prussian towns have adopted by-laws under the statute of 1907. Saxony, Würtemberg, and the Free City of Bremen have since adopted laws on the same lines. In Bremen no plan for a new building or the alteration of an existing one is passed until it has received the scrutiny and sanction of a standing committee consisting of four officers belonging to the municipal public works department, three architects, and two art experts.

Many Prussian towns have gone further and have established special municipal offices for advice to builders and architects upon matters of style and taste. No charge is made, and there is theoretically no obligation to follow the advice given unless the builders' plans infringe the local regulations, yet the good offices of the municipality are both freely used and highly valued. The municipality of Baden-Baden adds rewards to advice, for it gives premiums every year to architects and builders whose erections are adjudged to comply most nearly with certain prescribed conditions as to artistic design and quality of materials, and best harmonise with the general architectonic scheme of the town. By the adoption of these and similar common-sense methods, and by insisting that the building like the planning of a town should be considered as a whole, it is hoped to prevent the architectural anarchy which has often reigned in the past, and even to rectify many mistakes which have been inherited from times when the building speculator was left to his own devices. The amenity of civic life in Germany is further protected by a law, applying to the whole country, providing that before industrial or trading undertakings which would cause injury or even inconvenience to the neighbouring residents can be established the consent of the higher State authorities must be obtained.

TOWN PLANNING AS A STUDY.—Finally, in its town planning schemes and its endeavour to add dignity and decorum to the outward aspects of municipal life, Germany shows unwavering fidelity to the national belief in the expert and the efficiency of education and training. Instead of trusting to the intuition and judgment of the practical man—that precious town builder by " natural " methods, who has made so many of our English industrial towns the hideous abominations they are— Germany acts on the assumption that as town planning is a science and an art, it ought to be studied like any other science or art, and indeed more thoroughly and laboriously than most, since the vital welfare of entire communities is at stake. Hence it follows as a matter of course that some of the technical universities regularly offer courses of lectures on town planning, both from the theoretical and the practical side. These lectures attract large numbers of students who are preparing for a career in the administrative service either in connection with the State or the local government bodies. A special seminary for town planning has been attached to the Royal Technical University in Berlin since 1907; the lectures cover every phase of the subject, and all incidental questions are treated from the architectural, technical, sanitary, and financial standpoints. In Saxony the Government instituted a similar seminary in connection with the Dresden Technical University in 1910, and a seminary is attached to the Technical University of Danzig. The colleges for communal administration and social science at Cologne and Düsseldorf likewise provide courses of lectures on this subject as a part of their regular work. Town planning exhibitions and conferences also play an important part in the development of a healthy official and public opinion upon this important question. The exhibitions held in Berlin in 1910, Düsseldorf in 1910 and 1912, and Leipzig and Karlsruhe in 1913 have given a great impetus to the town planning movement both in Germany and abroad, and have been fruitful in stimulating interest in local government in many ways.

ADMINISTRATIVE AREA OF GERMAN TOWNS.—It will be convenient to give here some indication of the extent of the more important German urban districts. English students of municipal government visiting Germany are invariably surprised at the apparent large area of the towns whose acquaintance they make. While there are large German towns with a far less density of population than any towns of the same size in this country, on the whole the conditions in the two countries do not greatly differ. A classification of the areas of 93 German towns with 50,000 inhabitants or more, with a total population in 1910 of 16,711,600, contained in the "Statistical Yearbook of German Towns" for 1913, shows an average area of 10,138 acres, and a ratio of 17·7 inhabitants per acre. A classification of the areas of 81 English towns of corresponding size, with a total population in 1911 of 11,459,800, shows an average area of 7622 acres, and a ratio of 18·6 inhabitants per acre. The collective area of the 93 German towns had increased by 78 per cent. since 1870.

Dividing the towns into three groups, according as they contain (a) more than 200,000 inhabitants, (b) between 100,000 and 200,000 inhabitants, and (c) between 50,000 and 100,000 inhabitants, we get the following comparative figures :—

GERMAN TOWNS.

No. of towns.	Population.	Aggregate area.	Average area.	No. of inhabitants per acre.
		Acres.	*Acres.*	
A—22.........	10,106,700	381,348	16,582	26·5
B—24.........	3,423,000	227,121	9,463	15·1
C—46.........	3,181,900	334,411	7,270	9·5
Together—93 ..	16,711,600	942,880	10,138	17·7

ENGLISH TOWNS.

A—15.........	5,864,800	240,177	16,012	24·4
B—23.........	2,929,800	137,223	5,966	21·3
C—43.........	2,665,200	240,168	5,585	11·1
Together—81 ..	11,459,800	617,568	7,622	18·6

THE PLANNING OF TOWNS

Of the German towns with the largest area relatively to population, the most important are the following (the figures relate to 1910) :—

German Towns.	Population.	Area.	No. of inhabitants per acre.
		Acres.	*Acres.*
Münster	90,300	16,564	5·8
Bonn	46,700	7,708	6·1
Mülheim (Ruhr)	112,600	17,315	6·5
Saarbrücken	105,100	12,693	8·3
Remscheid	72,200	7,815	9·2
Magdeburg	279,700	26,683	10·5
Hagen	88,600	8,114	10·9
Crefeld	129,400	11,737	11
Düsseldorf	358,700	28,899	12·4
Frankfort-on-Main	414,600	33,345	12·4
Aix-la-Chapelle	156,000	12,503	12·5
Duisburg	229,500	17,470	13·1
Oberhausen	89,900	5,150	17·5
Cologne	516,500	28,916	17·9

The town with the largest area is Hagenau in Alsace, with 45,600 acres to a population of 19,000, or 2¼ acres per inhabitant.

Many of the larger areas are of comparatively recent growth, being the result of successive incorporations of adjacent communes and rural districts. Thus the area of Nuremberg increased during the years 1825–1905 from 400 acres to over 16,000 acres, due to the absorption by the old walled town of fourteen communes and seven other areas, effected by nine separate acts of incorporation. The population during this period increased from 33,000 to 294,000. Of other old towns, Munich has increased its area from 4200 acres in 1854 to 22,180 acres; Hanover from 2230 acres in 1859 to 24,800 acres; and Magdeburg from 1850 acres in 1867 to 27,010 acres. Of 94 towns which at the census of 1910 had over 50,000 inhabitants only seven had an area in excess of 12,500 acres in 1871; now the number of these towns is 27.

THE MODERN INCORPORATION MOVEMENT.—One of the outstanding facts of Germany's modern development has been the aggregation of urban population and the multiplication of "large" towns of over 100,000 inhabitants. At the beginning of last century there were only two towns of that size, viz. Berlin and Hamburg, and by the middle of the century there was only one more, Breslau, soon to be joined by Cologne and Munich. In 1870 the number of "large" towns had increased to eight by the addition of Dresden, Königsberg, and Leipzig; there were 15 in 1880, 26 in 1890, 33 in 1900, 41 in 1905, and 48 in 1910. More than one-fifth of the entire population of the Empire now lives in "large" towns.

The remarkable growth of the large towns that has fallen to the last generation is in part due to their incorporation of the growing suburbs. Legislation makes easy the amalgamation of willing communes. In Prussia, minor measures of incorporation can be effected by Royal Decree, and only in the case of the union of towns is a special law necessary, though the Circle Diet has a right to be heard if it objects. Where certain prescribed reasons of public interest are held to apply, adjacent areas may be compulsorily added to towns by resolution of the District Committee after the opinion of the Circle Diet has been taken, but appeal is allowed to the higher instances.

Of late years many large towns have been driven to incorporate adjacent areas by the necessity of room for expansion, for public works and institutions—sewerage, water, gas, and electricity, schools and hospitals, etc.—for the carrying out of housing schemes, for the extension of tramway systems, for the drainage of outside districts already appropriated for residences by the well-to-do, or for the equalisation of taxation within wider areas. Since 1880 Leipzig has gained a population of 180,000 by measures of incorporation, and in the same way Cologne and Dresden have each gained a population of 115,000, Essen one of 95,000, Saarbrücken one of 75,000, Duisburg one of 70,000, and Frankfort-on-Main one of 65,000.

On the other hand, the incorporated suburbs have often had a great inducement to join their lot to prosperous and well-governed towns. Hanging upon the skirts of large towns, many of them have had to drag on a penurious existence, conscious of liabilities and obligations of all kinds, yet unable, because of restricted resources, to fulfil them, and owing to the munificence of their wealthy neighbours most of the amenities of social life which they have enjoyed. For such places incorporation has been a great relief; they have secured public improvements beyond their own capacity to provide, they have on easy terms become partners in profitable undertakings of all kinds, and the privileges hitherto used by sufferance have become their rights.[1] Dortmund, in Westphalia, for example, carried out in 1913 a large scheme of incorporation the financial benefits of which were entirely on the side of the eight adjacent rural communes taken in. In most of these communes Dortmund already had substantial proprietorial interests—in one a park, in another a cemetery, in two others docks, and so on—but the determining motive was the need of space for expansion and for a large and rational housing plan. So favourable were the terms offered to the incorporated communes that four of them will pay local income tax at a much lower rate than heretofore, while all were able to conclude hard bargains securing to them preferential treatment for a long term of years in regard to other taxes, to electricity, water, and sewerage charges, and other matters. To Dortmund a larger area was essential, however, and it was willing to pay the price. As a result of the incorporation its area was increased from 5700 to 12,500 acres and its population from 214,000 to 248,000.

Some of the great towns, however, owe their growth pre-eminently to industrial expansion. Thus the population of Düsseldorf by natural increase of population and immigration alone grew from 40,000 in the middle of last century to 95,000 in 1880, 145,000 in 1890, 214,000 in 1900, and 290,000 in 1910, while the increase of its administrative boundaries in 1908—the first time for five centuries—brought in a population of 70,000, making the total 360,000 at the last census. Its area was thus increased from 12,170 to 27,790 acres. Here and

[1] "Often a measure of incorporation is the only means of rescuing a commune from its economic perplexities and of relieving it from the threatened danger of being no longer able to fulfil its communal duties. And if at the outset the step often entails heavy sacrifice upon the economically stronger commune concerned, the proceeding, though at first perhaps regarded as one of dire necessity, in the end usually proves a blessing to both parties, and hence to the newly created unity."—Kappelmann, " Verfassung und Verwaltungsorganisation der Städte," p. 10 (Verein für Sozialpolitik).

there several communes of large size have been united to form a single town ; as, for example, the union of Duisburg, Ruhrort, and Meiderich on the Rhine in the town of Duisburg in 1905, and the union of Saarbrücken and two other large communes in the town of Saarbrücken in 1909.

The most remarkable exception to the incorporation movement is the city of Berlin. Twenty years ago the incorporation of several of the suburbs of Berlin, which have since grown into large towns, was favoured by the Government and urged by it upon the municipal council, but this body deliberately declined to enlarge the city's boundaries. Owing to the permanent domination in the local administration of the party of what in Germany is regarded as an advanced Liberalism and to the steady growth of the Social Democrats in the representative assembly the Government's attitude has entirely changed, and to-day it is questionable whether incorporation of any of these suburbs, even were they willing, would be allowed.

CHAPTER VII

HOUSING POLICIES

Character of the housing problem in German towns—The evil of land and house speculation—Remedial measures adopted by the communes—The reaction in favour of small houses—Miscellaneous administrative measures—Erection of houses by local authorities—Public assistance to building societies—Municipal inspection of dwellings—Municipal house registries—Building regulations.

TOWN planning has been raised to the dignity of a science in Germany, but in house planning and building the communes have not proved equally successful. A well-known German housing reformer, Dr. Stübben, of Berlin, said recently :—" The price which we pay (in Germany) for the possession of the best planned towns in the world is the destruction of the home. High prices of land, high rents, and high taxes prevent the building of small houses and lead to the erection of huge barracks, with the result that the workman, like many others, seeks recreation not in his home but in the public-house." The housing question is at least as acute in German towns as in others, though opinions will differ greatly as to the extent to which the German system of town planning is responsible, and it is doubtful whether Dr. Stübben's dictum would be largely endorsed without careful reservations by other housing authorities in his own country.

About the facts of the question, however, there can be little difference of opinion. Outwardly the streets of a German town usually give the impression of order, cleanliness, comfort and well-being. Except in the older quarters the streets are wide and well kept, and if the observer keeps to the streets he will detect few signs of bad housing and will rarely come across property that can be fairly described as of the " slum " order. It is only when the high portals on the street front are passed, the courtyards entered, the dingy staircases climbed, and the interior of the dwellings inspected that the special character and the seriousness of Germany's housing problem will be properly understood. "Behind the straight streets and within the chess-board planned building blocks," wrote a contributor to the "Soziale Praxis" (September 10, 1910), in reference to the towns of the Rhineland, "there are found, owing to perverse building regulations, made to suit the requirements of building speculators, narrow courtyards without air or sun, frightful ventilation shafts, the ever dark landings, semi-dark rooms, and other defects which are a parody on the simplest requirements of hygiene. The present generation will have to suffer for decades from the exploitation of speculators and the neglect of duty shown by the authorities. Gradually, however, we are coming to a new housing culture which cannot indeed wipe away inherited sins, yet which is endeavouring to give us whatever is possible under the existing system of property and the existing structure of society."

CHARACTER OF THE HOUSING PROBLEM IN GERMAN TOWNS.—The congestion which exists in many towns is an obvious product of historical and physical conditions. In proof of this statement it is only necessary to point to old fortified towns, like Danzig or Cologne, in which in earlier times buildings were almost necessarily huddled together within the walls without regard for sanitary considerations, to maritime and river towns like Hamburg and Kiel, whose building was largely determined by the natural traffic ways, and to towns settled in narrow valleys, like Elberfeld, where people built just where and as they could, and systematic planning was out of the question. In all such towns defective housing arrangements were to a large extent inevitable in the past.

But the evil is far more widespread and extends to towns whose natural conditions offer no excuse for bad housing. It is, indeed, no exaggeration to say that, after allowing for much quite exemplary building, housing conditions are nowhere so bad with so little justification as in many of the newer industrial towns of Germany. Some of these towns have been in possession of conditions which, if wisely used, would have secured the highest standard of working-class housing known anywhere—extensive administrative areas, with an abundance of open land, excellent town-building plans worked out to the smallest detail, large estates in municipal hands, wide powers whereby to regulate house building in every direction, and unlimited opportunities of helping building societies by the sale of public land and the loan of public money. Instead, however, of building its towns on the extensive principle, Germany has committed the inexpiable sin of creating the barrack house, consisting of any number of floors, up to seven, upon which small dwellings jostle against each other like cubicles in a doss-house.

The large barrack house is specially characteristic of the east of Prussia and in a less degree of the west, though in the west there are seldom found the " side " and " back " houses and the arrangement of four or six dwellings on a single floor peculiar to Berlin and its suburbs. While the new houses built at Charlottenburg in 1910 contained on the average 24·4 dwellings per building, the ratio for the houses built at Essen and Aix-la-Chapelle was 3·7, at Crefeld 3·5, at Cologne 5, and at Düsseldorf 5·7.

The most notorious home of the barrack house is, of course, Berlin. The average number of persons per inhabited house in that city is 77, so that Breslau with 52, Leipzig with 35, Halle with 26, and Frankfort-on-Main with 20 persons per house are almost exemplary by comparison. Berlin's high average of 77 inhabitants per house, however, implies a far more appalling congestion in the thickly populated working-class areas, for this average is kept down by the relatively small average prevalent in the well-to-do districts of the west, where whole districts have an average no higher than 26. In contrast to that relatively low figure there are large districts in the north and east of the city with an average of over 100 persons per house. The consequence is that, in the words of Dr. H. Preuss, " Berlin is, in ratio of area to population, the smallest city of over a million inhabitants on the face of the earth." If tuberculosis is a housing disease, as medical authorities more and more agree that it is, there is room for serious reflection in the fact that owing to the intensive method of building adopted half the dwellings of Berlin contain only one room and a kitchen, that 33,000 of its dwellings have only one heatable room and 2400 no such room at all, and that 4090 dwellings consist simply of a kitchen.

Who conceived this enormity? How came it to dominate whole towns? There was no need for it, even in Berlin. Land was abundant always, and until the barrack house conquered it was not excessively dear; while fifty and even thirty years ago bricks and labour cost only half as much as now. There were large houses of four stories in Berlin two centuries ago, and in some of the old towns at a still earlier date, but they were not the prevailing type and often they were built for special purposes. Only when German towns began to renew their youth some forty years ago and house-building passed into the hands of speculators did the large "flat" house become really naturalised. Since then it has become an obsession.

Municipal authorities accepted it blindly as the last word in domestic architecture and assumed that no other form of building was possible in large towns. "The great barrack house owes its existence to accident and thoughtlessness," writes a well-known German housing authority. In part it was undoubtedly an expression of that unreasoning love of size and massivity which is so characteristic of modern Germany. It was this same characteristic that led the earlier town planners to lay down streets of great and often excessive width, irrespective of the purpose for which they were intended, just as their love of regularity led them to plan these streets in dismal straight lines. Only in recent times was the discovery made that the width of a street should bear some relationship to its purpose—whether for heavy or purely local traffic—and that long, straight, wind-swept streets lack in beauty what they gain in convenience. Meantime, the excessive width of streets insisted on by cast-iron regulations added greatly to the cost of house-building, and in order to recoup himself and make the most of his plots the builder began to extend his houses vertically instead of horizontally. The discovery that five or six stories could be built on a site which before had been occupied by three or four increased the value of the land, and even made dearer such land as was not intended for barrack houses, because of its potential use and value.

THE EVIL OF LAND AND HOUSE SPECULATION.—Infinite harm has also been done by wild and often unprincipled speculation. Much of the building enterprise in the larger German towns is unsound and unscrupulous, and behind it is the equally pernicious gambling of land companies ever eager to unload their property upon the public. There are in Berlin scores of land and estate companies, some perfectly honest, yet most of a speculative character, and some of the larger of these companies distribute princely dividends amongst their shareholders. The mischief done by many of these companies is not confined to the districts which, owing to their influence, are burdened permanently by excessive land prices and exorbitant rents, but extends to house property generally, and in the end the entire community is compelled to pay ransom to them.

Worse still, much—in some towns most—of the building is done by men of straw, working with money borrowed at high rates of interest. These speculative builders live from hand to mouth, they are provided with funds week by week to cover the current outlay, or as much of it as cannot be allowed to accumulate in debts that will never be paid, and by the time they have completed a block of dwellings the interest paid or accrued on advances and on the heavy outstanding mortgage that remains often represents a standing charge quite out of proportion to the intrinsic value of the property, and this charge the tenants have to pay.

A large amount of house property, at least in the towns of mushroom growth, is heavily mortgaged, thanks to the existence of an abundance of banks and moneylenders who are prepared to advance readily up to a very narrow margin of security. The effect is to draw into the web of house speculation hosts of people without either the brains or the conscience necessary to the responsible management of property. Not long ago a Berlin banking house published in a newspaper of that city offers of loans on a scale showing that a property of the value of £7650 might be had for a payment on account of £500 (6½ per cent.), the balance remaining on mortgage; a property valued at £8150 for £600 (7½ per cent.), one of £9500 for £750 (8 per cent.), one of £10,100 for £800 (8½ per cent.), and so on. In other words, on this system of speculation, the nominal buyers were only required to pay down between one-fifteenth and one-twelfth of the purchase price, the truth being, of course, that a person operating on these conditions no more owns his house than the stock exchange gambler who speculates in margins owns the securities for whose ups-and-downs he makes himself responsible. The margin of profit shown on these house transactions, after paying interest, but without allowances for repairs, rates and taxes, etc., ranged from 1 to 1½ per cent. on the purchase price, and proportionately more upon the sum actually invested.

This system of pseudo-house-ownership largely explains the short tenure of house properties in Berlin and towns offering equally favourable opportunities for unsound speculation. An investigation made by the Charlottenburg Statistical Office showed that 41 per cent. of all properties in that town changed hands during the five years 1900 to 1905. This rapid turnover of property bears out the common observation of housing investigators that Germany more and more lives in rented houses. Dr. H. Wolff, of Halle, estimates that whereas in the middle of last century 50 per cent. of all dwellings in the large towns of Germany were rented and 42 per cent. owned by their occupiers, the proportions in 1900 were 85 and 11 per cent., and in 1910, 88 and 9 per cent. It is estimated that in Berlin 97 per cent. of all inhabitants live in rented houses; in Breslau, 96; in Hamburg, 94; in Leipzig, 93; in Munich, 92; in Essen, 90; and in Cologne, 86 per cent. In large towns the tradition of the householder settled upon his own little domain survives only where the single family dwelling has kept at bay the flat and barrack house, as in Bremen, in this characteristic perhaps the most English-looking of German towns, Oldenburg, Lübeck, and a few other towns.

Incidental to the practice of frivolous borrowing is the pernicious custom of house farming. A large owner of working-class property will let a whole " book " of dwellings—often as many as a hundred—to a middleman agent whose only capital is his capacity to screw out of the tenants a shilling or two a week beyond the amount which he agrees to pay the landlord in chief. These parasites live by rack-renting, perform no useful service, and have no legitimate place in the social economy.

In some towns harm has been done in the past, and is done to-day, by the curious stipulation found in the communal electoral law of some of the States—Prussia and Saxony among the number—to the effect that one half or more of the members of a town council, and it may be of the municipal executive as well, must be house-owners. The provision dates from a time of limited franchises, when a large proportion of the freemen of a town lived in their own houses, and when the burden of local taxation fell predominantly upon property owners. In general the effect of this arrangement upon the housing policies of the towns has not been beneficial, and in some cases it has been obstructive in a high degree. Indeed, when one allows for the conscious and unconscious play of self-interest and prejudice, it might seem remarkable that German towns have been able to do so much of late years to help forward housing reforms and to ameliorate the entire conditions of their areas, in view of the theoretical power of the statutory party of property to direct policy in accordance with its wishes.

The effect of all these forces and influences, inelastic building regulations, intensive building, the mania for huge blocks, inordinate land speculation, professional building by men of straw, and heavy mortgage indebtedness—from nearly all of which dear land follows as certainly as night follows day,—is seen in excessive rents, a tendency to pinch house room to the utmost, and a condition of congestion which is all the more deplorable since the areas of German towns are, in general, so large as to show a very favourable general ratio of space to population. In spite of the fact that the predominant dwelling of the British working classes contains four or five rooms while that of the German working classes contains only two of three, the former, as a rule, pay no higher rent. Other classes of the population suffer equally from the dearness of house room, and only seldom is the accommodation fully adequate to the need. As a consequence, rent takes a specially prominent place in the domestic budget, for one-seventh or one-sixth of a man's income is regarded as a nominal expenditure on this one item, and in the case of the working classes a fifth and a quarter are very common. Speaking of the results of his own observations, a German housing authority, Herr Folsen, in a study of English and German housing in relation to land values, comes to the conclusion that house rent in Berlin is from 30 to 50 per cent. higher than in London, and that in general English housing is far cheaper than either German or French. Dr. Landmann said at the second German Housing Congress held at Mannheim in 1911, " If the price of land in the large towns, and even in those of medium size, does not fall, the classes of the population with only moderate means are doomed to suffer from ever-increasing housing difficulties."

REMEDIAL MEASURES ADOPTED BY THE COMMUNES.—Resuming the special aspects of the housing problem as presented to German municipalities and reformers, the principal are the existence of a large amount of property, particularly in the old towns, insanitary in surroundings and internal arrangements, high land prices, excessive rents, a great lack of small dwellings within the reach of the working classes and other people of small means, and above all the need for a decentralisation movement, so as to relieve the congestion in the heart of the large communities by diverting population to the outskirts. It is necessary now to inquire what is being done to grapple with a problem which forces itself upon all thinking persons at so many points.

Relief is being sought in various directions, and by every town according to the special aspects presented by its own problem and its special facilities for dealing with the resulting difficulties. Improved legislation will admittedly be necessary before the question is done with, but meantime the local authorities are doing their best with the powers at their disposal. In many towns the old slums have been cleared away wholesale at enormous expense. Hamburg has already expended several million pounds in this way; costly clearances have also been made at Cologne, Frankfort-on-Main, Dortmund, Augsburg, Strassburg, and other towns, and as a result light, air, and health have been introduced into dark and foul places. The Strassburg improvement scheme embodies novel methods of procedure. The town has acquired for about £600,000 a large area of narrow streets in the Old Town and intends to demolish this property and construct a wide and handsome boulevard from the central railway station into the heart of the business quarter. Instead of itself building or negotiating the sale of the land that will be available for buildings the town has entered into an arrangement with a bank, which will dispose of the available sites at minimum prices and pay the town a fixed share of the profit. Where possible the land will be sold on lease for a term of 65 years, but the rest will be sold outright. Leaseholders will pay interest only slightly above that payable by the town on its loan, and at the end of the term the whole of the buildings will become public property without further consideration. Where the land is sold outright 20 per cent. of the purchase price has to be paid down at once, and the balance must be paid with interest in ten years.

Improvement works of this kind can be carried out by the aid of the Expropriation Laws where necessary. In Germany as everywhere, however, the displacement of population under such circumstances creates the problem of its future housing. No law or local statute requiring provision to be made for the re-housing of working-people who may be so displaced is known to exist. Nevertheless, when after the cholera epidemic of 1892 the State of Hamburg cleared a large insanitary area in the inner town it sold the land subject to the condition that it should be used for dwelling-houses, a certain number of which should be for the working class, and the same principle has been followed in relation to later clearances.

THE REACTION IN FAVOUR OF SMALL HOUSES.—In some respects the German towns are simply endeavouring to retrace the ways unwisely chosen half a century ago, and just as Germany has taught England the importance and value of good town planning, so Germany is learning of England how to build good houses.[1] Happily a strong and wholesome reaction has set in against the barrack house. The speculative builder will cling to it as long as possible, just as Demetrius clung to his shrines, but amongst housing reformers no one can be found who has a good word to say for it ; the architect has rebelled against it, and the municipal authorities are more and more throwing difficulties in its way. " We must emancipate ourselves from the barrack house," said Government Councillor Freund, a high official of the Prussian Ministry of the Interior not long ago, " for the crowding together of dwellings is responsible not only for much sickness but also for much crime." " The modern tendency," writes Dr. Most, as an active representative of municipal government, " is in favour of the small house in distinction to the barrack house, and in spite of opinions to the contrary this is now in general regarded as the most suitable and most favourable form of house."[2] " This form of dwelling," says, finally, a building expert, Herr Geusen, municipal surveyor of Düsseldorf, where the barrack house has found a far too cordial welcome, " must be opposed with all the means available, not only for sanitary but for social and ethical reasons, and its abolition must be the principal aim in the remodelling of our towns. In contrast to it, the building of one-family houses, where they appear to be suited to the population, must be furthered in every way."[3]

And so testimony to the discredit of the barrack house might be multiplied almost indefinitely. But yesterday it stood against the world, with its crude, oppressive proportions, and barbaric ugliness ; now none is so poor as to do it reverence. The police and municipal authorities are giving

[1] The compliment to this country is paid by Germany. Dr. Stübben, of Berlin, writes : " In house-building we must learn from England. Just as English people have during recent years studied town planning with us, so we Germans have gone to England in large numbers in order to study house-building, and particularly the building of small houses."
[2] " Die deutsche Stadt und ihre Verwaltung," Vol. II, p. 52.
[3] *Ibid.*, Vol. III, p. 22.

effect to this accumulating condemnation of the barrack house by amending building regulations so as to restrict large houses to the inner districts of towns, while the permissible number of stories diminishes with the distance from the centre, and by abolishing the deep blocks with their double and treble courtyards. Thus the municipal authority of Mannheim divides its area into three zones or districts for building purposes; within the first zone houses may be built to a height of five stories, within the second zone to a height of four stories, and within the third zone to a height of three stories, while detached side and back houses may not have more than four, three, and two stories respectively. So, too, the building regulations of Munich recognise five types of houses on the " closed " method of building (i.e. building in rows), and four on the " open " method (i.e. detached blocks); in the former case the permissible height is graduated from ground floor and four stories to ground floor and one story, and in the latter from ground floor and three stories to ground floor and one story.

On the other hand, every inducement is now being offered for the erection of small houses for one or two families on the periphery of towns, for the ideal of the " English home " is in the ascendant. "The Germans like to live together," writes Professor Vogt, of Frankfort; "they fear having far to walk, and at first they even looked askance at suburbs." That was true of the generation that took its outdoor exercise in bowling alleys and that had never heard of garden towns, but it is no longer true to-day. A veritable migration to the country has set in, and around every large town may now be seen colonies of villas and *maisonnettes,* planted in the midst of field and woodland.

Something is being done to alleviate the housing problem by administrative measures. With a view to cheapening the cost of house-building and thus of keeping down rents more, elasticity is being shown by the regulations relating to street construction; wide streets are no longer insisted on where the probable needs of traffic do not require them, so that a given property can be used for a proportionately larger number of dwellings. The municipality of Bremen, in its desire to facilitate the building of small houses, to be occupied by their owners, and to preserve the reputation of the town as a town of one-family houses, decided in 1913 to allow such houses to be built on unmade roads not intended for through traffic and lined by front gardens. It is estimated that small houses can be built at a cost of £200 to £250, exclusive of the land.

MISCELLANEOUS ADMINISTRATIVE MEASURES.—Among other measures of an administrative character, yet of wider scope, which are more or less within the power of all municipalities in proportion to their financial resources, and are being increasingly employed, are the extension of the communal boundaries by the incorporation of rural suburbs, with a view to bringing in new areas for building purposes, and of diverting population outward, the planning of these areas on systematic lines, the purchase of land and its disposal to building societies, the extension of tramways and other transport arrangements, so as to facilitate traffic between the towns and their suburbs,[1] the encouragement of building societies by the loan of money or the concession to them of rating privileges, the formation of mortgage funds for the advance of building money on easy terms to private individuals, subject to conditions as to the size and type of dwelling to be erected, the building of houses for municipal employees and for small occupiers generally, the division of the administrative district into zones and their assignment to special purposes (industrial works, residences, parks, etc.), the development of the land and building taxes, particularly in the direction of taxing all transactions in real estate, with special taxation of " increased value " or unearned increment, the increase of parks, recreation grounds, and open spaces, the introduction of an efficient system of house inspection, and the establishment of municipal house registries. Many of the foremost men in municipal government claim a wide extension of the existing limited powers of expropriation, so as to enable communal authorities to acquire and either use or redistribute

[1] The subject of urban transport is fully dealt with in the chapter on " Municipal Trading Enterprises," pp. 232–240.

whole areas of their districts, according as circumstances may dictate. The action taken by many of the towns on some of these lines deserves special notice.

ERECTION OF HOUSES BY LOCAL AUTHORITIES.—In all the States the first public experiments in house-building have invariably been undertaken in the interest of municipal workpeople. As long ago as 1901 (March 19) the Prussian Ministers of Trade and Commerce, for Education, and for Home Affairs issued a decree on the improvement of housing conditions, directing the Presidents of Government Districts to use their influence with communal authorities so as to persuade them to increase their real estate as much as possible, with a view to counteracting private speculation in land, yet urging them not to sell but only to lease such town land for building purposes. They were also to encourage communal authorities in small as well as large towns to " provide for their minor officials and the working-men engaged in public undertakings wholesome and convenient dwellings at as low rents as possible." The decree added :—" A further means whereby influence can successfully be exerted towards the improvement of housing conditions is the facilitating of communication with the outer districts of the larger communes. Wherever abuses in housing conditions exist, care should be taken to develop the system of municipal communications, and to provide the necessary facilities for conveying working-people and school-children from and to the outer districts. In so far as the communes grant new concessions for tramways, etc., special provision to that effect should be introduced in the contracts." Similar decrees were issued more recently by the Governments of other States.

These decrees powerfully stimulated the local authorities in many parts of the country, and a large number of towns have since provided dwellings for a portion of their employees, invariably upon town land on the outskirts. These houses are in general cheaper than similar houses in private ownership, for the municipalities are satisfied with the return of bare interest, and sometimes do not press for that. Of 106 towns with over 50,000 inhabitants, 42 (including Mannheim,

Frankfort-on-Main, Düsseldorf, Munich, Stuttgart, Cologne, Mülhausen, and Essen) had in 1909 built such houses. Some of the best of these municipal working-class dwellings are to be found at Mülhausen, for they combine, in a high degree, both comfort and elegance. They are built detached, each block surrounded by a considerable piece of land, and the style of architecture suggests rather a *bijou* suburban villa than a working-man's abode. The dwellings consist of three rooms and a kitchen, with a portion of the attic, and the use of a common drying-ground.

Many towns go further, however, and build small houses for people of limited means generally. Of 15 of the larger towns which have been specially active in house-building one has built over 200 houses, five between 100 and 200 each, and the remaining nine 50 each. In Bavaria a number of small towns and even villages have built dwellings for the working classes.

Two comparatively small towns, Freiburg in Baden and Ulm in Würtemberg, have built houses on a specially large scale and their experience deserves more detailed reference since it represents a serious practical attempt to alleviate the housing problem by public action on commercial lines, and as such has attracted great attention throughout Germany. Freiburg's house-building enterprise dates from 1862. It began by building houses to sell at cost price, but when it was found that the owners were selling out at a profit it ceased to part with its houses and has since let them on a commercial basis to working-people, small officials, and others. The town owns, or manages as custodian of charitable funds, over 500 dwellings, and these it lets at rents which, while moderate, yield a satisfactory profit, but if to this number are added the dwellings provided by building societies receiving public assistance the town directly or indirectly controls over 1000 dwellings, or 6 per cent. of the total number in Freiburg. The houses contain from one to three living- or bedrooms, with kitchen and other accommodation, and a garden, and the rents range from 10s. to 33s. a month. The town council has explained its housing policy as follows:—
" It is the purpose of the town to set a beneficent example in the

domain of house-building and to attempt as far as possible to equalise the fluctuations in supply. When it is satisfied that private enterprise meets all justifiable demands it will move slowly, while, on the other hand, it will be more active when abuses threaten. We can affirm with satisfaction that no serious complaint has yet been made of private individuals having been injured by the action of the town."

The municipality of Ulm follows a different method in that it builds houses and sells them outright. It also sells land for building purposes, but subject to the right to buy it back with the buildings thereon during a period of a hundred years whenever the property changes hands or the owner fails to observe his obligations. The town further reserves a special right of re-purchase for a period of 200 years in regard to front garden ground in the event of its being needed for street improvements. Ulm began to build in 1894, when the town council assigned a vote of £10,000 for this purpose, and it has now built and sold some 175 dwellings to artisans, factory and other workmen, small officials, and others. Two types of houses are built—two-story houses containing two dwellings, each with two rooms and a kitchen, etc., and a garden, costing with the land £300; and one-story houses, likewise containing two dwellings of the same size, costing £410. Buyers are expected to pay 5½ per cent. on the purchase price yearly, 3 per cent. as interest and 2½ in repayment of loan, making a payment of £16 10s. and £22 11s. respectively for the two types of buildings. An additional sum of from £3 to £4 is payable for repairs, taxes, and water. It is required by the contract of sale that the buyer shall live in one of his two dwellings, and he may not charge for the other a higher rent than the town council approves; if these and other conditions are not faithfully observed the town can exercise the right to buy back the land with the building. Where re-purchase takes place the value of the property is fixed by a committee of experts, of whom the owner nominates one; the method of valuation followed is to take the cost price as a basis and to increase this by the unexhausted value of improvements made and decrease it by depreciation due to use. The sum so arrived at, less interest and balance of purchase price due by the owner, is paid by the town.[1]

PUBLIC ASSISTANCE TO BUILDING SOCIETIES.—The policy of municipal house-building has many strong opponents in local government circles. These critics contend that housebuilding must in the main be left to private enterprise always, and that the most local authorities can do is merely to palliate unsatisfactory conditions where they exist; hence that the more private capital can be attracted to this enterprise the more surely will the play of competitive forces tend to a reasonable level of rents and to an adequate supply of houses of the kinds needed. They claim, however, that municipal competition has the effect of frightening private capital away and that if carried to an excess it is capable of accentuating the very evils which it desires to remove. Towns which adopt this attitude restrict their action to the encouragement of building societies and the provision of credit facilities. These societies are as a rule of the " public utility " type, and exist for a semi-philanthropic purpose. They consist of public-spirited citizens who bind themselves by the rules to receive no more than 4 per cent. interest on their money. Most of the capital with which they work is, however, obtained from the State Pension Boards, communal and provincial authorities, savings banks, and other public sources, at a low rate of interest. Where municipalities lease or sell land to the societies or otherwise assist them they usually impose conditions as to the size and character of the dwellings to be built and the purpose to which they shall be put, and guarantees are required to prevent their becoming objects of speculation; in some cases a right of purchase is reserved by the town in certain eventualities.

Leipzig is one of the towns which has on principle refrained from building houses, but which all the more readily assists co-operative building societies by the sale to them of land on easy terms. It was, indeed, one of the first towns to place leasehold land at the disposal of these societies. In 1901 it

[1] See Appendix V, "Agreement relating to Municipal House Building at Jena."

leased to a "public utility" society for 100 years 125,000 square metres of land, at 1·4d. per metre yearly, for the purpose of cheap dwellings for the working classes. At the same time it became surety for loans to the amount of £185,000 granted to the society on favourable terms by the Saxon Pension Board. The municipality has the right to exercise supervision over the buildings with a view to ensuring that they are maintained in a good condition. At the expiration of the lease the houses will become the property of the town without any payment. Since then the municipality has disposed of further areas of land on the same tenure, and it now lends money direct to building societies to the extent of 85 per cent. of the value of the buildings erected, redeemable in 50 years, charging interest at 4 per cent.

The municipality of Mannheim leases land on easy terms to co-operative and other societies for the erection of small and cheap dwellings. Interest is charged at the rate of 3½ per cent. of the leasehold value of the land, as fixed at three-fifths of its actual market value. If the houses so built are placed at the disposal of municipal officials, teachers, or workmen, a further 30 per cent. of the value is deducted in arriving at the leasehold value, and interest is charged at the rate not exceeding 4 per cent. The duration of the lease is 75 years. The contracts on which land is so leased impose on the building societies the following obligations :—

1. To submit plans to the town council before beginning the work of building and to carry out all amendments required.

2. To complete the work of building within a fixed time.

3. To make no structural alteration to dwellings without permission of the town council.

4. To keep all buildings, both above and underground, in a good state of repair during the term of the lease.

5. To take steps to prevent sub-letting and the keeping of lodgers, and the use of the dwellings in a manner injurious to the health and morality of the inhabitants.

6. To obtain the assent of the town council to all rents charged and to observe the rents so approved.

At the expiration of the lease the town may require the society to remove the buildings within six months at its own expense, or to transfer them to the town, free from all liabilities, in which case the town must pay to the society one-fifth of the value of the buildings, as determined by experts.

Similarly Frankfort-on-Main has sold to building societies land upon which some 1700 dwellings have been or will be built, and has advanced £200,000 towards the cost. A large part of the land has been reserved as recreation grounds and gardens. Among many other towns which sell or lease land and advance money to building societies on favourable terms are Cologne, Düsseldorf, Barmen, Strassburg, Essen, Dresden, Bremen, Aix-la-Chapelle, Magdeburg, Munich, Augsburg, and Nuremberg. The Munich Statistical Office recently published a list of 43 towns which had lent money to building societies to the aggregate amount of £1,085,000. The usual rates of interest varied from 3 to 4 per cent. In some of these towns the municipalities bear either the whole or a portion of the cost of street and sewerage works and of the laying of gas and water pipes in the case of houses built by " public utility " societies for the working classes, and in others the land and building taxes are reduced or remitted for a term of years. In Bavaria these societies have the benefit of a law which enables the State to exempt from the house tax for twelve years small dwellings built by co-operative enterprise. In some towns the funds of the municipal savings banks are largely used in financing " public utility " building societies, and here and there, as at Strassburg, the savings banks build at their own risk.[1]

The practice of municipalities guaranteeing loans made to building societies by the State Pension Boards is becoming increasingly common. In addition to the cases mentioned, Frankfort-on-Main has undertaken a guarantee of the kind to the extent of £306,000, Essen one of £200,000, several other towns one of £100,000 each, and in 1912 sixty-five towns

[1] This is quite independent of the loans on real estate in general advanced by the municipal savings banks, the sum of which in the case of 222 towns was in 1912 over £160,000,000.

had together become surety for loans to the amount of two and a quarter million pounds, advanced for the most part by the State Pension Boards. The towns of the Prussian province of Rhineland have been specially active in the matter, as in housing reform generally. Many towns also take shares in building societies, thus both helping to raise capital for building purposes and sharing the risk. Like the building societies, some of the municipalities themselves obtain money for building schemes from the Pension Boards, and in several States they are able to borrow from Government. Thus in Würtemberg the State lends money for house erection to communes to the full value of the buildings.

Altogether a work of the utmost value is done by the municipalities on these various lines. Some time ago the German Labour Department instituted inquiries as to the extent to which the towns promoted housing schemes or assisted in their promotion. It was found that of 106 towns questioned, 42 had provided municipal work-people with dwellings ; 25 of these towns were in Prussia, five in Baden, three each in Bavaria and Würtemberg, two each in Saxony and Hesse, and one each in Brunswick and Alsace-Lorraine. Fifteen towns had built dwellings for people of limited means in general, Freiburg having done most in this direction. Professor Albrecht, of Berlin, estimates that the building societies, generally with public assistance in some form, had up to 1912 erected houses to the aggregate value of ten million pounds, and that they are building at a rate of 4000 a year.

A recent inquiry into the action taken on the housing question by the municipal authorities in Prussia showed that of 122 towns with a population above 25,000, 38 had sold land at a cheap price (sometimes under cost) for the erection of small dwellings, 50 had established mortgage funds intended to encourage the same enterprise, 38 had taken shares in building societies, and 30 had reduced the taxation and other contributions (e.g., on account of street construction) due in respect of small houses.

So far as the quality of housing accommodation goes, it is probable that the indirect effect of the action of municipal authorities and building societies is greater than the direct. The influence of house-building on semi-philanthropic lines on rents in general may have been insignificant, but the influence upon the working classes, upon their standard of taste, and so upon the builders who supply the housing needs of these classes, has been great. Owing to the enterprise of public authorities and building societies, the working-man becomes used to a better type of dwelling; he learns to appreciate conveniences which he never enjoyed in the past—balconies, larders, bathrooms, and the like—and so private builders have to fall in with his requirements, and the general level of housing is gradually raised.

As an offshoot of the housing reform movement the garden-town idea has materialised in many parts of Germany, and in the neighbourhood of Berlin, Dresden, Nuremberg, Mannheim, Karlsruhe, Magdeburg, Strassburg, Königsberg, Posen, and Essen attractive rural colonies have sprung up, while several propagandist societies have been formed in furtherance of the movement. Some municipalities have offered the garden-town societies practical help. Mannheim and Strassburg have both given security for large mortgage loans obtained by such societies and have taken shares in the undertakings.

MUNICIPAL INSPECTION OF DWELLINGS.—There is no Imperial legislation on the subject of house inspection. The subject is regarded as an internal one which every State must settle for itself in accordance with its own traditions and circumstances. In most States the matter is not even regulated by general law but is left to local decision, with the result that the utmost diversity of practice may exist within the same State. As a rule, inspection is confined to dwellings containing not more than three rooms and to those in which lodgers are taken. The inspection of dwellings has been introduced on the largest scale in Bavaria, Würtemberg, and Hesse, in all of which States inspection is compulsory, and is carried out in conjunction with a central State inspectorate. Bavaria has specially distinguished itself in the matter. There inspection is exercised by the police authority, except where a town forms its own housing committee with special inspectors, as has been done at Munich, Augsburg, Nuremberg, and elsewhere. A Royal Decree of February 10, 1901, required the introduction of house inspection in all communes in the kingdom, with the object of " keeping a continuous and careful watch over the housing system, the improvement of housing conditions, especially as concerns people of limited means, and of adopting measures for the removal of evils." The Decree required the formation of Housing Committees in the larger towns, the members to be chosen by the local authorities (the medical profession being represented) for six years at a time. Where necessary, housing inspectors were to be appointed and special investigations to be made into housing conditions. The Decree also prescribed certain regulations on the subject of light and ventilation, heating and firing, the location and condition of rooms, and the keeping of lodgers, and provided for the issue of police regulations dealing with details. As a result of the Decree nearly all the communes with a population exceeding 10,000 appointed inspectors, and by 1906—when a Central State Housing Inspector was appointed—housing committees had been formed in over 900 communes. Housing censuses and systematic investigations had also been made in Munich, Nuremberg, Bamberg, Augsburg, and other towns.

On the whole the system of house inspection depended on honorary service, and remedial measures progressed slowly. In consequence of this the Government in 1907 required that trained inspectors should be appointed in all towns of 15,000 inhabitants, while in towns with a less population the appointment of such inspectors was to depend upon circumstances. The larger towns were also urged to create Municipal House Registries and to affiliate them to the existing Labour Registries, and this has been done at Munich, Nuremberg, and elsewhere. At present the Bavarian system of house inspection or " house care," as it is called, is a combination of official and voluntary service. The housing committees are, as a rule, composed of representatives of the house-owners and tenants (the statutory sickness funds and building societies being represented), members of the municipal authority, Poor Law officials, municipal doctors, and women chosen for their interest in social work. Stress is laid upon friendly advice rather than coercion; only when such advice fails of effect does the executive intervene with stronger measures.

In Baden house inspection is compulsory in the larger towns. Ministerial Orders of June 27, 1874, and November 10, 1896, empower the State District Councils (*Bezirksräte*), working hand in hand with the communes, to institute investigations into housing conditions where there is reason to believe that structural, sanitary, and moral abuses exist. These investigations are made by the local Boards of Health (*Gesundheitsräte*) or special *ad hoc* commissions. Systematic inspection of dwellings may also be introduced, this being exercised by the State District Board (*Bezirksamt*), which is the building authority in Baden. These administrative orders were strengthened by a law of September 1, 1907, requiring a system of house inspection to be introduced in all towns with over 10,000 inhabitants in conjunction with housing committees. For the purpose of such inspection Mannheim is divided into ten districts, to each of which an inspector (*Wohnungskontrolleur*) is attached. It is the duty of the inspectors to visit all houses in the town periodically and to report the defects noticed to the District Board, which promptly takes remedial measures.

In Würtemberg all dwelling-houses consisting of from one to four rooms must be inspected once every two years. Inspection is exercised by the local police authorities, but in Stuttgart it is carried on in conjunction with the municipal house registry. There the municipality first tried a system of honorary house-visitors, the town being divided into 210 districts (each containing a definite group of houses), to each of which was assigned a visitor whose duty it was to visit the dwellings and see that they were kept in sanitary condition and in a good state of repair. The plan did not succeed; the voluntary visitors did not in general take well to their duties, and house-owners were disposed to throw obstacles in their way whenever possible, in spite of their being armed with official entrance warrants; and in course of time most of them resigned office. As a consequence, the voluntary system was abandoned, and paid officers have since been introduced.

The principal towns of Hesse have inspection by trained officers, and the same system is adopted in Strassburg, Mülhausen, and Metz, in Alsace-Lorraine, and in the free cities of Hamburg, Bremen, and Lübeck. Hamburg has a very thorough system, in which room is found for much valuable voluntary service. The town is divided into " circles," and these again into " districts " ; for every " circle " there is a house-visitor (*Pfleger*) and for every " district " a chairman (*Vorsteher*). The chairmen and two senators form the " Authority for House Care," which has under it a staff of technical officers.

Most of the towns in Saxony with a population above 5000 have introduced house inspection on more or less systematic lines; Leipzig and Chemnitz have done so more thoroughly than the rest.

In Prussia housing legislation still hangs fire, though Bills have been brought forward by the Government for public discussion, and the question of house inspection is a matter for local by-laws.[1] Many of the large towns have introduced efficient systems of inspection, exercised by technical officials working hand in hand with honorary visitors or house curators. In several cases the entire work of " house care " is vested in Municipal Housing Boards, with which are affiliated House Registries. The majority of Prussian towns have still no system of house inspection, however, though the exceptions include important towns like Essen, Berlin, Düsseldorf, Cologne, Charlottenburg, Aix-la-Chapelle, Breslau, Cassel, and Elberfeld, where inspection is exercised by the municipal authority, and Barmen, Crefeld, Bonn, and other Rhenish towns, where the police authority acts. While in some towns inspection is exercised by special officers trained for the work and devoting all their time to it, in others there is a combination of paid and honorary service. The Essen system is regarded as one of the most efficient. It was introduced in 1899 as a branch of the town's social welfare work, and is directed by a Public Health Committee consisting of the

[1] At the time of printing this book (March, 1914) an important Housing Law is before the Prussian Diet, and its provisions, if enacted, will remove or abate existing defects in this and other directions.

chief mayor or an *adjoint*, the district medical officer, the poor relief doctors, and a number of citizens, working in conjunction with district committees.

One of the most recent systems of municipal house care is that which has just been established in Charlottenburg. Here all matters relating to housing are placed under the supervision of a Housing Board. This body is subject to a special Housing Deputation of the town council, consisting of 21 members, of whom five are members of the municipal executive, seven are members of the town council, and nine are co-opted citizens, election being for three years. Besides conducting a house registry this Deputation is responsible for the inspection of all dwellings consisting of not more than two habitable rooms and a kitchen, all dwellings in which lodgers are taken, and all dormitories for work-people and other employees who sleep in the houses of their employers. The house curators or visitors are paid officers. In order to facilitate the work of inspection and house registration, house-owners are required to notify to the police all dwellings vacant or let, and the police inform the municipal house registry. It is the intention of the Housing Deputation to collect periodical housing statistics and to endeavour to regulate the supply of houses in the town. For the purpose of inspection, the town is divided into fourteen districts, and each district is supervised by a small housing committee, the members of which include a doctor and a woman. The practical work of inspection is done by house curators whose duty it is to co-operate with house-owners and tenants in the removal of unhealthy conditions where they are found to exist.

Where house inspection is seriously carried out special attention is given to lodging-houses and the lodger system generally. The lodging-house system is regulated by State law in Bavaria, Würtemberg, Baden, and other States, while in Prussia, in the absence of a general law, uniform regulations on the subject are issued for large administrative areas. Mannheim has distinguished itself by the thoroughness with which it has for many years endeavoured by administrative measures to minimise the evils incidental to the practice, common amongst working-class households in German industrial towns, of letting to lodgers rooms which should be occupied by the younger members of the family.

The introduction of house inspection has inevitably raised the old controversy on the subject of municipal and police functions. Where towns were willing to take upon themselves this responsibility they naturally wished to exercise real and not merely illusory powers, and hence some of them endeavoured to induce the police authority to stand aside and abdicate its rights in the matter. The municipality of Berlin, for example, before it settled the details of its new system of house inspection petitioned the Government to transfer to it the powers in regard to housing matters hitherto exercised by the State police authority. There as elsewhere the Government politely but firmly refused, on the plea that the control of dwellings could not be separated from that of building operations, public health, and public morals, all matters regulated by the police. All the Government would do was to promise to confer upon the housing officials who might be appointed by the municipality powers of entry similar to those exercised by the police, and with this crumb of concession the administration of the first city in the Empire had to be satisfied. The consequence of the reservation to the police of all their old rights is that the municipal housing departments and their inspectors have no compulsory powers. Their work is in the nature of social welfare work; for while they can visit, inspect, and advise, they cannot coerce, punish, or even threaten offenders.

While experience is being gained on many different lines of experiment, it seems to be agreed that the best system of housing control is that which combines trained officers with a sufficient body of honorary visitors and advisers. Thus, when Berlin in 1913 set up its new Housing Board it was formed of 20 salaried officials and 740 honorary members, these being divided amongst 118 district committees, each with from four to twelve members, according to the social character of the district. The police system of inspection has been found to be too uniform and rigid to produce the best results. What is needed is the neighbourly advice of sympathetic visitors imbued with the social spirit, and this is best secured when the services of civilians are employed. Many towns have been sufficiently enlightened to recognise the importance of women's work in this branch of municipal government. Women inspectors and officials have been appointed in a few towns, and the housing committees now almost invariably contain a fair proportion of women.

MUNICIPAL HOUSE REGISTRIES.—The Municipal House Registry is a development of the new system of house inspection. These institutions are now found in at least forty towns, mostly in West and South Germany. They are intended to register offers and wants of dwellings of two and three rooms. The registry places before house-seekers plans and other details relating to dwellings likely to interest them, thus saving them much useless wandering and loss of time. In Munich, Stuttgart, Nuremberg, Charlottenburg, and some other towns the owners of these small dwellings are required to report them when empty to the public registry. As a rule no charge is made for registering or letting working-class dwellings, but a small fee (2d. or 3d.) is usually charged for middle-class houses and applicants. The experience of these registries is said to have been very favourable on the whole, for once established they soon prove a great boon to the small householders. One of the largest is that of Stuttgart, which receives in the course of a year as many as 10,000 offers of and applications for dwellings, while the Cologne and Essen registries deal with between 4000 and 6000. In general, from 40 to 60 per cent. of the house-seekers' wants can be met, though the proportion is higher where the supply of dwellings is very limited.

In relation to this question of housing reform the German confidence in the value of statistics has received practical illustration, for, recognising that the first condition of useful action is a knowledge of the facts, many towns publish continuous returns of the number of unoccupied dwellings, and these present a fairly faithful picture of the movement of the house market. It is assumed that a normal relationship between supply and demand exists when there is a surplus of 3 per cent. Some of the larger towns go further and make periodical enumerations of all the houses within their areas, with returns of their accommodation, rent, etc. The Cologne Statistical Office also publishes annual returns from all the larger towns of Germany, showing the extent of their building activity during the year.

BUILDING REGULATIONS.—While the town plan lays down the general lines which the development of a town must follow, including the street and building alignments, the building regulations prescribe the general structural conditions, such as the proportions of a building site to be built on and left free respectively, the height of buildings, of stories, and of rooms, the size or air space of rooms, the lighting and ventilation arrangements, building material, etc. The regulations may also stipulate where the " open " and the " closed " system of building may be adopted; the " open " system being building in small blocks with intervening spaces; and the " closed " the unbroken or terrace form of building.

In Baden, Würtemberg, Brunswick, Hesse, Anhalt, and other States general codes of building regulations have been introduced for the whole State, these being adopted by the local authorities with such modifications as circumstances require, subject to the sanction of the competent State supervisory authority. In Prussia such general regulations do not as yet exist; uniform regulations have been issued for several Government Districts in the Rhineland and other provinces; but for the rest each commune has its own regulations, framed, as a rule, by the local building police authority with the acquiescence of the Government. Most of the recent building regulations prescribe differential conditions for the inner and outer districts of a communal area respectively; in the former less latitude is allowed to the builder in such matters as the style of building, height, number of stories, and proportion of plot to be left free. Not infrequently the regulations are relaxed in the case of small dwellings intended for persons of limited means, with a view to reducing the costs of construction.

Where uniform rules are not laid down by law, there is considerable diversity in the building regulations of different States, and even of different towns within the same State, and only the general principles can be indicated here. A common rule as to the height of buildings is that this may not exceed the width of the adjacent street, including the side walks and the gardens, but everything depends upon whether the building is in an inner or an outer district of the town. In some towns a separate maximum is specified for back buildings, the measurements being here either definitely specified or proportionate to the size of the courtyard. Most building regulations prescribe the maximum portion of the building plot which may be built upon, or conversely how large a proportion must remain free ; the area that may not be built upon varies as a rule from 20 or 25 per cent. in the inner districts of a town, but it may be 50 or 60 per cent. in outer districts. The maximum number of stories permissible depends on circumstances, and the requirements as to the size of dwellings also differ greatly. The Bavarian regulations state that a dwelling must, as a rule, contain at least one heatable room, one bedroom, and a kitchen, with storeroom ; while in Saxon towns a dwelling must contain at least one heatable room and one bedroom, with a kitchen if possible. Most regulations also contain provisions as to the minimum cubic contents of rooms intended for habitation, their height, the size of windows, etc.

It will be understood that the provisions of the modern codes of regulations are, as a rule, enforced only in relation to new buildings, and that much of the existing house property in old towns falls far short of the official requirements. In these towns earnest efforts are being made to level housing conditions all round to a tolerable hygienic standard, but except within very narrow limits the task is often a hopeless one. In such cases the only comfort of housing reformers lies in the fact that in the populous towns there is a steady movement of population from the centre to the circumference and the suburbs. There is also some ground for the hope that in course of time the old and insanitary areas often found in the inner " city " districts will be abandoned as residential quarters and will be used or reconstructed for business purposes.

CHAPTER VIII

PUBLIC HEALTH

Public health authorities—The public hospital system—Inspection of foods and drinks—Sewerage, drainage, and scavenging—Public swimming baths—Parks, gardens, and recreation and sports grounds—Municipal cemeteries and crematoria.

A PAST high death-rate is one evidence amongst others that German local authorities in general have not until quite recent times devoted as much care and expenditure to the sanitary as to some other branches of administration. Great progress has been made during the last twenty years, however, and simultaneously the mortality rate has fallen as a consequence. For forty years prior to 1891 the general rate of mortality (including the stillborn), averaged over periods of ten years, had ranged from 26·5 to 28·8 per 1000 of the population; the rates for the two succeeding decennial periods were 23·5 and 19·7 per 1000, and from 1905 to 1910 the rate steadily fell from 20·8 to 17·1. On the whole the decrease has been greater in the urban than the rural districts, and many of the larger towns in particular have a far more creditable record than small places, where natural conditions might seem to be more favourable to health. Nowadays the German municipalities regard their public health work as amongst the most remunerative as well as most urgent of their many activities, and shrink from no expenditure that can be usefully incurred on its behalf. As an example, the costs to Charlottenburg of public health administration in all its branches, including the expenditure on hospitals, baths, dispensaries for infants and consumptives, school hygiene, the care of consumptives, disinfection, scavenging and drainage, increased from 4s. 2d. a head of the population in 1900 to 8s. 8d. in 1910.

PUBLIC HEALTH AUTHORITIES.—To some extent past indifference to sanitation may be attributable to the absence of that constant pressure from a central authority, responsible for the general oversight of public health, which has done so much to stimulate English local authorities, and to give to this country its relatively high standard of sanitary administration. The Imperial authorities which have to do with public health are the Imperial Board of Health and the Imperial Council of Health. The Imperial Board of Health was formed in 1876 to assist the Imperial Ministry of the Interior (or Home Office) in dealing with questions bearing upon public health and sanitation generally. It is essentially a research and advisory department upon a national scale, and its four sections deal with such important matters as water supply, sewerage, disinfection, and the disposal of trade effluents. The Council of Health, with nine committees for different branches of work, is affiliated to it. The Imperial Board of Health advises local authorities upon questions of sanitation, and the valuable results of its own constant investigations are placed at the disposal of these authorities in the form of reports and statistics. But neither the Imperial Board of Health nor the subordinate Council of Health possesses compulsory powers of any kind.

In the States public health questions come under either the Ministry of the Interior (or Home Office) or a department of the Ministry for " Ecclesiastical, Educational, and Medicinal Affairs " (commonly known as the *Kultusministerium*). The medicinal department of the Prussian Home Office organises all measures for the combating of infectious and certain other diseases as well as for the care of cripples ; it examines local schemes of water supply and sewerage, and generally advises local authorities upon matters affecting public health and sanitation. Though its functions are not so far-going as those of the British Local Government Boards, they are by no means of a negative character. In addition, a Royal Institution for the examination and testing of water supplies and sewerage has existed in Prussia since 1901. It investigates questions relating to water supply, the disposal of sewerage, and the purification and utilisation of trade effluents, and has an experimental station in connection with the Charlottenburg irrigation works.

The municipalities would probably have done more for public sanitation in the past, and have done it sooner, had the sole responsibility for sanitary administration rested with them instead of being to a large extent entrusted to the police authority and only exercised by the local authorities indirectly in virtue of the fact that the mayor of a commune is usually invested with police functions in the name of the Crown.

In all the larger States the municipal authorities are required to form committees for the purpose of co-operating in the administration of the public health laws. In Prussia (under a law of September 16, 1899), standing health committees must be appointed in all communes with more than 5000 inhabitants, while for smaller communes they are optional. Such a committee must be constituted in accordance with the provisions of the Municipal Ordinances relating to all such devolution of the duties of town councils; the number of members is determined by the council, but where possible a medical practitioner and a building expert must be on the committee. Sometimes one or more of the Poor Law doctors are also appointed. District sub-committees may be formed in the larger towns. In every case the term of office is fixed by the town council, but the minimum is six years. Membership of such a committee is honorary and may not be declined except for the reasons which exempt from honorary service in general.

It is the duty of these health committees to acquaint themselves, by inquiry and inspection, with the sanitary conditions of their districts, to support all sanitary measures taken by the police authority, acting in accord with the " circle " medical officer, to give opinions on questions relating to the public health which may be addressed to them by the municipal and police authorities, to instruct the public upon such questions, to investigate evils which may have a tendency to lead to the outbreak and spread of disease, and to initiate proposals for the removal of insanitary conditions generally, for the improvement of existing arrangements, and for the introduction of timely innovations. The questions to which the attention of the committees is particularly directed by the law include the condition of dwelling-houses and habitations in general, the cleanliness of the streets, public places, etc., water supply in all its branches, the pollution of water courses, trade in food-stuffs, public abattoirs, the relation of industrial undertakings to the public health, the condition of schools, the condition of the poor and sick and of institutions for their care, first-aid arrangements, bathing and swimming establishments, cemeteries, and mortuaries.

Committees are expected to meet at least once in three months and to make visits of inspection at least once a year, and at other times when necessity arises, as on the occasion of floods, epidemics, etc. The "circle" medical officer has a right to attend and vote at all meetings of a committee, and he may require it to be convened at any time; while a local committee is expected to meet that official at his request when he makes his periodical visits of inspection.

Municipal medical officers are appointed, corresponding closely in status and duties to the same officials in this country. Some towns give to their principal medical officer a higher, some a lower rank, in so far as he is either given a place in the executive (as a "magistrate" or alderman), or is simply made the head of a department dependent upon that body. Berlin and Charlottenburg have lately created "medicinal councillors," with seats in the executive, who are responsible for all public health and sanitary matters falling within the province of the local governments.

In Baden similar local health committees (called councils) have to be appointed, and are composed of the chief mayor of the town (as chairman), an officer of the District Board (*Bezirksamt*), a State authority responsible for the execution of the sanitary laws, two district medical officers, the Poor Law doctors, the district veterinary surgeon (a State official), members of the municipal executive, town councillors, a chemist, and the principal surgeon of the general town hospital. This council meets at irregular intervals, but the principal part of its work is done by committees. The divergence of the German from the English system of public health administration may be illustrated by the wide extent of police functions in this domain exercised in Baden. There, the District Board, as the police authority, administers the State laws and local by-laws and regulations relating to the sale of milk, the inspection and sale of meat, the trade in poisons, the manufacture of mineral waters, the use of beer stills, the sale of bottled beer, and the businesses of barbers and hairdressers, masseurs, knackers, quack doctors and uncertificated dentists. Quack doctors are required to be registered, to notify every change of address, and to inform the police of every case of death by violence, serious physical injury, poisoning, crime and offence against human life that comes within their knowledge while following their barely tolerated vocation.

THE PUBLIC HOSPITAL SYSTEM.—Highly developed though the German system of public hospitals is, the provision of these institutions, other than for infectious disease, is voluntary on the part of the local authorities, at least to the extent that they are not expressly required by statute to build them. An indirect form of compulsion may be said to exist, however, owing to the obligation of the communes to care for the poor in sickness. Thus in Prussia this liability arises in virtue of section 1 of the law in execution of the Imperial Settlement Law, viz.: "Every necessitous German shall receive at the cost of the poor relief union liable for his maintenance shelter, indispensable subsistence, *the necessary care in sickness*, and in the event of death seemly burial." Until two or three decades ago, indeed, the public hospitals were almost exclusively used for the sick poor, and it was only after the social insurance laws were passed and the need arose for a sufficiency of institutions affording to the working classes all the advantages of modern medicine and surgery that any great extension of the hospitals took place.

Here, however, as in so many other directions, where the interests of the less favoured sections of the population are concerned, the towns have ignored the letter of the statute and have considered only the welfare of the communities for whose good government they are responsible, and to-day treatment which was formerly the luxury of the rich is regarded as the necessity of the poor. The total number of public hospitals in Germany in 1885, shortly after the sickness insurance legislation came into force, was 1706, and the number of beds provided was 75,000. In 1907 the number of such hospitals had increased to 2222, and the number of beds to 138,000. There was an increase of 30 per cent. in the number of hospitals and of 83 per cent. in the number of beds, comparing with an increase of 42 per cent. in population. The ratio of beds to population increased from one to every 616 inhabitants in 1885 to one to 450 in 1907. These figures relate to public hospitals only. There had been a still greater relative increase in the number and accommodation of the private hospitals. These private hospitals, like private homes and asylums, can only be established under concession from the higher administrative authority, and in certain circumstances the local authority and the local police must be heard before such a concession is granted. In Prussia hospitals of all kinds are subject to State supervision. In 1911 over three million pounds was paid for the treatment of insured persons in hospitals under the Sickness Insurance Laws, and by far the greater part of this sum went to the institutions under communal or other public management. As a rule the maintenance fees charged to insurance societies are under cost: the usual rates vary from 2s. to 3s. 6d. a day. The Government, however, fixes rates uniform for the whole country for patients who are maintained in hospitals at the expense of Poor Law authorities, with a view to preventing unfair charges.

The cost of " a large municipal hospital meeting only the moderate hygienic and scientific requirements " is estimated by German authorities at from £350 to £500 per bed, but while a few modern hospitals of the kind have cost more—e.g. the Virchow hospital in Berlin, £625; and the latest Munich hospital, £535—probably most of the existing institutions have been erected and equipped at much less expense.[1] There would appear to be a strong disposition to give the doctors too free a hand, with the result that expenditure often goes far beyond actual needs. In 1913 the Prussian Minister

[1] Dr. F. Schrakamp in " Die deutsche Stadt und ihre Verwaltung," Vol. I, p. 132.

of the Interior issued a rescript to the Chief Presidents and District Presidents, calling attention to the growing tendency of local authorities to incur excessive expenditure upon the unnecessary embellishment of hospitals, and urging them to use all their influence in the direction of greater economy. It was stated in this document that an expenditure of from £150 to £200 a bed should suffice to build and equip hospitals meeting all the requirements of modern science. Such, however, is not the opinion of the larger municipalities.

The larger institutions are worked by permanent staffs, but in the smaller towns part-time surgeons and doctors are usually appointed, and as a rule patients may be attended only by the staff doctors.

Many of the larger towns have supplemented their general hospitals with institutions for the treatment of special diseases, children's hospitals, sanatoria, infant dispensaries, convalescent homes, forest resorts, etc. Thus Weissensee, a working-class suburb of Berlin, beginning with an infants' dispensary, has just built a special hospital for infants containing 40 beds, at a cost of about £20,000, including model stalls for cattle. Staffs of outside nurses usually support the work of the dispensaries for infants and consumptives, and of the school doctors, or the local authorities subsidise district nursing associations which undertake this duty on their behalf. A remarkable awakening of interest in the condition and welfare of crippled children has occurred of late, and in many towns hospitals and homes for their treatment and education have been provided by the municipal authorities or by these in conjunction with private philanthropy.

An admirable movement has of late been introduced in some towns by philanthropic societies with municipal encouragement in the form of what is known as "hospital care" work. It is the object of these societies to look after the dependants of patients while in hospital, to prevent that too common tragedy of sickness amongst the poor, the break up of homes, and to help the patients on discharge to get back either to their old or to new employment. For efforts of the kind there is always need in large towns, and the movement has called forth much generous enthusiasm.

Mention must also be made of the " Samaritan," first-aid, and rescue work carried on or subsidised by the local authorities. Berlin grants £3750 a year, Leipzig £1300 and Frankfort-on-Main £750 to agencies engaged in work of this kind. There are rescue depots in more than 130 of the larger towns, and in nearly 100 cases medical aid is provided on the spot.

The provision of communal hospitals for the isolation and treatment of infectious diseases of certain kinds is compulsory under the Imperial Law of June 30, 1900, and in Prussia under a supplementary law of August 28, 1905. Here the supervisory authority is empowered to require local authorities to take the necessary steps. As a rule provision is made in connection with the general hospitals, but in order to meet the contingency of an epidemic the large towns usually have in reserve suitable buildings which can quickly be adapted to the purpose of isolation hospitals, and also sites upon which emergency hospitals can be at once erected.

The Imperial Law of June 30, 1900, makes notification compulsory and empowers the sanitary authority to require disinfection in the case of certain infectious diseases, viz., leprosy, Asiatic cholera, spotted fever, yellow fever, oriental bubonic plague, smallpox, and anthrax, but the number of notifiable diseases is increased in many States by statutes and by-laws. The Prussian law of August 28, 1905, promulgated in execution of the Imperial Law, empowers the sanitary authority to require notification in cases of illness or death from diphtheria, puerperal fever, relapsing fever, dysentery, typhus, scarlet fever, hydrophobia, cerebro-spinal meningitis, trichinosis, trachoma, glanders, and in the case of deaths from tuberculosis of the lungs or throat. The administrative regulations of September 15, 1906, issued under this law provide that " measures " in this sense shall include rooms for the observation and isolation of persons infected or suspected of infection, disinfecting apparatus, appliances for the conveyance of sick and dead persons, mortuaries, and burial places.

All the larger towns have efficient disinfecting arrangements, but the extent to which the disinfection of dwellings after the occurrence of disease is compulsory varies greatly in different towns. Of 86 towns upon whose practice in the matter the "Statistical Yearbook of German Towns" reports in 1913, the disinfection of dwellings is compulsory in the case of diphtheria in 72 towns, in the case of cerebro-spinal meningitis in 57, in the case of puerperal fever in 54, in the case of trachoma in 49, in the case of tuberculosis of the lungs or throat in 68, in the case of relapsing fever in 58, in the case of diarrhœa in 68, in the case of scarlet fever in 71, in the case of typhus in 78, and in the case of dysentery in 64. In a majority of towns disinfection is carried out by police officials. In some towns disinfection is free for all households, but in most places a charge is made, this being reduced or remitted in the case of small dwellings or households with small incomes, the limit varying from £45 to £150.

There is great diversity of practice in various States in the degree to which notification and disinfection are enforced in case of tuberculosis. In Prussia compulsion applies in the case of deaths from pulmonary tuberculosis, but not in cases of infected persons who remove from one dwelling to another. Hence some local authorities offer to disinfect free of cost in the latter event. Compulsory notification goes farthest in Baden, Saxony, and Bavaria, and a few of the smaller States. In Baden not only have all deaths from tuberculosis to be reported to the sanitary (police) authority, but doctors in attendance upon advanced cases of pulmonary tuberculosis are obliged to notify them in the event of a change of dwelling or of risk to neighbours; and cases occurring in the schools have likewise to be notified. House disinfection is carried out by the urban sanitary officials, but the cost may be claimed from the persons concerned. In dangerous cases, without change of residence, it is the duty of the authority to adopt preventive measures, even to the extent of requiring the removal of the patients to a hospital.

INSPECTION OF FOODS AND DRINKS.—The inspection of foods and drinks is the duty of the sanitary police, but the local authorities co-operate in various ways. There is a tendency to make this inspection increasingly stringent. Animals slaughtered for food are inspected at the abattoir and all imported meat is also inspected there unless it has already been passed by official veterinaries. A specially thorough system of food inspection is enforced at Munich. There, inspection is exercised by four different bodies of officials. All food which enters the municipal markets is examined by market inspectors; all milk brought into the town and the milk trade in general are inspected by six special officials and tested at times by two chemists under the supervision of veterinary surgeons; there are 21 district inspectors, with assistants in addition, for the inspection of food stuffs in general in all parts of the town; and all meat coming from outside the town is examined at the railway stations by veterinary surgeons.

Great care is taken to secure not only the purity but a high quality of milk, and in Würtemberg the Government has recently placed a special responsibility upon the communes of origin. Believing that much milk is adulterated before it reaches the towns, the Government has introduced a regulation requiring the police to take and analyse periodically samples of milk in all rural communes which send away more than ten gallons daily, and the communes concerned are charged with the cost.

A number of the larger towns have analytical laboratories for the examination of foods offered for sale, with a view to the detection of adulteration and of injurious constituents, while in some towns the services of State or university laboratories are available for this purpose. Berlin has a municipal laboratory intended to serve both for the analysis of foods and of materials used for industrial purposes, and for chemical and bacteriological investigations generally. The public disinfection service is also under it, and it helps in the training of nurses and assistants for the hospitals of the town.

SEWERAGE, DRAINAGE, AND SCAVENGING.—In referring to this branch of the province of municipal activity all technical questions must necessarily be passed over. As in other countries, the usual methods of treating sewage are either land filtration on the extensive or farm system, or artificial filtration on the open and septic tank systems. The difficulty of obtaining the necessary land and the heavy cost incurred are often insuperable obstacles in the way of the adoption of the former and " natural " method of irrigation. The largest irrigation farms are those of Berlin, 44,000 acres in area ; Königsberg, 5720 acres ; Breslau, 4350 acres ; Magdeburg, 2800 acres ; Neukölln, 2650 acres ; and Dortmund, 2500 acres. In many ways Berlin's sewerage system, planned by the late Rudolf Virchow, and begun in 1873, is regarded as a model of its kind. Nearly one-half of the total area of the sewage farms is used for irrigation purposes, and about 400,000 cubic yards of sewage, drawn from the city and a number of adjacent towns and rural communes, are treated daily. Of the rest of the area, 11,660 acres consist of corn land, meadow land, garden land for small holders and labourers, dykes, water, railways, and roads, and there are 8750 acres of forest. Some of the farms produce fruit and vegetables for the Berlin market. The Farm Administration provides dwellings for married men and a large lodging-house for unmarried labourers who are unable to find accommodation in the nearer villages.

The influence of an efficient system of sewerage is shown in the case of Berlin by a marked decrease of typhoid fever. In 1870 no fewer than 15,000 properties in the city—then only about one-third as large as now—were without connection with the sewerage system, and the rate of mortality from typhoid was 7·7 per 10,000 of the population ; in 1885 only 4500 properties were still unconnected and the deaths from typhoid numbered 1·6 per 10,000 ; and in 1900, when the sewerage system was in full operation, the typhoid rate had fallen to one in 25,000, and it is now one in 30,000.

In most States the communes are empowered by law to levy contributions on account of sewerage works upon the adjacent owners of the streets drained. The usual rule is to charge the costs of construction proportionately to the length of frontage, and to levy an annual due for permission to connect with and use the main sewers. This sewerage due is based either upon the length of frontage, the number of connections with the sewer, the rental value of the property served (a common method of assessment in Prussian towns), the amount of the land and building taxes payable in respect of the property, or the quantity of water carried. The owner is liable for the due and pays it in the first instance, though he may try to transfer it wholly or partially to the tenants in the rent. In Berlin the sewerage due is 2 per cent. of the rental value of the property connected, but here the large size of the blocks must be remembered. In small towns the charge, when similarly assessed, is usually less. Frankfort-on-Main is one of the few large towns in which the sewerage due falls on the occupiers. Dwellings the rents of which do not exceed £15 per annum are exempted, but those rented at from £15 1s. to £20 pay ½ per cent. of the rental value, and from £20 1s. upwards the charge is 1 per cent.

The cost of street scavenging is also as a rule charged to the property owners and only in exceptional cases is it made a common charge. The methods of charging are either according to the length of the frontage of a property or the superficial area of street before it, a distinction being sometimes made between sites which are built upon and those which are free. Scavenging is now almost invariably done by the local authority or by contractors on its account.

The removal of house refuse is done variously by the local authority or by contractors, but in either case the property owners are usually responsible for the cost in the first instance. In some towns, e.g., Berlin, Dresden, and Leipzig, the owners make their own arrangements. In some towns the necessary vessels are provided by the local authority, and for every vessel removed an empty disinfected vessel is left. The charge levied on the owners may be either a percentage of the building tax, a percentage of the rental value of the entire house or building, or it may be proportionate to the number of rooms, the number of stories, or the number of families. In some towns no charge is made in respect of small dwellings. The disposal of house refuse has been greatly simplified by the various devices adopted for turning the refuse into value and by the use of destructors, which were first introduced from England. The municipality of Charlottenburg has a contract with a company which undertakes, in return for a payment of 1s. 9½d. per head of the population, to collect all house refuse in its own vessels on the " three-part system." For each house or block three vessels are provided, one for ashes and sweepings, one for food refuse, and one for paper, rags, broken pots, and similar rubbish. The ashes and clean refuse are sent away by rail and used for filling up marshy land, the food refuse is converted by patent process into dry feeding stuffs for horses, cattle, and sheep, and the clear refuse is sorted and turned as far as possible into money. The municipality recoups itself by charging house-owners a fee based on the rental value of their properties. The fee is fixed every year and is now about 1 per cent. In more than a hundred towns the street and house refuse is utilised, after treatment, for the generation of power.

PUBLIC SWIMMING BATHS.—Few if any towns of consequence are without public baths, and in most large towns the principal baths belong to the local authorities. Many German towns are encouraged to enterprise of this kind by the nearness of running water, and the towns on rivers like the Rhine and Elbe and their tributaries use this advantage to the utmost. In 1910 there were 335 separate bathing establishments in public hands in 51 towns with a population exceeding 50,000, while the number of establishments owned by companies and private individuals was still larger. Nearly all these towns owned swimming baths in number from one to six. Further, 72 of the 85 towns whose public bathing facilities are reported on by the " Statistical Yearbook of German Towns " for 1913 are shown as having equipped nearly 500 school buildings with baths. Many of the municipal baths have been planned and equipped with apparent disregard of expense, and of their kind are probably without rivals in any other country. One of the largest and most sumptuous of these establishments was a gift to Munich, though it is under municipal management. It contains swimming basins for men and women measuring 450 and 225 square yards respectively, a Turkish bath, and a number of tub and shower baths. Over 600,000 persons use the various baths in a year, and though the charges made are very moderate, 1½d. and 3d. for the working classes, the institution pays its way. Munich has also four open air river baths, and baths at 30 of the elementary schools. Mannheim has just built a swimming bath at a cost of £91,000, towards which the town contributed £60,000, while the balance was a benefaction; it contains covered basins for both sexes, a series of special baths (steam, electricity, wave, etc.), and a wash-house. The municipal authorities take care to preserve the utmost cleanliness. Not only are all the appointments kept in perfect order and the water frequently renewed, but the rule of requiring bathers to cleanse themselves with soap and water before entering the bath is rigidly enforced.

Many towns have gone beyond the standpoint of cleanliness in the provision of public baths, and have introduced medical baths of various kinds for the special benefit of insured persons. Open air, light, and air baths on a large scale have been instituted for public use by the municipalities of Düsseldorf, Metz, and a dozen smaller towns. Almost invariably the public baths are carried on at a considerable money loss to the town, but this consideration does not count with authorities bent on promoting the public health by the adoption of every measure approved by science.

PARKS, GARDENS, AND RECREATION AND SPORTS GROUNDS.—One of the incidental results of the social welfare work done by the German towns is the increasing importance attached to parks and recreation grounds. The large towns in particular nowadays spend lavishly in the provision of ample facilities for outdoor recreation. Berlin, Düsseldorf, Cologne, Aix-la-Chapelle, Munich, and Dresden are particularly well provided for in this respect. In some towns the rule is observed of setting aside a fixed proportion—say 5 per cent.—of the area of all new districts incorporated as park and recreation ground. In spite of their strongly developed industries many of the populous towns of Westphalia and the Rhineland have within their administrative areas a large reserve of green open spaces—for example, Duisburg 12·4 per cent. of the total area, Barmen 12·5 per cent., and Mülheim 37·2 per cent. Barmen has 20 square yards of green surface to every inhabitant, Düsseldorf 24, Duisburg 22, and Mülheim 268, land in private and State ownership being included.

In recent years many towns have acquired adjacent forests and woodland and converted them into natural parks. This has been done already by Aix-la-Chapelle, Düsseldorf, Mannheim, and other towns. The municipal authorities of Dresden are considering the possibility of forming a girdle of woodland around the town, and the Traffic and Town Planning Board for Greater Berlin contemplates a still more ambitious project on the same lines, involving the purchase from the State of some 25,000 acres of forest at a cost of several million pounds.

While in the extent of their public parks, gardens, and recreation grounds the large German towns are on the whole still behind the same towns in Great Britain, they have a far greater extent of forest and woodland. A comparison based on returns received from seven German towns with a population varying from 155,300 to 431,900 (in the aggregate 1,981,500) and nine towns in Great Britain with a population from 165,300 to 1,015,200 (in the aggregate 4,026,300) shows that the former owned in 1912 parks, gardens, and recreation grounds in the ratio of one acre per 1000 inhabitants, and forest and woodland in the ratio of 8·5 acres per 1000 inhabitants, while the corresponding figures for the towns in this country were 1·8 acre and 0·2 acre per 1000 inhabitants. Gathering ground for purposes of water supply was not included.

It is said that the first thing done by a German visitor on arrival in London is to go to Hyde Park in order to walk on grass. Most of the German parks are of the decorative order—made to be seen but not handled too closely—and do not offer the facilities for free movement which the town dweller so sorely needs. Of late, however, more attention has been given to the provision of parks of a truly recreative character—people's parks in the widest sense, offering to adults and children equally unrestricted opportunities for healthy exercise and sport—walking, games, swimming and bathing, gymnastics, etc., and where, above all, everybody may everywhere walk on the grass at will. The Treptow Park in Berlin is a park of this kind, and Hamburg, Düsseldorf, Cologne, and Lübeck are only a few of many other towns which have departed from the conventional idea of the park as a sort of barred-and-bolted museum in green.

At many of the modern recreation and sports fields there is provision for most of the games followed in their season by English youth of both sexes, including cricket and tennis in summer and football and hockey in winter.

Above all, German town children are again being taught to play. Hitherto, owing to the exigent claims of school on the one hand, and the paucity of playgrounds on the other, the little folk who inhabit the barrack houses of the large towns, where even the dismal courtyards are forbidden to the noise of children at play, have been strangers to many of the pleasures of open-air life, and for them childhood has been robbed of much of its natural and rightful gaiety. Happily this wrong to childhood is being rapidly repaired. Berlin devotes 310 acres to playgrounds for children, 70 acres being grass, 25 acres gravelled ground, and 130 acres open spaces and squares reserved for this purpose. A recent enumeration showed that Breslau had 84 public playgrounds for children, Cologne 54, Hamburg 46, Erfurt 39, Mayence 43, Posen 42, Munich 34, Essen 30, Chemnitz 37, and Dresden 36, and that nearly all towns with 50,000 inhabitants had a larger or smaller number. At Frankfort-on-Main the experiment has recently been introduced of grouping four schools—elementary schools for boys and girls, a higher grade school, and a Kindergarten—round a large open grass playground which serves for all the children.

The children's playgrounds usually take the form of portions of parks set aside for them, special recreation grounds or spaces, and the ordinary courts attached to schools; but in addition some of the larger towns have playgrounds in the open country, which are, as a rule, resorted to during the holidays. The holiday games movement is a boon of untold value to the children of the working class in the large towns. The school authorities of Berlin, in conjunction with philanthropic associations, provide over twenty playing-grounds to which the children are taken daily during the holidays. Some of these playing-grounds are situated outside the city boundaries and in woodland. The day is passed in games out of doors, or, in the event of bad weather, in large tents; and necessary meals are supplied at a nominal charge. From 1000 to 2500 children can be received at once at each of these resorts. Over a quarter of a million children used these rural playgrounds during the summer holidays of 1913, and 40 per cent. of those who travelled thither by rail were given free tickets, the cost of which and of meals was defrayed by the city (to the extent of £3000) and the societies which co-operate in organising juvenile games. Children who because of age or other reasons cannot be sent so far away from home are received at play-centres in the city.

A noteworthy variant upon the holiday playgrounds are the holiday walks which have been introduced by the school authorities in some towns in conjunction with the labour organisations. At Wiesbaden the parents are expected to pay 6d. a week per scholar towards the cost of fares and food; the town makes a grant of £500 a year, and the remaining funds are supplied by private individuals.

A work of equal importance, if more restricted in character, is done by the Country Holiday Associations (*Vereine für Ferienkolonien*), which, assisted liberally by the local authorities, have for many years taken the children of poor parents for a stay varying from four to six weeks to health and rural resorts during the summer months. The municipality of Ludwigshafen has bought a small forest estate, where in a suitable building the children of the poorer classes are lodged in turn for several weeks during the summer months. The "holiday colony" movement, as it is called, has succeeded so well that in some towns the same boon has been extended to children of middle-class families, from whom as a rule so much is expected by the local authorities, and for whom so little is done.

MUNICIPAL CEMETERIES AND CREMATORIA.—The provision of cemeteries becomes a communal duty only where existing churchyards are inadequate to the needs or prejudicial to the health of the community. In Prussia the obligation to provide burial-places rests in general with the parish churches. A special liability is sometimes thrown on the commune, however, owing to the illiberality of the ecclesiastical authorities. As a rule, the old town graveyards belong to the parish churches, and are administered by them. When a man withdraws from the State church, however, he forfeits his right to be interred in the graveyard serving his parish, and for such outsiders the local authorities are required to make provision. Nevertheless, in Berlin the old parish churches, on the ground of ancient custom, claim burial fees in respect of persons buried elsewhere than in the official graveyards of their parishes, and the claim appears to have a legal justification. Some of the modern cemeteries have been laid out as parks and gardens, entirely free from the depressing characteristics of the conventional burial ground. The park cemeteries of Hamburg, Kaiserslautern, Bremen, and Munich are unique in this respect, and have been copied on a smaller scale by many other towns. The Berlin Central Cemetery at Friedrichsfelde is also regarded as a model.

The law does not contemplate that cemeteries shall be regarded as a source of profit, and in Prussia the fees for grave sites and other services rendered must be fixed so as to cover only the costs of providing and administering the cemeteries. Some towns follow the principle of graduating the charges according to the income of the deceased or the relatives, a test easy to apply, since all the necessary information is collected by the authorities for the purpose of the local income-tax assessment. Frankfort charges different fees for incomes above £300, incomes between £150 and £300, incomes between £75 and £150, incomes between £45 and £75, and incomes below £45. A grave space may cost as a rule any sum from 5s. up to 30s. or more, according to the town.

Many towns, including Düsseldorf, Stuttgart, Frankfort-on-Main, Karlsruhe, Wiesbaden, Mannheim, Heidelberg, Magdeburg, and Strassburg, carry on the business of undertaking, from the laying out of the body to the interment; and in some cases the use of the town's hearse is compulsory. Karlsruhe charges an inclusive sum for every service involved (including the coffin), viz., from 30s. to £9 for adults and from 25s. to £6 for juveniles.

The cremation movement is making rapid progress. The

first crematorium was established at Gotha in 1878, and owing to the hostility of the Governments, incited by the ecclesiastical authorities, twelve years passed before another was built. Nevertheless, there were 29 in Prussia in 1913, and 11 in the other States, nearly all owned by the communes; in that year 10,168 cremations took place in all Germany. The cost of cremation alone varies from 20s. upwards, with an addition for non-residents, and an extra charge is made for storing the ashes. Stuttgart is the only town in which cremation is free.

CHAPTER IX

TRADING ENTERPRISES

The old German tradition—The modern revival of municipal trading—The system of concessions combined with royalties—Scope of modern municipal enterprise—Revenue and profits from trading enterprises—Gas supply—Electric light and power works—Water supply—Tramways and transport—Docks and quays—Furtherance of trade and industry—Public abattoirs, market halls, and food supply—Municipal savings banks—Mortgage and rent-charge banks—Insurance enterprises—Miscellaneous trading enterprises—The execution of public works: régie versus contract—Municipal workpeople: conditions of employment.

GERMANY has applied the principle of municipalisation to economic undertakings upon a far more extensive scale than any other country, and it has done this as the result not of any considered acceptance of economic theories, but of the force of tradition and still more of modern conditions. Yet so large a conquest of this domain of enterprise as has been effected would have been impossible but for the wideness and elasticity of the powers possessed by the municipal authorities. As we have seen, German legislation upon town government does not prescribe certain powers as competent to be employed and rule out all others that are not formally specified. What it says to the communal bodies in effect is: "Govern your towns well. How you do it is your own concern. Devise measures and exercise the powers that seem necessary, and if new powers not contemplated by existing law and custom are needed, take and use them." It is easy to see how this view facilitates public action, encourages experiment, stimulates ingenuity and inventiveness, and lifts local government to the level of constructive statesmanship.

THE OLD GERMAN TRADITION.—Readiness to engage in trading enterprises on a small scale was evidently characteristic of the old German towns. In the middle ages they frequently owned large tracts of forest and common lands. In the fourteenth century the governing council of Cologne built warehouses, mills of various kinds, a clothworkers' hall, dyeworks, weaving sheds, and slaughter-houses.[1] Many towns still retain to-day warehouses which have been in their possession for centuries. Communal corn, wine, and fruit businesses, even inns and bathing establishments, were not uncommon in the distant past. Two centuries ago Berlin and its sister town Kölln followed dairy-farming among other communal enterprises, and carried on depots for the sale of farm produce in these towns and the neighbouring places. Survivals of the early tradition of collective enterprise remain still in the most unexpected places, as in the form of the communal bakeries carried on in many villages on the Rhine and elsewhere for the use of the settled families, which use the ovens in turn as determined by lot.

As, however, the towns lost in autonomy under the absolutistic *régime*, so the power and the disposition to engage in any activities outside the narrowest limits of civil administration became weakened, and for practical purposes the municipalisation movement belongs to quite modern times. Stein's Municipal Ordinance of 1808, devised though it was to revive communal life in Prussia, clearly did not contemplate the development of activity on the economic side. Liberalistic ideas had gained the upper hand in Germany as in England, and the theory of municipal government had been reduced to its simplest terms.

From that time until the middle of last century, and even later, little land was added to the public estates, and trading enterprise of every kind was at a discount. Like the State the communal authorities had fallen back on the dreary and sterile police conception of government; deeming their purposes fulfilled when they had made provision for public security and had secured for private enterprise a fair field.

The recognition of this limited view of the function of local government is seen in the origin of the first gas and water

[1] H. Preuss, " Die Entwickelung des deutschen Städtewesens," Vol. I, p. 85.

works. For these were established with no intention of gain, and hardly of ministering to the convenience of the public as something separate from its security. The governing consideration in the case of gas was the order and safety of the streets, hitherto insufficiently lighted with oil ; the domestic use of gas was encouraged much later, and even then mainly with a view to reducing the cost of public lighting. Similarly, the provision of a regular water supply was called for by way of protection against fire, in contending with which the well supplies proved inadequate, and for the better cleaning of the streets. It is significant also that gasworks, like tramways at a later date, were first introduced as private enterprises—in some towns by English companies ; only later, when they were proved to be remunerative, did the towns become eager to own and work them. Waterworks, on the other hand, offered less attraction to the private capitalist, and he was, as a rule, content to allow the commune to supply its needs at its own risk. Berlin and Hamburg were among the few important exceptions, and here again it was English capital which led the way.

THE MODERN REVIVAL OF MUNICIPAL TRADING.—The middle of last century saw a return to the old collectivist practice, and the movement grew so rapidly that long before the end of the century Communal Socialism may be said to have triumphed in civil life as completely as State Socialism has triumphed in political. For though in one sense this triumph merely represents the revival of an ancient principle, this principle is nowadays applied with a boldness and thoroughness unknown in the past. " The question whether the communes should engage in trading enterprises," writes Dr. Leidig, " was answered in the affirmative in Germany centuries ago. Both the German peasant communities and the mediæval towns promoted the economic interests of their inhabitants on a large scale, and amid changing times and needs it has so remained until to-day. In Germany the only question that can be discussed is not whether the communes shall so occupy themselves, but how far they should go, and what forms such enterprise should take."

Nevertheless, the communalisation movement takes even to-day three distinct directions. For practical purposes the old individualists are a negligible quantity, yet their lineal descendants still cling tenaciously to the doctrine that economic enterprise, and particularly enterprise which promises profit, is only proper for the individual, and not for the community. They would not altogether debar the communes from carrying on enterprises of the kind, but they would only allow them to step in when private capitalism is unwilling or unable to provide the public with the conveniences of which it stands in need.

At the other extreme is the uncompromising party of militant Social Democracy—strong in numbers and in the conviction that it alone holds the key to social progress—which on principle advocates the socialisation of all enterprises that impose no insuperable technical obstacles, whether the prospect of gain be large or small.

Midway between these irreconcilable groups is a thoroughly practical party favourable to a progressive policy of communalisation and quite indifferent as to theories one way or the other, and its policy is the one which holds the field in all the most wide-awake towns of Germany. The spokesmen of this party contend that the extent to which the communes should carry on trading undertakings cannot be decided by appeal to abstract principles, and that the best test is the test of experience and results. They urge also that in these days of highly developed social organisations the convenience and welfare of large populations cannot be subordinated to the material interests of private individuals eager only for gain and often indifferent as to the manner of obtaining it. They admit that the most efficient of municipal administrations will at times commit errors of judgment and fail in their endeavours, but they claim that it is as unreasonable to expect perfect success of public enterprise as of private. From the financial standpoint they contend that municipal enterprises afford a convenient method of raising revenue, for if the profits from public trading are in effect taxation, it is taxation in a form that falls lightly upon the community, and that leaves no sense of inequity, since the inhabitants know that in return for the tax they enjoy material advantages.

Furthermore, this party of sane communalisation can point convincingly to the fact that but for the willingness of the public authorities to step in and shoulder the burden many institutions of great public utility would never have come into existence at all. For example, many towns have dredged rivers, built docks, and otherwise developed their natural trading facilities on a scale beyond the power of private enterprise, and so gained new life, and safeguarded their industrial and commercial prosperity for all time. The growth of a town like Mannheim has been promoted and directed into progressive lines almost solely by the enterprise of the governing authority, which long ago had the foresight to buy land freely for extensions and for the accommodation of new industries.

THE SYSTEM OF CONCESSIONS COMBINED WITH ROYALTIES.—In the past, however, a small minority of towns—among them Berlin and Hanover are specially noteworthy—have favoured the French system of " concessions " in regard to such undertakings as tramways, gasworks, and electricity works, granting the concessionary companies the use of the streets in return for the payment of fixed royalties or otherwise a share in their profits. For this system certain practical advantages can, of course, be claimed. Under it a municipality is freed from the necessity of raising large amounts of capital for trading enterprises and from the risks attending its investment therein ; it escapes the responsibilities and worries which are incidental to all large undertakings, successful or otherwise, and it reduces the sum of the labour force for whose employment and contentment it is responsible. From the public standpoint the principle of " concession " means that the concessionaries bear all the losses while the local authority shares in the profits, and there are instances of municipalities which, by acting on this principle, in Mill's words, " grow rich in their sleep." For example, Berlin in 1910 received royalties from electrical works in private hands to the amount of £314,180, Königsberg received £29,650 from the same source, Schöneberg £18,900, and Strassburg £18,860, while the royalties paid by tramway companies to 28 of the larger towns exceeded £400,000. From concessions of all kinds Berlin in that year derived a revenue of over £500,000. On the other hand, the granting of concessions in respect of valuable privileges, unless carefully guarded, may hand a town over, lock and stock, to the mercies —which are not always tender—of monopolists, without securing to it any equitable share in the exactions upon which the unrestrained monopolist so often waxes fat.

To some extent, of course, a town may protect itself against undue exploitation by limiting its concessions to short periods, and by inserting into all agreements provisions securing to it a progressive share in profits, an equal voice in the determination of trading conditions, rights of purchase, ultimate reversion of the property, and the like. Nevertheless, the concession system in its old form may be regarded as moribund, though it has received an unexpected stimulus in the form of " mixed undertakings "—to be referred to later—in which public authorities and private capitalists nowadays join for the promotion and supply of electric current for light and power.

SCOPE OF MODERN MUNICIPAL ENTERPRISE.—Allowing for local circumstances, the advantages, like the disadvantages, of public as compared with private enterprise are the same in all countries, and any theoretical consideration of that aspect of the question is superfluous. In general, however, it may be said that municipal enterprise is favoured where one or other of the following considerations carries special weight : (*a*) where the enterprise is concerned with the health, convenience and safety of the community, as in the case of waterworks, sewerage works, scavenging, etc. ; (*b*) where the commune is the largest consumer, as often in the case of light and power ; (*c*) where the enterprise involves the use of public property, as the tramways in relation to the streets ; (*d*) where important monopolies are at stake, as in the case of water and several of the utilities already named ; (*e*) where private capital is not attracted, as in the case of abattoirs and stockyards ; (*f*) where the community can distribute more efficiently than private individuals, as in the case of gas and electricity; and (g) where uniformity of action is desirable, and conflict of authority should be prevented, a consideration which applies to most public enterprises. Behind nearly all these enterprises, however, there is an equally powerful financial motive —the desire to raise revenue freely in other ways than by direct taxation, and this motive, as we shall see, is strongly emphasised by the German Governments.

The laws relating to municipal government and taxation do not attempt to define the directions in which local authorities may engage in trading undertakings, but give them a perfectly free hand, subject to some extent to control by the State supervisory authority. How wide is the scope of public enterprise in Germany at the present day may be shown by a return relating to 1279 Prussian towns of all sizes, prepared in 1906. It was found that the following undertakings were in public hands in these towns:—

561 waterworks.
440 gasworks.
201 electricity works.
 54 tramways.
426 abattoirs and stockyards (one for horses).
 19 docks and quays.
 38 market halls.
370 bathing establishments.
 13 sea and therapeutic baths.
  5 salt and mineral springs.
  1 milk cure establishment.
 10 warehouses and sale halls.
  1 wine business.
 42 stone and lime quarries, turbaries, and sand and gravel pits.
 17 breweries.
104 inns and restaurants.

 15 hydropathic establishments.
  2 fruit preserving factories.
  2 wine cellars.
  2 refrigerating works.
  1 timber warehouse.
  2 mines.
  2 bakeries.
  4 factories.
 45 brickworks.
 23 mills.
  2 lock-smitheries.
  2 rope works.
  2 dairies.
 17 dancing halls.
 16 ferries.
  2 fishery enterprises.
  1 livery station.

Of these 1279 towns only 310—nearly all small places with less than 5000 inhabitants—were without trading enterprises.

TRADING ENTERPRISES

The variety of enterprises carried on by the communes would be further increased if the survey were to be extended to other States. While owning and working undertakings common to other places, some towns have enterprises peculiar to themselves. Munich, Frankfort-on-Main, Düsseldorf, and Magdeburg, for example, have wine business and restaurants. Dresden, Düsseldorf, and Neukölln (Rixdorf) have printing works. Nuremberg has an orchard, and also stone quarries, from which it paves the streets. Breslau, Hanover, Mayence, Worms, and a number of smaller towns own, and in some cases carry on, pharmacies. Cologne carries on a brewery and Leipzig a bakery to meet the needs of the assisted poor. The municipal newspaper, devoted to official reports and notices, has already been mentioned ; in two towns, however, Dresden and Elberfeld, the municipal daily newspaper has all the characteristics of a public journal. A number of towns, again, own theatres and concert halls. Some towns own so large an area of forest that they find it necessary to have a special department to manage this section of their estates, to sell timber, re-afforest as may be necessary, etc.

The wide range of enterprises carried on by individual towns may be illustrated by the case of Mannheim, whose larger undertakings include gasworks, waterworks, tramways, abattoir and stockyard, docks and quays, a land trading department, river and other bathing establishments, theatre and concert hall, milk kiosks, and a large amount of house property. Some towns, in addition to having important commercial undertakings of their own, have large share interests in industrial, tramway, and power companies ; the municipality of Düsseldorf places at the disposal of the mayor and executive a special fund for participating in industrial undertakings.

An interesting illustration of the readiness of German municipalities to give hostages to the future where there is a prospect of ultimate benefit is afforded by their present enterprise in encouraging aeronautics and aviation. Enormous sums have been expended by the larger towns in particular in the provision of airship sheds, aerodromes, landing stages, etc. Brunswick, for example, has just agreed to provide a

Frankfort Airship Company with a site for a landing place for its airships and also for an aerodrome, and to subsidise the company to the extent of from £1250 to £1600 a year, while the company undertakes in return to make Brunswick a place of call in journeys between Frankfort, Hamburg, Berlin, and Düsseldorf. In making grants and subsidies of this kind the towns act entirely on their own responsibility, and without seeking Government or other permission. They also invariably subsidise the local improvement and similar associations formed for the purpose of attracting visitors and ministering to their convenience.

The "public utility" services are now largely owned and worked by the local authorities. A census taken in 1908 relating to 2309 urban districts showed that these services were so owned to the following extent :—

Towns with a population of	Total No. of towns.	No. of these towns which owned—				
		Water-works.	Gas-works.	Electricity works.	Tramways.	Abattoirs.
Under 2,000	615	206	19	22	—	56
2,000 to 5,000	873	404	180	154	—	223
5,000 to 20,000	602	426	333	112	17	352
20,000 to 50,000	134	123	112	62	27	101
50,000 to 100,000	44	41	32	30	17	43
Over 100,000	41	38	33	33	18	39
TOTALS	2,309	1,238	709	413	79	814

Some of the undertakings here specified are obviously beyond the means of small places, but it will be seen that nearly all the towns with a population exceeding 50,000 owned waterworks and abattoirs, four out of five owned gasworks and electricity works, and two out of five owned tramways. Corresponding figures for 1911 published by the "Statistical Yearbook of German Towns" show that of 87 towns reported upon 77 then owned waterworks, 72 gasworks, 67 electrical works, 78 abattoirs, 47 tramways, and 69 bathing establishments. It has been estimated that a capital of two hundred and fifty million pounds is now invested in the trading enterprises of German towns. In most towns about one-half, and in some as much as three-quarters, of all the outstanding loans has been contracted on behalf of these enterprises, a fact to be remembered when the heavy indebtedness of German towns is considered.

In the past each of the large trading enterprises has been worked as an independent undertaking and administered by its own special committee and executive officer. Of late, however, many municipalities have recognised the advantage of placing certain undertakings under the same management, and this is particularly the case with gas and electricity works, the success of which depends upon so many factors common to both, e.g., favourable purchase of raw material, rates of charges, and other conditions of service, interchange of labour, etc.

REVENUE AND PROFITS FROM TRADING ENTERPRISES.—The only available comprehensive estimate of the revenue derived by the communes for their trading enterprises is one published in 1908 by the Imperial Ministry of Finance and relating to towns and rural communes with over 10,000 inhabitants. It was then estimated that the receipts from undertakings of all kinds—those carried on without special regard for profit equally with those conducted upon strictly commercial principles—amounted in the aggregate to £25,350,000, or 26 per cent. of all communal receipts, and the expenditure to £22,650,000, or 23 per cent. of all communal expenditure, showing an apparent surplus of £2,700,000.

The power of the local authorities to carry on certain enterprises at a profit is subject to important restrictions. The Prussian Communal Taxation Law distinguishes between enterprises which may be legitimately worked for gain and those, described as " communal institutions " (*Anstalten*), which are intended to fulfil a public purpose yet are not primarily intended to yield profits. The fees which may be charged for the use of the latter must be limited to such an amount as will cover the costs of construction and working. Thus the law does not allow communes to charge higher fees for the use of abattoirs than are needful to yield 8 per cent. of such costs. In practice over one-third of the public abattoirs show a return ranging from 4 to 6 per cent., and over one-quarter a return of from 6 to 8 per cent. On the other hand, the communes have a right to fix at will their charges for the products or services of the trading enterprises, and the law provides that these enterprises shall be so administered that the revenues shall at least cover the costs caused to the commune, inclusive of interest and the redemption of the capital invested. Dr. Most emphasises the legal difference between fees in the former sense and ordinary trading charges in the latter. Inasmuch as " communal institutions " come under the public law and trading undertakings under the civil law, fees in respect of the former may be collected like taxes—by summary process; while trading charges can only be recovered by civil action. Further, according to the Municipal Ordinances all the inhabitants of a town have a right to use its " communal institutions," while the use of its trading undertakings is based on a personal contract.[1]

The line of demarcation between trading enterprises and " communal institutions " as above defined is often difficult to define, but Dr. Most points out that by general agreement hospitals, poor relief institutions of all kinds, pawnshops, abattoirs, and provision for refuse removal and street cleaning all rank as non-trading " communal institutions." On the other hand, tramways, gas and electricity works, breweries and inns, where these are carried on by local authorities, are enterprises from which a town is entitled to extract as much profit as may be possible and expedient. In the list of doubtful cases, Dr. Most places waterworks, market halls, and bathing establishments—all institutions of greater practical utility than profit-yielding value. In his view the proper test by which to decide whether institutions of this kind should be worked for profit is the question whether the use of them is obligatory upon the inhabitants or not, since the exercise of compulsion is not, as a rule, justified if profit-making is a governing motive.[2]

[1] " Die deutsche Stadt und ihre Verwaltung," Vol. I, p. 12.
[2] *Ibid.*, Vol. I, p. 13.

Prices and charges are often graduated for the purpose of encouraging the use of a service offered or of affording relief to small incomes. Thus in the case of water, gas, and electric current, less is charged for industrial than for domestic consumption, and gas and electricity used for heating and cooking are charged less than the same for lighting. Similarly the refuse removal and water dues and school fees, where charged, are commonly reduced in favour of persons of narrow means.

The vexed question whether gas, electricity, and water works, tramway systems, and similar undertakings should be made to contribute towards the reduction of the rates or should be carried on as nearly as possible at cost price is debated as much in Germany as in other countries, and with no more likelihood of agreement. The question is obviously not settled by the superficial plea that the consumers make the profits and should therefore have the benefit of them—a plea which ignores the fact that all trading undertakings are carried on by the credit and at the risk of the whole community, and by the use of the community's streets, roads, and other property; and, further, that their directors and the workmen engaged in connection with them are the servants of the whole community and not of the consumers at all. Municipal authorities there as elsewhere, however, are finding that the larger the profit made the greater become the demands of labour. More than one commune has sold paying undertakings to private capitalists or refrained from adding to its trading enterprises in order to avoid the constant friction with employees who are taught to regard all profit as a "surplus-value" created by and wrongfully withheld from labour, and who in wages controversies are not always amenable to reason as understood by the official mind.

On the whole, German towns work their economic undertakings both efficiently and profitably, and the public has every reason to be satisfied with the way in which it is served. Instances might be given without end of towns which owing to foresight and good husbandry are to-day in possession of valuable properties which contribute largely towards the general costs of administration, and cases are not rare of small communes which for this reason are altogether exempted from local taxation.

Undoubtedly German municipalities in general work their "public utility" enterprises far more systematically from the standpoint of profit than is the case in this country. In so doing they are simply following the injunctions of the Governments, which, through the supervisory authorities, are constantly urging the local authorities to make the most of these opportunities of raising revenue before falling back on taxation. While, for example, the water service, when in public lands, is not usually regarded in this country as a legitimate source of profit, the larger German towns levy charges which yield a very considerable contribution towards the general funds. Thus in 1910 62 towns with a population of 50,000 or more, for which returns are given in the "Statistical Yearbook of German Towns" for 1913, reported a combined surplus, before charging interest and depreciation, equal to 7·7 per cent. of the total capital invested, and one of nearly twice this figure on the amount of capital as written down by all allowances for depreciation.

The larger profits derived by German municipalities from trading undertakings can best be illustrated by the cases of the gas and electricity works and the tramways. In the comparisons here made profits actually available for the reduction of local taxation or rates, after allowances for renewal and reserve funds, are taken; in the case of German towns royalties received from private companies, where these have been allowed to work undertakings of the kinds named, are included in such profits; and in each case losses have been deducted. The figures relate to groups of towns of the same size, and while the German figures are for the administrative year 1910 or 1910–11, the figures for Great Britain are for the administrative year 1911–12[1] in the case of electricity works and tramways, and for the year 1910–11 in the case of gasworks.

The aggregate profits on their gasworks available in 1910–11

---

[1] The source of the German figures is the "Statistisches Jahrbuch Deutscher Städte" for 1913, and that of the figures for Great Britain the "Municipal Year Book" for 1913.

TRADING ENTERPRISES

for the reduction of taxation in 72 German towns with 50,000 inhabitants or more were £2,653,700, equal to 3s. 6d. a head of the combined population of 15,139,700. In 21 towns with 200,000 inhabitants or over the profits were equal to 3s. 9d. a head of a combined population of 9,897,700 ; in 20 towns with from 100,000 to 200,000 inhabitants they were equal to 3s. 2d. a head of a combined population of 2,814,900 ; and in 31 towns with a population of from 50,000 to 100,000 they were equal to 3s. a head of a combined population of 2,427,100.

The corresponding profits made in 1911–12 by 37 towns of the same size in Great Britain were £446,200, equal to 1s. 3d. a head of the combined population of 7,130,100. Grouping the towns, it appears that in 11 towns with 200,000 inhabitants or over (in the aggregate 4,651,600) the profits were equal to 1s. 0½d. a head ; in 11 towns with from 100,000 to 200,000 inhabitants (in the aggregate 1,396,400) they were equal to 1s. 4d. a head ; and in 15 towns with from 50,000 to 100,000 inhabitants (in the aggregate 1,082,100) to 2s. a head.

Again, net profits, available for the reduction of taxation, were made on their electricity works in 1910–11 by 72 German towns with 50,000 inhabitants or more, having a combined population of 14,116,000, to the amount of £1,817,900, equal to 2s. 3½d. per inhabitant. In 20 towns with a population of 200,000 or more the profits were equal to 2s. 8½d. a head of their 8,413,000 inhabitants ; in 19 towns with a population of from 100,000 to 200,000 they were equal to 1s. 11½d. a head of their 3,319,000 inhabitants ; and in 33 towns with a population of from 50,000 to 100,000 to 9d. a head of their 2,383,500 inhabitants.

The corresponding profits devoted to the reduction of the rates in 1911–12 in 100 towns in Great Britain with a population of 50,000 or more, and having a combined population of 15,164,000, were £173,600, equal to 2¾d. per inhabitant. The profits in 19 towns with a population of 200,000 or over (in the aggregate 7,322,000) were equal to 4d. a head ; those in 35 towns with from 100,000 to 200,000 inhabitants (in the aggregate 4,698,000) were equal to 1½d. a head ; and those in

46 towns with from 50,000 to 100,000 inhabitants (in the aggregate 3,144,000) were equal to 1¼d. a head.

Taking finally the profits from the tramways available for the relief of local burdens, the amount yielded in 1910 in 74 German towns with 50,000 inhabitants or over was £718,000, equal to 10d. a head of a combined population of 15,883,300. In 22 towns with a population of 200,000 or over (in the aggregate 9,804,200) the profits were equal to 1s. 5d. a head; in 24 towns with from 100,000 to 200,000 inhabitants (in the aggregate 3,423,000) they were equal to 1½d. a head; and in 28 towns with from 50,000 to 100,000 inhabitants (in the aggregate 2,656,100), they were equal to 1¼d. a head.

The corresponding profits for the year 1911-12 in 58 towns in Great Britain with a population of 50,000 or over were £458,800, equal to 9d. a head of the combined population of 12,005,000 inhabitants. In 16 towns with a population of 200,000 or over (in the aggregate 7,396,000) the profits were 1s. 1d. a head; in 23 towns with a population of from 100,000 to 200,000 (in the aggregate 3,252,000) they were 3½d. a head; and in 19 towns with a population of from 50,000 to 100,000 (in the aggregate 1,357,000) they were 2d. a head.

The combined profits from these three sources in the towns considered were equal to 6s. 7½d. a head of the population in German towns, and to 2s. 2¾d. a head of the population in Great Britain. The question whether and how far larger profits in German towns are counterbalanced by a higher cost of services is one upon which no general statement is possible.

The material value of trading enterprises to the large towns in particular may be illustrated by the following statement showing the amounts of profits and royalties which accrued in 1910 or 1910-11 to the common funds of twelve such towns from the four most fruitful sources of gain, viz., water, gas, and electricity works, and tramway undertakings. The profits shown are the surpluses remaining after all allowances for depreciation, redemption of capital, and additions to renewals and reserve funds. Where these towns received royalties from companies holding concessions from them in respect of any of the services specified the amounts are indicated by asterisk. The amounts received from these companies were independent of all payments on account of paving and maintenance, street cleaning, and the usual local taxes :—

Towns and population (1910).	Gasworks.	Electricity works.	Waterworks.	Tramways.	Total.
	£	£	£	£	£
Berlin (2,071,300).....	387,980	314,180*	141,020	8,550 198,020*	1,049,750
Breslau (512,100)	131,810	62,100	52,640	26,380*	272,930
Charlottenburg (306,000)	129,240	64,590	—	7,020*	200,850
Cologne (516,500)......	65,730	54,990	56,770	58,480	235,970
Dresden (548,300)	156,440	80,050	9,130	54,360	299,980
Düsseldorf (358,700) ..	58,630	38,870	39,870	4,430	141,800
Frankfort-on-Main (414,600)	32,290*	145,080	34,180	73,710	285,260
Hamburg (931,000) ...	239,820	—	—	91,690*	331,510
Leipzig (589,900)	32,880	45,400	31,550	19,810*	129,640
Munich (596,500)	69,200	67,550	5,460	77,810	220,020
Nuremberg (333,200)..	75,190	30,470	6,000	11,740	123,400
Stuttgart (286,200) ...	56,140	36,580	32,000	5,630*	130,350

The profits here shown, in the aggregate £3,421,460, were equivalent to 9s. 2d. a head of the combined population of 7,464,300.

Perhaps nowhere in Germany does the "magic of property" perform a greater feat than in the little Bavarian town of Klingenberg, for the trading undertakings of the town not only defray all public expenditure, but yield to each of its 2000 inhabitants a yearly dividend in cash. For Klingenberg owns, in addition to a large amount of forest and other lands, some valuable clay pits, the profits from which amount to as much as £32,000 a year. After the costs of local government had been paid and a large addition had been made to the reserve fund, now £100,000, there remained in a recent year a gift of £20 a head for each freeman. Naturally Klingenberg sells its citizenship dearly. To be a freeman of the town it is necessary to have lived there for 25 years and to pay a fee of £10 in the case of natives and £80 in other cases. In the same way the ownership of a large estate together with several profitable undertakings enables the small East Prussian town of Seeburg to dispense with local taxes altogether. At Enkirch, on the

Moselle, the revenue from the public lands relieves the inhabitants from local taxes, and in addition each householder receives a small holding rent free, with wood for fuel. A number of favoured communes in the Prussian provinces of Westphalia and Hanover receive from their forest estates revenues ranging from £2000 to £12,000 a year.

It will be of interest to indicate briefly the directions in which municipal trading enterprise is most developed and the general lines upon which the larger undertakings common to the principal towns are conducted.

GAS SUPPLY.—The first experiments in gas lighting in Germany were made at Freiburg in 1817, and the first gasworks were introduced in Berlin and Hanover by English companies, which still retain the right to supply part of the municipal areas. For a long time private enterprise kept the communes at bay, but the communalisation of gas undertakings has made rapid progress during the last thirty or forty years, and it is estimated that about two-thirds of all town gasworks are now in public hands, as compared with barely one-half of the electricity works, in regard to which public enterprise is losing rather than gaining ground. The proportions are more favourable to municipal enterprise in the large towns. In 1911, of 23 towns with over 200,000 inhabitants, 16 owned and worked the public gasworks, of 23 towns with from 100,000 to 200,000 inhabitants 14, and of 41 towns with from 50,000 to 100,000 inhabitants 29; the corresponding numbers of towns which owned and worked electricity works were 15, 15, and 28, while three towns owned and leased such works. The whole of these 87 towns had both a gas and an electricity supply.

Nevertheless, the domestic use of gas is far from general even in the large towns; oil is still largely used as an illuminant, though the increasing use of automatic meters introduces gas more and more into working-class households. It was found in 1910 that gas was used as an illuminant in only 34 per cent. of all dwellings in Hanover, but in 75 per cent. for cooking and heating, while 5 per cent. of all households used electricity. Conservative habits and still more the dearness of gas explain the persistence of the oil lamp in small homes. It is estimated, however, that half the population of Germany lives in communes whose principal illuminant is gas, and that 50 per cent. of the total production of gas is supplied to private individuals. The predominant prices of gas in 83 of the larger towns of Germany in 1911 were about 4s. 6d. per 1000 cubic feet for lighting and 3s. 5d. for cooking and heating and industrial purposes; but the local rates varied from 3s. 5d. to 6s. in the former case and from 2s. to 5s. in the latter. With a view to more successful competition with electricity lower rates are invariably charged for gas used for motive power, and most towns have an elaborate system of discounts, ranging in Berlin from 5 to 20 per cent., devised for the encouragement of large consumers. The municipality of Berlin goes so far as to instruct scholars in the elementary schools in their final years in the use of gas for cooking and heating purposes.

Thanks to their monopolist position and to the high price charged, the municipal gasworks are generally able to show high profits. The Berlin gasworks in 1912 yielded a surplus of £425,000, available for the reduction of the local taxes, and a few other large towns in this way relieve the taxes to the extent of between £100,000 and £200,000 a year. Where private works are carried on they are generally liable to the payment of royalties to the town, and in 1910 Frankfort-on-Main received £32,300 from private gasworks companies, Hanover £43,800, and Schöneberg £16,700.

A recent innovation in gas engineering which seems destined to have an important future is the supply of gas to large areas from central works. Many of the larger towns have for a long time supplied adjacent communes and rural districts, and in 1909 there were known to exist 105 central gasworks from which 340 places were supplied, the largest belonging to a company in Silesia and supplying 13 communes with a population of 180,000 by means of 63 miles of main pipes. The municipal gasworks of Berlin supply gas to some 30 communes, large and small, within a radius of many miles; Chemnitz supplies 11 other communes, Meissen 12, Lübeck seven, and many towns supply from four to six neighbouring areas.

The special development of this method of central distribution from which the greatest results are expected is the utilisation of coke-oven gas, which hitherto has to a large extent been wasted. It has been estimated that more gas is wasted at the collieries of Westphalia than is used both for industrial and domestic purposes in the entire province. Several of the Westphalian collieries already supply gas to many adjacent towns, some of which, like Essen and Bochum, have either sold their gasworks to the contracting companies or have agreed not to extend their production. At present the competition of the colliery companies is confined within a narrow radius of the base of operations, and towns situated at a large distance from the coal measures are not yet threatened by this new competition, but the volume of coke-oven gas available is so enormous and it can be sold at so low a price that its ultimate distribution over wide areas would appear to be only a matter of time.

ELECTRIC LIGHT AND POWER WORKS.—The relation of the communes to electrical enterprise has undergone a great change during recent years. Having made the mistake of allowing private capital to capture the gas supply in the first instance, with the result in many cases that public ownership and control could be acquired only at great sacrifice, the communes early took steps to reserve to themselves the right to supply electric current within their areas. There were noted exceptions, however, and Berlin amongst other towns held back a long time and granted concessions to companies in virtue of which these were allowed to serve specified areas in return for royalties taking the form of a share of the gross receipts or profits. The largest of these undertakings is the Berlin Electricity Works, which paid the city in 1912 royalties to the amount of £195,000, while returning its shareholders a dividend of 12 per cent. The agreement is that the municipality shall receive half the net profit in so far as the latter exceeds a dividend of 6 per cent. on a capital of £1,000,000, and 4 per cent. on a capital beyond that sum, with 10 per cent. of the gross receipts from the supply of light and power in Berlin. Essen has an agreement with a large central power company under which it receives 5 per cent. of the gross

TRADING ENTERPRISES

receipts and a share of the profits, and Stettin, Schöneberg and other towns have also concluded agreements with concessionary companies on the same lines.

The agreement under which the Berlin electrical company works provides for the transference of the above named concern to the municipality in 1915, and at the time of writing the future relationships between the company and the city had not been decided. The adjacent town of Charlottenburg, in the exercise of its contractual powers, took over in 1910 the electrical power and light works which had hitherto held the ground.

The possession of these works is the more important for the towns, since electricity has captured the tramways entirely, insomuch that horse tramways are only to be found in the most backward of small towns. It is estimated that from 40 to 60 per cent. of the current produced is used for traction. Another direction in which electricity has made great strides is in its application to industrial purposes. In some towns as much as 50 per cent. of the current produced is sold for motive power, and in towns dependent upon small and house industries new life has been given to threatened trades by the provision of current at a cheap rate.

As yet electric lighting is rare in small dwellings, but in order to tap this source of revenue some towns have an arrangement whereby for a fixed yearly sum the unlimited use of one or more lights (as may be agreed on) is allowed. Thus at Treves householders may subscribe for current at the rate of 3s. 7d. a year for ten watts, with a minimum of 60 watts, costing 21s. 6d., for which sum the subscriber may burn two lights of 25 candle-power as often and as long as he likes; any number of lamps may be installed in the house, but only two may be used simultaneously for this amount; three lights cost 32s. 4d., four cost 43s. 2d., and so on. As Germany lives on the flat system and as the dwellings of the working and lower middle classes seldom contain more than three rooms, a small installation suffices and the subscription system works well. In the larger towns the price of electric current for light ranges from 3½d. to 8½d. per kilowatt hour, with an average of 6d., and for power from 1½d. to 3½d., with an average of 2½d.

The modern tendency is in favour of large overland or central stations owned and worked exclusively by unions of communes or jointly by communes and promoting companies, these latter being, as a rule, offshoots of one of the great electrical corporations. The first overland station was instituted in 1891, when power was conveyed from the Neckar to Frankfort-on-Main, a distance of 109 miles, for the purpose of an electrical exhibition then being held there. Now a large part of the country is served by large central works, the number of which in 1911 was nearly a hundred, all but four or five established within the last fifteen years. As a rule the communes are financially interested in the central works from which they obtain their supply of current, and in many cases their influence predominates. The Westphalian town of Bielefeld supplies 35 rural communes, under agreement, with electric current in bulk, and the local authorities lay down all cables and distribute to the inhabitants within their areas.

One of the largest "mixed" or joint undertakings is the Rhenish Westphalian electricity works at Essen, which supply more than 50 communes, covering an area of no less than 2300 square miles, with current for lighting and power for general purposes. Behind this great undertaking, whose capital is three million pounds, are some of the foremost industrialists of Western Germany, and it works hand in hand with several of the large colliery companies under an agreement by which it buys their superfluous current and supplies them with current when required. The company is able to supply current so cheaply that many of the communes have either sold to it their electricity and gas works or keep them as reserves. A number of tramway systems likewise obtain their power from this source. Nearly one-half of the shares are held by the communes concerned, and the local authorities are represented on the board of directors and by means of committees. Current is supplied at the price of 3½d. per kilowatt hour for light and 1¾d. for power, and as the company can produce at about ½d. these rates allow of large dividends being paid.

Several of the great central electrical works belong to a still larger extent to the communes which they mainly serve. Thus the "Mark" Communal Electricity Works of Hagen, in Westphalia, are almost entirely owned by eleven towns and rural districts, whose holdings in the undertaking vary from £3750 to £40,500 in the case of Hagen. Similarly the " Westfalen " Communal Electrical Company of Bochum is owned for the most part by some thirty communes. Central works on a joint basis are also common in the South. Thus the municipality of Munich is interested to the extent of 51 per cent. of the capital—so as to give it a balance of influence—in a company which has been formed for the supply of electric current to the town and neighbourhood by the use of water obtained from a stream in the Bavarian Alps, while the rest of the capital is in the hands of a group of banks, firms, and individuals.

While the Governments of Bavaria, Baden, and Hesse have encouraged the formation of mixed undertakings, other Governments, like that of Saxony, are of opinion that the towns are disposing of their electrical works too readily, and in 1913 the Saxon Minister of the Interior issued an order to the State supervisory authorities instructing them to use all their influence to persuade local authorities to keep this branch of enterprise in their own hands. Certainly the belief is widely held that the great electrical companies already possess far more power than is good for the public interest, and that the safest form of combination for the establishment and working of these large overland power stations is that which restricts membership to the communal and other local government authorities interested as consumers.

WATER SUPPLY.—Where water for domestic use is not obtained from house wells, which in towns no longer serve even as an important auxiliary source of supply, the local authority is almost invariably responsible for the water service. Waterworks seldom offer great attraction as an investment ; for not only is the expenditure involved as a rule very heavy, and the financial return seldom large and not always certain, but the risks involved, owing to the relation of water supply to public health, are apt to deter private capital from disputing this field of enterprise with the communes. There are, however, notable exceptions to the rule. Some of the large communes around Berlin obtain their water from a powerful company which bought from the Government for a mere song the right to drain the Grunewald district abutting on the river Havel. Most of the contracts bind the local authorities to the company for fifty years and several run until the year 2000. Neukölln (Rixdorf), one of these suburbs, with a population of 237,000, rather than face the cost of constructing works of its own, in 1910 renewed its contract with the company until 1997. The company has a capital of one and a half million pounds and it is able to pay dividends of from 14 to 17 per cent. Berlin itself received its first water supply from an English company, which received a monopoly from the Government in the middle of last century, and had to be bought out at a high price when it no longer kept pace with the growth of the city. The works are now entirely in municipal hands and the principal supply is derived from deep wells at Tegel and at the Müggel Lake, the former on the Havel and the latter on the Spree. These sources are no longer sufficient, however, and water is being taken from the Müggel Lake itself until the completion of two new works now in progress at the Heiligen Lake and Wuhlheide.

The rivers and lakes are an important source of supply for the towns situated on the North German plain generally. On the other hand, many towns in the hilly districts of West, Central, and South Germany obtain their water from large reservoirs formed by barrages thrown across narrow valleys, whereby the double purpose of water supply and motive power can be served simultaneously. Thus the Ruhr Valley Water Board obtains water from eleven barrages, and supplies a number of communes. Not infrequently the rural communes join for the construction of large waterworks; and in one part of Saxony as many as 85 small communes own a joint undertaking. In Prussia small communes with limited resources are helped in their water schemes by the Circle Governments, which sometimes make grants-in-aid and for a few years pay the interest upon the capital expended, while the grouping of rural communes for the construction of waterworks is common.

In Würtemberg the Government both advises local authori-

TRADING ENTERPRISES

ties and helps them financially. A noteworthy instance of the reinforcement of local by State action occurred at Stuttgart in 1910. For some years the water supply of this town had been inadequate, and as the municipality was unable to carry out a favourite project of its own the Government made an independent examination of other sites, and having found a suitable supply secured the rights over 1300 acres of gathering ground and announced that with or without co-operation of Stuttgart it intended to carry out a large water scheme for that town and a number of others at a cost of over three-quarters of a million pounds. When finished the works will either be bought by the communes affected or the State will retain them and charge interest on the outlay ; in neither case will the State seek to make a profit.

Water dues or rates in German towns are usually levied either according to the quantity of water which passes through the meter, or the rental value of the entire house or of the separate dwellings it contains. Where the charge is based on the rent it usually forms a percentage, e.g., 2 and 3 per cent., according as the house is a small or a large one, with in some cases a reduction for business premises. Thus at Karlsruhe the charge is 2s. 6d. for every £5 of rent, representing a rate of 2½ per cent. Elsewhere the charge is per tap, e.g., 5s. as at Freiburg. Another method is to charge for each room in the house or the separate tenements respectively, independently of the rental value, the charge being differentiated according to the character of the premises, and a cruder method is to charge according to the superficial area of the rooms, regard being had here likewise to the type of house. Some towns, however, only supply by meter. If the rate is levied on the entire house in one sum the owner pays it in the first instance and divides it amongst the tenants, with or without an addition ; if it is levied on the separate dwellings the tenants pay direct, though working-class dwellings are often let at a rent which includes the charge. Tenants in general object to this collective arrangement, inasmuch as it enables a landlord to restrict the use of water unduly, and to charge more than he actually pays. Frankfort-on-Main, Cassel, and other towns supply water for domestic purposes free to small dwellings rented up to £12 10s. a year, and in a large number of towns such dwellings are supplied at a reduced rate.

The consumption of water is a valuable index of social as well as of hygienic progress, and it is significant that this shows each year a steady increase. In 1910 the average consumption per inhabitant in 75 of the largest towns (with an aggregate population of 15¼ millions) was 25¼ gallons per diem. The highest consumption was over 44 gallons in six towns only, while 25 towns had a consumption above and 50 towns one below the average.

TRAMWAYS AND TRANSPORT.—The provision of transport facilities is regarded by the modern German town as belonging exclusively to its province. Many of the tramways constructed in the tertiary era of street traction were private undertakings, and some of these had to be bought at great cost—as at Cologne, Düsseldorf, and Frankfort-on-Main—before they could be electrified under communal management. The first municipal tramway undertaking was that of Düsseldorf, dating from 1892. Between that year and 1900 many other towns either bought up existing companies or built their own tramways, and to-day public enterprise holds the field.

Germany may be said to have gone over from horse to electric traction almost at a step, without passing through the intervening stage of steam. The first electric tramway to be constructed in Germany was that at Halle, dating from 1894. In that year the total length of electric line in Germany was 64 miles; in 1911 there were 2700 miles. The number of municipal undertakings in 1912 was 132, 95 of these being in Prussia. The largest of the municipal tramway systems are now those of Dresden with a length of 72 miles, Munich 58 miles, Frankfort-on-Main 53 miles, Cologne 50 miles, Düsseldorf 47 miles, Nuremberg 24 miles, and Chemnitz 23 miles.

On the whole the towns which own and work tramway systems have laid more stress upon the provision of ample and efficient transport services than upon securing large profits. The fares are, as a rule, moderate and cause little complaint. There are two systems of rates: the uniform fare and the zone or sectional system. In Berlin, Bremen, and

Leipzig a fare of 10 pfennige (1¼d.) is charged for any distance, while Düsseldorf, Frankfort-on-Main, Mannheim, and Freiburg-in-Baden have tried and abandoned this system. The sectional system is now almost general. The minimum charge is 1¼d. for about 2½ miles, rising by about ½d. a mile to a maximum which seldom exceeds 2½d. even when the lines run far out into the suburbs. Cheap workmen's and scholars' season tickets (either weekly or monthly) are common, and less cheap season tickets for the public generally are issued in some towns. As a rule, workmen's tickets cost 6d. a week for two journeys a day, but are only available during the early hours and in the evening, and sometimes by special cars. Single-decked cars are universal in Germany; apart from the German objection to the cumbrous double-decked cars from the standpoint of appearance the smaller cars are found to facilitate a quicker service and to entail less cost in the wear and tear of track.

In Berlin, urban and suburban traffic is divided between the street tramways, underground and elevated railways in private hands, and the State Metropolitan and Circular Railways. Berlin is wonderfully well governed, but in the application to trading enterprises of the principle of municipalisation it has so far lagged behind, true to the individualistic traditions which its rulers imbibed from a now obsolete form of political Liberalism. The error of the old policy of abstention is frankly acknowledged by the municipality, however, and for some years energetic measures have been taken with a view to repairing the mischief which that policy brought in its train.

In no department of municipal government has the mistake of handing over valuable public monopolies to private capitalists inflicted such harm on the community as in that of transport. Until several years ago the city of Berlin did not own a single mile of tramways, though the municipal area was intersected in every direction by tramways, the owners of which have made enormous profits. Unfortunately for the city's finances also, a large part of the in-and-out traffic between the city and the suburbs, and even of the urban traffic, falls to the Metropolitan and Circular Railways. In 1912 no fewer than 156,000,000 local passengers were carried by these railways, which the Government was shrewd enough to get hold of more than thirty years ago, while the city fathers slept. Now, however, a new spirit has come over the City Council and Executive. Municipal enterprise is no longer taboo; two tramway lines have already been built by the city, there are more to follow, and it is now engaged in constructing two underground railways, following the streets from north to south and from north-west to south-east respectively, at an estimated cost of some seven million pounds. Both the prosperity of the companies and its own success in transport enterprise justify the city in adopting a bold forward policy. The city's two tramway lines, with a length of 21 miles, carried 22,000,000 passengers in 1912 and out of receipts of £101,480 yielded net profits of £32,290, equal to 14 per cent. of the capital, after allowances for depreciation.

While, however, Berlin has in the past left the construction and working of tramways and railways to companies, it has made its consent to the use of the streets dependent upon the payment of rents or royalties, an arrangement which secures to the city a substantial yearly revenue. These royalties are, of course, independent of the local taxes which transport companies have to pay like other companies and private individuals, viz., income-tax, trade or occupation tax, land and building tax, etc., which correspond to local rates in England. Thus in the year 1912-13 the receipts of the municipality of Berlin from nine tramway, overhead and underground railway, and omnibus companies in taxes, royalties, and shares in profits (exclusive of all payments on account of street and track maintenance) were as follows: income tax, £14,818; trade-tax, £10,160; royalties, £165,005; shares in profits, £56,373; total, £246,356, equal to nearly 2s. 6d. a head of the entire population.

Not only so, but the municipality has inserted in all agreements a clause reserving to it the right of purchase. Such a clause was in the agreement under which the powerful Greater Berlin Tramway Company, which carries over 80 per cent. of the tramway traffic of Berlin, worked until 1911. That agreement secured to the company a municipal concession until 1919, when the undertaking was to pass into the hands of the municipality. The city's expectations were, however, thwarted in a way which to English minds will appear incomprehensible. Under the Prussian Local (Light) Railway Act the consent of the Government is first necessary to the construction of tramways, and it is possible for this permission to be given without the assent and against the will of the local authorities. It is even possible for the Government to override agreements concluded between transport companies and the local authorities by granting concessions over the heads of the mayor, executive, and town council. This is what happened in Berlin. While its agreement had still some years to run the tramway company went to the Government with a request for the prolongation of the requisite State assent until 1949, and without communicating with the municipal authority the Government granted it. Naturally the city was not disposed to accept this rebuff humbly, and had not a compromise been proposed the matter would in due time have been fought to the bitter end in the law courts. This compromise secured to the company a continuation of its virtual monopoly of the streets, yet on terms more favourable to the city.

A glance at the main provisions of the document will show how tightly a German municipality controls private enterprises of this kind. The agreement will have force until December 31, 1939. Under it the company renounces the State concession obtained for the ten years 1939 to 1949, undertakes not to apply to the Government for the extension of the present sanction, and agrees to pay to the municipality a lump sum of £1,150,000 by way of solatium and of consideration for the new permit. The company agrees to bear the cost of all street works which become necessary owing to its undertaking and of all alterations, renewals, etc., caused by the same, also of paving for a distance of one foot on either side of each rail. Further, it agrees to contribute towards the cost of certain street extensions and improvements carried out or to be carried out by the city. All services and fares, all the general conditions of traffic (in so far as they are not regulated by the police authority), such as the type of car, provisions for lighting, warming, etc., are subject to the approval of the municipality. There will as hitherto be a uniform fare of 10 pfennige or 1¼d. for any distance, but this rate may be revised on the requisition of either side to the agreement at intervals of ten years, and from January 1, 1920, the company may be allowed to charge 15 pfennige (1¾d.) for distances longer than 5 kilometres (about 3 miles) and 20 pfennige (2½d.) for distances exceeding 6¼ miles. (At present it is possible to travel 12 miles for 1¼d.) The company undertakes to issue cheap season, scholars', and workmen's tickets on such lines as may be prescribed by the municipal authority. It also undertakes if required to carry the street and house refuse of the city by night in return for a " moderate payment," and to transport corpses to the cemetery if the city should in future act as undertaker, as many German towns already do. In the interest of convenience of traffic the company is required to connect up with other lines and within limits to allow to the latter running powers. The company can only increase its capital with the consent of the municipality.

In return for permission to use the streets the company must pay to the city 8 per cent. of the gross receipts (increasing to 10 per cent. if and when fares are raised beyond the uniform 1¼d.) in respect of all lines upon streets for whose maintenance the city is responsible. In addition, whenever the divisible profits exceed 12 per cent. of a share capital of £1,143,750 and 6 per cent. of the remaining capital, the company must pay to the city one-half of the excess, and when the profits exceed 10 per cent. of the entire capital the city takes two-thirds of the excess. The city reserves the right to take over the entire undertaking on January 1 of the years 1920, 1930, 1935, and 1940, by giving the prescribed notice to that effect, the price being fixed at 25 times the average dividend distributed to the shareholders out of ordinary profits during the preceding seven years, excluding the year of maximum and that of minimum profits. If the share capital has been increased the dividend upon the old and new capital will be averaged separately. There is the proviso, however, that if the right of purchase should be exercised on January 1, 1920, the price shall be in no case less than 200 per cent. or more than 250 per cent. of the share capital. On the other hand, if the city does not decide to take over the undertaking until January 1, 1940, it may then acquire the permanent way and appurtenances, the land and buildings belonging to the tramways, and the rolling stock, either at their book value (less 40 per cent. in the case of the permanent way) or on a valuation.

In 1912 this company, working with a capital of £5,041,000, carried 463,300,000 passengers, and had receipts of £2,207,400 from passenger traffic. Its profits were sufficient to allow of the distribution of £425,350 in a dividend of 8½ per cent. Besides paying £47,160 in " welfare " expenditure (insurance contributions, grants to special pension funds, special bonuses, etc.), it paid £47,200 in taxes of various kinds (taxes corresponding to the State income tax and local rates in this country), and for the privilege of using the streets it paid to the communes affected, though mainly to Berlin, the handsome sum of £165,330 in " pavement rents or royalties," and in addition it handed over to Berlin the sum of £55,920 (against £68,960 in 1911) as its special share of the profits.

As with the tramway so with the other transport companies of Berlin—permission is given to use the streets, but a fair consideration is exacted for the privilege. Thus under its agreement with the city, running until 1987, the Elevated and Underground Railway Company has to pay to the municipal treasury by way of royalties for way-leaves, etc., 2 per cent. of its gross revenue up to £50,000, 2¼ per cent. on a gross revenue of from £50,000 to £56,250, 2½ per cent. on from £56,250 to £62,500, and ¼ per cent. extra for every additional £6250 of revenue, while in the event of its net profits exceeding in any year 6 per cent. of the share capital half of the excess goes to the city. The agreement gives to the city the right to buy the undertaking as at November 5, 1927, and thereafter at intervals of ten years, and binds the company not to increase its fares for ten years if wages have not advanced by at least 15 per cent. during that period. The agreements under which concessions have been granted to other transport companies follow the same lines.

Two aspects of the local transport problem which are receiving attention to-day in all the great centres of population are the increase of facilities for reaching the suburban districts and the provision of inter-urban tramways. The old idea of the tramway as merely a cheap and expeditious means of travelling from one part of a town to another has been abandoned owing to the spread of population outward, the growing tendency to incorporate rural suburbs, the removal of industrial works to the open country, and the extension by the larger towns of their land-purchase schemes to extra-communal areas, suitable for development as building land. The extent of the in-and-out traffic which has to be carried by the Berlin transport systems may be judged from the fact that over 100,000 persons travel to and fro between the city and the suburbs every day. Hence the old street tramway has in many places grown into a large system of lines stretching out into the country in all directions, and tendencies point to further developments on the same lines.

On the other hand, the ordinary railways, with their limited services and higher fares, have proved insufficient for the needs of populous districts where town joins on to town almost without intermission. This need for quicker means of continuous communication between adjacent towns has led to the formation in the industrial districts of West Germany of multi-communal companies for the joint construction and working of tramways and light railways serving wide areas. Such are the Rhenish-Westphalian Railway Company of Düsseldorf and the Upper Rhenish Railway Company of Mannheim. In some cases the Circle (*Kreis*) Diets have stepped in and constructed and worked tramways intended to carry inter-urban traffic. Not infrequently enterprises of the kind are opposed by the State, which, as the owner of the railways, is jealous of competition and regards with disfavour every extension of the inter-urban tramway system. For a long time some of the largest towns of Rhineland-Westphalia, from Düsseldorf to Dortmund, have vainly endeavoured to obtain consent to the construction of a series of lines intended to connect these two towns and to bring them into communication with the intervening industrial centres. The railway legislation of Prussia (July 28, 1892) does indeed leave to communes, other local government bodies, and corporations the construction of what are called " small " or light railways, to which class of lines tramways belong, but State sanction is necessary even to the building of a tramway by a commune though it be restricted to its own streets, and herein lies the Government's power to obstruct local enterprise. The same thing has happened in Saxony for the same reason. There likewise, the State, in general, leaves the building and working of tramways to the towns, yet, in order to protect the State railways from competition, it has constructed several local lines near Dresden, then leasing them to the municipal authority.

Should the Düsseldorf-Dortmund project be approved it is intended that there shall be thirty stations, passengers being carried in two classes of carriages by a ten-minute service, and a speed of between 30 and 40 miles an hour is promised. The scheme is expected to cost five million pounds, but most of the towns affected have already undertaken to subscribe their proportionate shares of the necessary capital.

For the purpose of securing efficient transport facilities for their populations and of obtaining a controlling influence, some of the large municipalities have acquired a share-interest in the local tramway systems worked by companies. Düsseldorf owns shares in the Rhenish Railway Company to the value of £307,500 (out of a total capital of £500,000) and has invested £640,000 in tramway undertakings of all kinds ; nearly all the shares of the Barmen Bergbahn Actiengesellschaft are held by the municipality of Barmen ; the city of Lübeck has invested £25,000 in a company formed for the construction and working of a light railway from that place to some of the Baltic Sea bathing resorts ; Cologne has invested £905,000 in tramways, and Dortmund £436,000.

Isolated experiments in railless electrical traction have been made, but as yet without decided success. The municipality of Munich in 1911 gave a concession to a company formed for the working of railless motor-bus services between the city and the suburbs. The municipality receives 25 per cent. of the net profits, it has the sole right to supply the current needed, and it reserves the power to take over the undertaking on payment of twelve times the average net profits of the last three working years, in addition to a sum diminishing from £2500 to £500 according to the time that elapses before this power is exercised. A similar experiment has been tried at Mülhausen in Alsace. A short time ago a municipal omnibus service was instituted at Neukölln, near Berlin, but as soon as the tramway company undertook to extend its lines the town sold out. Many towns, however, maintain regular suburban omnibus services, and a far larger number subsidise private undertakings of the kind.

DOCKS AND QUAYS.—The German idea that towns should be managed like business concerns has caused municipal authorities to devote great attention and expenditure to the development of their water communications. Towns that do not lie upon a river are ambitious to connect themselves with one by means of a canal; if so situated, they seek communication with the sea. Hence such towns are prepared to spend enormous sums and to pledge their resources and credit for decades in the development of natural and artificial waterways and the construction and improvement of their dock facilities. Cologne, Düsseldorf, Duisburg-Ruhrort, Mannheim, Ludwigshafen, and Strassburg on the Rhine, Hamburg, Magdeburg, and Dresden on the Elbe, Bremen on the Weser, Breslau and Stettin on the Oder, with Berlin linked to that river by its tributary the Spree, are examples of towns which have shown a keen appreciation of the importance of water communications and have invested money freely in the provision of large and well-equipped docks, provided with all necessary warehouses. Emden, at the mouth of the Ems, owes its remarkable growth entirely to the far-sighted policy of the municipality which saw in the completion of the Dortmund and Ems canal the opportunity for converting Emden into a great North Sea port.

An inquiry made by the Central Office of the German Municipal Congress in 1911 relating to the measures adopted by 113 towns for the furtherance of trade and industry elicited the fact that 27 of these towns had constructed docks equipped with extensive quays, warehouses, railways, electric cranes, and all other necessary auxiliaries. The inland towns which had done most to develop their river advantages and traffic were Mannheim, Breslau, Dortmund, Karlsruhe, Frankfort-on-Main, Offenbach, Bamberg, Würzburg, and Worms.

Often the construction of docks has been part of a great scheme of industrial development. Mannheim, Bremen, Frankfort-on-Main, Emden, and many other towns have purchased large areas of land adjacent to their docks and by selling it on easy terms have attracted new industries and trades. The inquiry made by the Central Office of the Municipal Congress showed that nearly half of the 113 municipal authorities questioned had acquired land for industrial purposes and had systematically offered it to capitalists on advantageous conditions, and that in many cases their land was in communication with the municipal docks. It appeared that in one case the town sold land at half the cost price solely with a view to attracting new industries, while in others mortgages on the land sold were accepted at a low rate of interest.

In many river ports it is the duty of the Municipal Harbour Board, besides administering the general traffic of the docks and warehouses, to promote the sale of town land for industrial purposes. Mannheim's land business is so large, however, that it has set up a special office for this purpose. The methods followed are just those which any wide-awake business man desirous of extending his connections would be likely to adopt —free advertising in likely publications, prompt replies to advertisers who are in search for sites, and judicious feelers wherever there seems a chance of success. So well has Mannheim used its natural and created advantages that a new town has arisen on the area bought by the municipality and sold again for factories, warehouses, and undertakings of many other kinds.

Berlin itself, though situated so far inland, has of late years expended large sums in dock enterprise. Thanks to the development of the rivers and canals Berlin has long been in direct water communication with Hamburg by the Havel and the Elbe, with Magdeburg by the Plauen canal, with Breslau by the Spree and Oder, and with Stettin by the Finow canal and a deep water canal now being completed. In order to make the fullest use possible of its water facilities the municipality has just constructed, at a cost of £870,000, on the right bank of the Spree, several miles from the centre of the city, a large dock known as the East Dock, with a wharfage front of 1500 yards and an area of over 20 acres, and it is about to construct a much larger West Dock on the Spandau Canal at a cost of nearly two million pounds, one-third of which will be spent in the purchase of land. The Berlin Chamber of Commerce and the Corporation of the Merchant Elders have shown their faith in the first of these projects by guaranteeing a minimum annual revenue.

FURTHERANCE OF TRADE AND INDUSTRY.—While trade and industry in general are assisted by measures of a large kind, the claims of the smaller *entrepreneurs* and the handicrafts are not overlooked. Many municipalities supply electric current at a cheap rate to small workshops and to home workers, and in some old centres of the textile trades the transition to the factory system has in consequence been retarded. Instances of public action of the kind are Pforzheim, the seat of the gold and silver trade, where the town has for this purpose constructed at a cost of £80,000 a central station worked by water power obtained from a neighbouring stream; Elberfeld, where electric power is supplied to the home weavers; and Solingen, the seat of the cutlery industry. The commune of St. Johann-Saarbrücken, in the Saar colliery district, supplies small artisans both with gas engines and electric motors, and in some cases advances money to a maximum of £300, repayable within five years, for the equipment of workshops with machinery. Many communes of the Rhineland have assisted small industries by taking shares in the establishment of a co-operative society for supply to handicraftsmen and others on favourable terms of tools, machinery, and materials. Similarly the Saxon town of Elsterberg recently gave a site worth £1250 free to a company to enable it to introduce a new industry. The small industry is assisted less directly yet no less surely by institutions formed for the purpose of bringing the handicraftsmen into contact with progressive ideas. An institution of the kind is the newly formed Institute for the Advancement of Industry created at a cost of £30,000 by the city of Cologne, assisted by the Rhine

Province, the State, and several Chambers of Commerce. Under one roof are found a technical college for young men and apprentices, training workshops, exhibition halls, testing rooms for machinery and materials, an advice and information bureau, a library, etc.

All these efforts are voluntary, and the communes are able to extend them at will. There is little, indeed, that German towns cannot do in this direction, and the fear of transgressing their powers never seems to trouble the authorities responsible for their government and welfare. Their principal statutory obligations towards trade and industry are those imposed upon them by the Imperial laws which make the communes responsible for the establishment of and maintenance of courts of industry and of commerce for the adjustment of civil disputes of certain kinds.

PUBLIC ABATTOIRS, MARKET HALLS, AND FOOD SUPPLY.—The duties of the municipal authorities in relation to the food supply do not, as a rule, include its control and inspection with a view to the prevention of adulteration and the protection of health, for this is a function of the police authority. The principal exception is meat. There are now few German towns of any importance which do not own abattoirs, often with stockyards attached. The local authorities are empowered, by the adoption of by-laws to that effect, to require butchers to use the public abattoirs and to prohibit the slaughtering in any other place of animals intended for human food. There are now in Germany about 1000 public abattoirs, 100 connected with stockyards, and only about 50 are still in the hands of Butchers' Guilds or private persons. Before the meat is allowed to enter the market it must be passed by official inspectors. Although the public abattoirs are primarily established in the interest of the public health and convenience, they are managed on business principles. The Prussian Abattoir Law of 1868 empowered the local authorities to charge for their use such fees as would cover the costs of maintenance and also of inspection, but in order to prevent the abattoirs from being regarded too much from the profit standpoint, which would have led to the indirect taxation of important articles of food, the interest on capital chargeable was limited to a maximum of 6 per cent., viz., 5 per cent. as interest and 1 per cent. for amortisation. The Communal Taxation Act of 1893 increased this rate to 8 per cent., and authorised the communes to levy higher charges on meat imported into the town and hence liable to inspection, unless it has already been inspected by official veterinaries, in which case it may be sold without passing through the abattoir.

The regulation of the open weekly markets for the sale of country produce, which are still very common in German towns even of large size, is a police function, exercised by the mayor, however, where he is appointed the State commissary for police purposes. On the other hand, where a town provides closed market halls their control remains in its own hands. These halls are found in most large towns, and are used principally for the sale of vegetables, fruit, farm produce, meat and fish—in general, for all perishable food stuffs of which daily supplies come to the town. Berlin has built fifteen of such halls, in addition to a large central wholesale market, but several have been disused owing to movement of population from the inner districts to the periphery and the suburbs. At present the municipality is erecting a second large wholesale market hall for the exclusive use of the fruit and vegetable trade. Some towns have added to their market halls large ice works for the supply of ice for their own purposes and to the public.

Stringent control is exercised by the municipal and police authorities, acting in conjunction, over the food stuffs offered for sale and the conditions under which they are sold. Many towns have their own chemical laboratories for the analysis of food stuffs, and their use by retailers and the public is encouraged in every way. Stringent regulations often apply to shops and other places of sale, and particularly to the sale of meat, milk, and bread. In Munich the regulations go so far as to prohibit the open sale of milk in the streets, or even in house entrances or courtyards.

In some States the price of bread is still regulated by the local authorities, and the prices fixed have to be displayed by all retailers. Nor are these authorities slow to use their influence in breaking down food monopolies when the public is being unfairly treated. Where, in 1910, the abolition of the octroi duties on meat (as provided for by the Imperial Customs Tariff Law of 1902) was not followed by a reduction in prices the town councils promptly called the butchers to account, and by establishing public meat markets or threatening to do so secured the result desired. Many towns have by-laws requiring butchers and other meat sellers to display in their windows or before their shops the prices of all kinds of meat, and at Stuttgart and elsewhere the prices of meat, uniform for the whole town, are fixed once a month by a joint committee representing the town council and the Butchers' Guild.

Until recent years the only important direction in which the communes directly engaged in food enterprises was in relation to milk and other farm produce. The supply of pure milk takes a foremost place amongst the measures by which the excessive mortality amongst infants is being combated in Germany, and many towns produce milk on their own farms and sell it in public depots. The whole of the milk supplied to the mothers who frequent the nine infant dispensaries of Berlin is produced at the dairies on the municipal irrigation farms and after being sterilised is distributed from 70 centres (usually schools) scattered throughout the city, and the produce of the same farms is also supplied to the city's sanatoria, orphanages, houses of correction, and to persons in receipt of outdoor relief. Dortmund has a municipal model dairy, with baths for the hinds and milkers, where milk is produced for the public hospitals. Bielefeld subsidises a co-operative dairy company and provides it with five kiosks for the sale of milk. From the depot milk is supplied in carts to the working-class districts of the town. Some of the co-operative societies and labour organisations share with the town in the cost. Mannheim has a municipal central milk depot which obtains its supplies from co-operative dairies.

Other towns, like Leipzig, Magdeburg, and Ulm, carry on dairy farming and stockbreeding on a commercial basis. Several years ago the town council of Stuttgart seriously debated the question whether the municipality should take up the retail sale of milk and cut out the middleman altogether, and it was only after the proposals made to this end had been examined by experts that it was decided to refrain from such action and, instead, to encourage the formation of co-operative associations of consumers for the purchase of milk direct from the producers.

The large administrative powers enjoyed by German municipal authorities and the fact that these powers are exercised by permanent officials who are independent of interests, and under no necessity to resort to vote-catching devices, make it possible for towns to embark at any time upon such new enterprises as circumstances may seem to call for. Hence the exceptional dearth of meat which occurred in Germany in 1911 and 1912, leading to prices which often placed this article beyond the resources of the working classes, caused many local authorities all over the country to engage directly in the business of food supply. Herein they were encouraged by the Governments, which (as in Prussia) urged them to " take steps to induce butchers to sell meat at reasonable prices, or failing this to set up their own meat depots, to obtain supplies of cheap fish and sell them in public markets, and to ensure regular and abundant supplies of vegetables and other food stuffs, so that the daily food outlay of the working classes might be reduced."

Over two hundred towns in all parts of the country concluded contracts for the supply of foreign meat, and either sold it direct to the public or arranged for its sale by butchers at agreed prices. The municipal authority of Berlin sold foreign meat in the latter way to the amount of £375,000. Although it was possible to sell the meat from 20 to 30 per cent. cheaper than fresh meat, most towns worked with a profit and few made a loss. Some towns went still further. The municipality of Offenbach-on-Main, for the time being under Socialist influence, went systematically into the meat business, opened shops, and set up a sausage manufactory; other towns began pig fattening and rabbit breeding on a large scale, or, by grants or loans, assisted co-operative societies and private individuals to do so, binding them to supply for local consumption a given amount of produce annually. Other towns concluded with Chambers of Agriculture and other farmers' organisations contracts for the supply of definite quantities of meat at fixed times. In many towns the mere threat of such municipal competition induced the butchers to moderate their demands.

A still larger number of town councils further relieved the shortness of the meat supply at that time by purchasing sea fish and selling it as nearly as possible at cost price. In most places the fish was sold direct to the public, and the popularity of fish as an article of diet was increased in many towns by classes for instruction in fish cookery arranged by the same authorities. Almost as common was the sale at public depots of potatoes and vegetables at cost price. The municipality of Barmen in 1913 began the cultivation of vegetables on a commercial basis on an area of six acres of town land.

Although these municipal experiments in food purveying have continued since, sufficient experience has not yet been gained to prove the permanent utility of public action of the kind. It was established, however, that the towns were able to carry on undertakings of the kind described without loss and with undoubted advantage to large sections of the population. Inquiries made by the Berlin Statistical Office in sixty-two important towns showed that in sixty of these towns, with a combined population of over fifteen millions, the authorities had in 1911 and 1912 organised a meat supply in order to relieve the prevailing scarcity and counteract the high prices. Meat had been imported from Russia, Holland, Servia, Roumania, and Bulgaria, and the conclusion was drawn that while it was impossible to prove by figures that municipal competition in the meat trade had reduced prices, it had unquestionably had the effect of preventing the butchers from exploiting the needs of the moment as much as they might otherwise have done. Many of the arrangements devised to meet a temporary emergency have now been placed on a permanent basis, and it is probable that German towns will in no distant future add to their other enterprises practical measures for making certain branches of the food supply independent of the interest and convenience of private traders.

MUNICIPAL SAVINGS BANKS.—There are municipal banks in two German towns only, Breslau and Chemnitz; but few towns, even of small size, are without municipal savings banks, which exist in the main for the encouragement of thrift, but also for the purpose of increasing the credit facilities of the local authorities themselves. Many of these banks have a large cheque business. Although created originally as welfare institutions in the interest of small depositors, the savings banks have far outgrown their first purposes, and they are now largely used by the lower middle class, shopkeepers, artisans, small officials, and the like. Hence it is a fallacious idea that the deposits in these local banks represent working-class savings or can in any way serve as a standard of working-class thrift or well-being. An analysis of the 102,800 depositors in the Königsberg municipal savings bank made in 1909 showed that the working classes and persons corresponding to them in social condition were represented by only 30 per cent. of the depositors and 28 per cent. of the total savings. The wide scope of the operations of these banks is reflected by the growing tendency to extend the limits of individual accounts. Many banks only accept deposits up to £50 in any one name, though allowing several accounts to run in the names of different members of a family; but a larger limit is usual; the Berlin and Munich banks accept individual deposits up to £150, other banks go as far as £250 and £500, and some impose no limit at all. The usual rate of interest is from 3 to 3½ per cent.

A large part of the money lent by these banks goes in financing the administrative work and trading enterprises of the town. Some towns have been enabled to pursue an energetic land and housing policy owing to the resources placed at their disposal by the savings banks, from whose funds loans are often made to building societies. As showing the large operations of the more important municipal savings banks it may be stated that the accumulated funds of the banks of 55 large towns amounted in 1910 to 171¾ million pounds. The Berlin savings bank alone receives deposits to the aggregate amount of over three million pounds per annum, and has accumulated deposits to the amount of over fifteen million pounds.

Great efforts are made by the local authorities to popularise their savings banks and to make it easy for working-class households to invest even the smallest sums. In many towns branches of the savings bank are carried on in connection with the elementary schools, and in others—Munich, Bremen, Schöneberg, etc.—deposits of any amount are collected once a week at the homes of the depositors, without charge. Home saving is also encouraged by means of boxes, stamps, and even automatic machines. Some town councils or school authorities present every child born in the commune with a savings bank book in which the sum of one or two shillings is credited to the holder.

The laws of the various States differ in their provisions relating to the application of savings bank profits. In general these profits have to be used for purposes of a philanthropic character lying outside the statutory obligations of the communal authorities, and some laws state expressly that they must be applied " for the benefit of the poor." Nevertheless, many towns systematically use the savings bank surpluses for ordinary public purposes, like school building, or transfer them direct to the common account. Even when the surpluses are used " for the benefit of the poor " the effect in most cases is simply to relieve the general taxes.

The communal savings bank system of Saxony is particularly well developed, and in many towns large annual surpluses are shown. Begun originally from motives of philanthropy, the banks have grown into credit institutions of the highest importance, for they serve not only the working classes but the middle classes and the communes themselves, which are able to borrow from them on a large scale and by means of the surpluses realised to help many objects which cannot properly be aided from the rates. The number of accounts in 1910 was 67 for every 100 inhabitants, whereas the ratio for all Germany was 30, for Prussia 35, for Bavaria 15, and for Würtemberg 31. While the average deposits in the public savings banks of Germany as a whole were £12 6s. a head of the population, and the average for Prussia £13 11s., for Bavaria £4 8s., and for Würtemberg £10 13s., the average for Saxony was £17 17s. Deposits are received to a maximum amount of £250 in any one account and the interest paid is usually 3½ per cent. There are small communes in Saxony in which the savings bank yields in profits a larger amount than the local taxes, and a return from this source of from 10s. to 20s. a head of the inhabitants is not uncommon. Many of the communes devote a portion of the savings bank surpluses to church and school building, but more generally grants are made to philanthropic and social welfare objects.

MORTGAGE AND RENT-CHARGE BANKS.—Many towns have established mortgage and rent-charge banks or loan funds for the purpose of advancing money to land and house owners and contractors to enable them to build and to develop their property. This is a comparatively recent form of municipal enterprise and has been resorted to owing to the increasing difficulty with which private individuals who needed money for building purposes had to contend so long as they were dependent upon the ordinary credit facilities. No less than 38 towns—for the most part in Prussia—are known to have mortgage banks or funds which make advances for building, while eight of these towns and thirteen others have rent-charge banks and funds which advance money for improvements, such as drainage, water supply, and pavement works. The towns which have assigned the largest funds to this purpose are Dresden with £4,310,000, Düsseldorf with £2,081,000, Neukölln with £3,050,000, and Aix-la-Chapelle with £1,000,000. Up to 1911, 33 towns had lent money on mortgage to the amount of £7,875,000, while eleven towns had lent £800,000 for improvement works, the loans in this case being repayable, as a rule, in yearly instalments spread over a short period.

Money is lent on first mortgage to the extent of from 60 to 75 per cent. of the value of the property, and on second mortgage to the extent of 80 per cent., but in this case conditionally on repayment within a fixed period, and the usual rates of interest are from 3½ to 4½ per cent., and from 5 to 6 per cent. respectively. Some towns give loans on second mortgage only in respect of small dwellings intended for persons of limited means. Charlottenburg lends money on mortgage by means of a mortgage bank association formed with a municipal guarantee to the amount of a million pounds. Any house-owner of the town may join on paying an entrance fee of £25, and after a year he will be entitled to borrow so far as the available funds permit.

There is reason to believe, however, that in some cases the mortgage banks have been formed for the special purpose of stimulating building operations in the interest of town extension, and that in general these banks, without careful guarantees, may simply play into the hands of the speculative land companies and builders, who are sufficiently mischievous already. Hence the Prussian Government, in a circular letter issued in February, 1912, urged local authorities to insist upon the systematic redemption of all loans, failing which house property would inevitably become more encumbered with debt than it is at present.

These are not the only or the principal ways in which municipal authorities assist local building enterprise and exercise a steadying influence upon the money market. Other measures adopted to the same end are the loan of money on mortgage from the accumulated funds of the municipal savings banks, and from funds belonging to charitable foundations under municipal management, the lease of municipal land and the advance of money on mortgage in respect of it, loans on special conditions to " public utility " building societies formed for the erection of small dwellings, and the giving of surety for loans obtained by such societies from other sources.

In 1913 the Municipal Statistical Office of Munich published an interesting report on the operations of German towns on all these lines.[1] It showed that 223 municipal savings banks had lent money on first mortgage to the amount of £155,556,000 and 45 banks on second mortgage to the amount of £10,423,000, the usual rate of interest being from $4\frac{1}{4}$ to $4\frac{3}{4}$ per cent., while 16 towns had lent a further £1,008,000 from charitable and other funds, chiefly for the building of small dwellings. Thirty-nine towns had leased land to building and garden town societies and private persons, and twelve had advanced £426,000 on mortgage in respect of the buildings erected thereon. Forty-three towns had advanced together £1,085,000 in loans on mortgage to building and co-operative societies

[1] " Die Wirksamkeit der deutschen Stadtgemeinden auf dem Gebiete des Realkredits," Munich, 1913.

formed for the erection of small dwellings, the usual rates of interest ranging from 3 to 4 per cent. The towns which had made the largest loans for this purpose were Munich with £465,000, Stuttgart £205,000, Freiburg-in-Baden £65,900, Hamburg £59,000, Breslau £21,750, Eisenach £25,750, and Essen £25,000. Finally, 65 towns had become surety for other advances made to these societies, chiefly by the Statutory Pension Boards, to the amount of £2,290,000. The largest guarantees were undertaken by Frankfort-on-Main, viz., £305,600, followed by Essen £245,700, Leipzig £185,000, Neuss £154,600, Barmen £117,500, and Bremen £100,000.

From all these financial operations the motive of immediate gain is absent, the object being rather to benefit the community indirectly by increasing credit facilities, making builders independent of the professional usurers, and enabling the growing demand for small dwellings to be sufficiently and cheaply supplied.

INSURANCE ENTERPRISES.—Many towns engage in insurance enterprises of various kinds. The principal undertaking of the kind is the municipal fire insurance society as carried on in Berlin and elsewhere. The usual method of operations is for the town to form a company for the purpose, providing all the necessary capital, carrying on the business as an ordinary public enterprise, taking all risks, and receiving all profits. Neukölln, the largest suburb of Berlin, encouraged by the latter's success, recently formed an insurance company on the same principles, beginning with the insurance of new buildings. In 1910 the total value of property insured in public insurance enterprises was £3,781,000,000, of which £3,357,000,000 represented immovable property. The year's net profits were £670,000 and the accumulated funds stood at £12,664,000.

In Westphalia a combination of communes has been formed for mutual insurance against liability for compensation for damages of all kinds. It was found that many municipalities were paying year by year in premiums to insurance companies twice, four times and in some cases ten and twenty times the amount of their actual liability, as shown by the compensation claims which had to be met by the companies. The towns of Gelsenkirchen, Herne, and Bochum have, therefore, united in an organisation known as the " Mutual Liability Association of German Towns," and it is expected that other towns will come in as soon as the financial stability of the undertaking is proved. A similar but larger organisation of German towns for mutual insurance against the consequences of accidents occurring upon their tramways has been in existence for many years. Other towns have their own general accident insurance funds. Frankfort-on-Main has had such a fund since 1888, and it is estimated that between £9000 and £10,000 was saved during the first 20 years as the result. Some towns carry foresight so far that they insure all the children attending the primary schools, with their teachers, against accident sustained while going to and from school, or while on the school premises.

MISCELLANEOUS TRADING ENTERPRISES.—Among other notable public properties are the pharmacies owned by six towns—the largest of them Breslau, Hanover, and Mayence. In the first two of these towns the pharmacies are carried on as municipal undertakings, while in the others they are leased to private individuals. In 1910 Breslau made profits of over £2000 by drug selling. A far larger number of towns have hospital pharmacies, which supply drugs and appliances for all municipal institutions. The municipality of Duisburg, in conjunction with the local Chamber of Commerce, both owns and carries on a hotel, and several Bavarian towns own hotels and restaurants. Until recently Aix-la-Chapelle carried on its famous bath as a municipal institution, and though, owing to the want of success, it has been transferred to a company, the town is interested to the extent of 70 per cent. in the company's capital.

An acceptable source of revenue to most municipalities are the pillars erected at street corners and elsewhere for the posting of bills. As a rule, the right to erect and use these pillars throughout the entire town area is leased to companies or individuals—at Chemnitz and Freiburg the town carries on the posting business *en régie*—the municipality retaining full control as to position, number, and the kind of placards permissible, but with their erection the pillars become the property of the town. The contract under which the posting pillars of Berlin are leased to a company provides that municipal and police notices shall be exhibited free of charge, all repairs and additions be made at the cost of the lessees, and the interiors of the hollow pillars, which are reached by hinged doors, be placed at the disposal of the municipal authorities, serving for the reception of street cleaning appliances, etc. When the posting pillars were introduced over 30 years ago the city was content to receive from them a revenue of £250 ; under the contract concluded in 1911 it will receive £27,750 a year for twelve years from this source. The convenient and not unsightly public posting pillars enable the authorities to obviate much of the ugliness inseparable from hoardings.

THE EXECUTION OF PUBLIC WORKS: *RÉGIE* VERSUS CONTRACT.—The question of the extent to which public works should be executed by contract or *en régie* is a constant source of controversy on municipal bodies on which the Labour party has secured a voice and influence. The relative advantages of the two systems were severely contested, however, long before the Labour party arrived. At all times the towns have executed with their own staff of workpeople a large amount of work which is unsuited to be given out to contractors. Aix-la-Chapelle is specially noteworthy amongst the towns which have gone beyond this negative principle and kept as much work as possible in their own hands. The *régie* system was introduced there just over 20 years ago, and for a time was confined to street and road maintenance. Before that time work was done by contract, and the results both as to quality and cost were so unsatisfactory that the town decided to have all such work done henceforth by its own men. Experience justified the decision, and other branches of public work have been added since—all cartage, scavenging, and the like. There is a large provision for stores, which are under the control of the municipal surveyor and his assistants. Many towns have special Stores Offices (*Materialämter*) whose sole duty it is to purchase materials and stores needed by the various departments. One of the best of such offices is that of Mannheim, which has existed for many years. The whole of the building materials, furniture, books and stationery, and requisites of all kinds required for the municipal service pass through the office, whose business it is to test the quality of all goods received and dispose of old stores which are no longer suitable for use. Before the beginning of the financial year each department sends in an estimate of its probable needs, and the office buys in the manner it thinks most expedient.

In the giving out of work the three methods of open public contracting, limited contracting (i.e., competition between invited firms), and private treaty are followed, each according to the character of the work to be done, but public contracting predominates in the case of large transactions. An effective form of local protection is very common, especially in regard to work which can be done or goods which can be supplied as well by resident tradesmen as by outsiders; while many local authorities divide their work as much as possible with a view to enabling the small handicraftsmen to share. There is no general rule of accepting the lowest tender. The wide range which is notoriously shown by competitive tenders led the municipality of Mannheim to give work on the " mean price " principle in the case of certain contracts; that is, the mean of all tenders was taken and offers deviating by more than 20 per cent. from the figure so arrived at were at once rejected. The plan was abandoned after two years' trial, and Elberfeld similarly adopted and abandoned it. At Barmen the cost of any given work is estimated by a committee of experts, and only tenders that approximate to the estimate are considered.

In spite of all the care taken to secure honest dealing, rings of contractors are not uncommon and are difficult to circumvent. A ring discovered too late in a suburb of Berlin not long ago cost the ratepayers on a single contract £7500. The bribery of minor officials is rare, but it happens at times, and the municipality of Berlin has found it necessary to insert in agreements with contractors a clause binding them to pay a heavy fine on proof of any practice of the kind. There is no general rule resting on statute or by-law disqualifying members of town councils from tendering for or executing public works. Such a disqualification is regarded as wholesome, however, and some towns enforce it in the case of work which is not submitted to open competition.

The "standard rate" clause has an equivalent in the provision introduced in contracts by some municipal bodies requiring contractors to pay rates of wages not lower than those fixed by collective agreements, should they exist, or otherwise be recognised as usual in the trades affected, while a few towns, as in France, schedule the actual rates to be paid in the contracts. This recognition of "standard" or "fair" wages rates is far from general, however, though the communes have accepted the principle on a larger scale than the State in its dealings with contractors.

MUNICIPAL WORKPEOPLE : CONDITIONS OF EMPLOYMENT.—The large extent to which the towns have embarked in trading enterprises has swelled the army of communal workpeople to a force estimated at over 160,000. Often the town is the largest of local employers and sets the level of wages and the standard of labour conditions. Berlin leads, for it employs in its various undertakings over 18,000 workpeople, but it is followed closely by Hamburg with over 15,000 ; Breslau, Cologne, Dresden, Frankfort-on-Main, and Munich employ between 5000 and 6000, and Bremen, Chemnitz, Düsseldorf, Leipzig, Magdeburg, Mannheim, Stuttgart, Danzig, and Darmstadt employ between 2000 and 3000 ; while 20 other towns employ over 1000, and 50 more employ over 500. On the whole, two-thirds of the communal workpeople are unskilled.

The great majority of communal workpeople labour under the formal disadvantage that the Imperial Industrial Code does not apply to them ; to that extent they are deprived of the protection given to industrial workers by certain useful regulations relating to the limitation of the hours of labour, the general conditions of employment, factory inspection, and other matters. For the same reason the communal authorities are exempted from the obligation to issue works regulations such as are required in the case of all factories and workshops in which, as a rule, at least 20 workers are employed.[1] Nevertheless, many communal authorities have voluntarily adopted rules of the kind setting forth in the utmost detail the conditions of employment, the scale of remuneration, the pension and other benefit arrangements, if any, to which workpeople can look forward, and the like.

Many social reformers contend that a municipality should pay better wages than private employers, inasmuch as its trading enterprises are nearly all of a monopolist character and in any case are rarely subject to effectual competition. On the whole the difference is probably very slight, and is favourable to municipal labour in one town and unfavourable in another. If, however, as the labour organisations assert, the towns pay somewhat below the standard of the best private employers, there must in fairness be set against this fact the advantages of fairly continuous employment, and often of certain valuable subsidiary benefits rarely enjoyed by industrial workers in private service. Not only so, but municipalities as a rule show themselves very willing to meet, as far as circumstances will allow, any reasonable demands made by their employees where inferior rates of payment and other exceptional conditions can be shown to exist. It is not unusual to require employees to serve for a term of years varying from one to ten before they gain the status and come into enjoyment of the benefits of "permanent communal workpeople."

Where the rates of wages are in continual flux and where the hours of labour differ so greatly it would serve no useful purpose to quote illustrations, though the annual reports of the Federation of Communal and State Workpeople contain comprehensive and reliable data on the subject. It may be said, however, that minimum rates are laid down by many municipalities, and that most apply a graduated scale to the

[1] These regulations must show the hours of beginning and ending work, the intervals for meals, and the mode of calculating and the time of paying wages, the period necessary to giving notice, and the conditions under which no notice is required; fines of all kinds, the reasons for the same, and the purposes to which they are applied. Before such regulations can be issued or altered all employees of age must be given an opportunity of expressing their opinion regarding them, or if a workmen's committee exists that committee may be heard instead.

S

principal departments, rising according to years of service. Some towns pay married men higher wages than single, and in addition give an allowance in respect of children under 14, 15, or even 16 years. Thus the municipality of Charlottenburg gives its workpeople, like its other employees of all ranks, family supplements to their agreed pay, beginning with four children. In the case of workmen 5 per cent. extra wages is paid where there are four children and 10 per cent. where there are five, up to a maximum of £15; 15 per cent. where there are six, with a maximum of £22 10s.; and 20 per cent. where there are more than six, with a maximum of £30. In the case of officials there are fixed rates of £7 10s., £15, £22 10s., and £30 in the four cases named. Here and there grants are made in aid of rent to enable workpeople to take dwellings proportionate to the size of their families. As a rule, 25 per cent. extra is paid for all ordinary overtime, and from 25 to 50 per cent. extra for night and Sunday work. Some municipalities allow their workpeople to use the tramways free in going to and from work.

An eight-hours day is worked by gas-workers in many towns, and here and there by workpeople employed in other undertakings or departments; a day of nine hours is more common; while the general range of hours is from 8 to 12 in summer and from 7 to 12 in winter, shorter time being as a rule worked when the shift system prevails and where the conditions of employment are specially arduous.

Hitherto the communal authorities have refused to conclude wages agreements with their workpeople on the lines now common in the building and allied trades. The objection to the wages agreement is probably dictated less by fear of extravagant claims than by indisposition to bargain with the trade unions. On the other hand, many of them require contractors as a condition of receiving public contracts both to pay the rates of wages and work the hours fixed in local agreements concluded for their trades.

The most important of the special benefits granted by many towns to their workpeople, as a part of their " social welfare " work, are the extra allowances in sickness beyond the provision made by the statutory insurance organisations, and the retirement pensions. Many municipalities pay to workpeople on the sick list the whole difference between the sickness insurance pay and the normal wages, though often this is due only after the lapse of a certain number of days of absence, varying from three to thirty. Other towns pay wages during the time occupied by military service in the reserve, and on public holidays. Some towns, like Frankfort and Düsseldorf, provide a sickness insurance and maternity benefit for the wives of workmen, either without charge or on the payment of half the cost.

Retirement and disablement grants supplementing the statutory provision are given in many towns, generally without contributions, and pensions to widows and orphans are also common. These retirement pensions are usually given only after ten years of service and on the attainment of the age of 30 or more years, and the allowance usually varies from a minimum of 25 per cent. of the wages to a maximum of 75 per cent.

Annual leave, with wages, is now given very commonly, and soon it will be the rule. The holidays allowed vary from three to twelve working days in the year, but a waiting time of from one year to five years of service is often required to qualify for the boon. Some towns not only pay wages, but give in addition a bonus ranging from 10 to 30 per cent., according to the years of service, by way of contribution towards the costs of travel.

Statistics published in 1913 by the Federation of Communal and State Workpeople show that, as far as can be ascertained, 307 towns grant summer holidays, 123 pay the difference between sickness insurance pay and wages in times of illness, 147 pay wages during short absences and annual periods of military service, 98 pay wages on public holidays, 29 grant family bonuses, 124 pay retirement pensions, 111 make provision for survivors, and 9 contribute to special pension funds. Finally, as has been stated in the chapter dealing with housing, many of the larger towns provide dwellings at a low rent for a portion of their workpeople and other employees, particularly those whose employment requires that they should have a settled address.

CHAPTER X

RELIEF OF THE POOR

Characteristics of the German poor relief system—Organisation of the poor relief authority—The Elberfeld system of poor relief—Character of assistance given—Assistance in return for work—Forced labour houses for workshies and loafers—Cost of poor relief in German towns.

THE relief of the poor is one of the statutory obligations imposed upon communal authorities by Imperial legislation, supplemented by State statutes. Now that Bavaria has abandoned its particularist traditions and the French system has been abolished in Alsace-Lorraine the Imperial laws apply equally to the whole Empire. The main principle of the German Poor Law is that destitute persons must be relieved in the first instance by the commune in which they become destitute, subject to the right of this commune to call upon the commune of settlement or persons liable to refund the cost. Each State determines by its own laws how much or how little shall be connoted by the term " poor relief." In Prussia it comprises shelter and necessary subsistence, care in sickness, and seemly burial in the event of death. Disputes between poor relief unions within the same State in relation to questions of liability are decided by the District Committees, and similar disputes between unions in different States are decided by the Imperial Board for Settlement Questions (*Bundesamt für Heimatwesen*), which also serves for Prussia and some other States as a court of final appeal in Poor Law questions generally.

CHARACTERISTICS OF THE GERMAN POOR RELIEF SYSTEM.—The bare statement of the legal liabilities of the communes towards their poor gives no true indication of the actual practice of poor relief in Germany. Every poor relief union interprets the law according to its discretion, with the consequence that the assistance given often goes far beyond the statutory requirements. The poor relief authority of Berlin, for example, adopts a test of eligibility which is capable of a very wide interpretation, for it regards as needing assistance any person, not being workshy, or of drunken or immoral habits, who " in consequence of lack or diminution of work or of the loss of the bread-winner is unable by his (her) own work or resources to provide for himself (herself) and his (her) family the necessary food, clothing, shelter, household utensils, and care of health." As in their tests of poverty entitling to assistance, so in the measures by which need and distress are relieved, the utmost variety exists, and it must be the object of this summary treatment of the question to emphasise only those lines of procedure and experiment which lie outside the common routine of Poor Law administration in this country.

The English social worker, with practical experience of Poor Law administration at home, who studies German methods of poor relief must be prepared for surprises and for some revision of his preconceived notions. He will seek in vain in the German Poor Law vocabulary for any term corresponding to the ugly word " pauper." Not only so, but he will fail to find the odious attitude towards poverty which is reflected by this word in a country whose social and moral standards have been so confused by its opulence that wealth has almost come to be synonymous with respectability and poverty with disgrace. In Germany, as everywhere, poverty may be honourable or dishonourable; but while English legislation, institutions, and methods for relieving poverty have long inflicted upon the dependent poor a stigma hardly less cruel than the brand invented for the vagrant in the sixteenth century, the idea underlying German poor relief is that the poor man who temporarily loses his foothold in crossing the treacherous sandbanks of social life does not for that reason forfeit the respect and consideration due to him as a citizen. The Germans speak simply of their " poor," whether they be dependent or independent ; with us the poor who claim assistance from the public funds are ringfenced as a class apart, and we have abused past recognition an honourable Latin word in our eagerness to stamp poverty as discreditable.[1]

A recent German writer on Poor Law questions, Dr. A. Weber, regards it as " a deplorable anachronism " that public relief should " entail serious legal disadvantages."[2] It is true that the Imperial Electoral Law of May 31, 1869, disqualifies from voting in elections to the Reichstag any person who during the preceding year has received poor relief, and that the laws of the various States apply the same disqualification in relation to elections to the State Diets, but recent Imperial legislation has removed certain kinds of public assistance from the index. There is also a strong body of public opinion averse to all provisions of the kind, and the franchise regulations relating to many town councils are far more charitable to the poor than those relating to the legislatures.

Just as we do not find the equivalent of the word " pauper " in Germany, so also we do not find " workhouses " in the English sense. The German " work " or rather " labour " house is an institution of quite another kind, for it is devised for the detention at forced tasks of the loafer, the workshy, and the shirker of domestic responsibilities. And though Germany has " poor houses," they are, as a rule, small local institutions, and are intended in the main for the old and infirm who are unable to obtain proper attention amongst relatives or friends. The general basis of public assistance is not, however, institutional but outdoor relief.

A further difference is that in Germany the work of relieving the poor is a part of the general administration of the town, and falls to the town council and executive (helped by co-opted citizens) just as does the administration of education, hospitals, and libraries, or any other public enterprise. Not only so, but in discharging this work the commune is entirely

[1] As its rehabilitation is impossible, is it quixotic to hope that the word " pauper " may soon be relegated to the limbo of certain other discredited Poor Law anachronisms—the workhouse uniform of children (adults must wear it yet), and the like ? The Local Government Board could abolish the word with all its variants by a stroke of the pen if it would. Let it disappear from official reports and the thing would be done. There is no reason in the world why the term " assisted poor " should not be used instead.
[2] " Armenwesen und Armenfürsorge," p. 38.

free from Government or any other outside influence. Because the poor relief authority is so organised, the care of the poor does not in Germany, as is so often the case in this country, fall into the hands of men without special qualifications, many of whom join boards of guardians for the purpose of being put on assessment committees, and of having the pleasure of assessing their neighbours' property, or quite incidentally as members of rural district councils, but is usually—and in large towns invariably—the special business of citizens chosen for their intelligence and practical sense, and by them is regarded as amongst the most responsible branches of civic duty.

Nor may this duty be shirked at will. The Prussian law relating to settlement says explicitly: " Every parishioner entitled to take part in parochial elections is liable to discharge unpaid duties in the poor-relief administration of the parish during a period of three years, or longer, as may be provided by the by-laws of the parish," and " any eligible person who without legal justification shall refuse to accept, or to continue, voluntary duties in the poor relief administration may be deprived for a period of from three to six years of the right to take part in parochial elections or to occupy honorary civic positions, and may be assessed to the extent of an eighth to a quarter more to the direct parochial rates." This punitive measure is enforced by the local authority itself when necessary. Exemption from honorary service can be claimed only on the score of age, illness, or insuperable obstacles, but a person who has served for one term may be excused from service during a similar period.

On the whole, the standard of poor relief provision and administration is singularly high. For some of the rural districts of Germany the treatment of the poor is unquestionably as bad as it can be, but we are concerned here with town government only, and the intelligence, sympathy, and high ideals brought into the service of poor relief by the hundreds of honorary workers who in every large town engage in this work must excite the admiration of anyone who knows how mechanically and perfunctorily the Poor Law is administered by the average English Board of Guardians.

Further, because the poor relief system is administered by

the municipal authority its cost is a charge on the common funds out of which all the other needs of local government are defrayed. In some parts of the country, certain revenues are earmarked for application to the relief of the poor—in Saxony, Bavaria, and Alsace-Lorraine the proceeds of the amusement tax, and in Saxony part of the profits of the municipal savings banks—but the "poor rate," as levied in this country, is unknown. Like the other departments of the administration, the poor relief authority prepares its estimates once a year and they are considered and approved or amended with the rest of the municipal budget.

Two other notable characteristics of German poor relief are the wide range of assistance offered to the needy and the great importance attached to preventive as distinguished from mechanical palliative measures. Here, as in so many other directions, the administrative authorities have complete discretion; there is no official policy of poor relief imposed from above; there are no Government rules or standards to which local action must conform; every municipal government decides upon its own policy, and the measures by which the poor are helped are as various as their needs. Disputes may occasionally occur between communal bodies and the supervisory authorities as to whether the former go as far as they should, but such disputes seldom arise out of any imputed excess of powers, for that, on the German theory of local government, is almost impossible.

ORGANISATION OF THE POOR RELIEF AUTHORITY.—The work of poor relief—sometimes to the exclusion of the care of orphans—is usually placed under a special Deputation, Commission, or Direction, composed of several members of the executive, the president or chairman being usually a paid member of that body, with members of the town council and often a number of citizens co-opted from outside. In large towns a member of the executive may be made responsible for this special work alone. This is the case in Berlin, where the Central Poor Relief Board consists of 44 persons, five being members of the executive, 17 members of the city council, ten burgher deputies or co-opted citizens, and 12 minor members of the official staff who are attached to this branch of work. The city is divided into 26 principal poor relief districts or " circles " (*Kreise*) and 466 sub-districts, each with its own committee of almoners or guardians (*Pfleger*). For each district an honorary superintendent is appointed, except in the case of three districts, for which central offices (*Armenämter*) under salaried officers exist, and the chairmen of the local sub-committees form the district meeting, which meets once a month. In 1910 the total number of guardians in Berlin was 5857, of whom 136 were women. Similarly Leipzig is divided into 105 districts, with 1254 guardians; Breslau into 63 districts, with 1946 guardians; Hamburg into 121 districts, with 1683 guardians; Frankfort-on-Main into 63 districts, with 1090 guardians; and Essen into 41 districts, with 490 guardians.

THE ELBERFELD SYSTEM OF POOR RELIEF.—The object of the system of decentralisation above described is to obtain the utmost individualisation in the consideration and treatment of poor relief cases. The system is in effect that known for more than half a century as the Elberfeld system, though in Germany that term no longer bears any such definite and distinctive meaning as is commonly attributed to it abroad. The Elberfeld theory of poor relief presupposes the cultivation of intimate knowledge of the social conditions of a community by a more or less minute division of labour, accompanied by individual treatment as determined by such knowledge. The idea is that every single application for assistance should be reported on by someone who is familiar with all the circumstances of the case, and be followed up by the same person. To this end a town is divided into districts and these again, in the case of Berlin and other large towns, into sub-districts. For each district or sub-district, as the case may be, a superintendent and a number of resident guardians are appointed, and the guardians of a district or the superintendents of districts, where there is a further division of the administrative area, form the " district meeting," which usually comes together once a fortnight for the consideration and decision of cases. The district superintendents in their turn are called together by the president of the central body as may be required, but the local guardians have no direct communications with that body.

To each guardian is assigned the duty either of exercising friendly oversight over certain families or of inquiring into the circumstances of special cases of poverty, according to the plan of procedure adopted. Where a guardian is given the continuous oversight of a few families he or she is expected to assist them with advice when desired, and to put in operation the poor relief machinery when necessary.

Domiciled residents needing assistance apply to the local guardians, and their applications are considered in the first instance by the committee for the district. In urgent cases the local guardian, with the consent of the chairman of his committee, may give immediate relief and he may do so on his own responsibility when there is danger in delay, but in the latter event his chairman must be at once informed and the case must be reported to the next meeting of the guardians of the district. Should a guardian refuse to entertain an application for relief he must likewise report his decision to the chairman or committee with the reasons for refusal. The spirit in which the guardians are expected to act is reflected in an instruction issued to the poor relief committees of Charlottenburg, which runs :—

" In the case of persons who apply for relief for the first time the committees are requested to reflect upon the position of needy persons who have sought assistance and who wait day after day for someone to appear and investigate their condition and bring help. Often enough it is impossible to judge from an application for relief, particularly when written by an unpractised hand, whether it may not be one of extreme urgency. Prompt response may save the town much later expenditure."

Applications for relief from persons without a settlement are dealt with by the central board, which also decides whether persons shall be admitted into institutions under its management, and exercises a general superintendence over all decisions of the district committees, which decisions it may reverse or alter at its discretion. The relief votes are, on the direction of the president of the central board, paid over to the district superintendents, who in turn assign to the local guardians the sums which they are authorised to pay to the applicants resident in their areas, these receiving relief at intervals of a week, a fortnight, or a month, according to local usage.

Strassburg some years ago adopted certain modifications of the Elberfeld system, and they have been imitated by other towns. There the administration of poor relief falls to a council consisting of twenty members, viz., the mayor, the medical officer of health, and persons nominated by the town council for five years, these including women and workingmen. The council exercises complete supervision over the arrangements for the care of the poor, but delegates all executive duties to a poor relief board, a body of permanent officials, which is assisted in its duties by twelve district committees each consisting of a member of the central council as chairman and six honorary members chosen from the 800 guardians who co-operate in visiting the poor and inquiring into the causes and circumstances of all cases of poverty assisted.

It would be a mistake to suppose, however, that the methods of relief for which the Elberfeld system nominally stands are consistently and generally applied in German towns. In its complete form this system may be said to have broken down in the large towns, less owing to defect in the principles themselves than to the difficulty of finding a sufficiency of capable honorary workers, for it is a common experience that the capable citizen is not always willing and the willing not always capable. Nor is it found that the Elberfeld system invariably ensures the desired expedition. Hence some towns have gone over partially or altogether to a plan of official paid relieving officers, appointed for the work of investigation and control, while still enlisting as much as possible the service of honorary guardians. These officers broadly correspond to the relieving officers of the English Poor Law system, except that they are expected to have undergone training before appointment instead of learning their craft more or less satisfactorily by experience.

Under this system of paid officers the principle of individual treatment based on careful inquiry into the causes and circumstances of poverty is applied with even greater method and thoroughness; for, like the guardian, the relieving officer is required to visit the homes of the poor and to familiarise himself with their special conditions, difficulties, and needs. But the official almoner has the advantage over the honorary that as a public official whose work is co-ordinated with that of the entire administration of the town he is able to decide whether and how needy persons can be assisted in other and better ways than by the giving of money; e.g., in the case of able-bodied men, by the municipal labour registry, the labour home, the distress works, or the offer of a piece of land for cultivation; and in the case of his children, by the day nurseries and cribs, the special schools for defective scholars, and the like; or it may be by finding for the family a cheaper dwelling by the aid of the municipal house registry. In Posen a number of women have been appointed to act as inquiry officers, and their services are utilised simultaneously in connection with the dispensaries for consumptives and dipsomaniacs.

So far the innovation of paid relieving officers is reported to have given satisfaction, insomuch that in some towns the voluntary workers who at first resisted it have come to recognise its expediency. Naturally, the Social Democratic party and its spokesmen on the poor relief committees strongly advocate the system of official almoners, for it is quite in keeping with their endeavour to take from poor relief all suggestion of charity and patronage, and to convert it into a right to be claimed instead of a benefaction to be asked for.

Possibly the difficulty of finding honorary workers would prove far less serious if the service of women were more readily enlisted, or accepted when volunteered. Nowhere in the world is the woman's movement directed by more reasonable and moderate counsels than in Germany, where all that women ask at present is to be allowed to enter the lowliest spheres of public life and there employ for the common good their best powers of brain and heart; yet even this modest request meets with formidable resistance. Women cannot sit upon local government bodies in Germany, and the men who monopolise local offices in some towns are determined that the intruders shall only enter the council and committee rooms over their prostrate bodies. It is not principle but prejudice, and in many cases sheer stupidity, that bars the way. When only several years ago the late Dr. Emil Münsterberg, president of the Berlin Poor Relief Administration—to the last a persistent and unwearying advocate of women's right to take part in public life—proposed to add women to the local relief committees in that city, whole committees threatened to resign office rather than be subjected to such indignity. Even to-day Berlin finds room for only 160 women in its army of nearly 6000 poor relief visitors, though a much larger number serve on the orphan care committees. Some other large towns have no better record. Thus (taking figures for 1910) of 1946 members of poor relief committees in Breslau only 59 were women, in Hamburg there were 12 out of a total of 1683, in Leipzig 28 out of 1254, in Frankfort-on-Main 95 out of 1030, in Cologne 60 out of 993, in Munich 40 out of 510, in Bremen 49 out of 420, in Essen 90 out of 490 ; while on the poor relief committees of Dresden and Stuttgart there were no women at all. Large proportions were shown by Karlsruhe, with 98 out of 167, and Strassburg, with 322 out of 812. On the whole about 6 per cent. of the members of these committees in the large towns are women. Women are represented still more sparingly on the central poor relief bodies, answering to the English Boards of Guardians. Only in thirty or forty towns are they so represented at all.

Baden is the only State of importance which gives to women's work statutory recognition. When the revision of the Town and Communal Ordinance of Baden took place several years ago the provision was introduced that in communes with more than 4000 inhabitants women shall sit on all bodies concerned with the care of the poor and of orphans.

Working-men have hardly fared better, though one reason for this may be that they are unable to devote to this work all the time they would like. Inquiries made in 1911 of all communes with a population of 50,000 and upwards showed that in 58 per cent. of the towns answering working-men were upon the poor relief committees but that they formed on the whole only 5 per cent. of the honorary members.

CHARACTER OF ASSISTANCE GIVEN.—In most towns outdoor relief is granted on the principle of ascertaining what may be regarded as the "minimum subsistence incomes" necessary for individuals and for families of different size living at home, having regard to the principal factors in the cost of living, and such grants are made as are needed in order to bring the receipts of the applicants from other sources (if any) up to these amounts. The allowances naturally differ greatly in various towns. Assuming the absence of independent sources of income, the grants for a man or woman living alone range in the larger towns from 15s. to 37s. 6d. a month, though most rates fall between 20s. and 24s.; the usual rates for a family consisting of parents and three dependent children range from 45s. to 55s. a month, with 6s. or 7s. less per child where there are fewer children. Allowances both lower and much higher are given in some towns. Grants towards the payments of rent are also common.

While money payments are the rule in most towns, payment is made in kind where there is reason to believe that money would be wrongly spent; money's worth in food is then supplied by approved tradesmen in return for vouchers, which are duly honoured by the local guardians. At Mülhausen, Freiburg, and Lübeck from 40 to 50 per cent. of the relief is paid in kind, and proportions of 15 and 20 per cent. are very common. In Berlin, on the other hand, relief in kind forms only 3 per cent. of the total cost of outdoor relief. The value of food ordered by the poor relief doctor is not counted as part of the grant. Articles of furniture (especially bedding), cooking utensils, fuel, clothing, and food are supplied in suitable cases, and other common forms of relief in kind are tools and material for work. Leipzig, Strassburg, and Metz have their own bakeries for the production of the bread given by the poor relief administration. Medical attendance, medicine, help in confinement, and burial belong everywhere to the usual range of poor relief, and the Federal Settlement Board has decided that sanatorium treatment and salt baths fall within the obligations of the public relief authorities towards the poor.

Often help is given, to persons with a settlement, in excess of the official relief granted by the central administration, this coming from special funds or from money placed at the free disposal of the president of the Poor Law Administration by societies or private individuals for use in this way.

As a rule, a town has at command the services of a large number of medical practitioners, who attend cases at the written request of the local guardians or district chairmen ; the drugs ordered by doctors are usually obtained from any apothecaries, but instruments and appliances are sometimes supplied by the central authority. Midwives are similarly called in at the discretion of the local guardians.

Outdoor relief, as has been stated, predominates, and institutional relief is the exception and only figures prominently in the poor relief budgets of the large towns which cope with need and misery in a great variety of ways. Even in Berlin the cost of indoor relief—including in this term the maintenance of the public infirmaries, shelters for the homeless, the labour house for loafers and the like, the orphanages, and of boarded-out children—makes only about 25 per cent. of the total expenditure on poor relief.

In Prussia the provision of institutions for imbeciles, lunatics, epileptics, the deaf and dumb and the blind, and the relief of persons without settlement are the duty of the provinces, but inasmuch as the provinces derive most of their funds from local taxation, on the plan of the English county rate, much of the cost is borne by the towns. Some of the large towns, however, have their own institutions for the care of defective persons.

Moreover, indoor relief would appear to be in less favour than ever. " Formerly," writes Dr. Franz Schrakamp, " it was believed that the poor could be helped best in the event of illness by sending them whenever possible into hospitals. This view has been abandoned. To-day it is regarded on ethical, sanitary, and financial grounds as more proper to send such a sick person to the hospital only where the successful treatment of his disease cannot be effected at home, and for the rest to keep him as far as possible in contact with his family."[1]

[1] " Die deutsche Stadt und ihre Verwaltung," Vol. I, p. 134.

This preference for the home treatment of the poor has led to various important modifications of practice. Charlottenburg, Nuremberg, and other towns own or rent blocks of dwellings which are let to suitable applicants either free or at a nominal rent, and wherever possible the dependent poor are assisted in their struggle against the breaking up of the home by contributions towards the rent and the gift, or loan, of articles of furniture. The new Municipal Housing Office of Charlottenburg has an arrangement with the poor relief department of the town whereby it is authorised to supply beds and bedding to families which are found by the visiting officers to lack sufficient provision of the kind. A nursing staff is also placed at the service of the poor in many towns.

A further change of policy has taken place here and there in relation to the medical service. The old rule was to appoint a few part-time Poor Law doctors as in England, and to require the poor to go to them and no others. In contrast to this rule the principle of " free choice of doctor," borrowed from the practice of the statutory sickness insurance societies, has been introduced in a number of towns—following the lead of Strassburg—and in these towns the poorest of men is now in the hour of sickness equal to the richest in his power to ask for treatment by the doctor in whom he has most confidence. Other towns go further and allow the poor to consult specialists for any diseases, while some towns employ whole-time specialists for certain common diseases. Thus Charlottenburg has municipal doctors for eye, throat, nose, and ear diseases, for nerve and gynæcological diseases, and for skin diseases. Where part-time doctors are not paid by attendance the usual stipends range from £30 to £40 in towns of medium size and from £50 to £75 in the large towns. Where payment is by attendance the doctors are required to accept the minimum fees specified in the official scale sanctioned by the Government.

As a rule, a separate committee known as the Orphan Board (*Waisenrat*) is entrusted with the care of the orphans and other children for whose maintenance a commune is responsible. Here again large towns are divided into districts for administrative and supervisory purposes, and honorary service occupies an important place. Thus the municipal area of

Düsseldorf is for this purpose divided into 51 districts, in each of which a large number of citizens act as visitors. More and more the poor relief administrations are endeavouring to board out these children in the country, partly because it is cheaper to maintain them there than in towns, but also for reasons of health and better control. The result in some towns has been that the institutional care of children has almost disappeared except in the case of the defective. Dresden boards a hundred orphans with families for every five maintained in institutions. Most of the boarded-out children live in rural districts, and the town pays for their keep 14s. a month in the case of those up to two years of age, 12s. for those from two to four years, and 10s. for older children, with an allowance of clothing in addition in each case. Once a year the children are taken by their guardians to specified centres for inspection by a municipal doctor and another officer of the poor relief authority. Similarly Frankfort-on-Main distributes its children in over a hundred different places, at the rate of from one to twenty in a place. Berlin follows the same system on a smaller scale, but first receives the children into a temporary home. After being kept under observation here for a short time the children are assigned to the care best suited to them, whether to families or special institutions, as the case may be.

In some towns a serious attempt is made to co-ordinate public relief with the work of the various philanthropic and " social welfare " associations and institutions. Thus there has existed for some years both at Munich and Mannheim a central municipal agency known as the " Information Agency for Philanthropy and Poor Relief." It is a sort of clearing-house, whose object it is to prevent overlapping in the bestowal of charity and to check fraud upon the public. The poor relief department is the nucleus of the organisation, and most of the philanthropic societies of the town are affiliated under a rule which binds them to confer together before dispersing their charities. Every organisation retains complete control of its affairs and funds, but it is helped in the efficient administration of both. Institutions working on the same lines and conducted by the municipal authorities or associations

T

exist also at Frankfort-on-Main, Charlottenburg, Leipzig, Breslau, Hamburg, Berlin, and other towns.

ASSISTANCE IN RETURN FOR WORK.—The relief of the poor is not all giving, however; for it has a disciplinary and also a repressive side as well. Many Poor Law authorities exact from able-bodied applicants for relief work in poorhouse, hospital, or elsewhere, and there is a growing disposition to substitute what the French call "*assistance par le travail*" for doles. In thus acting the communes are carrying out the injunction contained in the old Common Law of Prussia of 1794, viz., "Work suited to their powers and capacities shall be supplied to persons who lack the means and opportunity of earning their own livelihood." At Bielefeld and Charlottenburg, for example, an attempt is made to find work for all able-bodied applicants for relief on this healthy principle of reciprocity. No matter how limited their capacity may be, they are expected to work in return for the assistance given. They may be offered outdoor employment in some department of the public service if fit for nothing else, or work may be found for them with a private employer, who is expected to pay only reduced wages, while the balance necessary to make up a living wage is defrayed from the poor fund. At Posen the able-bodied poor are employed in cultivating town land, while at Cologne, Strassburg, Danzig, and other places they are given plots of land to cultivate for their own benefit, potato and other seed and manure being supplied free. Breslau has recently established a labour home for unemployed applicants for relief. Labour tickets costing ¼d. are also issued to householders, who are encouraged to give them to mendicants instead of alms. A ticket will secure the bearer admission into the home, where food and lodging are given to him in return for such work as he can perform.

In Bavaria the same principle is applied on a larger scale at Nuremberg. In administering the Poor Law the municipality of that town acts on the principle: "Whenever possible, not alms but work should be offered to those who, owing to age, crippled condition, and other physical defects, vainly seek employment in the ordinary labour market." For the purpose of so helping these unfortunates the town has established a special training institution at which industry and agriculture are carried on simultaneously. The buildings include, beside the administrative block, workshops for both sexes, dwellings, a bakery and kitchens, and farm buildings. Married couples are allowed to live together in two-room apartments. Berlin and several other towns have begun to experiment with the sending of able-bodied applicants for relief to the labour colonies of the Bodelschwingh type and the farm colonies carried on by the Inner Colonisation Society, formed for the reclamation and settlement of waste lands. In consideration of the municipality of Berlin making it a loan of £5000 free of interest for two years and bearing interest of 4 per cent. afterwards, this society has undertaken to receive on its reclamation works an average of 200 unemployed workmen assigned to it by the city authorities, maintenance grants being payable on an agreed scale.

FORCED LABOUR HOUSES FOR WORKSHIES AND LOAFERS.—Finally, the poor relief authorities have at command in some States various devices for coercing the loafers and workshies who become chargeable, or allow their dependants to become chargeable, to the public funds. One is the forced labour house. Detention in such a house may be enforced under the Penal Code in case of (a) vagabonds, (b) any person who begs or causes children to beg, or neglects to restrain from begging such persons as are under his control and oversight and belong to his household, (c) any person so addicted to gambling, drunkenness, or idleness that he falls into such a condition as to be compelled to seek public help himself or for those for whose maintenance he is responsible, (d) any female who is placed under police control owing to professional immorality when she acts contrary to the police regulations issued in the interest of health, public order, and public decency, or who, without being under such control, is guilty of professional immorality, (e) any person who, while in receipt of public relief, refuses out of sloth to do such work suited to his strength as the authorities may offer him, (f) any person who, after losing his past lodging, fails to procure another within the time allotted to him by the competent authority and who cannot prove that, in spite of his best endeavours, he has been unable to do so, and (g) persons who live on the immorality of others.

The maximum period of detention is two years, but whether the detainee obtains discharge at the end of a shorter sentence depends entirely upon himself. If he shows distinct signs of improvement as the result of his discipline, he may be released after six months. If not, the sentence is probably prolonged for six months, or in bad cases to the maximum term, at the end of which the prisoner must unconditionally be discharged, whether reformed or not. The labour houses provided in Prussia for offenders of these classes are maintained by the provinces, but in other States the communal poor relief authorities have for a long time had the power to keep at forced labour in disciplinary institutions of their own men or women who fall on the poor funds by reason of slothful or immoral habits. In Saxony this power has existed since 1840 ; the same power was enacted in Wurtemberg in 1889, in Hamburg in 1907, and in Bremen in 1911. The forced labour houses at Rummelsburg, near Berlin, Leipzig, and Dresden are particularly deserving of note.[1] Since 1912 Prussia has had a Workshy Law (July 23), aimed particularly at men who neglect to provide for those for whose maintenance they are legally liable, e.g., chronic drunkards, wife deserters, and the like. This law empowers poor relief authorities to keep such persons at forced labour for a period not exceeding twelve months as a rule. At the expiration of the term fixed the detainee may be released on probation on condition that if he finds regular employment within three months his discharge will be permanent. The poor relief authorities of Frankfort-on-Main and Berlin, among other towns, have already put the law in operation.

COST OF POOR RELIEF IN GERMAN TOWNS.—No useful comparison can be made of the cost of poor relief in German and English towns or of the cost in different German towns. In the first case comparison would be entirely vitiated not merely

[1] For a full consideration of labour houses and the system of disciplinary detention in Germany and other countries the reader is referred to " The Vagrancy Problem : the case for measures of restraint for tramps, loafers, and unemployables " (P. S. King & Son, 1910), by the present writer.

by the varying standards of destitution and relief applied but still more by the very different range of expenditure embraced by such returns as are available. Before the comparative statistician ventures to set side by side the crude poor relief returns of German and English towns he would do well to digest the fact that the German expenditure will as a rule embrace items like the feeding of necessitous scholars, the free supply of milk and other food to pregnant women, the support of children's country holiday societies, the sending of sick and weakly children to baths and other health resorts, possibly also the cost of shelters for the homeless, of public dispensaries for consumptives, and, almost certainly, liberal grants to a host of philanthropic societies and movements working on lines parallel to those of the poor relief authority.

A comparison of the expenditure of German towns would be equally inconclusive as a test of relative poverty, liberality of treatment, or efficiency of administration, inasmuch as the cost of poor relief everywhere is largely affected by local conditions, such as the occupational character of the population, the amount of public charities available for the poor, the extent to which outdoor is preferred to indoor relief, etc.

Germany is like England, however, in the fact that the burden of poor relief is very unequally distributed. Many of the poorer communes have to bear a load far beyond their capacity, while adjacent rich communes enjoy a virtual immunity from poor relief charges. The disparity is naturally most glaring in the case of the metropolis and its suburbs. Thus the net cost of poor relief, estimated per head of the population, is ten times higher in Berlin than in some of its villa suburbs. In more or less acute form the disparity occurs, however, in every great centre of population, where wealthy independent suburbs cluster round industrial towns. It is misfortune enough for any community that it should be poor, but that the poor should, unaided, have to relieve their own poverty is a refinement of irony. With a view to repairing this anomaly, Poor Law reformers are urging the equity of some method of equalisation either by the grouping of districts or the conversion of poor relief into a national, or at least a provincial—or, as we should say, a county—service.

Enough will have been said to justify the claim that the policy pursued by German Poor Law authorities is emphatically positive and constructive, whatever be its tangible influence upon the condition and habits of the poor. Herein lies its immeasurable superiority to our own system of public relief. To the spirit of that system any wider conception of society's duty to the poor than the granting to them of doles and their collection, on more or less indiscriminate principles, in large institutions when better oversight can there be given, is entirely foreign. For a poor relief " policy " in the true sense of the word the English Poor Law offers neither encouragement nor scope ; hence the public-spirited citizen who believes that dole-dealing is a cowardly device for cloaking social evils and evading social responsibilities has perforce to turn to voluntary agencies like the Charity Organisation Societies.

It is possible, indeed, that the highly developed systems of public assistance peculiar to some of the large German towns are not entirely free from danger. Danger will certainly arise if by any chance their efficiency as agencies of relief should tend to obscure the fundamental truth that the object of all public assistance should be the removal of the causes of impoverishment, and hence that the final test of the success of any poor relief system or authority must be the degree to which it is able to make itself unnecessary. Nothing could be worse for the cause of charity, public or private, for the poor themselves, and for society at large than the common disposition to regard our relief systems as a permanent part of the social machinery, instead of as unsatisfactory makeshifts, as an end in themselves instead of a means to larger and more intelligent and more beneficent purposes, as virtuous evidences of public and personal sacrifice, instead of as a penalty which society is paying for past and present default, and, like all penalties rightly apportioned, branded with reproach and discredit. Such a danger does not threaten us in this country, at any rate, and for a long time we may safely study all that Germany has to offer for our instruction.[1]

[1] These remarks must be read in connection with the following chapter on " Social Welfare Work."

CHAPTER XI

SOCIAL WELFARE WORK

Scope and purpose of social welfare policy—The crusade against infant mortality—Municipal guardianship of illegitimate children—School doctors—School dentists—Feeding of necessitous children—Children's care centres—The crusade against tuberculosis—Convalescent homes—Municipal lodging-houses for single men—Municipal labour registries—Assisted unemployment insurance funds—Public works for the unemployed—The poor man's lawyer—Municipal pawnshops—Miscellaneous welfare work.

THE admirable reports in which German municipalities review their administrative work from year to year often contain a special section devoted to a kind of activity which to the average English municipal politician, whose mental horizon is limited by drains, building plans, and road making, will in such a connection appear anomalous, if not incomprehensible. This is " social welfare " work. What, he will ask, have municipalities to do with social welfare in the personal sense ? Once more it is necessary to recall the fact that nothing human is alien to the German conception of town government, and that it excludes no activities and no measures which aim at advancing the well-being of the community in any direction.

SCOPE AND PURPOSE OF SOCIAL WELFARE POLICY.—The " social " spirit which nowadays informs the governing authorities of all large towns, and not less many of the smaller towns within their capacity, from the mayor down to the committees of the representative assembly, is to a large extent a by-product of the insurance legislation dating from the early 'eighties of last century. The effect of that legislation was to set in movement new social forces and new philanthropic ardours in many directions ; and under their influence current conventional conceptions of public health administration have been widened and the consciousness of social obligation has everywhere been stimulated and deepened. Just as Molière's hero discovered that he was speaking prose without knowing it, so many municipalities, responding more and more to the new influences that were abroad, came to engage in social welfare work unconsciously long before they began to organise this work on systematic lines.

All municipal policy may be said to have a social side, since directly or indirectly its concern is with men and women, their well-being and convenience. Yet a distinction must be drawn between the formal routine social policy into which a municipality falls, as it were, by necessity, and schemes of social reform deliberately devised and co-ordinated for the attainment of certain definite objects. In social welfare work of the latter kind many German towns excel, and in no department of local administration can their example be studied with greater profit.

Most of the measures which fall within this definition lie entirely outside the obligations imposed upon local authorities by statute, and because the scope of welfare work is thus limited only by the discretion of the authorities it is continually expanding. The measures more or less common to most progressive towns comprise housing schemes of various kinds, sanatoria and other institutions for the treatment of tuberculosis, convalescent homes for the poorer classes, dispensaries for infants, for consumptives, and for dipsomaniacs, medical advice offices for mothers, measures for the protection of illegitimate children, maternity homes and other assistance for women before, at and after childbirth, school kitchens for the feeding of necessitous children, school doctors and dental clinics, labour registries, and shelters for the homeless. These and other measures akin to them in purpose will be referred to more particularly in later pages.

It will be seen that most of these measures are of a preventive character, and all of them fall within the meaning of the phrase "social therapy," which aptly describes the lines upon which German social reformers are to-day endeavouring to combat the ills of modern civilisation. The course of reasoning which has induced the severely logical German mind thus to revise preconceived ideas and to trace evils to their source is well expressed in a recent exposition of the municipal welfare work carried on in Charlottenburg, and published by its mayor and executive.

" The insurance organisations, which had to bear the cost of occupational risks to health, soon learned that it was remunerative to prevent illness, and expended large amounts in prophylactic work. Success in this endeavour was, however, dependent upon the opening up of new ways in the domain of care for the public health. While such care had in the past been restricted in the main to the creation of a sanitary environment, the efforts of the new hygiene were directed to the protection of the man himself from threatened dangers by observation, advice, and treatment. The experiences collected by the insurance organisations were so favourable that a demand for their extension was raised on all hands.

" The insurance authorities can only provide for the working classes who are insured by law ; the extension of their benefits to other sections of the population, the uninsured men, women, and children, needed the intervention of other efficient bodies, and these could only be the communal authorities. For while private philanthropy, enlisting itself enthusiastically in the great mission, freely offered personal service, its monetary resources were limited, and the needful co-ordination of effort was also wanting. Hence just as after the first outbreak of cholera in the first half of last century the German towns did not wait for science to decide which were the best methods of prevention, but boldly and with extraordinary sacrifice began to experiment in public sanitation on their own account, so to-day in the domain of personal hygiene they are launching out into new ways in the hope that their success, though it may not be witnessed by the workers of to-day, will justify in the estimation of the rising generation the sacrifices which are now being made."[1]

Charlottenburg has distinguished itself more than most towns by bold experiment in the domain of " social therapy."

[1] " Die gesundheitlichen Einrichtungen der Königl. Residenzstadt Charlottenburg " (1911), pp. 5, 6.

The voluntary welfare institutions and agencies which it has established or promoted during the last few years are not exhausted by the list given above, for it has in addition a large maternity hospital, a home for aged people, a special housing department with a house registry, dwellings for persons in receipt of poor relief, day nurseries, forest schools, special schools for mentally and physically deficient children, home instruction for children who cannot attend school, and a series of recreation grounds fully equipped for games of various kinds. Charlottenburg spends £15,000 a year—equal to 8d. a head of the entire population—on its dispensaries for infants and its various measures for helping women before, at, and after childbirth. Its provision for consumptives, in the way of dispensary, sanatorium, and home care, costs an equal amount, and there is a still larger outlay on school hygiene, i.e., school doctors and dentists, and the other branches of welfare work specified above.

Nor do the municipalities limit their philanthropy to official efforts, for they support readily and generously all sorts of outside agencies and movements following the same lines. The benevolent subscription list of a large German town runs into thousands of pounds, for it is subject to no statutory restriction such as would make it impossible to obtain money from English local authorities for charitable purposes, even if the disposition to give existed.

No responsible institution or organisation which is able to show that it is engaged in useful public work on purely philanthropic lines is refused a share, greater or less, in the ample grant assigned to social welfare objects. Thus the municipality of Frankfort-on-Main gives £21,000 a year in this way. Among the objects followed by the societies so assisted are the combating of consumption and of intemperance, the care of the aged poor, infant dispensaries, dental treatment for scholars, district nursing, convalescent homes, cribs and nurseries, children's games, excursions, and holidays, school meals, popular libraries and lectures, shelters for the homeless, aid for discharged prisoners, legal advice agencies, writing-rooms for unemployed clerks, and a multitude of other worthy objects. In the same way the municipality of Berlin contributes amounts varying from £10 to £500 to associations established for the following among other purposes: child and juvenile care (*crèches*, play centres, etc.), instruction in crafts for boys and in housekeeping for girls, flower culture in schools, the feeding of necessitous children, the support of women in childbirth and their infants, private maternity homes, district nursing, housing reform, labour colonies, shelters for the homeless, work amongst discharged prisoners, general rescue work amongst the young, legal advice agencies, temperance work, popular libraries, concerts, theatrical performances, and associations for the promotion of a love of art, literature and knowledge generally amongst the working classes. No question is ever asked as to the political or religious auspices under which efforts of these kinds are made; the one and only claim to support is concern for the public good.

It is also a common and laudable custom for municipalities to vote sums of money for the establishment of philanthropic institutions in commemoration of great national events and anniversaries. Sometimes a town in this way acquires a new park or library, or the money may be earmarked for a special purpose—the endowment of a maternity hospital, or a convalescent home, scholarships for poor children in the higher schools, and the like. Thus the city of Berlin, in commemoration of the bicentenary of the creation of the kingdom of Prussia, set apart the sum of £50,000 to be used in promoting the erection of cheap dwellings for the working classes. So, too, in 1911 Düsseldorf erected a lodging-house for single men at a cost of £10,000 in commemoration of the silver wedding of the Emperor and Empress.

The stern individualist, solicitous for the virtues of self-reliance and independence—virtues which, after all, flourish only in a rich and fertile soil—may be inclined to ask whether this ready offer of public assistance does not deter people from helping themselves and encourage the growth of an insidious form of parasitism. The Charlottenburg municipal authority answers the question in the statement already mentioned, and its answer is that these measures are carried out as much in the interest of the community as a whole as of the individuals who immediately benefit.

"The care of the poor and the maintenance of necessitous sick persons in institutions," it writes, "are obligations imposed on the communes by law, and according to the decisions of the highest courts measures for the prevention of sickness may also in certain cases be regarded as obligatory. The measures for the protection of health, on the other hand, are altogether voluntary, yet they are not merely adopted from humanitarian considerations and motives of pity, but are imperatively necessary in the interest of the health of the entire population. The fear is often expressed that the benefits thus voluntarily provided may diminish the sense of responsibility of parents and guardians, and that the town relieves these of obligations which properly belong to them. But this view is not tenable. The classes of the population to which these health measures apply are now very inadequately cared for, and are in consequence a source of danger not only to the physical, moral, and economic well-being of their descendants, but to the entire population. But, further, the influence of these measures is pre-eminently educative, and its effects will be seen in the cultural advance of the coming generation."

Let it be admitted that the social welfare work done by German towns is not dictated exclusively by altruistic considerations, and that expediency is often a powerful though an unacknowledged motive. In the main, however, this work, so many-sided and so fruitful in results, unquestionably reflects a genuine philanthropic spirit and an earnest desire to soften social antagonisms and lessen social inequalities, by offering to the less favoured members of the community, not in the form of a private charity but of a public gift, advantages and amenities of inestimable value which otherwise would be beyond their reach. Such a policy may not altogether realise yet it is true to the spirit of words used by the late Dr. E. Münsterberg, one of the heralds of this new movement in municipal life : " When we no longer divide the members of the community into the rulers and the ruled, but regard all as comrades in the good old sense of the word, then only do we think socially, and the commune which discharges its obligations in this sense will be carrying on communal social policy."

Where official initiative in this work is slow, impetus is supplied in abundance by the Labour or Social Democratic representatives on the town councils, and it speaks volumes for the humane spirit which inspires the middle-class parties in power that, in spite of much reckless imputation of apathy to social evils, so much is done and done so readily at the request of a party which is never weary of asking yet is never grateful for what it receives. Too often the Socialist sees in these manifold activities only an evidence of human misery, and the very efforts of the much maligned " bourgeois society " to right the wrong he forges into a new weapon for his war against the social order; what he does not recognise, or refuses to admit, is the fact that behind these measures is an enthusiasm for humanity and a rebellion against social ills not less sincere and ardent than his own, but informed by a suaver and more charitable spirit and directed on the whole by a more practical because a more patient and more discriminating judgment.

As social welfare work has grown, new machinery has been called for with a view to economy and co-ordination of effort. The governing authorities of between twenty and thirty of the larger towns have formed Social Commissions for dealing with all questions which come under this head. In this way experts upon the various problems which have to be faced are brought together, and their knowledge and advice are placed at the disposal of workers without the same experience yet wishful to learn ; questions are viewed together and no longer in isolation, and reformative measures are similarly adopted as part of a concerted plan. To the Social Commissions, or departments corresponding to them though differently named, are committed many advisory functions relating to such branches of the general administration as are concerned directly or indirectly with social conditions. For example, they may be entrusted with the preparation and revision of the regulations relating to the labour registry, the legal advice agency, the conditions of service of municipal employees, industrial insurance, the industrial and commercial courts, and the like.

The municipality of Breslau has recently erected in different parts of the town buildings, known as " Welfare Houses," intended to serve as centres for social welfare endeavours of various kinds. There are four institutions of the sort, each adapted to the special needs of the locality in which it is situated. All of them have baths for adults and children, cribs, infants' dispensaries, milk depots, libraries and reading-rooms, and savings banks, and several have gymnasiums, laundries, and sewing-rooms to which women and girls can resort for the purpose of instruction and help in the making and mending of clothing. Curators live on the premises. From £6000 to £18,000 each has been spent upon the building and equipment of these institutions.

Some of the more important branches of social welfare work may now be reviewed.

THE CRUSADE AGAINST INFANT MORTALITY.—Germany has still one of the highest infant mortality rates in Europe, in spite of a considerable improvement during the past ten years. The rate in 1912 for the whole empire was 14·7 per cent., but in Prussia 14·6 per cent., in Bavaria 17·7 per cent., in Saxony 15·6 per cent., in Würtemberg 13·8 per cent., and in Baden 13·8 per cent. It is, however, no accident that in Prussia the rate is lowest in the industrial provinces, since it is there that the most energetic measures have been adopted with a view to preventing unnecessary waste of infant life. Apart from the humanitarian aspect of the question, the husbanding of its population is a matter of vital importance for Germany as an industrial and a military country. In the crusade against infant mortality attention is first given to the time prior to the birth of the child. Thus in Charlottenburg no woman, married or unmarried, who is undergoing the physical and mental strain incidental to childbirth need lack friends, food, or shelter. If only food is needed she can have it for the asking, for the municipality has an arrangement with the Mothers' Association by which its agents are authorised to supply, at the cost of the town, soup, milk, and other food to needy women during four weeks preceding confinement, with the services of a doctor, nurse, and midwife as required. Single women left to face motherhood alone are offered shelter and care in one of several maternity homes, admission through whose ever-open doors is attended by no formality whatever. After confinement mothers and infants are looked after until permanent arrangements can be made for them, and meantime the infants have been placed in the legal care of a public guardian, a municipal official, whose duty it is to see to their welfare and to assert their rights and those of the mothers against men who are too often ready to shirk their responsibilities.

Only one German town is known to provide medical and midwife's assistance gratuitously independently of the Poor Law, and that is Offenbach; but many other towns, like Charlottenburg, subsidise associations and institutions which offer this service to the poorer classes. Although only a small minority of all maternity hospitals and homes in Germany are in public hands, in Prussia 22 out of a total of 65, with 2670 beds, belong to municipal or other public bodies. One of the largest municipal institutions is that already partially built at Charlottenburg; when completed it will contain over 400 beds and the total cost is estimated at £270,000.

Dispensaries for advice to mothers on the nursing of infants are now almost general in the towns; and in most cases they are either carried on or largely subsidised by the local authorities. Berlin has nine of these institutions, and during the administrative year 1912-13 nearly 17,000 infants were taken to them for examination, and counting the infants still under oversight at the beginning of the year advice and help were given in 20,000 cases. While nearly one-third of all the infants born during the year were taken to the dispensaries, the proportion in the case of illegitimate children was over one-half. The total number of consultations given by the doctors in attendance was 178,000, and in addition 75,000 visits were paid by nurses and other helpers to the homes of the parents; nearly £10,000 was paid to 9000 mothers in premiums, ranging from 2s. to 5s. a week, to encourage natural feeding; and a large quantity of milk was also distributed. While most dispensaries are intended for infants, those at Charlottenburg take children up to six years of age. Both at these towns and elsewhere wet nurses are supplied at the public expense in special cases. Apart from the help rendered by the visiting nurses medical treatment is not given.

In Berlin the police authority exercises oversight over children given out to nurse under a power conferred upon it by a Cabinet Order of 1840, since which time all foster-mothers in Berlin have been licensed and subject to constant control.

Premiums to encourage natural feeding are very common, and as a rule are paid in connection with the infant dispensaries. The Dresden town council draws on the profits of the municipal savings bank for the purpose. A common rule is to offer these premiums only in cases where the family income falls below a fixed amount, e.g., 20s. a week. The amount ranges from 1s. 6d. to 3s. a week, with an addition during the months of the year specially favourable to infantile diseases. The premiums may be given in milk in lieu of money. In all cases the condition of natural feeding is insisted on.

Great importance is attached to the supply of milk either gratuitously or at a reduced charge to mothers of the poorer class. At Posen a municipal "milk kitchen" has been established for this purpose. It is managed by an experienced dairyman under the oversight of a doctor, and the milk is sold at 18 depots located in different parts of the town. Poor people are supplied free on the order of the poor relief doctors. In connection with the "milk kitchen" a dispensary for infants is carried on, and here, too, feeding premiums in the form of milk and money are given.

Municipal *crèches* are also common, and the towns in general subsidise institutions of this kind carried on by philanthropic societies. Where a charge is made it is nominal, e.g., 3d. or 4d. a day for nursing and food. The municipality of Weissensee, near Berlin, has just built a special hospital for infants at a cost of £18,000. It is intended solely for the treatment of children up to two years of age, and 65 patients can be taken at once. No diseases are refused, and provision is even made for the treatment of infectious cases. All the milk used in the hospital is produced on an adjacent farm belonging to the town.

Another noteworthy municipal experiment which has been made at Karlsruhe and at Sebnitz, in Saxony, is a plan of assisted maternity or motherhood insurance. Sebnitz set the example in 1911. The town is one of the centres of the artificial flower industry, in which women are mostly employed. The maternity insurance fund is intended to supplement the meagre provision made by the statutory sickness insurance societies, and it is on a voluntary basis. All women living at Sebnitz whose income does not exceed £85 can become members and remain in membership so long as their own or their family income does not exceed £125. The contribution is 6d. a month, and when it has been paid for a full year the member receives back in the event of the birth of a child the total amount paid (6s.) together with a bonus of 14s.; after two years she receives the sum of the contributions paid (12s.) and a bonus of 18s., and after three years the sum of the contributions (18s.) and a bonus of 22s. Milk is also supplied free. The fund is subsidised by the town and by philanthropic citizens.

While the general infant mortality is steadily falling, in spite of fluctuations due to exceptionally hot summers and other special causes, the effect of these concerted efforts is best seen in the case of individual towns. Thus Munich in 1886 had an infant mortality rate of 33 per cent.; in 1896 the rate had fallen to 26 and in 1906 to 20 per cent., and the improvement was attributed largely to the infant dispensaries, milk depots, and *crèches*, the encouragement of natural feeding, the improved supervision of foster-children, and the systematic instruction of mothers in the proper nursing of their infants. Similarly at Stettin, where the municipality has for some years co-ordinated the various public measures for the reduction of infant mortality by means of a Board of Health, the rate of mortality has fallen from an average of 27·9 per cent. during the years 1901 to 1905, to 22·6 per cent. during the years 1906 to 1910, and in 1912 it was 17·5 per cent. At Regensburg, owing to similar efforts, the infant mortality rate has been reduced from 43 to 24 per cent., and that of Freiburg in Baden from 25 to 10 per cent. So, too, the infant mortality rate of Hanover fell from 17·3 to 10·9 per cent. between 1896 and 1910, and rates of from 10 to 12 per cent. are now no longer rare in the large towns, e.g., Frankfort-on-Main, Kiel, Essen, Bremen, Düsseldorf, etc.

U

MUNICIPAL GUARDIANSHIP OF ILLEGITIMATE CHILDREN.—
The system of municipal guardianship (*Vormundschaft*), under which illegitimate children become at birth the legal wards of officers appointed by the local authorities, is one of the most effectual of the measures by which the terrible mortality amongst these children is being combated. High as is the general rate of infant mortality, the rate amongst illegitimates in many parts of the country, and not alone in the large towns, is appalling. Germany had in 1911 a general infant mortality rate of 19·2 per cent., but while the rate amongst legitimates was 18·2 the rate amongst illegitimates was 29 per cent. In Prussia the two rates were 17·1 and 31·1 per cent. respectively, in Bavaria 21·3 and 29·3 per cent., in Saxony 21·6 and 29·6 per cent., in Würtemberg 18·4 and 26·4 per cent., and in Baden 16·8 and 24·7 per cent. In some of the provinces of Prussia one in every three illegitimate children dies within the first year, and in the large towns the rate of mortality sometimes exceeds 40 per cent., and is twice as high as amongst legitimates.

The public guardian is an extension of the obligation placed on the communes in relation to orphans and deserted and illegitimate children by the Imperial Civil Code. Guardianship may extend to illegitimate children only or to all children coming under the Poor Law, though other classes of children may be taken into protection in special cases, and the power is exercised in virtue of an arrangement with the Court of Wards (*Vormundschaftsgericht*) whereby the latter constitutes a definite communal officer the legal guardian of certain classes of children except in cases where there is some other approved guardian who is unwilling to retire in his favour or where the appointment of another guardian is desirable for special reasons.

The institution of municipal guardianship in respect of Poor Law and friendless children was begun in Dortmund in 1898, and it has since been adopted by more than 150 towns, one-half of them in Prussia. The scope of this public guardianship differs in the various States. In Nuremberg, in Bavaria, it extends to all children who fall upon the Poor Law, whether maintained in institutions or boarded out with families, to

SOCIAL WELFARE WORK

illegitimate children maintained in part at public cost, to foster-children nursed in Nuremberg, and to children and juveniles under disciplinary care for whose welfare the municipality is responsible. As a rule the guardianship lasts until the expiration of school age or the age of 14 years.

For the reason given above illegitimate children are the principal object of attention. The method of procedure is as follows. The public guardian receives notification from the civil registry of every illegitimate birth, but where women have been received for confinement into hospitals or other institutions he enters into communication with them before the birth of their children and deputes his women assistants to look after them and to continue oversight over the children when the mothers have returned to work. Later personal oversight is usually exercised by the poor relief committees appointed for the care of orphans, consisting of the head of the orphans' department, orphan visitors or guardians, and the municipal medical officer, but for the first two years the services of the nurses attached to the infant dispensaries are freely utilised. After the wards have left school they may still continue in the legal care of the municipal guardians, if necessary until they come of age. The guardians often have central offices where, during hours fixed for consultation, information and advice can be obtained upon legal questions affecting the custody and maintenance of children.

Not only are the infants and the mothers cared for under this system, but the fathers are also looked after. One of the most important duties of the public guardians is to see that these men discharge their legal liability, and the success which attends this part of their efforts alone justifies the expense and labour involved. In the administrative year 1912-13 the public guardians appointed by the city of Berlin took over the charge of 4200 illegitimate children, and gave advice and assistance in a large number of additional cases. Pressure of some kind had to be brought to bear upon most of the fathers, and legal proceedings to be taken in 638 cases, but as a result alimony to the amount of £15,000 was paid either direct to the mothers or to the municipal guardians on their behalf. In the first four years (1907 to 1910) of his work the Dresden public guardian collected £25,000 from fathers of illegitimate children, one-half of this sum being collected in 1910.

One of the principal reasons which led the municipality of Düsseldorf to introduce the public guardianship of illegitimate children was the wish to enforce the rights of these children against their fathers. It is found that 90 per cent. of all proceedings for maintenance taken by the guardian are successful and that 60 per cent. of all the payments awarded or otherwise due are paid. Magdeburg introduced the institution in 1906, and the number of illegitimate children in its care increased from 788 at the end of the first year to 3763 at the end of 1910; during this period the municipal guardian had taken proceedings against defaulting and putative fathers in 844 cases, in nearly all cases successfully, and had received £10,800 in alimony. At Leipzig the public guardian was able during the ten years 1900 to 1909 to extract from the fathers of illegitimate children—apart from payments made voluntarily—no less than £87,500, of which £15,800 was received in 1909. Hitherto not 40 per cent. of the alimony due had been recovered where the children had private guardians; now that the town undertakes the responsibility of looking after the fathers the leakage is small.

It is worth while calling attention to this aspect of the public guardians' work in view of the indifferent success of English Boards of Guardians in the same direction. In Germany it is found that the municipal authority can often enforce claims on behalf of illegitimate children where the mothers acting alone would have no chance. The very knowledge that the community, in the person of the public guardian, is behind the mother and child is, as a rule, sufficient to bring the most callous deserter to heel. It is interesting to read that so energetically do the municipal guardians protect the interests of unmarried mothers—and incidentally of the rates —that an "Association of Fathers of Illegitimate Children" has been formed for mutual counsel and defence.

CHILD AND JUVENILE CARE.—When the years of infancy are passed, other agencies, either provided or assisted by the municipalities, are ready to help the child at various stages of the journey to adolescence. Here come into play the many and diverse activities comprised within the term "juvenile care" or "juvenile protection," and co-ordinated in some towns — like Charlottenburg, Bremen, Hamburg, Mayence, Magdeburg, and Schöneberg—under municipal direction in special Juvenile Care Boards.

(a) *School Doctors.*—Inasmuch as this survey is confined to social welfare activities of a non-statutory character, the first place may properly be given to the institution of school doctors as introduced in Frankfort-on-Main so long ago as 1883, in Breslau in 1887, and now universal in the towns. The peculiar significance of the German policy of school hygiene lies in the fact that no legislation or Government pressure of any kind has been needed to call it into existence, but that the movement was due to the spontaneous action of the local authorities and has continued on voluntary lines. It was estimated in 1913 that altogether 1786 school authorities had appointed school doctors. With few exceptions part-time officers are engaged, but some medical authorities contend for whole-time appointments, and this system has been adopted at Chemnitz, Mannheim, Halle, and other places. Chemnitz used to have 17 part-time doctors, each having charge of two schools and 2500 scholars ; it now finds that their work can be done by three whole-time practitioners, each being responsible for 12 schools and 14,000 scholars. Some towns, like Düsseldorf and Barmen, entrust the inspection of schools and the examination of scholars to the ordinary municipal medical officers and their assistants.

Hitherto the work of the school doctors has been confined to examination and advice, but the Labour party on the town councils and school committees strenuously advocate. the treatment of children as well ; and far-going though the proposal may appear, it is possible that before long some enterprising municipality may experiment in that direction. Meantime, the Labour party is being met half-way in many towns. Thus Fürth in Bavaria has a polyclinic—the equivalent of the out-patients' department of the English public hospitals —at which scholars of necessitous parents receive not only advice but medical treatment and medicine in all ailments, without charge, while ill-fed children are there supplied with milk daily.

In a number of towns school nurses have been appointed to support the work of the doctors, taking the children to the surgeries, visiting homes, and seeing that the treatment advised is carried out. Charlottenburg has for many years entrusted to school nurses the duty of watching over the welfare of poor and sickly children. A certain number of schools is assigned to each nurse, and these schools are visited in turn on the direction of the headmasters and the school doctors. Where necessary the parents of children needing medical attention or special care are visited in their homes and assisted in carrying out the doctor's orders. Amongst other miscellaneous activities falling within the scope of school hygiene are the provision of spectacles, trusses, and other inexpensive appliances to poor children, independently of the Poor Law, which is made by some local authorities, and the special classes for cripples.

(b) *School Dentists.*—Dental treatment is given on a large scale and the school dentist is fast coming to be regarded as a natural coadjutor of the school doctor. Treatment is given as a rule in special school clinics or surgeries. The first municipal clinic of the kind in Germany was established in 1903 at Strassburg, in which town the children attending the elementary schools had since 1888 had free dental treatment at the university polyclinic. To-day there are over 200 school dental clinics in some fifty towns, and the number increases every year. In most cases a charge varying from 6d. (as in Berlin) to 3s. a year, in respect of each child treated, is required from parents who can afford to pay, but treatment is usually given free to the children of poor parents. The number of children treated in large towns like Berlin, Düsseldorf, Nuremberg, Essen, and Stuttgart varies from 11,000 to 19,000 a year. In Alsace-Lorraine caravan clinics have been introduced for use in the villages; an entire equipment is found to cost about £125. The same institution has been introduced in the interest of town children at Dortmund, in Westphalia.

(c) *Feeding of Necessitous Children.*—The feeding of necessitous children is almost general in the larger towns, which here likewise have undertaken this heavy financial liability voluntarily and not in virtue of any statute or Government injunction. In some towns the work is done by the municipal authorities direct, but it is more convenient and usual to finance philanthropic societies formed for the purpose of carrying on this humane and necessary work. The municipality of Berlin began with a grant of £3500 in 1908, and it now votes over £11,000 a year towards this object. The tendency is more and more for the children to be fed at their own or neighbouring schools, to which end kitchens are equipped in suitable schools. These kitchens form an indispensable feature of all new buildings, and are also used in connection with the cookery instruction given to girls in the higher forms and at continuation classes. Usually the children of the very poor receive both breakfast and dinner free, but parents able to pay are charged a small sum—often not more than 1¼d.—for the midday meal. In some towns the school dinners are continued during the holidays.

(d) *Children's Care Centres.*—An invaluable work is done by associations assisted by public funds on the lines adopted by the children's care committees of London, though on a larger scale. The special purpose of these associations is the care of boys and girls of school age during the absence from home of their parents at factory or workroom. How important is the place filled by these societies may be judged from the fact that, according to the latest occupation census, four and a half million married women (widows and divorced and deserted women included) were in 1907 working for a livelihood in Germany. The movement began by the local authorities lending to these societies schoolrooms to which scholars came in the afternoon to do their homework, and afterwards stayed for other light occupation and games. Out of these simple children's work-and-play centres grew in some towns large institutions, like the model " Juveniles' Home " (*Jugendheim*) of Charlottenburg—founded and carried on by a philanthropic association subsidised by the town—where care begins with the infant and ends with the upgrown youth or maiden, for under one roof are gathered cribs, nurseries, and rooms for school work, games, and practical instruction in housekeeping and simple handicrafts. The "children's care centres" held in the schools are for the most part directed by voluntary workers, but some of the "Juveniles' Homes," like that at Charlottenburg, are staffed by trained women, assisted by girl volunteers of the higher middle class. When school years are over the children who frequent these centres are helped in the choice of occupations, and often ties are formed which last into married life. The "children's care centre" idea is naturally most developed in the large towns. Berlin, for example, has between sixty and seventy such centres, scattered in various parts of the city, most of them carried on in school buildings. At the present time (1914) some 35 municipalities are known to have established juveniles' homes, while the still more numerous institutions promoted by societies and individuals are as a rule liberally assisted from the public funds. Altogether there are in 256 towns about 1250 of these homes making regular provision for over 84,000 children, at a cost of £100,000 a year.

The Crusade Against Tuberculosis.—In no country is the crusade against tuberculosis being prosecuted more systematically and more vigorously than in Germany, and though the crusade specially owes its existence and its success to the insurance legislation, the municipal authorities are, at great cost, taking a prominent part in the work. So far their energies have been specially directed towards the development of the dispensary system. These institutions now exist in nearly all important towns, and in many small ones; they are often carried on by the local authorities, but if established by philanthropic societies they are invariably subsidised by the towns.

Of municipal agencies alone there are no fewer than 170 at the present time in various parts of the country. The majority are for men, others are for women, others again have departments for both sexes, and many are exclusively intended for children. The number of public dispensaries of all kinds, however, is estimated at between 800 and 900, Prussia having 187, Baden 537, Bavaria 54, and Saxony 39. The larger dispensaries are usually staffed with at least one trained practitioner, with assistants and nurses, and at all advice and assistance are given free. If home treatment is sufficient patients are required to visit the dispensary at intervals in order that the doctors may assure themselves that their advice is being faithfully followed. If admission to a sanatorium is desirable the needful steps are taken.

In the case of a person insured against sickness or invalidity the statutory insurance organisation to which he belongs undertakes the responsibility. In some towns examination at the municipal dispensary is a necessary preliminary to application for sanatorium treatment under the insurance laws. In the case of an uninsured patient without means, the Poor Law administration bears the cost.

Another form of treatment is that of the home for recuperation, admission to which is likewise conditional upon examination at the public dispensary. The incurables are dealt with as far as possible in special homes or separate sections of the municipal hospitals. The dispensary is only a single link in a chain of institutions created for combating one of the most terrible while one of the most preventable of diseases, yet its work is the starting-point for other measures, and upon its efficiency the success of these largely depends. Of dispensaries for consumptives Berlin and its suburbs have now fourteen, besides eleven for dipsomaniacs (one for women), and four for the diagnosis of cancer.

The Charlottenburg dispensary differs from most others in that while its medical staff advise the consumptives who report themselves, its nurses and visitors seek out the victims of tuberculosis in the homes of the working classes and the poor with a view to obtaining for them the special help which they need. The dispensary works in close association with the municipal school administration, the Industrial Insurance Organisations, and the National Women's Association for the Care of Consumptives, and though it does not undertake actual treatment, it procures for suitable patients admission to the proper institutions, while those undergoing domiciliary treatment are provided where necessary with nourishing food, clothing, beds and bedding, and fuel. Special attention is given to the care of children in the early stages of consumption with a view to increasing their resistibility to disease at a later age. Latterly the Charlottenburg dispensary has been developed into a "care office for consumptives." The cost of carrying on the "care office" in 1912 was about £2000, but in addition the town expended £9000 in sending patients to sanatoria, convalescent homes, and similar institutions, besides a large sum in treating patients in ordinary hospitals.

The municipal institutions for the special treatment of consumption known to exist in 1913 comprised, in addition to the dispensaries and advice agencies, ten sanatoria for adults, 36 institutions or sections of hospitals reserved for incurable cases, 20 sanatoria for children, five forest schools, five convalescent homes, and eight observation stations. Berlin, Munich, Hamburg, Bremen, Cologne, Nuremberg, and Aix-la-Chapelle are among the towns which have established sanatoria for consumptives, but the great majority of these institutions—the total of which exceeds three hundred, with some 27,000 beds—are owned and worked by the Statutory Insurance Organisations and philanthropic societies. Berlin receives consumptives in four sanatoria (with 426 beds), two for each sex, and it is about to build a special hospital for these sufferers at Buch, where it owns a large area of land and forest. The hospital is to accommodate 500 patients at first, but ultimately 1000, and is to be built upon a site 56 acres in extent, one-half of which is and will remain forest. The cost will exceed £400,000.

Charlottenburg is at present erecting an institution, situated in the midst of a large forest estate, in which tuberculous patients of three classes will be received, viz., serious cases of the type now treated in a special hospital in the town, incurable cases unsuited to admission into ordinary sanatoria, who will be offered a comfortable home until the end of their lives, and cases in the early stage. There will be accommodation for 200 persons, and children as well as adults will be received.

A preventive measure of a special kind is adopted by the municipality of Cologne, which provides tuberculous families with dwellings with gardens in open suburbs, in the hope that under the influence of healthy surroundings the scourge may be wiped out in the second generation. Görlitz, in Silesia, has followed Cologne's example. So, too, the town of Halberstadt has a municipal nursery garden for the employment of consumptives during the period of after care, until they are able to return to their past work or more suitable work can be found for them. While employed in this outdoor work they are under constant medical oversight. In many towns the municipal authority undertakes the cost of disinfecting all houses in which deaths from tuberculosis have taken place or in which tuberculous persons have lived.

Thanks to the energetic measures taken by the insurance organisations, the municipal authorities and philanthropic organisations jointly, the rate of mortality from consumption has already been reduced from a high to a moderate figure, and every year further progress is being made. According to Professor Kirchner the reduction in Prussia during the past 30 years has been nearly 50 per cent.

CONVALESCENT HOMES.—Although provision of this kind is made on a large scale by the statutory insurance organisations—chiefly by the Pension Boards which administer the Invalidity Insurance Law, but also by many of the sickness insurance societies—the larger towns are more and more regarding it as an essential part of their social welfare work. Where municipalities establish convalescent homes, homes of rest, and recuperative institutions akin to them, they do it mainly in the interest of the working classes, and in practice most of the persons received in these places are sent by their insurance organisations, yet admission is restricted to no section of the population, and the lower middle class is not slow to use the facilities offered. Except where admission is by order of the poor relief authority a charge is made, but this seldom or never covers the cost to the town.

The municipality of Berlin maintains a series of excellent and popular homes for convalescents and persons on the threshold of disease or breakdown for whom rest and recuperative treatment are necessary. There are seven of these homes, all pleasantly and healthily situated at a moderate distance from the city, from which they are conveniently reached by railway or tramway. There are three homes for each sex, two in each case being for consumptives and the third for general convalescents, and there is a home for children. Together the homes have accommodation for 650 persons. A feature of the convalescent home for women is the provision made for care after confinement. From all homes epileptics, dipsomaniacs, and persons suffering from certain other diseases are excluded. An inclusive charge of 2s. 6d. per day is made for each person, and this is often paid by the sickness insurance society to which the patient belongs. Cases of straitened means are met out of a charitable fund at the disposal of the municipal authority, allowing of free maintenance for several hundred persons for varying periods in the course of the year. There is a public office in a central part of the city at which applications for admission are received any day in the week.

The little town of Buch, where the home for male consumptives is situated, promises before long to become in its way a municipal " colony of mercy " after the pattern of the famous Bodelschwingh institution of " Bethel " near Bielefeld. A municipal infirmary, under the poor relief administration, intended for the aged and infirm poor, with room for 1500 persons, and a large lunatic asylum with room for 1800 persons are already located there ; a further lunatic asylum, the fourth municipal institution of the kind, is being erected ; and a large hospital for consumptives is contemplated.

Other towns have institutions of the same kind of a size proportionate to their needs, and it is noteworthy that increasing provision is being made for children in many ways. Thus Schöneberg recently built a convalescent home for children suffering from tuberculosis and scrofula.

MUNICIPAL LODGING-HOUSES FOR SINGLE MEN AND SHELTERS.—The municipal Rowton House for single men (*Ledigenheim*) is an institution of quite recent date whose origin must be sought in the insufficiency of the old practice of lodging with families, due in the main to two causes, viz., the severer lodger regulations now enforced and the curtailment of house space imposed on working-class families by the pressure of high rents. A number of towns have either built lodging-houses of this kind or have assisted philanthropic societies in so doing by the grant of land or money or by loans at a low rate of interest. Since 1908 Charlottenburg has had such a lodging-house, built by a society on land given by the municipality. It has 340 beds, mostly in separate rooms or cubicles, and the cost of bed and light breakfast is from 10s. to 15s. a month. The building is open from 5 a.m. until midnight. Attached to the institution are a branch of the municipal library, reading rooms, a common room, a restaurant, and baths. Weissensee has more recently built a lodging-house with three flats, one for women and two for men, and it is carried on as a municipal institution. Strassburg and Düsseldorf have similar institutions. The municipalities of Berlin and Posen have given to public utility building societies sites for houses to contain several hundred beds, and Munich proposes to erect two houses of still larger size.

In the interest of the homeless waifs and strays of town life municipal shelters of various kinds are provided, from the warm " kitchen," simply equipped, it may be, in a railway arch or some other odd corner, where food may be had for a coin of the lowest denomination, to the public doss-house where a mattress is offered free for the night, " with no questions asked." Few of the too regular frequenters of these institutions belong, however, to the work-seeking class. Berlin has two large shelters, one for single men and women and the other for families, and between them they house on an average 3000 persons every night of the year. The municipality also subsidises a smaller shelter working on the same lines. The municipality of Dresden has just opened two shelters, one for families who are unable to find or rent dwellings, and the other for the general homeless wanderers of the street. The former are assigned small apartments at a charge of 6d a day if they can afford it, and the latter are received without charge. When completed the two blocks will have cost the town £37,500.

MUNICIPAL LABOUR REGISTRIES.—Germany set the world an example in the creation of public labour registries, and other countries have gone to it for instruction in the working of these institutions. While, however, Great Britain and, on a small scale, some of the United States have adopted a State organisation of labour registries, this field of activity is still left in Germany to the municipal authorities and welfare associations, the latter being almost invariably assisted by grants of public money or the loan of public buildings or both, and to trade and labour organisations. Of registries either conducted or assisted by the communes there were in Prussia only three in 1880 and 29 in 1890, but 266 in 1911 ; in the last-named year there were in Bavaria 67, in Saxony 43, in Würtemberg 16, in Baden 18, in Hesse 27, and in the rest of the Empire 38, making a total of 475. The importance attached to the subject by the municipalities may be judged by the fact that of 123 Prussian towns with a population in excess of 25,000, 115 now either maintain or subsidise labour registries. According to the " Statistical Yearbook of German Towns," 57 of the larger towns in 1911 expended on their own labour registries the sum of £27,870, an average of £490, independently of the cost of rent, light, and heating.

This large expenditure is the more noteworthy since it is entirely voluntary. Some of the public labour registries are organised on a bureaucratic basis, that is, they are conducted by municipal officials like any other local institution, but what is known as the " paritative " principle is usual, the executive here consisting of employers and workpeople in equal numbers, though here, too, a municipal official may be chosen as chairman. Invaluable as is the service which the registries perform both for labour and capital, however, their influence is not as great as it might be owing to the fact that the larger employers and the larger industries more and more remain aloof.

There is a tendency to combine the general work of the labour registry with activities of a cognate character ; thus some registries endeavour to find employment for children leaving school, for domestic servants, for consumptives and other persons of limited physical capacity ; or the registry keeps a list of foster-parents for use in the boarding out of orphans and other children maintained by the poor relief authority ; and the municipal house registry, the legal advice agencies, and writing-rooms for unemployed clerks and others are sometimes worked along with the public labour registry.

As in France, the private employment agencies are subject to severe public control. Under the Industrial Code all employment agents need to be licensed, and for the protection of the public it is required that their charges shall be submitted to the police authority for approval, shall be displayed conspicuously in their rooms, and shall be notified to applicants before business is done. In some towns these private registries are subject to the oversight of the local authorities.

In some States many of the communal authorities contribute liberally towards the cost of the " relief stations " established for the benefit of wandering work-seekers, and in Bavaria one-third of the three hundred institutions of the kind are maintained by the communes, rather more by the district authorities, and the rest by associations. At most of these stations only relief in kind—board and lodging, with clothing occasionally—is given, and as a rule a labour task has to be performed in return. A Prussian law of June 29, 1907, provides for the establishment by the local authorities of labour yards for the same class of itinerant workers. The law can be put in force by resolution of the Provincial Diets, and the Provincial Committees then decide which communes shall take action and the character of the provision they shall make, but the provinces contribute largely towards the costs of maintenance. Many towns have been required to establish labour yards for the itinerant unemployed, and their existence has in some places led to the application of severer police measures against mendicancy and loafing than were formerly regarded as justifiable.

ASSISTED UNEMPLOYMENT INSURANCE FUNDS.—A few towns have introduced unemployment insurance on what is known as the Ghent system. So long ago as 1896 an unemployment insurance fund was formed at Cologne in the special interest of workpeople engaged in the outdoor trades and, with municipal help, was carried on during the winter months. Some time ago the fund was reorganised on a broader basis and passed into municipal care. Leipzig has had a similar assisted fund since 1903, providing benefits all the year round.

More important, however, are the experiments which have been made on the Ghent lines by the municipal authorities of sixteen towns up to 1914, including Strassburg, Freiburg, Stuttgart, Schöneberg, Mannheim, Mülhausen, and Offenbach. Under this system the public authority usually grants to recognised trade unions an agreed proportion—often 50 per cent.— of the unemployment benefit which they pay to their members. As a rule, the town's subsidy is paid out of a fund which is under the same management as the public labour registry, an arrangement which makes it possible to exercise close control over the applicants for benefit and also to afford many of them work instead of money. At Strassburg, which introduced this system in Germany, unmarried men must be willing to accept work out of the town, if offered, on pain of forfeiting claim to benefit, and recipients of benefit must report themselves daily at the labour registry at the times fixed. Subsidies are only given in respect of workpeople who are unemployed owing to causes other than strikes, lockouts, sickness, accident, and disablement (provision is made for the last three cases by statutory insurance funds), and in order to be eligible to receive a subsidy a workman must have lived in the town uninterruptedly for a year prior to losing his employment. Strictly speaking this system of helping the unemployed is not insurance in the technical sense of the word. The mutual principle is adopted to the extent that workpeople pay special contributions to a common fund for the purpose and receive benefit from that fund, but both contributions and benefits are fixed in a more or less arbitrary manner.

In practice the boon of public assistance falls in the main to the skilled workers, inasmuch as unemployment benefit is rare in the unskilled trades. In order to meet this difficulty some towns encourage individual saving for the contingency of unemployment by the offer of premiums, but neither in Belgium nor Germany has this feature of the Ghent system proved very successful. Although the Labour party, both by its newspapers and its representatives on the town councils, has made vigorous attempts to commend to local authorities this system of assisted unemployment insurance, and although the Governments have strongly urged its adoption, the great majority of towns refuse to take action, holding that this is a question for Imperial legislation.

Without creating insurance machinery, several towns, like Munich and Mayence, relieve unemployed workpeople by direct payments of public money, which do not count as poor relief and hence do not entail civil disqualifications. Such payments are, as a rule, confined to the winter months, and with a view to the prevention of fraud organised workmen in receipt of help are required to report themselves daily to the officials of their unions, and unorganised workmen to municipal controllers. In order to be qualified for this benefit applicants must have lived in the town and have been out of work for a specified period, and at Munich only men are eligible. During the wide-spread unemployment in the winter of 1913-14 the municipality of Berlin set aside a sum of £15,000 out of which loans free of interest were made to deserving persons.

PUBLIC WORKS FOR THE UNEMPLOYED.—The larger towns have found it necessary to supplement the work of the labour registry by more positive measures. Wherever possible suitable unemployed persons who come before the notice of the poor relief authority are offered work, usually of an unskilled, out-of-door character, in connection with one or other of the many departments of the administration. In times of exceptional unemployment this can often be done on a large scale owing to the care taken to anticipate pressure of the kind, and to hold over for periods of trade depression public works the execution of which is not urgent. This policy of reserving work for bad times is not confined to local authorities, but is followed on an even larger and more systematic scale by the Government departments, and particularly the Railway Ministries. In so acting the local authorities of Prussia are following instructions issued by the Government as long ago as 1894. When trade depression increased unemployment in Berlin in the winter of 1913-14 the municipality was able to put in hand public works involving an expenditure of half a million pounds which would not have been executed under ordinary conditions of the labour market, and employment upon these works was offered only to Berlin workmen.

Where the normal works of the municipality do not suffice to absorb the unemployed, public distress or relief works are commonly undertaken. Such works were first organised on a large scale during the period of acute trade depression 1891–5, then again in 1900–3, and once more in 1907–9. More than a hundred and fifty towns now resort to distress works in case of need, and in a few towns distress works are carried on from year to year and all the year round. Here and there writing-rooms are opened for skilled applicants for employment, but the great majority of the unemployed are offered outdoor work, such as road and street making, excavating, digging, sand getting, stone breaking, and faggot cutting—in general, just such works as were suggested by the Order of the Local Government Board issued by Mr. J. Chamberlain in 1886, empowering Boards of Guardians to furnish to the unemployed work instead of poor relief, for the purpose of protecting them against the demoralising influence of dependence on public assistance.

Almost the only merit that can be claimed for the distress works is that they enable the authorities to exact some sort of equivalent for what in many cases is, in effect though not in law, public relief. While not confined to digging holes and filling them up again, much of the outdoor work is work of an uneconomic kind, in the sense that it would not be undertaken except on compulsion and as an alternative to poor relief, and that it is, as a rule, done at a loss as compared with the price of contract work. Unquestionably, too, distress work is looked down upon not only by workmen in general but by the men who do it. Naturally workmen of the better class only go to the distress works as a last resort. As a rule the work is restricted to persons who have lived in the town for a certain qualifying period varying from three months upwards, applicants must hitherto have been in regular employment, and sometimes preference is given to married men.

The rates of payment are almost invariably below those usually paid for similar work; yet even so the towns usually find that they pay dearly for whatever is done. " The past experience of distress works," writes Dr. Thissen, " has not in general been satisfactory. In most cases the work done has not covered the cost, and in many cases a very considerable over-expenditure has taken place."[1] Thus in the winter of 1908-9 the municipality of Düsseldorf employed 2350 men on distress works at a cost of £29,900, which amount was £10,000 larger than the cost that would have been incurred had the town employed ordinary labourers on normal conditions, and during the entire period 1901 to 1910 the loss on its distress works varied from 30 to 50 per cent. Similarly Berlin paid distress workers 23s. per cubic metre of stone broken by hand as compared with a contract rate of from 3s. 6d. to 4s. 6d., and one of 1s. if done by machine. It has been estimated that distress work in general is quite one-third dearer than similar work done under ordinary conditions.

THE POOR MAN'S LAWYER.—Another institution of great and growing utility which belongs to the social welfare work of German municipalities is the Legal Advice and Information Agency (*Rechtsauskunftstelle*), which assists persons of small means in the many legal difficulties that arise in industrial, civil, and family life—e.g., in regard to the relationship between employer and workman and between landlord and tenant, rates and taxes, industrial insurance, liability for the maintenance of relatives, the labour laws, marriage contracts, military service, school and Poor Law questions, and the like. In most cases advice is given free, but a small charge is often made when documents have to be prepared. The office is usually in charge of a municipal official with legal training. This is a branch of work in which the municipalities have been induced to engage owing to the remarkable success of the earlier Trade Union agencies of the same kind, the number of which exceeds 500, three-quarters of them belonging to the Socialist organisations. In addition to the agencies of these two types a large number are carried on by public utility and religious organisations, by societies working exclusively in the interest of women, and a few by employers' associations and political bodies, the total in all Germany being nearly a thousand.

In 1912 there were over 110 municipal advice agencies,

[1] " Soziale Tätigkeit der Stadtgemeinden," p. 47.

nearly all established within the preceding ten years, and in the course of the year they gave advice in over 300,000 cases, chiefly to working-people and other persons of small means. Sometimes the municipalities, instead of conducting these agencies by their own officers, subsidise philanthropic societies formed for the purpose. Schöneberg, for example, provides such a society with offices free of rent, and in addition grants it £100 per annum. In Würtemberg the State pays one-half of the salaries of officers engaged in connection with the municipal legal advice agencies. In many towns these agencies extend their functions in various directions. At the Hagen municipal information office women and girls are advised as to occupations. Information is given to them not only upon the duties of and qualifications for various callings—i.e., nursing, teaching, domestic service, and commercial and other work specially suited to women—but the labour laws are explained to them, and intelligent applicants are able to learn all that they need to know in order to protect themselves against exploitation. At Schöneberg the municipality keeps a register of experts—both societies and individuals—and applicants who visit this clearing-house for inquiries are promptly referred to the proper quarter.

MUNICIPAL PAWNSHOPS.—Few of the larger towns are without public pawnshops, which transact a large amount of business on terms more favourable to borrowers than those offered by private establishments. The latter are stringently regulated by Imperial and State laws. Not only does the business of a pawnbroker require to be licensed, but a town may adopt a by-law making permits dependent upon proof of need. The effect is to protect the municipal pawnshop, where it exists, from competition and the working classes from a good deal of imposition. Germany borrowed the idea of public pawnshops from Italy, and Augsburg established the first at the end of the sixteenth century. There are now 49 such pawnshops in Prussia, 34 in Bavaria, and 15 in other parts of the country, and most of them are of old standing. The Munich pawnshops, dating from the middle of the eighteenth century, are among the best examples of municipal enterprise of this kind. There are four of these institutions, under the direct control of the municipality, which provides the buildings, appoints the officials, and finances the undertakings. In general, the articles that are taken in pawn comprise all movables which may be stored easily and without danger, and also State and municipal bonds, mortgages, and other securities. No articles of furniture are received, partly because of the large amount of warehouse room that would be required, but also because it is a fixed principle to discourage the pawning of articles which belong to the primary comforts of the home. Documents relating to debts (promissory notes, etc.), wages and pension certificates, orders and medals, and furriery are also refused. For the better security of the municipality whose credit is employed, the appraiser who values the articles received on pawn is held personally responsible for each sum advanced being realised in the event of sale. Should the amount then realised fall below that advanced, he must either take the article himself and pay the institution the sum advanced, together with interest and pawn-ticket fee, but without the auction fee, or, as in Paris, must pay the deficiency. The effect of this arrangement is that the valuations are kept fairly low, but this is not regarded as an unmixed evil, for it encourages the owners to reclaim the goods pawned. On the other hand, should an article be sold for more than was advanced upon it (plus interest to the day of sale and auction fees) the excess may be claimed by the late owner within a year of the day of sale, after which date it becomes the property of the institution.

The Municipal Pawnshop Law of Bavaria accords with that of Prussia in requiring that the profits from these agencies shall be applied to the relief of the poor, which means in effect the special relief of the larger taxpayers. In the other States the profits are assigned variously to the public poor funds, to local charities, or direct to the municipal treasury, but in some towns a portion is divided amongst the officials concerned. It is sometimes objected that pawnshops encourage thriftlessness. If they are to exist at all, however, it is better that they should be accompanied by the guarantees of moderate interest and honourable dealing which municipal management offers.

MISCELLANEOUS WELFARE WORK.—In addition to all the foregoing activities, which are more or less common to the larger towns, many voluntary benefits of a minor and miscellaneous kind are offered to the poorer classes as local conditions suggest. For example, at Dessau the municipal authority systematically helps heads of large families to pay their rents. Should such households be willing to take houses of a size proportionate to their requirements, a grant of one-third of the rent may be made, but the condition is imposed that lodgers may not be received. Strassburg holds evening sewing and mending schools at which women and girls after work-hours are taught to make and mend their own clothes. A small fee is charged to those who can afford to pay, but all women of the poorer classes are welcomed. The municipality of Nuremberg supplies coke made at the town gasworks at a reduced price to persons of limited means (the income limit for the purpose being fixed at £110), with the condition that not more than 25 cwts. may be bought by any one individual in the course of a year. Essen has a marriage dowry fund for working-girls. These girls are encouraged to lay by savings for the purpose in the municipal savings bank, and in addition to 3½ per cent. paid by the bank a further 3½ per cent. is added by way of bonus.

Most of the measures mentioned in the foregoing survey relate specially to the working and the poorer classes. Nevertheless, some towns extend their solicitude to other sections of the community, and particularly to the handicrafts and the small industries. A sympathetic endeavour is being made in many parts of the country to strengthen the position of these deserving and hard-pressed interests by the promotion of technical and continuation schools, the establishment of workshops for the training of apprentices (as in Munich), the supply of cheap power for industrial purposes, the establishment of permanent industrial museums and exhibitions, the promotion of co-operation, arrangements for allotting public work to handicraftsmen and small employers, and other measures.

CHAPTER XII

INTELLECTUAL LIFE

Public libraries and reading-rooms—Primary schools—Secondary schools—Continuation and technical schools—Municipal expenditure on education—The drama and music.

TRUE to their large conception of municipal government, as embracing the entire corporate life of the community, the local authorities act as official patrons of learning, of the arts and sciences, and by the use of the resources of the community bring the influences of culture within reach of the population in forms and on a scale which would be impossible were this domain left to the uncertain action of private individuals. German towns are rich in art galleries and museums of various kinds, and the buildings in which these collections are housed are seldom unworthy of their purpose; the public schools have been claimed as " the pride of the towns," and their work is supported by well-equipped public libraries; municipal theatres, or theatres subsidised by the municipalities, are regarded as an essential part of the intellectual life of even small communities; and many towns add to their patronage of the drama equal concern for the plentiful provision of good music.

The pride shown in the architecture and appearance of the streets and public buildings may fairly be taken as indicating a high estimate of the place of art in municipal life. Prodigal outlay is incurred upon town halls, public theatres and concert halls, museums and art galleries, bridges and monuments. In the State capitals some of the finest public buildings and monuments owe their existence to Government necessities or to the liberality or dynastic piety of the rulers, but such examples only encourage the municipalities to more willing emulation in adorning and beautifying their towns. Many of the old town halls, besides being monuments in themselves, are literally treasure-houses of art in the most diverse forms—painting, sculpture, wood-carving, gold, silver, metal, ceramic and glass work—and stimulated by the tradition of past public munificence modern towns, with history still to make, are proving that the old spirit of municipal pride to which these memorials bear witness is still as vigorous as ever.

Some towns, while endeavouring, so far as their means allow, to obtain examples of the best modern art both of Germany and foreign countries, specially collect *Heimatkunst*, i.e., works by noted painters born in or otherwise connected with their respective localities. In the place given in their galleries to " local " art, Cologne specialises in Leibl, Frankfort-on-Main in Thoma, Trübner, and Boehle, and Leipzig in Klinger. Hamburg, however, has still more distinguished itself in this direction, and its collection of local art, made by its art director, the late Alfred Lichtwark, is regarded as a model for all Germany. Of late years many towns have established, on the same lines, museums devoted to the special products of local industries, to local antiquities, costume, and the like. All such efforts are in sympathy with the modern policy of the public schools, which aim at cultivating the national and patriotic spirit by strengthening local attachment and pride.

In the larger towns all public artistic property is administered by special committees composed in the usual way of members of the town council and the executive, with co-opted citizens. In some towns, however, Advisory Art Committees have been formed to assist the local authorities in spending wisely the public grants and private benefactions made in promoting the interests of art. At Cologne a committee of this kind consists of the chief mayor, members of the city council, the directors of the museums, with a number of painters, architects, and art connoisseurs.

The activity of the municipal authorities in this domain may be shown by the following summary of the expenditure of large towns on miscellaneous purposes of culture, viz., libraries, art and science, theatre and music, etc., exclusive of all expenditure on schools, in the year 1912 :—

INTELLECTUAL LIFE

Towns and Population.	(a) Libraries and Reading-rooms.	(b) Art and Science.	(c) Theatre and Music.	(d) Miscellaneous.	(e) Total.
	£	£	£	£	£
Aix-la-Chapelle (158,800)	1,720	4,850	16,680	2,800	26,050
Düsseldorf (390,000)	5,725	8,350	26,500	4,105	44,680
Essen (307,000)	2,350	5,520	15,320	270	23,460
Cassel (155,300)	930	—	—	3,580 (b) (c) (d)	4,510
Chemnitz (287,800)	2,850	3,130	18,130	—	24,110
Danzig (173,900)	3,750	7,140	500	120	11,510
Frankfort-on-Main (431,900)	7,660	32,530	30,280	5,460	75,930
Mannheim (217,700)	1,080	16,800	27,930	2,870	48,680
Totals (pop. 2,122,400)	£26,065	£78,320	£135,340	£19,205	£258,930
Expend. per inhabitant	2·9d.	8·9d.	15·3d.	2·2d.	29·3d.

The aggregate expenditure thus shown, viz. £258,930, was equivalent to nearly 2s. 6d. a head of the combined population of over two millions.

Figures relating to certain large towns of Great Britain, also for 1912, may be given for comparison:—

Towns and Population.	(a) Libraries and Reading-rooms.	(b) Art and Science.	(c) Theatre and Music.	(d) Miscellaneous.	(e) Total.
	£	£	£	£	£
Leeds (445,600)	12,992	1,033	346	—	14,371
Cardiff (184,600)	7,706	—	—	—	7,706
Dundee (165,300)	6,506	—	—	—	6,506
Birmingham (840,200)	21,726	23,662	—	—	45,388
Glasgow (1,105,200)	27,306	13,324	4,585	29,348	74,563
Manchester (731,700)	31,792	10,427	5,609	4,126	51,954
Huddersfield (107,800)	2,028	5,069	—	—	7,097
Newcastle (271,300)	848	2,569	495	10	3,922
Leicester (227,200)	4,020	13,091	284	—	17,395
Salford (231,400)	7,778	1,619	—	—	9,397
Bradford (290,300)	8,295	2,280	—	—	10,575
Bolton (180,900)	6,718	—	—	—	6,718
Sheffield (454,600)	9,720	4,183	2,872	—	16,775
Bristol (359,400)	8,674	1,500	—	—	10,174
Total (pop. 5,595,500)	£156,109	£78,757	£14,191	£33,484	£282,541
Expend. per inhabitant	6·7d.	3·4d.	0·6d.	1·5d.	12·1d.

The expenditure per head of the aggregate population of over 5½ millions shown by these figures is 1s. It will be seen that the higher German expenditure was chiefly incurred on account of the theatre and upon science and art, while the English towns had a larger *per capita* expenditure upon libraries and reading-rooms. This larger expenditure appears to be explained by the multiplication of branch libraries and reading-rooms in these towns, their average number of libraries and branches being twelve, as compared with four in the German towns, and of reading-rooms eleven as compared with three. The public libraries in the English towns named had a total of 3,479,000 volumes, equivalent to 630 volumes for every thousand inhabitants; while the libraries in the German towns had a total of 1,113,100 volumes, equivalent to 520 per thousand inhabitants.

PUBLIC LIBRARIES AND READING-ROOMS.—The efforts which are made on behalf of popular enlightenment are deserving of all praise. No public body will freely spend money upon objects unappreciated by those for whom they are intended; hence the fact that German municipalities do so much, at so large a cost, for the spread of enlightenment amongst the working classes is of itself proof of a genuine popular regard and demand for knowledge. Most towns have excellent public libraries and reading-rooms, often with branch institutions of both kinds in convenient centres, and if, as statisticians say, from 60 to 70 per cent. of the books lent out are novels, the remnant represents a very respectable margin of serious reading. Some towns, including Munich, Frankfort-on-Main, and Charlottenburg, have of late introduced a novel extension of the public library principle by lending out collections of music in the ordinary way with books. In 1910, 329 German towns were known to have public libraries, and 168 to have reading-rooms. The principal municipal library of Berlin now contains 125,000 volumes, but affiliated to it and scattered about the city are 28 smaller libraries containing from 5000 to 15,000 volumes each, and connected with 14 of them are reading-rooms. One of the Berlin public reading-rooms is intended for children from six to thirteen years of age; at fourteen they are allowed to use the reading-rooms for adults. In many other towns children are similarly provided for by societies subsidised by the local authorities.

Many towns regularly arrange winter courses of popular lectures on scientific, literary, and historical subjects, and still more assist associations and institutions which in any way whatever aim at bringing knowledge of the kind within the reach of the working classes. In this work of popular enlightenment as carried on in Prussia the State is not able to claim a very meritorious part, for its action has been directed for the most part towards preventing the working classes, if Socialist, from educating themselves in their own way and the municipal authorities from helping them to do so. Private associations, on the contrary, have done much honourable work, and particularly the Humboldt Association, the German Society for Ethical Culture, the Gehe Foundation of Dresden, the Scientific Association, the Roman Catholic Borromeo Association, the Society for the Spread of Popular Education, the Comenius Society, and the University settlement and extension societies which exist in some of the larger towns.

In their concern to advance the education of the working classes, to stimulate their interest in culture, and to refine their tastes and habits, the municipalities are simply carrying further endeavours which began with the workers themselves. Since the middle of last century working-men's educational associations have been common in German towns, and indeed it was to these associations that the modern pioneer of the German Socialist movement, Ferdinand Lassalle, addressed himself when he sought to gain the popular ear for his ambitious scheme of a Universal Working-men's Productive Association, which was to combine all working-people in a national movement for the purpose of supplanting private capitalism. The desire of the working classes for a larger share in the satisfactions of culture has never been overshadowed by their striving for a fuller part in the gains and benefits of material progress, but rather has deepened with the growth of their class solidarity. The remarkable development of the trade union movement in Germany within the last decade impresses all observers, both at home and abroad, but the educational movement which is part of it, and is directed by the same men who are foremost in the work of labour organisation, is often ignored, though in some respects its significance is greater.[1]

PRIMARY SCHOOLS.—The name of the primary or elementary schools of Germany—*Gemeinde,* or communal schools—tells their origin. For centuries the communes have been responsible for the provision and maintenance of these schools. Lübeck had town schools as early as the middle of the fourteenth century, and at the Reformation the communes more and more assumed responsibility for popular education. Luther himself, in 1524, addressed a strong appeal to the senates of all towns in Germany to " establish and maintain Christian schools." As a rule, the towns encountered bitter ecclesiastical opposition in their claim to establish these schools, and often they won it only subject to the condition that the clergy should give the instruction.

To-day, therefore, the communes are doing for elementary education on a larger scale just what they were accustomed to do in the days prior to the passing of education laws, and still the old conflict with the Church goes on. The elementary school system of nearly all the States rests on a distinctly "confessional" basis, i.e., the children attend schools intended for Protestant, Roman Catholic, or Jewish children respectively. Of about 6½ million elementary school children in Prussia, only some 370,000 attend schools for mixed confessions, and in these they are instructed as far as possible on confessional lines. Moreover, the clergy have the right in some States to give religious instruction and to inspect the schools, or co-operate in that work, and throughout the country they occupy a prominent place on the administrative boards and committees. In no part of Germany is clerical influence in the primary schools so strong as in Bavaria, where the clergy almost monopolise the work of local inspection, and in some districts are able to determine the choice of teachers

[1] The answer of a poor old farm labourer of Westphalia to the question (put to him by a friend of the writer in 1913), what would he do if he had unlimited leisure, " I would read myself full " (" *Ich würde mich satt lesen* "), is a touching expression of the craving for knowledge which is one of the most honourable traits of the German working class.

and the character and methods of instruction, even to the choice of text-books.

To state these facts, however, is not to imply that the local governments recognise the existing division of authority as expedient or tolerable ; for the schools of the people are the scene of quite as much conflict in Germany as elsewhere, the only difference being that, as in that country the interest and influence of the State are on the side of the Church, the struggle is unequal and the prospect of victory for the secular side at present hopeless.

As a rule the State contents itself with laying down normal regulations in regard to buildings and their equipment, teaching staffs and their salaries, and the curriculum, and leaves the communes to do as much more as they like, while retaining the right to confirm certain appointments and to inspect all schools through its special officers.

The local administration of the primary schools is vested in bodies more or less representative in character—usually known in Prussia as School Deputations, in Saxony as School Committees, and in South Germany as School Commissions. These bodies are composed of members of the municipal executive and of the town council, representatives of the clergy, and other co-opted citizens deemed to be specially fitted for the position, with one or more headmasters or other teachers of elementary schools, while the school inspector of the " circle " has a right to attend all meetings in his capacity as commissary of the supervisory authority, and the mayor of the town can also attend at his will and take the chair. Often, however, the chairman is a permanent municipal official known as the school councillor, who is responsible for the executive work. In the larger towns committees are often formed for groups of schools.

For the consideration and determination of technical questions many towns have created special bodies known as School Boards (*Ämter*), composed of municipal officials who are chosen as educational experts. In Hamburg these questions are referred to a school synod, of which all teachers on the establishment are members. One of the latest departures in education is the experimental school, the purpose of which is to do for education what experimental farms and stations, for example, do for practical agriculture—to test teaching methods and appliances on a small scale before they are introduced into regular use. The idea took root first at Munich in 1909, and it has since attracted attention in other parts of the country. Frankfort-on-Main and several other towns have school museums for the exhibition of school appliances, with libraries for teachers attached.

For expositions of educational policy and internal administration the reader must be referred to special works, which are no longer rare. Nor is it possible to dwell upon the enlightened policy of school building followed by all progressive towns. All that can be said on this subject is that in no department of administration is money spent on a more lavish scale than in the provision and equipment of schools, which are equally excellent whether intended for fee-paying middle-class scholars or the children of the people. Upon the portal of many of these fine buildings, as imposing without as they are attractive within, might well be written the words which Shakespeare puts in the mouth of Miranda : " There's nothing ill can dwell in such a temple."

Here it is only pertinent to call attention to distinctive features of the general organisation of the primary school system. Great changes have been wrought in recent years owing to the institution of a system of inspection and examination by municipal school doctors. The old mechanical method of treating all children alike, whether normal or abnormal in physical and mental capacity, has been abandoned, and special schools for defective children are now common. Schools for stammerers, for the deaf and dumb, for children suffering from defective hearing, for cripples, and for the mentally deficient are found in all the large towns, and the results have proved successful beyond expectations. The Düsseldorf school authority several years ago began orthopœdic gymnastic courses for deformed children, and its example has since been followed in other towns. What is called " lip reading " instruction for deaf children, the object of which is to develop their observation and enable them to interpret lip movements in terms of sound, is also common.

The School Deputation of Berlin instituted "auxiliary" schools for defective children of various kinds in 1910 and the number has since increased to twenty. If satisfactory progress is made the children are sent back to the ordinary schools, otherwise they receive separate instruction throughout the school course. Where possible these auxiliary schools are carried on in the ordinary school buildings, and the teachers are chosen from amongst the permanent elementary teachers of both sexes who have been for some years in service and have shown special fitness for the work. Munich has twenty-six of these schools, and the children attending them are cared for out of school hours by a philanthropic society, which provides them with food, clothing, and medical attendance where needed, and after the school course is over endeavours to find them suitable employment if capable. Charlottenburg, Dortmund, Mülhausen, and München-Gladbach have established municipal forest schools for physically defective children, and in other towns the local authorities subsidise schools of the kind. As a rule, the children remain at the schools from morning until evening, but in several cases they are boarded as well as taught.

Among the miscellaneous activities of the school authorities, traceable to a wider conception of social obligation—some of which are referred to in greater detail in the chapter dealing with the social welfare work of the municipal authorities—may be mentioned the arrangements for feeding scholars, for organised games suitable to all seasons of the year, for country rambles, for holidays at the seaside and elsewhere, the school baths, the school libraries and museums, the concerts and theatrical performances arranged for scholars only, and the school gardens. Recently the school authorities of many towns have recognised the educational value of the "picture theatre" when properly conducted, and special exhibitions are often arranged for children of the higher forms, bearing as a rule on subjects of daily instruction. The local authorities also subsidise the day nurseries, afternoon work-and-play centres, and children's clubs which are carried on in the larger towns by philanthropic societies.

School gardens have been common in Germany for half a

century; Berlin has had them since 1875, Leipzig, Breslau, and Mannheim since 1888. The amount of land devoted to this purpose varies from an acre to over sixty acres at Magdeburg. School rambles in the company of teachers are an important feature of the summer term in all towns. The children of the elementary schools as a rule set out from a convenient point on the railway (nominal fares being charged for the purpose) and return home in the evening, but the rambles taken by boys and girls of the higher schools last several days or even a week, and often take them far afield.

There is not so clear a class division between the primary and higher schools of Germany as that which exists in this country. In the rural districts especially it is still a common practice for the children of the lord of the manor, the State chief forester, and the local clergyman to pass several years in the elementary schools before going elsewhere. In Bavaria the children of all classes, whether high or low, are in theory obliged to attend the primary schools for the first three or four years, though it is not difficult to obtain exemption from the rule, and the children of well-to-do parents usually attend private schools or receive home teaching until they are able to enter the higher schools. In Berlin and other towns the education authority provides preparatory schools for those who can afford to pay.

Although Germany is "a land of schools," education is no more free in that country than in this. Fees, often of large amount, are universal in the higher and middle schools, and Prussia is the only important State in which the primary schools are free. In Saxony fees of from 5s. to 8s. yearly may still be charged in these schools, though in many towns free places are given liberally, and in Dresden fees are charged only in respect of the first two children in a family. In Bavaria the fees may not exceed 2s. 10d. yearly, but in most towns no charge is made. In Baden so recent an education law as that of 1910 does not recognise the principle of free education, but only empowers the communes to relieve necessitous parents. Mannheim has two kinds of primary schools, "burgher" schools, in which fees of 28s. a year are charged, and free schools. School materials are charged for almost universally except in the case of persons with small incomes.

SECONDARY SCHOOLS.—The State is supposed to be responsible for the provision and, so far as fees are inadequate, for the maintenance of the higher schools in general, but here, too, the local authorities have shown great enterprise, with the result of relieving the State of much necessary expenditure. This has been the case particularly in Prussia and Saxony. Thus Berlin has 29 municipal higher schools of different types, eight being *lycées* for girls; Dresden has twelve, and Leipzig eleven. In Bavaria higher schools for boys are mostly established by the State, and those for girls by the local authorities. Of a total of 563 gymnasia in Germany in 1911, 331 were maintained by the State, 172 by the communes, and 22 by the State and communes jointly; of a total of 223 real-gymnasia the State maintained 51, the communes 159, and the State and communes jointly 11; while of the middle and higher-grade schools of other types the great majority were maintained by the communes. In Prussia two out of five of the gymnasia are municipal, while most of the other middle and higher-grade schools—including the " burgher " schools —are municipal. The middle schools (the " real " schools of various types), indeed, owe their existence largely to municipal initiative, and only tardily did the State agree to tolerate their competition with the old classical gymnasia. Nearly one-half of the higher schools for girls are municipal, and in many towns the local authorities subsidise private schools of this type. As a rule, the municipal higher schools are administered by a separate board or council consisting of members of the executive, town councillors, teachers, and other co-opted members, while the State higher schools in Prussia are administered by Provincial School Colleges, under the supervision of the Chief Presidents.

In many towns a serious attempt is made by the school authorities to open wide the doors of the higher schools to talent wherever found. In Bavaria every capable elementary scholar is afforded an opportunity of passing the examination for admission to the higher schools. In Berlin and other towns full or half exhibitions in the higher schools are systematically offered to elementary scholars who have given proof of capacity, diligence, and good behaviour. On the whole, however, the higher schools are principally used by the children of parents who are able to pay for the education given, and the fees are not in general low, though sometimes they are graduated according to income. Thus the fees charged in the higher boys' schools of Crefeld begin at £4 10s. per annum in the case of parents in receipt of income not exceeding £75, and are £5 for incomes between £75 and £90, £5 10s. for incomes between £90 and £120, £6 for incomes between £120 and £150, £6 10s. for incomes between £150 and £180, and £7 for incomes in excess of £180.

CONTINUATION AND TECHNICAL SCHOOLS.—The towns have been equally enterprising in providing continuation and technical schools. The continuation school system is regulated by State law, and the individual legislatures may make the establishment of these schools obligatory on communes or permissive at will. In order, however, to meet the case of States in which Government initiative is lacking, the Imperial Industrial Code contains the provision that where continuation schools are not compulsory under State law communes may adopt by-laws in virtue of which schools may be established, with obligatory attendance, for male workpeople generally under 18 years and for female shop assistants and apprentices of the same age, and wherever these schools exist employers are required to afford their workers liable to attend the necessary time for so doing. Should the local authorities decline to establish continuation schools on the requisition of employers and workpeople the supervisory authorities may require them to do so. Attendance at continuation schools is obligatory by State law for boys in Bavaria, Saxony, Würtemberg, Baden, Hesse, and other smaller States, but in Prussia only in several of the provinces by law, though elsewhere a large and increasing number of communes have adopted by-laws for the purpose. The age up to which attendance is compulsory is fixed variously at 16, 17, and 18 years. As a rule the course of instruction lasts three or four years, with attendance for six or eight hours a week. In Bavaria the obligation to attend a continuation school for three years begins immediately a youth has completed his elementary school course, which normally lasts seven years ; where, however, an eighth year is taken, the continuation school course is only two years. As far as possible the continuation schools have to be held on week-days, but part of the instruction may be given on Sunday afternoons.

The municipal continuation schools of Berlin provide special classes for forty occupational groups, including apprentices and others engaged in the building, metal, clothing, and food trades, barbers, shop assistants, and unskilled labourers, and the aggregate attendance exceeds 36,000. In some towns, like Munich, workshops for practical training are attached to the continuation schools.

Berlin, Munich, and Nuremberg have established continuation schools for shop-girls of certain classes. Three-quarters of the time allowed for instruction is given to subjects connected with their practical callings, and the rest to domestic economy. On the whole, however, little has been done for girls as yet, except in the large towns, and where continuation schools have been provided for them the instruction seldom goes far beyond matters intimately connected with housekeeping. " Housekeeping schools," with compulsory attendance, have for some years been successfully carried on in many of the larger towns in the Rhineland province, while Halle has a novel municipal continuation school for girls who have passed through the secondary schools. It is the object of the " Women's school," as it is called, to train girls for " their duties as women and mothers." The curriculum includes languages, civic science, hygiene, political economy, domestic economy, pedagogics, the history of art and culture, natural science, history, geography, and " social culture," and there are special classes for teachers of languages, gymnastics, housekeeping, needlework, librarians, kindergarten teachers, and apothecaries.

According to the " Kommunales Jahrbuch " for 1913-14 there were in Germany at the end of 1912 about 4400 industrial and trade continuation schools of a more or less urban character, the great majority subject to compulsory attendance and frequented by about 630,000 scholars in the aggregate, while the rural continuation schools numbered 5200 (of which 1700 were compulsory) and had an aggregate attendance of 84,000. In addition there were 17,000 continuation schools of a general character working on the lines of the ordinary primary schools.

The continuation schools are supplemented by trade, industrial, art, and general technical schools, one or more of which will be found in every town of even moderate size. Educational work of this kind the Governments endeavour to leave as far as possible to the local authorities, the various trade associations, and private effort, though in some States assistance in setting up technical schools is given from the public funds and in all the Governments are ready to afford advice and moral support. Naturally every town establishes the institutions most suited to the special requirements of its industries and trades, and no expense is spared in their equipment and in the provision of the best possible teaching staffs. The work done by the local authorities is largely supplemented by trade associations of various kinds and by the larger industrial firms, and any estimate of the extent and value of the continuation and technical schools of Germany which left out of account these private efforts would be very incomplete.

Some towns go still further and maintain commercial colleges having the status of universities. Perhaps the best municipal institutions of the kind are those of Cologne, Frankfort-on-Main, Mannheim, and Munich. Düsseldorf, Cologne, and Dortmund have recently established municipal academies or colleges for the administrative and social sciences, intended specially for the training of officials for the State and communal service, and smaller institutions of the same kind, intended for minor officials, exist in other towns.

Two attempts recently made by important cities to establish universities free from State control, which deprives the great centres of culture in Germany of independence, are of special interest. The first was made by Frankfort-on-Main in 1911. This city had already an important Academy of Social and Commercial Science, several scientific research societies, and many clinics, and the proposal was made that all these agencies should be combined in a " free " university, which should serve as a practical protest against the prevalent conception of universities as State institutions, and should revive the earlier tradition of the German university as a self-governing corporation. For the first German universities were entirely free from State control; they were self-governed, promulgated their own laws, chose their heads and teachers, and had their own courts. Although the whole of the necessary money was forthcoming from municipal and private sources, the Government promptly intervened with the warning that the projected university would have to comply with the official regulations applying to all existing institutions of the kind and would have to be regarded as a State institution. This was not the Frankfort ideal, but there was no room for argument, and the university is to be established and conducted on the orthodox lines. The university will have five faculties: for law, medicine, natural science, history and philosophy, and social and economic sciences. In addition to incurring large financial liabilities the town undertakes to supply land free of cost for various university purposes and to grant the use of its library, hospitals, and chemical laboratory, while retaining the right to manage these institutions. The municipality will also have strong representation upon the governing body of the university.

The other scheme originated in Hamburg. This City State has for many years maintained at its own charge a Colonial Institute for the training of men desirous of following an official or commercial career in tropical countries, and particularly the German oversea possessions. During 1912 and 1913 the city authorities endeavoured to combine this excellent college with the other local scientific institutions and make of them a university without theological and medical faculties, still keeping in view the special needs of colonial officials, pioneers, and farmers. An endowment fund of a million and a quarter pounds would have been necessary, and though the Senate was willing to vote the greater part of this sum the House of Burgesses declined, and the project fell to the ground.

MUNICIPAL EXPENDITURE ON EDUCATION.—In all the States the communes bear by far the greater part of the cost of primary education. In Prussia they are responsible for the building, equipment, and upkeep of the schools, as well as for a large part of the salaries of staffs, while the State contributes towards salaries and pensions and bears the cost of the training of teachers. Much more is done for the poor and rural districts than for the towns. A large part of the cost of the middle and higher schools is derived from fees, but here, too, the cost to the communes far exceeds that which falls to the State.

Of a total expenditure of £33,491,800 on the elementary schools of Germany in 1911 the various States paid £10,690,900 or 32 per cent., and the communes bore nearly all the rest. As the elementary scholars of Germany in that year numbered 10,310,000 the State grants amounted to a little over £1 a head.[1] In Prussia the State paid £6,366,700 (30 per cent.) out of a total of £21,044,900 ; in Bavaria the State paid £1,123,900 (36 per cent.) out of a total of £3,099,500 ; in Saxony £711,900 (24 per cent.) out of a total of £2,996,300 ; in Würtemberg £404,800 (36 per cent.) out of a total of £1,123,500 ; and in Baden £278,100 (26 per cent.) out of a total of £1,080,700. On the other hand, of a total expenditure in 1911 of £10,386,300 on the middle and higher schools (the universities not included) the States paid £2,675,100 or 25·8 per cent., the communes £3,300,000 or 31·8 per cent., and £3,998,100 or 38·5 per cent. was received from school fees.[2] These figures do not, of course, represent the entire expenditure of the States on education.

In Prussia State grants are made proportionately to the financial capacity of the communes, a far larger subsidy relatively to local expenditure being given to the agricultural than to the industrial districts, inasmuch as grants are only made in respect of 25 teachers in any one commune. Thus,

---

[1] In 1911 the Parliamentary grant on account of the ordinary elementary schools of England and Wales amounted to 11½ million pounds, or about £1 18s. per scholar, while the receipts from local rates in aid of these schools were 12¼ millions, together 23¾ millions. The contribution of the State was 48 per cent. of the whole cost. The population of Germany was 65¼ millions (estimated), and that of England and Wales 36 millions.

[2] "Vierteljahreshefte zur Statistik des deutschen Reichs," 22 Jahrgang, 1913, Zweites Heft, p. 192.

in 1911, 57 per cent. of the total cost of the primary schools in the Prussian province of East Prussia was defrayed by the State, 57 per cent. in the province of West Prussia, and 50 per cent. in the province of Pomerania, all these provinces being agricultural and poor, while in the industrial provinces of Westphalia and Rhineland the State bore only 20 and 19 per cent. respectively, and in Berlin less than 2 per cent. In illustration of the small assistance now given to the towns, it may be said that in 1912 Frankfort-on-Main received State grants in aid of education to the amount of 2d. a head of the population, while its own expenditure on that behalf was equal to 16s. per inhabitant. The education grant to Essen amounted to 7d. a head of the population, comparing with 17s. spent by the town; in the case of Cassel the corresponding figures were 5d. and 17s., and in the case of Charlottenburg 2½d. and 20s.

There is great disparity in the cost of elementary education in different towns. In the larger towns, where this cost forms from 50 to 75 per cent. of the total municipal expenditure on education, the usual outlay is from 10s. to 13s. a head of the population, out of from 15s. to 25s. a head spent on schools of all kinds.

The following figures show the cost of education in some of the larger towns in 1909, and hence understate the present outlay:—

Towns.	Cost per elementary scholar.	Cost per inhabitant. Elementary schools.	Cost per inhabitant. All schools.	Per cent. of all cost falling to elementary schools.
	£ s. d.	s. d.	s. d.	
Berlin	6 9 2	14 3	20 0	71·2
Breslau	5 7 10	13 5	20 4	65·8
Charlottenburg	7 2 7	11 8	20 2	57·9
Cologne	4 19 6	12 5	19 10	62·5
Cassel	5 14 2	12 5	20 11	59·2
Chemnitz	3 18 9	11 2	14 11	75·0
Dresden	3 14 0	8 10	17 7	50·6
Essen	3 4 4	11 4	16 1	70·4
Frankfort-on-Main	6 5 3	11 6	25 4	45·4
Hanover	4 10 6	9 10	21 2	46·6
Munich	5 7 1	12 3	14 10	83·0
Nuremberg	4 13 1	12 4	15 7	79·0
Stuttgart	4 19 1	6 8	12 11	51·4
Strassburg	5 8 11	10 1	13 1	77·2

The steady increase of the municipal expenditure on education may be illustrated by the case of Berlin. In 1890 Berlin's primary schools cost the city £2 8s. per scholar, in 1900 £3 5s., in 1910 £5 10s. 6d., but in 1912 £6 8s., while during the same period the municipal subsidy required by the higher schools increased from £5 to £14 12s. per scholar.

THE DRAMA AND MUSIC.—The budgets of most large and many small German towns contain an item, greater or less according to local circumstances, which is intended to cover " provision for the intellectual life of the town." This item is independent of expenditure on schools, and if analysed will be found often to include the maintenance of or subsidies to municipal theatres, bands, and orchestras, as well as grants to dramatic and musical societies of a miscellaneous order. In this provision the theatre takes an altogether dominant position, and the fact is significant as reflecting the great importance which in Germany is attributed to the drama as an educational and elevating influence in the life of the community. It may be that the practice of subsidising the theatre is not altogether independent of the fact that the repertory theatre is universal in Germany, except in the smallest of provincial towns, with the result that a far more intimate tie exists between the drama and the community than is possible in the case of travelling companies.

The municipal theatre is no new institution in Germany. Some of the oldest town theatres are those of Metz (1751), Mannheim (1777), Ulm (1781), and Nuremberg (1831), and most of the municipal theatres in the large towns of Germany can boast of a distinguished past. For the origin of these theatres it is necessary to look to that historical " particularism " which, while it has been attended by many political disadvantages, has ever exercised a powerful influence on behalf of culture. From early times each Court protected learning and the arts, and the drama being, according to enlightened German ideas, one of the greatest of educational agencies, the Court Theatre, maintained and directed by the Sovereign, was set up in the State capital or "residence" as a matter of course. But all large towns were not "residences," and it was impossible that a prince should provide every populous place within his State with a theatre. Hence it was that in such non-" residence " towns the municipalities stepped in, determined to keep abreast with the capital at least in the enjoyment of the drama. Broadly speaking it is still the rule to-day in Germany that in capital towns the theatre is under royal, princely, or ducal patronage, while in other large towns the municipalities are its patrons. Berlin, Munich, Stuttgart, Dresden, Karlsruhe, Brunswick, Meiningen, and Weimar are towns of the first class ; while most other towns of any consequence fall into the second class. At Mannheim, the second capital of Baden, Court and municipal theatres exist side by side.

In their support of the drama the German municipalities follow three methods. Either the town (*a*) owns a theatre and works it, or (*b*) owns a theatre and leases it, or (*c*) not owning a theatre, subsidises theatres in private hands, which are often entitled to describe themselves as municipal theatres. It is estimated that over fifty German towns own theatres outright, while four own two each ; thus the municipality of Charlottenburg, after building a theatre, has now built a costly opera house ; both are leased to companies. Of these towns thirty-two have over 80,000 inhabitants, and fifteen between 50,000 and 80,000 inhabitants. The list includes important places like Frankfort-on-Main, Leipzig, and Mannheim, which own two theatres each ; Cologne,[1] Aix-la-Chapelle, Charlottenburg, Nuremberg, Düsseldorf, Bremen, Erfurt, Breslau, Halle, Magdeburg, and Strassburg, all of which have a population exceeding 150,000 ; but also minor towns such as Würzburg, with a population of 80,000, Freiburg-im-Breisgau (83,000), Frankfort-on-Oder (64,000), and Liegnitz (60,000) ; though several towns with a population not larger than 30,000 also own theatres, for example, Oppeln, Schweidnitz, and Neisse.

[1] A writer in the "Cologne Gazette" recently recalled the fact that at the beginning of the seventeenth century companies of English "strolling players" visited Cologne year after year, and stayed for a week or a fortnight at a time. The writer concludes that Shakespeare was first introduced to Cologne playgoers by John Spencer, who had been invited to Germany originally by the rulers of Brandenburg, and who first performed at Cologne in 1613.

Of the towns which both own and work theatres the most notable are Mannheim (since 1839), Freiburg-in-Baden (since 1868), Strassburg (since 1886), Mülhausen, Kiel, Leipzig, Cologne, Dortmund, Colmar, and Königshütte. The usual practice, however, is to lease the theatre to an actor-manager ; though invariably on the subsidy principle. This principle is applied in two ways. Either the theatre is leased at a low or nominal rent and the lessee is left to make the most he can out of the enterprise, or a rent approximating to a commercial basis is fixed and the lessee is given an annual subsidy ; but variations of these two methods are common. Naturally, the liberality of the terms offered is governed by the extent and character of the population to be served.

The cost to a town of its theatre depends largely upon which of these two methods of management is adopted. It is a general experience that, whatever be the result from the standpoint of art, the town which manages its own theatre incurs far more expense than is entailed by the practice of leasing on the basis of a subsidy. Leipzig took over its theatre in 1912, with the result that whereas the cost to the town in 1910 was £13,200, there was an increase of £23,000, due in part only to special expenditure, and the deficit which had to be met in 1913 was £45,000. In 1911 the expenditure exceeded the revenue by £25,030 at Mannheim, by £8600 at Strassburg, by £5580 at Mülhausen, and by £13,460 at Kiel (two theatres). At Freiburg, where the town theatre (which cost £200,000) was taken into municipal management because (in the words of the chief mayor) " the town council regarded it as its most proper duty to raise this educational institution, like similar agencies for the elevation of the people, to a higher artistic standard," an outlay of no less than £16,000 a year is incurred, equal to nearly 4s. a head of the population.

By leasing their theatres the towns are able to limit their liabilities, and this most of them do, though on different methods. Thus Nuremberg places its theatre, which cost about £200,000, at the disposal of a lessee for a minimum rent of £1500 per annum, or 10 per cent. of the gross proceeds if this amount should be larger, and in addition it bears the cost of all important structural alterations, the cost of fire insurance and fire brigade service, and half the cost of the water supply; moreover, it sets aside a considerable sum yearly for the improvement of the decorations, furniture, fittings, and general conveniences of the theatre. This theatre, which was only completed in 1905, is one of the most attractive and best arranged in Germany, and took the place of a building which had stood for seventy years.

The Erfurt municipal theatre is leased to a private *entrepreneur* for £650 per annum, on condition that the profits after payment of this rent are divided between the town and the lessee, the latter first taking £650 and one-third of the balance, while the whole of the remainder goes to the town. During the summer months, when the theatre is closed, the town pays to each member of the chorus who has no summer engagement a weekly retainer of £2 10s., and to each member of the orchestra half this amount.

The municipality of Breslau pays a subsidy of £4500 to the theatre, imposing conditions in return, one of which requires the lessee to conclude written engagements with the members of his company.

The municipal theatre of Bielefeld is leased to an *entrepreneur* rent free, subject to the condition that one-half of all profits above £1000 shall be paid to the town.

Bremenhaven, a town of only 24,000 inhabitants, in building a new theatre at a cost of over £50,000 in 1911, decided to carry it on upon the partnership principle. The theatre has been leased to a director who will manage it in the common interest. The director has to account to the town for all receipts, and after the payment of all expenses subject to the approval of the municipal executive, the town first receives from the profits the sum of £250, and the next £1000 is divided equally between the town and the lessee; of the following £1500 the town receives one-third and the lessee two-thirds, and of later profits the town receives four-fifths and the lessee one-fifth. There are provisions in the contract to ensure that the theatre shall be conducted in the interest of art and education, for while the lessee has a right to fix the repertory he must submit weekly programmes in advance to the municipal executive, which is entitled to object to the presentation of worthless works.

In towns which are too small to support independent theatres the authorities often subsidise companies settled in adjacent places in return for periodical visits. A number of rural communes in Pomerania arrange every year for the formation and financing of a peripatetic company which visits each place in turn, and permanent dramatic companies are subsidised on the same terms in other districts. The most important of the travelling companies, however, is the Mark (Brandenburg) *Wandertheater*, which in the course of a season visits, in two sections, as many as 130 different places in the eastern provinces of Prussia. There are also two travelling companies of the same kind in the west of Germany, one operating from Frankfort-on-Main and the other from Düsseldorf. All these companies are run by associations of a " public utility " character, working not for money but for the educational interests of the people, and their services are highly appreciated.

In 1911 thirty of the larger towns owning theatres expended £216,480 in subsidies directly and indirectly, £181,820 being on account of the theatres and £34,660 on account of the theatre orchestras ; while eleven large towns not owning theatres expended in subsidies £33,500, £27,100 being on account of the theatres and £6400 on account of the orchestras. The total expenditure on the drama of these 41 towns was roughly a quarter of a million pounds, an average of over £6000 per town. Of subsidies, including in some cases special grants, paid to theatres belonging to the towns the highest in 1911 were £29,190, with £3810 for the orchestra, at Cologne ; £29,800 at Frankfort-on-Main ; £19,090, with £7040 for the orchestra, at Düsseldorf ; £25,030 at Mannheim ; £16,060, with £4320 for the orchestra, at Leipzig ; £16,320 and £2350 respectively at Dortmund ; £8600 and £7000 at Strassburg, £6910 and £3480 at Magdeburg, £11,890 and £2260 at Chemnitz, and £14,280 at Nuremberg. In many cases the town, in addition to paying a money subsidy, bore the whole or part of the costs of lighting, water, heating, and cleaning the municipal theatre. Of the towns which subsidise private theatres Stuttgart expended in this way in 1911 £7490, Hamburg £5290, Elberfeld £6890, Crefeld £3930, Cassel £3570, Munich £3070, and the other towns smaller sums. In addition, Stuttgart has just voted £60,000 towards the cost of building a new Court theatre, Cassel has voted £65,000 for the same purpose, and Stettin is building a concert hall at a cost of £50,000, towards which the town contributes £30,000, while the remainder is taken from a wealthy endowment for musical purposes.

Thirty Bavarian towns, for the most part small, spend on an average over £800 a year on theatres, and in addition they incurred special expenditure for this purpose in the course of ten years to an average amount of £14,460. In most of these towns the theatres are public property.

Important conditions are attached to the granting of municipal help to actor-managers in this way. In the main these conditions are intended to regulate charges, to secure fair treatment for members of the company and all employees, and to ensure the observance of a high standard alike in the choice of dramas and in their presentation. In many cases a minimum number of performances is stipulated, and in most towns a certain number of performances at popular prices have to be given for the benefit of the working classes and of children attending the elementary schools. The charge for admission to these popular performances varies from 1¼d. to 6d., and scholars are sometimes admitted free. The contract between the municipality of Bielefeld and the lessee of the town theatre stipulates for the presentation of dramas, operas, and operettas in specified number and sequence, and requires performances at low prices to be given on Saturdays for the special benefit of people with small incomes. The municipality of Hamburg assigns the sum of £250 a year towards the cost of dramatic performances for children in the senior classes of the primary schools, these performances being arranged by a committee of teachers. The tickets are sold to the children for 3d., or are distributed free according to circumstances. The town also pays £1500 a year towards the cost of popular performances on Sunday afternoons in May and September. The tickets for these performances cost 6d. and 2½d. (for seats and standing places respectively), and are distributed by the trade unions and other associations in touch with the working classes. Several years ago the municipal school authorities of Mannheim tried the experiment of taking to a special performance at the town theatre all the elementary scholars of both sexes who had at Easter completed their school course. Schiller's " Wilhelm Tell " was given, and 1400 boys and girls were present in company with their form teachers. A nominal charge of about 2½d. was made, so that the town had a large deficit to make up, but it was so pleased with the result that this scholars' performance has been made an annual event.

In some towns the municipal theatres are lent on easy terms to the trade councils and other working-class organisations for performances at popular prices. It will hardly be understood in England that these performances are almost invariably confined to classical works (dramas of Goethe, Schiller, and Shakespeare are almost equally in favour) or modern plays of the highest standard. The price of admission is as low as 6d., and however these theatres may be attended at other times the popular performances are invariably crowded. During 1912 the Leipzig municipal theatre, under public management, gave 326 performances, comprising 95 dramas (31 at popular prices), 70 operas (8 at popular prices), 57 operettas (21 at popular prices) ; 98 performances were arranged by societies of different kinds, and six were for school children. It may be noted also that the municipality of Berlin has just agreed to advance £100,000 on first mortgage to a company which is erecting a theatre for the people in one of the oldest and formerly most undesirable quarters of the city. The theatre, which will seat 2000 persons, will cost about £250,000, and the company undertakes to arrange at least ten day performances every year for the scholars attending the elementary schools, the price for admission not to exceed 7d. Similarly, in leasing to a company the opera house which it has just built, the municipality of Charlottenburg has stipulated that the company shall give every year for the benefit of the elementary school children four free performances, and ten more at which the charges for admission shall range from 6d. to 1s. 3d.

If the question be asked: Is the higher drama encouraged by the municipal theatre? the answer must be an emphatic affirmative, though the reason for this is probably less municipal action than the high standard of education in Germany. Speaking generally, no theatres in Germany maintain the drama at a higher level than the municipal theatres in the large towns. The lower forms of the drama will find no home here, for public taste looks for the best that the stage can offer, and as the demand is, so is the supply. Many a provincial theatre of this kind presents more Shakespearean plays in a week than the average English theatre outside London presents in a couple of years. A glance at the repertory of any of the municipal theatres which have been named is enough to convince one that an elevated aim is steadily kept in view. For example, in a recent year the two Mannheim municipal theatres presented 161 separate works, including 93 dramas, 62 operas and operettas, and six ballets, and of these works 442 repetitions were given in the aggregate, making for the year 604 performances, a number of which were at popular prices. The dramas given included 15 by Schiller, 10 by Shakespeare, three by Goethe, three by Lessing, five by Molière, four by Hans Sachs, four by Sheridan, 11 by Grillparzer, two each by Kleist and Hebbel, and several by Ibsen, while the operas included three by Beethoven, three by Cherubini, six by Mozart, three by Weber, and several by Wagner. Could an English provincial theatre—could all English provincial theatres together—show a record equal to this? That plays of this kind are given is proof that the German public looks to the municipal theatre for the cultivation of the highest possible standard of dramatic taste and achievement.

The figures given show that the patronage of the drama entails upon the towns no light burden, but it is a burden willingly borne. In all probability its weight will increase in the near future, for although the plan of leasing municipal theatres is still the rule, the opinion widely prevails that, by reason of the growing expense of maintaining the drama at a high artistic level, the towns will be compelled more and more to take over and work their own theatres. Even this prospect appears to have no terror for communities whose civic life is never governed on the elevating principle of " keeping down the rates." [1]

In addition to maintaining theatres or otherwise subsidising the drama many towns either maintain or liberally support orchestras on terms which secure their services for the public either gratuitously or at a nominal charge. In summer the concerts are usually given in the open air, and in the winter months in the public halls. Some towns even arrange for evening chamber concerts for the people. Berlin subsidises the Philharmonic Orchestra to the extent of £3000 a year, and in return the orchestra is bound to give 35 public concerts (two a week) for the charge of 3½d. between the beginning of June and the end of September, and in winter five similar concerts, with five afternoon free concerts for scholars. Nuremberg subsidises the Philharmonic Orchestra of that town to the extent of £600 a year, and in return offers to the public a series of thirty high-class concerts, indoor or outdoor according to the season, the former costing 4d. and the latter being free. Of 271 German communes with over 20,000 inhabitants 129 in 1911 expended in the aggregate £100,000 in the popularising of music, and seventy of these towns had their own orchestras. Among other municipal enterprises undertaken in the interest of popular entertainment may be named the cinematograph shows owned by many towns and also worked by the local authorities in several cases.

[1] See Appendix VII, " Municipal Theatre Regulations," pp. 491–495.

CHAPTER XIII

MUNICIPAL FINANCE

Sources of municipal revenue—The budget—Borrowing powers and loans—Extent of communal indebtedness—Improvement of municipal credit facilities—Balance sheets of municipal authorities.

SOURCES OF MUNICIPAL REVENUE.—The principal sources of municipal revenue, stated in the order of priority recognised by the laws of most German States, are—

(*a*) the proceeds of communal land and properties other than trading enterprises and of invested funds (*Kämmereivermögen*[1]) ;

(*b*) administrative and general fees and dues (including sewerage and scavenging dues) ;

(*c*) contributions in the nature of special assessments levied in consideration of material advantages conferred upon individuals or classes of individuals ;

(*d*) the profits of trading and other revenue-yielding undertakings, including the charges made in respect of undertakings and works which, while not regarded as profit-making enterprises, are either required or expected to pay their way ; and

(*e*) taxation, indirect and direct.

To these may be added (*f*) certain Government grants-in-aid made in some of the States.

Although the most important source of revenue, taxation (*e*) comes late in this enumeration, since the principle followed in the raising of revenue is that taxes have only to be levied if and to the extent that the commune cannot supply its financial needs in other approved ways. The forms of taxation usual in the towns and the yield of the local taxes, as also the

---

[1] "Its position in the communal budget corresponds to that occupied by the domains in the State budget" (Reitzenstein in Schönberg's "Handbuch der politischen Oekonomie," iii, p. 607).

character and productivity of the trading and other revenue-yielding enterprises (*d*), are considered in detail in the special chapters devoted to these subjects.

In all the States great emphasis is laid by the Governments on the importance of developing trading enterprises and of working them as profitably as possible. Thus the Ministerial rescript issued with the new communal taxation law of Saxony (which comes into force in 1915) urges the communes to raise all such revenue as may be feasible by their trading enterprises and to work no undertaking of public utility—even waterworks or baths—at a loss, so as to keep the taxes within moderate limits.

The dues and fees (*b*) are of many kinds and differ greatly in the various States. Most of the large towns charge the yearly costs of the sewerage system, of street scavenging, and of the removal of house refuse directly to the owners of the property concerned. In other towns these costs are charged to the land and building taxes, or part is defrayed in this way and part by special dues. In the case of sewerage dues the principle of assessment is either rental value, sale value, or the quantity of water passed into the sewers. In 1911, 75 towns with a population of 50,000 and upwards received in dues and charges on account of sewerage connections £1,333,480, on account of street scavenging £183,590, and house refuse removal £321,640, making a total of £1,838,710 received from property owners on account of these services. In addition, fees of a miscellaneous kind were received to the amount of £47,560. The aggregate revenue of these towns from the sources named was equivalent to a sum of 2s. 8d. a head of their total population of fourteen millions.

The communes are also empowered to charge fees for the use of institutions provided by the local authority for the common benefit, such as hospitals, bathing establishments, and certain of the schools for whose provision and maintenance they are responsible, though elementary schools are, as a rule, exempted from fees.

Among the miscellaneous dues and fees may be mentioned the pavement dues (a charge on horses and vehicles) levied in Bavarian towns, the bridge tolls still common in some parts of the country, fees charged in connection with building permits, the inspection of new buildings and the like, market tolls, fire brigade fees, and the fees for burgess or freemanship rights charged on a large scale in Bavaria and to a less extent in some other States.[1]

The principle of making special assessments (c) on property which benefits owing to works carried out at the expense of the municipality is expressly recognised by the communal taxation laws of Prussia and other States. For example, it is a general rule that adjacent owners (*Anlieger*) are required to contribute towards the first cost of sewerage works, either in the form of a single payment or by instalments spread over a certain number of years. In addition, special assessments may be made in respect of properties the value of which is increased owing to public improvements. Works of the kind are clearances of old property, the laying out of public parks and recreation grounds, the opening up of new areas for building purposes, pavement works, and the like. Reference has been made to these contributions, the revenue from which is naturally of an occasional kind, in the chapter dealing with town planning.

The State grants-in-aid (*f*) are no longer a very important source of revenue in the case of the large towns. Where given they are, as a rule, in respect of elementary education, poor relief, and road maintenance—in the towns, as a rule, only in respect of the first two objects.

The system of State subsidies to local authorities is, in fact, contrary to the theory of German national and local finance, and hence is but little developed in the German States.

The last amendment of the local taxation system of Prussia (that of 1893) was intended to open up to the communes financial resources ample for existing purposes, yet capable of being developed according to need, and so to make them independent of State aid. The one important exception to this rule are the grants on behalf of education. Such other grants as are assigned to the local authorities are made to the provincial and circle governments, mostly for their own use but partly for distribution to the communal authorities.

[1] For fees charged, see pp. 62, 63.

The Prussian State grants for certain special purposes, other than education, are as follows : (1) Under a law of April 30, 1873, towards the cost of provincial and circle government, the annual sum of £450,000. This grant is distributed to the extent of one-half in the ratio of area and to the extent of one-half in the ratio of civil population. (2) Under a law of July 8, 1875, towards the cost of provincial and circle government, the annual sum of £672,000, divisible on the same principles. This money has to be expended on main highways and township roads, the institutional care of lunatics, and deaf, dumb, and blind persons, reclamation works, the promotion of education by means of libraries, museums, etc. (3) **By the same law of July 8, 1875, the State transferred to the provinces and the municipalities of Berlin and Frankfort-on-Main the maintenance of a number of national highways for which it had hitherto been responsible, and made them a yearly grant of £950,000 to cover the costs entailed.** (4) Under a law of June 2, 1902, a further yearly grant of £350,000 was made to the provincial authorities for apportionment amongst the circles and communes towards the cost of poor relief and roads. The money is distributed according to the financial necessities of the various local authorities. (5) There are in addition a number of small grants to individual municipal authorities in respect of the maintenance of maternity homes and training establishments.

The sum of State grants (other than education grants) to local authorities in 1910 was £2,378,000, equivalent to 1s. 2d. per inhabitant on a population of 40,165,000.

In the administrative year 1910–11, the Government grants in Prussia towards the maintenance of the elementary, middle, and higher schools amounted to £7,425,800, or 26·5 per cent. of a total expenditure on these schools of £27,997,000. The bulk of the balance was borne by the local authorities. The State's share in the case of elementary schools was £6,367,000, or 30 per cent. of the total cost ; in the case of the middle schools £41,800, or 3·3 per cent. ; and in the case of the higher schools £1,017,000, or 18 per cent. The rural communes receive far more assistance from the State in proportion to their expenditure than the towns.

Prior to the passing of the Education Act of 1897 a commune received a State grant for every teacher. Since then communes or communal unions with more than 25 teacherships are supposed to be sufficiently well off to need no help, while to the necessitous communes the State makes a grant on a fixed scale towards the salaries of teachers, and bears the costs of their removal, and it contributes towards their retirement pensions and the pensions due to widows and orphans. The rule of exclusion is felt to be arbitrary and inequitable. The education burdens of the purely industrial towns with a predominance of working-class families, a high birth-rate, and a low level of income and therefore of taxing capacity, are often oppressively heavy, forming from one-third to one-half of the total expenditure. This fact explains the abnormally high local income tax payable in some of the Westphalian colliery and iron and steel centres.

A slight relief is sometimes afforded to over-burdened Prussian communes by a provision in the Communal Taxation Law intended to meet the case of communes which count amongst their inhabitants the workpeople of large industrial undertakings outside their administrative and taxing areas. In order to recoup such communes for the extra expense caused by the presence in their midst of this industrial population—education, poor relief, and police charges are specially mentioned—the law entitles them to claim from the commune in which the undertaking is situated a contribution proportionate to this extra expenditure.

A certain further relief to local taxation is afforded in virtue of the fact that the police service is claimed as a State service, for which reason the State bears part of the cost. It is impossible, however, to say what proportion of the State's expenditure on account of police administration might be held to rank as a grant in aid to local authorities comparable with the Exchequer grants in this country.

No comprehensive return of municipal revenue and expenditure exists of later date than that of 1907 relating to all German towns and rural communes with over 10,000 inhabitants and published by the Imperial Government in 1908. This return showed that 33·2 per cent. of the gross revenue came from taxation, 25·9 per cent. from communal enterprises and undertakings of all kinds, 5·9 per cent. from the administrations of communal estates and investments, 5·1 per cent. from educational and art institutions, 3 per cent. was received on account of poor relief, the care of orphans, and the hospitals, 4·7 per cent. from the building administration (fees, etc.), and the remainder (22·2 per cent.) from the general, police, and other branches of the administration.[1]

Of the gross expenditure 23 per cent. fell to the administration of communal undertakings and enterprises, 17·4 per cent. to that of educational and art institutions, 14·3 per cent. to the administration of debts, 11·8 per cent. to the general and police administration, 9·9 per cent. to the building administration, 7·6 per cent. to the administration of poor relief, the care of orphans, and hospitals, and the remainder (16·0 per cent.) to miscellaneous branches of administration.[2]

It may be noted here that there is no limitation of the expenditure which may be incurred on special objects, as with us on account of higher education, libraries, etc., nor are general taxes falling on the whole community earmarked for special purposes and assessed separately, as in the case of the general district and borough rates in corporate towns, and the general district and poor rates in urban districts. On the other hand, as will be shown, expenditure specially benefiting certain sections of the community, i.e., the property owners or the trading classes, is charged to taxes falling only on those persons.

THE BUDGET.—Yearly budgets are usual, but the Prussian towns have the option of budgeting for one, two, or three

[1] Of the total receipts of local authorities in England and Wales in the administrative year 1910–11, in amount £131,074,000, £21,165,000 or 16·1 per cent. came from Exchequer grants, £65,152,300 or 49·7 per cent. came from public rates, £32,947,600 or 25·2 per cent. from trading enterprises, and £11,809,300 or 9·0 per cent from other sources.

[2] Of the total expenditure of local authorities in England and Wales in the administrative year 1910–11, 21·8 per cent. was on account of education, 9·6 per cent. on account of poor relief (exclusive of the cost of pauper lunatics in county and borough asylums), 3 per cent. on account of lunatics and lunatic asylums, and 1·4 per cent. on account of hospitals other than Poor Law infirmaries. The service of loans is included in the foregoing expenditure, but stated alone it formed 22·8 per cent. of all expenditure.

years at once, and if a period longer than a year is chosen it may be for the entire administration or only for certain branches. In that country also the financial year is from April 1 to March 31, as is the case with Imperial and State administrations. The unrestricted control of the town council over the budget has already been explained in the chapter dealing with the constitution of this body and its position in the communal government.

Once a year, before the introduction of the new budget, the executive is required to give a full account of its stewardship in public meeting of the town council, and due notice of the meeting has to be published to the citizens. The estimates themselves must be published for a week, so as to give the public an opportunity of criticising and objecting to them, and only after the lapse of that time are they laid before the town council. A copy of the budget is also sent to the supervisory authority, but formal approval by this authority is not necessary except in so far as new taxes are proposed or old ones altered. Nevertheless, it is competent for the supervisory authority to object to proposed expenditure of an irregular kind or to require the inclusion of omitted items on account of services which the local authority is liable to provide ; in either event the latter may appeal to the Supreme Administrative Court.

The communal budget distinguishes between ordinary and extraordinary revenue and expenditure, and each department of local government prepares its own estimates, which need to be independently approved first by the executive and then by the town council. Revenue and expenditure are shown separately in each case. Dr. E. Scholz illustrates the method of division usual in Prussia by the following heads of a typical budget :—

- A. Ordinary part (*Ordinarium*).
  - I. Principal administration.
    1. General administration.
    2. Administration of estate.
    3. Finance administration :
       - (*a*) **Debts.**
       - (*b*) **Taxation and treasury.**

4. Police, Trade, and Traffic system.
5. Buildings :
    (a) Overground (*Hochbau*).
    (b) Underground (*Tiefbau*).
6. Poor relief, charities, and hospitals.
7. Education and Culture :
    (a) Schools.
    (b) Churches.
    (c) Art and Science.
    (d) Furtherance of objects of public utility.
8. Grants for State purposes.
9. Surpluses and subsidies of special administrations.

II. Special Administrations.
  1. Equalisation budgets :
      (a) Abattoir and stockyard.
      (b) Pawnshop.
      (c) Inspection of Weights and Measures.
      (d) Savings bank.
  2. Subsidy budgets.
      (e) Cemeteries.
      (f) Fire brigade.
      (g) Baths.
      (h) Destructors.
  3. Surplus budgets.
      (i) Waterworks.
      (j) Gasworks.
      (k) Electricity works.
      (l) Tramways.

B. Extraordinary Part (*Extraordinarium*).
  Such of the foregoing divisions as may be necessary.[1]

There is no Government audit of local finance in Germany. The accounts of each communal administration are audited by officers of the administration under the direction of the town council and the executive. In Prussia a " revision " of the local treasury (i.e., of the actual funds in hand) is made by the executive every month, on fixed days, and the

[1] " Die deutsche Stadt und ihre Verwaltung," Vol. I, pp. 58, 59.

town council is informed beforehand so that it may depute members to be present; and there is at least once a year a special surprise " revision " of which no notice is given, and at this either the chairman of the council or a member nominated by him must be present. A further means of controlling communal property is contained in the provision requiring the executive to keep and publish a register (*Lagerbuch*) of municipal estate, both personal and real. This register must be periodically revised and must be prepared in such a way as to offer to the citizens a clear presentation of the extent and character of the town's tangible assets.

Nevertheless, town councils often complain that effectual control over financial matters is impossible under the present system. Sheaves of figures are thrown at them, and without outside expert assistance there is no hope of testing them satisfactorily. Hence the desirability of some arrangement for an independent audit by approved accountants is widely recognised. Many of the larger towns accordingly have their accounts audited by professional accountants in the same way as the large British corporations. In some parts of Saxony the entire body of town councillors are, in virtue of regulations issued by the supervisory authorities, made jointly responsible for all losses caused by the insufficient or culpable control of finance.

BORROWING POWERS AND LOANS.—As a rule, loans may only be contracted with the sanction of the State supervisory authority, and rules are laid down governing such sanction, e.g., in regard to the purpose, amount, and arrangements for repayment (sinking fund); but in the past these rules have seldom been applied very rigidly and many towns have unquestionably borrowed very prodigally and injudiciously.

In Prussia the rule is that loans may be contracted only in respect of works of common benefit serving " not merely the present but the distant future," and not in respect of works which need to be renewed at short intervals; the latter have to be covered by ordinary revenue, i.e., taxation. In the case of school buildings the communes are urged to create building funds of sufficient amount by the assignment thereto of a yearly contribution.[1] Until such funds exist schools may be built in part out of borrowed money, but only on condition that the loans are paid back at a higher rate than in the case of other permanent works. The first paving of streets with a new material may be defrayed by loans, but the renewal and upkeep of such works must be defrayed out of ordinary revenue. Loans may also be contracted in respect of the building of theatres, concert halls, Town Hall restaurants, and the execution of other works of a kind which border on the definition of "luxuries," provided it can be shown that the expected revenue will sufficiently cover interest and repayment charges, or that such expenditure will not injure the financial credit of the commune or unduly burden the community As to State sanction in general, the Municipal Ordinance for the eastern provinces of Prussia says that "the sanction of the Government is necessary to loans by which the commune will have to incur a debt or an existing debt will be increased." The same provision applies to some of the western provinces, and where the Municipal Ordinances do not require such permission it is stipulated in Ministerial Decrees.

The Communal Ordinance of Bavaria empowers communes to conclude loans for the purpose of "repaying existing debts or of meeting unavoidable expenditure or such expenditure as will be for the permanent benefit of the commune when it cannot be met by other sources of revenue without overburdening the inhabitants." Arrangements for repaying all loans must be made and submitted to the supervisory authorities for approval, and the sanction of these authorities is needed in the case of all loans which would in the current administrative year increase the existing indebtedness to the extent of £42 17s. in communes with less than 2500 inhabitants, of £85 14s. in communes with from 2500 to 5000 inhabitants, £428 11s. in communes with from 5000 to 20,000 inhabitants, and £857 2s. in communes with over 20,000 inhabitants. In all cases the supervisory authorities can forbid the conclusion of a loan when the conditions above specified are not complied with. In general, loans are permissible on account

[1] Ministerial Decree of June 1, 1891.

of works which pay for themselves and provide a sufficient revenue for redemption ; but loans on account of extraordinary outlay which does not recur—or recurs only at long intervals— yet the revenue from which is uncertain, are only allowed when these works are intended to meet special needs and the ordinary revenues are inadequate to meet the cost. Loans are in general discouraged in the case of school buildings, street improvements, and works of a similar recurrent kind, and, as in Prussia, the formation of special funds to meet needs of the kind is urged.

In Saxony the supervisory authorities are given a general supervision over municipal borrowing with a view to protecting the communes against undue indebtedness, and their formal approval is necessary in the case of all loans which would within any one year increase a commune's indebtedness beyond £15 for every 1000 inhabitants; but loans intended to be repaid within a year do not require sanction. Corresponding provisions exist in the other States.

It may be added that loans are never contracted to cover deficiencies, and herein the communes are able to set the Empire a good example.[1]

In so far as the communes require and are empowered to borrow, their needs are covered by long term loans, issued as a rule through banks in the form of bonds, by loans from statutory insurance organisations and the public savings banks, loans on mortgage from mortgage banks and other bodies, and loans from minor miscellaneous sources. All but a minute fraction of the communal borrowing—hardly more than 1 per cent.—consists of long period loans, mostly in the form either of ordinary scrip or bonds payable to bearer, both redeemable at a fixed date and ranking as trustee securities. Short term loans are not usual.

It is nowadays the common rule to invite tenders from banks generally or from a selected list of banks. Where the sum is large banks often form combinations (*Konsortien*) for the purpose of taking up loans jointly, and most important municipal loans are now contracted in this way.

[1] Alex. Pohlmann in "Gemeindefinanzen," 2ter Band, 1ter Teil, p. 159 (Verein für Sozialpolitik).

The town accepts the most advantageous offer, and the banks or combinations issue the scrip to the public at a price agreed amongst themselves, first having the amount underwritten. A calculation made for the period 1897 to 1907 shows that the variation between the terms of acceptance by the municipalities and the terms of issue to the public was from 0·12 to 3·25 per cent., but these extremes were probably both due to the special conditions of the money market; and it is stated that the banks, as a rule, earn about ½ per cent. on the nominal value of the loans issued.[1] The old tender system, under which a town fixed a rate of issue to the banks and invited offers at this figure or the nearest to it, then accepting loans to the required amount on the most advantageous terms, is no longer followed, and there are also few open subscriptions nowadays. If a town wishes to issue a new loan it is to its interest to buy up the old scrip that may be on sale, so as to ensure an issue on favourable terms, and it may use the funds of the savings bank or charitable foundations under its management for this purpose. When bonds have to be repaid, a town will buy up its own scrip freely if it can be had under par, but here it has to contend with the banks, which are ever on the look out and are not slow to use effectual devices for keeping up the price.

The rates of repayment vary in different States—they are, for example, on the whole, higher in Prussia than elsewhere—and still more according to the purposes for which the money is borrowed. Although in past times a rate as low as ½ or even ¼ per cent. was common, loans are now seldom repaid on a lower scale than 1½ per cent. in Prussia, and this rate may rise to 10 per cent. in the case of works or improvements that need frequent renewal. In the case of trading enterprises it is sometimes stipulated that a part of the profits beyond a fixed amount shall be applied towards the more rapid repayment of the loan.

Municipal loans are regularly quoted 2 or 3 per cent. below the price of State securities giving a corresponding interest.

---

[1] Th. Kutzer, " Zur Organisation des Kredits der deutschen Städte," in " Gemeindefinanzen," 2ter Band, 1ter Teil, p. 194 (Verein für Sozialpolitik).

Apart from the question of credit two circumstances at present specially affect the relative unpopularity of municipal securities. One is the multiplicity of municipal loans on the market and the unsystematic manner in which they are issued, and the other is the uncertainty caused to bond holders under the arrangements for redemption on the principle of buying in bonds by lot. In order to meet the latter objection the municipalities of Wiesbaden and some other towns have of late adopted a new mode of redemption. The amount which would ordinarily be set aside yearly for this purpose is put to a special fund, which will be allowed to accumulate with a view to the repayment of the whole loan at once at the end of the prescribed period. This fund is invested in trustee securities and mortgages and is placed under the control of the State supervisory authority. It is said that a loan offered by Wiesbaden to the banks subject to these conditions was contracted on terms 2 per cent. more favourable than in the case of loans offered on the usual method of redemption, and that it is quoted higher by this amount than the other loans of the town bearing equal interest. With the idea of encouraging local investment in the town's loans many municipal authorities keep a register of municipal securities (*Schuldbuch*) in which holders of local bonds of all kinds may without charge register their securities, which they simultaneously deposit, so protecting themselves in the event of the loss either of the papers themselves or of the interest coupons. The town undertakes, as desired, to pay interest in cash at the municipal treasury or by post, to transfer it to the holder's banking or savings bank account, or even to credit it to him in part payment of his local taxes. Incidentally it also notifies bond holders of bonds drawn for redemption, and if desired reinvests in municipal securities the money thus liberated.

EXTENT OF COMMUNAL INDEBTEDNESS.—According to a statement published by the Imperial Government in 1908 in connection with its scheme of financial reform, the urban and rural communes of the Empire had in 1907 debts to the aggregate amount of £328,015,000, equal to £5 6s. a head of the entire population.

The indebtedness in the aggregate and per head of the population in towns with from 10,000 inhabitants upwards was £255,715,000, made up as follows:—

Towns with a population of	Total Indebtedness.	Indebtedness per inhabitant.
	£	£ s.
From 10,000 to 25,000	33,530,000	7 6
,, 25,000 to 50,000	28,080,000	10 3
,, 50,000 to 100,000	36,630,000	11 17
,, 100,000 to 200,000	46,445,000	14 7
Over 200,000 (excluding Berlin)	89,580,000	17 2
Berlin	21,450,000	10 10
	£255,715,000	—

Of this indebtedness £169,480,000 took the form of municipal obligations in bearer's name, £62,675,000 of loans for long periods, and £23,560,000 of mortgages, short term loans, balances of purchase money, etc.

A classification of the total indebtedness in 1910 of 84 of the largest towns in Germany, with a population of 15¼ millions, showed totals of £22,129,000 for Berlin, £84,847,000 for ten other towns with a population above 300,000, £84,998,000 for 34 towns with a population from 100,000 to 300,000, and £35,250,000 for 39 towns with a population of from 50,000 to 100,000; the debts of these towns in the form of loans amounted to £21,406,000, £79,051,000, £80,409,000, and £34,190,000 respectively. The aggregate indebtedness of the 84 towns was £227,223,000 and that in the form of long term loans (excluding mortgages) £215,059,000. The indebtedness of Berlin was equal to £10 14s. a head of the population, that of the other towns with a population exceeding 300,000 to £18 19s., that of the towns with a population between 100,000 and 300,000 to £14 3s., and that of the towns with a population between 50,000 and 100,000 to £13, while the average for all towns was £14 17s. a head.

Striking though these figures are, it would be easy to overlook their significance and to draw from them a wrong conclusion. The great indebtedness of German towns simply means that these towns are engaged on a large scale in carrying on enterprises which require considerable capital outlay, and much of their borrowing is just as necessary and desirable as is the increase of capital in the case of private commercial undertakings which are expanding on healthy lines. This view was expressed by the chief mayor of one of the larger municipalities (Bielefeld) at a recent congress of municipal officials. " It is not surprising," he said, " that we should hear to-day of heavy municipal debts and of a certain financial stringency in many towns. A town which contracts no debts is asleep. When towns borrow money to-day it means that they are fulfilling tasks so great that a later generation must share in the burden, and the undertaking of these tasks is meritorious so long as the capacity of a community to bear the cost is duly kept in mind."

On examination it will often be found that the major part of the loans of large towns has been contracted on account of trading enterprises of various kinds and other undertakings and works of a revenue-yielding character; and particularly gasworks, electricity works, waterworks, tramways, docks and warehouses, market halls, baths, abattoirs and stock yards, and sewerage and drainage works. A classification of the loans of 74 of the largest towns at the end of 1910, in amount £194,668,000, given in the " Statistical Yearbook of German Towns " for 1913, shows that £99,157,000, or a little over one-half, had been incurred on account of such works in the following amounts :—Sewerage (including pumping) works and sewage farms £19,400,000, waterworks £17,000,000, gasworks £15,548,000, tramway and light railways £13,686,000, electricity works £12,576,000, docks and warehouses £9,173,000, abattoirs and stockyards £7,320,000, market halls £2,173,000, bathing establishments £1,014,000, and other works yielding profit or regular revenue £1,215,000.

The proportion of such remunerative investments was largest in the case of Berlin, viz. 63 per cent. ; in the case of ten towns with a population of over 300,000 it was 49 per cent. ; in the case of 34 towns with a population between 100,000 and 300,000 it was 50·4 per cent. ; and in the case of 39 towns with from 50,000 to 100,000 it was 48·4 per cent.

Returns supplied by German and British municipal authorities enable an interesting comparison to be made of the indebtedness of some of the larger towns in the two countries and of the proportions in which this indebtedness is due to revenue-yielding enterprises. All the returns relate to the end of the year 1912 unless otherwise stated.

MUNICIPAL LOANS AT END OF 1912.

(1) GERMAN TOWNS.

Towns.	Total amount of loans.	Amount of remunerative loans.	Proportion represented by remunerative loans.
	£	£	per cent.
Aix-la-Chapelle	1,922,000	970,197	50·0
Berlin (1910)	21,406,500	13,477,200	62·9
Charlottenburg	9,346,274	2,772,712	29·7
Danzig	1,699,320	597,830	35·0
Düsseldorf	9,207,000	6,836,000	74·2
Essen	4,060,500	1,075,300	25·0
Frankfort-on-Main	16,112,500	12,250,000	76·0
Leipzig (1910)	8,064,500	4,246,400	52·7
Mannheim	4,108,700	2,214,800	54·0
Munich (1910)	13,706,000	6,124,600	44·7
Nuremberg (1910)	5,698,200	2,585,800	45·4
TOTALS	£95,331,494	£53,150,839	55·8

(2) TOWNS IN GREAT BRITAIN.

	£	£	per cent.
Birmingham	19,722,326	13,620,241	69·1
Bolton	5,535,236	2,657,805	48·0
Bradford	8,523,154	5,311,600	62·3
Bristol	8,055,613	6,374,811	79·1
Cardiff	3,873,099	1,947,704	50·0
Dundee	2,710,421	1,838,236	67·9
Glasgow	14,000,289	8,675,195	62·0
Huddersfield	3,381,832	2,424,987	71·7
Leicester	4,865,336	3,034,415	62·4
Manchester	23,336,611	11,108,226	47·6
Newcastle	3,210,034	1,431,751	44·6
Salford	3,234,345	1,418,383	43·9
Sheffield	9,692,742	6,336,445	65·4
TOTALS	£110,141,038	£66,079,799	60·0

Nevertheless, the feeling is prevalent that German towns have for some time been borrowing beyond the safer limits formerly observed. Each year new demands are made for new purposes, and every class of citizens presses its special claims upon the public funds, while there is a sort of conspiracy of consent to ignore the fact that all expenditure, however laudable the object may be, is at the cost of the common purse. According to the Prussian Statistical Office the long term loans, mortgages, and other debts of the towns of Prussia increased during the five years between March 31, 1906, and March 31, 1911, from £140,727,000 to £212,867,000, or at the rate of 51 per cent., and those of the rural communes from £6,808,000 to £13,394,000, or at the rate of 96·7 per cent. The indebtedness per head of the population increased in the towns during this period from £8 8s. to £11 5s., an increase of 33·6 per cent.

Not only in Parliament but in local government circles the opinion finds frequent expression that the present generation is carrying forward too large a portion of the responsibilities which it has incurred, and that sound finance and a due regard for the interests of the coming generation—which will have its own special duties and obligations to meet—require that local bodies should make a stronger endeavour to pay their way than they have done in the past. Considerations of prudence and self-interest point to the same conclusion. The great extent of municipal borrowing and the dearness of money have together had the effect of making it impossible for towns with even good credit to contract loans at a lower rate of interest than 4 per cent. Towns like Düsseldorf, Mannheim, Munich, Cologne, and Charlottenburg have recently had to borrow at this rate, which compares with habitual rates of 3¼ and 3½ per cent. twenty or thirty years ago, while other large towns have had to pay as much as 4½ per cent., and in addition to issue at 5 per cent. or more under par. Owing to the fall in the market value of communal securities it is possible nowadays to obtain from 4 to 5 per cent. interest on bonds having behind them the credit of large and prosperous towns whose tangible assets alone are far in excess of their liabilities.

With the object of meeting extraordinary expenditure of a kind uncertain in date but certain of occurrence without resorting to loans, the formation of emergency and new buildings funds has been recommended by the Governments, and in view of the severer conditions of amortisation now insisted on by the supervisory authorities this method has much to commend it. Düsseldorf has for some time set aside a yearly amount to meet the cost of new buildings, inasmuch as the supervisory authority now requires one-third of such cost to be raised otherwise than by loans, and Cologne and other towns do the same. The chief disadvantage of this method of meeting outlay is that it presumes a very accurate anticipation of coming needs and an exceptional spirit of sacrifice, for the average ratepayer is contented if he can meet the demands of the moment and is not disposed to provide for unforeseen and indefinite future needs. There is also a danger that the possession of such funds may prove a sore temptation to unnecessary or at least avoidable expenditure.

A greater effect has been produced upon the local authorities, however, by the admonitions of the Governments and the drastic action of the supervisory authorities both in the matter of sanctioning loans and in fixing the conditions of repayment. During the last few years the Governments of the larger States, as the final authorities in matters of supervision, have repeatedly endeavoured to call local authorities back to healthier financial policies and to encourage greater economy and a wiser husbanding of their reserve powers of taxation. Thus in 1907 the Prussian Ministers of Finance and of the Interior issued a joint rescript requiring communal authorities, both in town and country, to redeem their loans on a higher scale than heretofore; the minimum rate was henceforth to be $1\frac{1}{4}$ instead of 1 per cent. in general, while in the case of loans for street and similar works it was to be at least $2\frac{1}{2}$ per cent., and in the case of sewerage works 2 per cent. The rescript approved of the action of those authorities which had established special funds for the purchase of land for public purposes, and in view of their encouraging experience recommended the same measure to other towns, since " the existence of such a fund, when sufficiently endowed and kept at a constant level, relieves the town of the necessity of resorting to loans whenever it requires land for a public undertaking." The rescript added that there would be no objection to establishing land-purchase funds by means of initial loans. Funds to meet special expenditure on school buildings, paving works, and other recurring outlay were also recommended. In 1910 the Ministers decided that loans might not be contracted for the purpose of liquidating deficits—the disastrous policy pursued by the Imperial Government for some years—but only for meeting extraordinary expenditure which could not be defrayed otherwise without inflicting excessive burdens on the taxpayers.

In 1912 a further rescript was issued relating to towns with more than 10,000 inhabitants, directing that the supervisory authorities should in future exercise greater circumspection in the sanctioning of loans and should impose more stringent conditions in regard to their redemption. It was complained that local authorities had contracted the habit of beginning works in respect of which loans were needed before the loans had been sanctioned, employing, meantime, current revenue, floating debts, or other available money, with the result that the supervisory authorities were often compelled to give sanction against their better judgment and to that extent were deprived of their right to determine applications for power to borrow on their merits. Government Presidents and Landrats were enjoined to insist upon the presentation of plans for public works before the commencement of actual operations, so that they might be in a position to decide with freedom, and local authorities were warned that henceforth they would run a grave risk in beginning works without having loans at disposal.

These several rescripts have had a salutary effect in steadying local authorities, yet the Prussian Minister of Finance had to lament in 1912 in his place in Parliament that " the increasing indebtedness of the communes calls for the Government's most serious attention." Undoubtedly the gravity of the question, from the Government's standpoint, has been increased by the unsatisfactory state of national finance.

IMPROVEMENT OF MUNICIPAL CREDIT FACILITIES.—In general the municipalities are not satisfied with the existing arrangements for obtaining money, and various schemes have been put forward with a view to facilitating credit facilities and saving part of the profits that now go to the banks. Public banks have existed since 1848 in Breslau and Chemnitz as municipal institutions, both carried on profitably, but it is now proposed to establish a large central municipal bank to which all towns of a certain size should be affiliated. The project has been discussed by the German Municipal Congress more than once and in theory has been warmly approved. The idea is that such a bank should be established on the mutual principle, the associated communes supplying the requisite capital, and that all municipal borrowing and lending and all transactions with the money market should be done through it. The bank would transact business for the savings banks, buying and selling securities for them, and receiving funds for investment either with communes or otherwise. One form of bond would be recognised, and for every loan advanced to a commune the bank would issue bonds to the same amount. Inasmuch as such an organisation would have behind it the credit of all the towns represented, it is contended that its stock would rank with the best State securities.

It is significant that the idea of a central communal bank has been welcomed even more heartily by the rural communes and the provincial and "circle" authorities than the large towns, which on the whole are well able to look after themselves. Hence a rival project has been advocated in the special interest of these non-urban authorities, and a good deal of propagandism has been done on its behalf in Prussia. It is believed that a Communal Bank for this purpose could be started with a capital of £1,250,000, which should be subscribed by the towns, provinces, and "circles" interested in shares of a value of £50. The principal business of the bank would be the granting of loans to German communes, to which end communal bonds would be issued, the interest charged on the loans not to exceed that payable on the bonds plus a commission of from 0·5 to 0·7 per cent. to cover actual expenses.

The bank would also negotiate mortgages, receive deposits, and transact other non-speculative business, besides acting as a central agency for the public savings banks. A large number of "circle" authorities are said to be in favour of the scheme, and there seems a likelihood that it will soon take practical shape.

Meantime, many of the larger towns have associated experimentally for the establishment of a central credit agency (*Geldvermittelungsstelle*) for the negotiation of loans among themselves. It was begun at Düsseldorf in 1910, and after being removed to Cassel it has now followed its director, the chief mayor of Charlottenburg, to this town. Over fifty towns with a population exceeding 80,000 are affiliated to the bank and its transactions during the first three years represented an actual money turn-over of nearly nine million pounds. Applications for short term loans were received to the aggregate amount of £10,700,000, and loans to the amount of £4,080,000 were negotiated. Offers to the amount of £5,625,000 were received and to the amount of £3,800,000 accepted, and duly placed. Long term loans to the amount of £6,750,000 were applied for and to the amount of £975,000 negotiated. It was possible as a rule to obtain and lend money for short terms on very easy terms, sometimes at 1 and 1¼ per cent. below the Imperial Bank rate. The rules of the agency lay down the following purposes and procedure :—

1. The object is the exchange of money between towns which have money at disposal and those which are in temporary need of money.

2. All German towns with a population exceeding 80,000 are entitled to join the agency. Admission takes effect by a declaration of membership by the administration of the town concerned.

3. The towns affiliated to the agency are required to give notice as promptly as possible when they wish to deposit or borrow money. The notification shall state (*a*) the amount of the sum to be borrowed or deposited, and (*b*) the period for which the money is desired or offered to the agency. In the event of an alteration in the amount of money to be deposited

or borrowed, in the period of deposit, or in other conditions, the agency shall be informed immediately; and the same applies if a town withdraws an offer of or a request for money. In the interest of the efficiency of the agency it is desirable that the probable needs or funds at disposal—particularly the results of periodical estimates made in regard thereto—should be notified as soon as possible.

4. On the strength of the notifications received the agency undertakes to put the borrowing and lending towns in communication in the way that may seem to it most expedient. When this has been done the agency, as a rule, takes no further part in the transaction. The towns concerned are left to make their own arrangements. The agency shall be informed of every agreement arrived at, with the conditions of the same.

5. In all transactions between municipal administrations a strict observance of dates fixed is presumed, just as in Stock Exchange transactions. Money transactions between the towns are, as a rule, arranged by bills.

6. The agency charges no fees. Its expenses are covered by contributions from the towns affiliated, as fixed for the present at 10s. per annum, payable in the month of April.

There is a similar communal credit agency in Saxony, with its seat at Dresden.

BALANCE SHEETS OF MUNICIPAL AUTHORITIES.—A glance at the administrative reports of large German towns is sufficient to convince one that their governments spend money on the grand scale. Their ideas of local administration embracing so many spheres of activity which lie entirely outside the purview of municipal enterprise in this country, and their sources of revenue being so extensive, they spare no expense in making their towns attractive. Sometimes heavy expenditure is prompted by a mere spirit of ambition and rivalry, and the Governments are not slow to turn this weakness to good account. When State institutions needing costly buildings need to be established the Ministry concerned has only to give the sign and there is keen competition for the honour of providing site, structure, and it may be an annual maintenance grant as well. Even in the choice of towns to be garrisons the State is able to transfer a considerable part of the cost upon the communities so favoured, and the provision of the necessary barracks is the least concession expected. From the presence of State institutions in their midst the towns derive a certain indirect advantage—there are more officials to tax and more material wants to supply—but in the main it is the *cachet* of official recognition that attracts.

During the last decade in particular the expenditure upon general administration has shown an ominous increase, not merely absolutely but relatively to population. The reasons commonly advanced, in addition to the constant and inevitable multiplication of municipal duties, are the reduced purchasing power of money, repeated all-round increases in salaries and wages, and the growing tendency of the Governments to impose on the local authorities new liabilities which belong properly to the State, a tendency well illustrated by the extended duties given to the communes under the amended Social Insurance Law. Unfortunately the financial resources of the municipalities have simultaneously been crippled in some of the States owing to new Imperial and State legislation depriving the local bodies of sources of indirect taxation formerly open to them.

Thanks, however, to careful administration, to the elasticity of the system of local taxation, and not least to the fact that German mayors and municipal executives are not hampered by fear of burgesses whose only idea of local government is to spend as little as possible and keep down the rates, there are probably few German towns of consequence whose balance sheets do not show a substantial credit. For large as the liabilities of German towns are, this indebtedness is almost invariably a consequence of the fact, already noted, that the towns have borrowed capital in order to raise revenue independently of taxation by establishing and working trading enterprises.

The illustrations of municipal balance sheets given below have not been specially selected and hence may be regarded as typical of German large towns generally. All are given, however, with the reservation that while in statements of this kind it is safe to assume that the liabilities represent actual debts, there may not be the same certainty that all the assets represent actual and realisable values. Most of the figures have been supplied by the municipal authorities and refer to the end of the year 1912. It may be noted that the assets had in some cases been swelled by following the policy of executing public works in part out of revenue, and in others by judicious land investments, the value of which had in course of time greatly appreciated.

Towns and population.	Assets.	Liabilities.	Surplus.	Surplus per inhabitant.
	£	£	£	£ s.
Aix-la-Chapelle (158,800)	5,134,200	1,922,000	3,212,200	20 5
Augsburg (102,500)	3,044,000	1,829,000	1,215,000	10 17
Berlin (2,082,000)......	51,385,000	26,850,000	24,535,000	12 7
Cassel (155,300)	3,762,400	2,265,200	1,497,200	9 13
Charlottenburg (320,800)	11,876,400	9,346,300	2,530,100	7 18
Chemnitz (287,800)	6,215,800	4,109,800	2,106,000	7 6
Düsseldorf (390,000) ...	13,517,500	9,915,800	3,601,700	9 5
Erfurt (114,500)	2,039,000	1,489,000	550,000	4 19
Essen (307,000)........	7,714,100	4,060,500	3,653,600	11 18
Frankfort-on-Main (431,900)	27,425,000	16,112,500	11,312,500	26 4
Königsberg (246,000)...	4,410,000	3,334,000	1,076,000	4 9
Mannheim (217,700) ...	9,152,900	4,108,700	5,044,200	23 1
Mayence (110,600)	3,881,900	2,105,900	1,776,000	16 1
Nuremberg (333,100) ..	10,115,000	5,856,000	4,259,000	12 16
Wiesbaden (109,000) ...	4,744,000	3,010,000	1,734,000	16 0
TOTALS (pop. 5,367,000)	£164,416,300	£96,313,800	£68,102,500	£12 13

The same record of financial stability can be shown by smaller towns, with less resources at command. Thus Offenbach, with a population of 75,600, had in 1910 assets of £2,180,000, of which lands represented £600,000 and profit-yielding undertakings £1,062,000, against liabilities of £1,492,000, showing a surplus of £688,000, or £9 2s. per inhabitant. The small town of Menden, with a population of 11,000, in 1909 owned lands and forest with a value of £95,000 and counting its public buildings and trading enterprises, it had assets of £161,000, against liabilities of £74,000, showing a surplus of £87,000 or £7 18s. per inhabitant. Its forest

MUNICIPAL FINANCE

of 1660 acres is so well managed that it yields a net profit of over £1000 a year.

The following returns supplied by the town clerks of large towns in Great Britain and relating to 1912 compare on the whole not unfavourably with the German balance sheets given above :—

Towns and population.	Assets.	Liabilities.	Surplus.	Surplus per inhabitant.
	£	£	£	£ s.
Bradford (290,300).....	14,364,500	9,101,200	5,263,300	18 3
Bolton (180,900).......	6,193,900	6,064,400	129,500	0 14
Cardiff (184,600).......	6,329,700	4,686,300	1,643,400	8 18
Glasgow (1,015,200) ...	26,786,300	17,221,200	9,565,100	9 8
Huddersfield (107,800)..	4,615,600	4,238,500	377,100	3 10
Leeds (445,600)........	17,623,400	12,457,000	5,166,400	11 12
Leicester (227,200).....	8,422,800	4,866,500	3,556,300	15 13
Manchester (731,700)...	34,402,400	24,836,600	9,565,800	13 1
Newcastle (271,300)....	7,119,200	4,058,200	3,061,000	11 16
Salford (231,400)	5,518,500	3,567,300	1,951,200	8 9
Sheffield (454,600)	12,846,800	10,352,000	2,494,800	5 8
TOTALS (pop. 4,140,600)	£144,223,100	£101,449,200	£42,773,900	£10 7

CHAPTER XIV

MUNICIPAL TAXATION. 1.—THE LOCAL INCOME TAX

Local autonomy in taxation—Variety and incidence of local taxes—Individual basis of taxation—Communal taxation in Prussia—Principles governing the choice of taxes—The local income tax—Relief to small incomes—Local income taxes in the other States.

IN the later times of absolute sovereignty in Germany the ruler and his councillors determined the taxation of the towns, since they claimed to direct their government. Taxation was arbitrary and unequal, and as a rule was regulated less by what was done for the citizens than by their ability to pay or, it might be, to evade payment. The modern German idea of local government recognises the right of every citizen to share on equal terms in the benefits and conveniences provided by the communal authority, together with an equal obligation to contribute according to ability, in taxation,[1] towards the expenditure thereby entailed; if any section of the community enjoys special advantages it is expected, as a rule, to contribute in a corresponding degree. In general, assessment to local taxation may be said to follow the complementary principles of capacity and reciprocity.

Before reference is made to the taxes by which the towns in particular supplement their revenue from other sources, it will be useful to indicate briefly some of the special principles and characteristics of the German system of municipal taxation.

LOCAL AUTONOMY IN TAXATION.—Perhaps the most noteworthy are the wide taxing powers conferred upon the towns. These amount to a limited autonomy. That is to say, subject

[1] In writing and speaking of German local government it is necessary to accustom oneself to the words " tax " and " taxation." The English word " rate " and its derivatives have no meaning as applied to German conditions.

to certain duly defined rights of control reserved to the State, in the persons of its commissaries or supervisory officials, each town chooses the taxes which seem best suited to its conditions, and even the measure in which every tax shall contribute towards the revenue. There are certain local taxes which are common to most of the communes of a State, since they are assigned to them by general laws; yet the individual commune decides whether and to what extent it will levy even these taxes, and if it adopts them it may do so with its own modifications within limits, alike as to the form of their assessment, their amount, and their incidence, so as to meet its special circumstances. Beyond these prescribed taxes, each commune determines its taxes quite independently.

On the whole the widest taxing powers are enjoyed by municipal authorities in Saxony. Their large measure of liberty is reflected by the opening words of the Saxon Communal Taxation Law of July 11, 1913, viz., "The communes are entitled to raise direct and indirect taxes and to adopt measures for their introduction and regulation." Independence within generous limits, however, is the rule in all the States. The towns have reached their present degree of autonomy in taxing powers by the same course of evolution that has led to their wide independence in administration generally. "First, a time of extreme freedom and independence was followed by a period of complete dependence upon the State, and only the last century has witnessed a steady increase of the self-government of the towns in this as in all other domains."[1]

Further, apart from the statutory taxes referred to—taxes which in most States go back to the beginnings of modern communal government—local taxes are adopted not by virtue of special enactments or legislative procedure of any kind, but simply by the adoption of by-laws, which are almost as easy to put in force as the standing orders of an English town council. The power to introduce new taxes in this summary manner is not unlimited, yet the practical restrictions are not onerous. As much for the purpose of preventing undue demands upon the sources of State taxation, of securing a fair balance between different kinds of taxation, and of encouraging

[1] Dr. E. Scholz, "Die deutsche Stadt und ihre Verwaltung," Vol. I, p. 54.

uniformity within adjacent districts, as for the purpose of reminding the communes whence their powers of self-government issued, it is required that all new taxes and alterations of existing ones shall be submitted to the State's commissaries for approval. The Communal Taxation Law of Prussia states : " The introduction of new and the alteration of existing communal taxes can take place only in the form of Tax Ordinances, which require sanction." On the other hand, taxes can be repealed by mere resolution of the communal authority.

The law, indeed, places upon the Ministers of Finance and the Interior the primary duty of granting or withholding sanction, but it empowers them to delegate this duty to the authorities charged with the supervision of local government. In Prussia it is discharged primarily by the District Committee in relation to towns and by the Circle Committee in relation to rural communes, with right of appeal to the Provincial Council or District Committee respectively. The Chief President of the province must also give his assent, and in case of refusal appeal may be made to the Ministers of Finance and the Interior. In the case of the communes forming Greater Berlin the direct assent of the Government must be obtained. Sanction once given may not be revoked.

The fact that the communes are able to introduce taxes on their own initiative, and that all they have to do for the immediate enforcement of these taxes is to obtain the assent of an official who is in continuous touch with their work, and often lives in the neighbourhood, makes the revision of their taxation systems easy and expeditious. A noteworthy illustration of rapid procedure in the introduction of a new tax occurred in 1909 at Schöneberg, near Berlin. The town council had decided upon the adoption of a tax on unearned increment in land, and only the Order embodying it remained to be adopted, when it became known that a land development company was endeavouring to hurry through a large transaction with a view to escaping the new impost. There was a race between the municipality and the speculators, and the municipality won. On April 26 the municipal council adopted the Order, and the same day the executive gave its assent. The following day the District Committee met and passed a resolution of approval. On the third day the project was laid before the Chief President of the province, who ratified it ; on the fourth day the Minister of the Interior, and on the fifth day the Minister of Finance, gave their assent, and on the evening of the last-named day the Order was promulgated and entered into force. It is stated that this prompt action saved the municipal treasury some thousands of pounds in taxation. In Berlin a new tax upon sales of property was sanctioned by the municipal executive on March 4, 1910, and received the sanction of the Chief President the following day.

At times, of course, there enters into the question of sanction an element of uncertainty which proves embarrassing. State officials lightly come and lightly go. The personal equation is naturally powerful, and taxes approved in one town are, for no obvious reason save difference of official view, refused in another. Moreover, in a given district a change of officials may lead to a sudden change of policy ; a tax the introduction of which has been encouraged under one Chief President may be condemned by his successor. On the whole, however, serious inconvenience of the kind is infrequent, though, inasmuch as the decision of a Chief President is practically final, it is not surprising that his right of veto is obnoxious to many communal authorities, accustomed to the exercise of large executive powers, and that the demand is made at times that the communes should be given an effective right of appeal to the Supreme Administrative Court, or else that the refusal of taxes should be made dependent on clearly defined general grounds, with which a communal authority might be able to reckon beforehand.

It is significant, however, that no one appears to desire that legislation should specify the taxes which communes must introduce. It is also a fact that some of the towns which are most apt to complain of the alleged unnecessary checks upon their independence in matters of taxation—an independence which, nevertheless, is greater than any other towns in the world enjoy—have good cause to thank the provincial governors for their timely and successful efforts to equalise taxation and to curb unfair rivalries and small jealousies as between adjacent communities.

VARIETY AND INCIDENCE OF LOCAL TAXES.—Again, the German communes adopt as wide a basis of taxation as possible; the local taxes are many, and they are so devised as to draw into the net every individual citizen from whom contribution to the common fund can be expected without harshness. The citizen may be taxed in one or in several ways, according to the sources of his income. Thus, while every person in receipt of income of a certain amount, variable according to the State, pays a local tax upon that income or a portion of it, the owner of real estate is in addition subject to taxation as such, and not merely incidentally as an occupier, as is the case in England. So, too, the business man is taxed specially in respect of his enterprise; there are taxes intended to tap speculative profits on land, taxes on amusements, and a variety of indirect imposts. Two objects of taxation, however, are conspicuous in the Tax Ordinances of every commune—real estate and income; the gravamen may be real estate in one town, in another income, but it is safe to say that on the average of the towns as a whole, 80 per cent. of all local taxation properly so called[1] is derived from these two sources.

INDIVIDUAL BASIS OF TAXATION.—Another distinction of the German system of local taxation is that it knows nothing of the household basis of taxation as recognised in this country. Taxation there is individual, and its only condition is the receipt of income; the only condition of exemption, such a paucity of income as would make taxation inequitable. The mere accident of how or where a man lives does not enter into the question. To that extent the German principle of local taxation is that which underlies the State income tax, both in that country and in this. There the analogy ends, however, for in Germany the idea is held that every citizen should bear some direct share, however little, in the costs of local as of general administration, and upon this principle the State and

[1] Dues and charges for public services, like water and gas, fees for schools, etc., are here disregarded.

local income taxes are both based. The communal tax may only be 2s. or 4s. a year, but its payment is a formal attestation of the fact that every citizen has a share in and a responsibility for the good government of his town or village, and a reminder that the true conception of citizenship implies the recognition of duties as well as rights, since the services done for society, and not the claims made upon it, are the cement that most truly and securely knits any community together.

Hence a far larger proportion of a town's inhabitants is brought within the ambit of taxation than is the case in this country. As a rule, the separate assessments to the local income tax are equal to about one-third of the entire population, though where the exemption limit is low the ratio is higher. Inasmuch, however, as wives and children may in certain cases be assessed together with the head of the household the proportion of the population directly taxed is still larger. In this country the ratio of separate assessments to population is in general about one to four, though this figure includes a certain amount of duplication. Because of the variety of sources from which local taxation is drawn in Germany, however, it is possible to graduate the burden according to ability to bear it. Probably of no tax in common adoption in German towns can it be fairly said that it presses with undue weight upon persons of limited means.

The German system of local taxation is, of course, complicated, but that is because it is a system, and because it is the result of an endeavour to apportion taxation with some approximation to equity. The English mind, ever disposed to confuse system with pedantry, cares more for results than the methods of attaining them, and places singular trust in what are known as simple, common-sense solutions. But the problems which are evolved by highly developed social organisations seldom admit of adjustment by simple measures, and the reformer who makes short cuts in the search for illusory common-sense solutions runs a risk of losing sight of one-half of the problem at issue, and, in legislating for the other half, of doing so partially and ill.

No method of local taxation in the world is so simple as the English system of rating entirely on rental value, and none is so unjust. German economists are in the habit of calling the English local rate a " rent tax," and the view is still widely prevalent abroad that this tax is paid by the owners. The rate is, of course, simply and solely an income tax, assessed on the crudest and clumsiest of all standards, for it is devised so as to fall with special weight upon householders with large families and small incomes. There is not a service or a convenience for which the rate pays that is not enjoyed equally by the non-occupying inhabitants, yet they have these things free. Under this singular system of taxation, the wretched tenants of a tenement block in an East End slum may well pay together as much in local taxation as the wealthy occupants of a West End mansion. The rate is a progressive tax upon poverty, since the poorer the ratepayer the heavier he is taxed relatively to his income. It is consequently a tax upon living space, for its effect is to compel householders of limited means to content themselves with inadequate and inferior accommodation. Incidentally it further operates to increase the value of property without contribution from the owners, and hence to require every local community to pay tribute upon its own improvements. As we shall see, German local taxation is so devised as to have precisely the opposite effect.

The operation of this unsocial and undiscriminating tax is to some extent veiled by the system of compounding for rates, by which the owner of small dwellings makes himself responsible for the rates upon his property in consideration of these being reduced—an arrangement adopted not, indeed, for the benefit of the tenants, but for the purpose of facilitating the collection of revenue, much of which would otherwise never pass beyond the stage of the demand note. No one has ever pretended, however, that the house-owner pays the rates himself, and their ultimate incidence is hardly a matter for uncertainty. What the rating system actually means to the pockets of the working classes can be best understood by considering the ratio of rate to rent in any industrial town.

Equitable taxation is a science, and cannot be devised except by the application of scientific principles, but the working of the English rating system requires no more science than is necessary to the use of a ready-reckoner or the turning of a thumbscrew.

MUNICIPAL TAXATION—LOCAL INCOME TAX

Minor taxes on the principle of the English rate upon rental value used to be common in Germany, but they were merely incidental, and took a quite insignificant place in the local plan of taxation, and they have now almost entirely disappeared. In Prussia the Communal Taxation Law of 1893 prohibited the introduction of new taxes of the kind, and made the continuance of existing ones subject to renewed State sanction, failing which they were to lapse in five years. Since that time the general recognition of the inequity of these imposts has led to their abandonment in all but a few towns, where they survive in a harmless form.

COMMUNAL TAXATION IN PRUSSIA.—In considering how towns tax themselves for common purposes, it will be convenient to give special prominence to Prussia, since that State contains nearly two-thirds of the Empire's population, and that two-thirds of all German communes with a population exceeding 10,000 (388 out of 576) are in Prussia. It is the more permissible to centre attention upon the system of communal taxation prevalent in Prussia since, while every State has peculiarities of its own, the general lines are the same, and the principal difference is in the varying degree in which stress is laid on one or other of the two main sources of taxation, real estate (as in parts of Prussia) and income (as in Saxony). Moreover, the whole tendency of modern taxation laws and regulations in Germany is in the direction of uniformity and of assimilation to Prussian practice, a tendency well illustrated by the laws passed in Bavaria and Saxony so lately as in 1910 and 1913 respectively.

The Prussian Municipal Ordinance of 1853 provided that, in so far as local taxes were necessary owing to the insufficiency of a town's revenues from other sources, they should consist in (a) percentage additions to the direct taxes levied by the State, and particularly the income tax, subject to the condition that the assent of the Government should be obtained to all additions to the income tax and to additions above 50 per cent. in the case of all other State taxes, and in (b) special direct and indirect taxes, all of which needed the Government's sanction. In the main, the communes at that time raised their revenue by means of taxes of the first class, though various subsidiary taxes were introduced, such as duties on articles of consumption, particularly on corn and flour, and on animals slaughtered for food in the commune, rent and house taxes, taxes on luxuries (horses, crests, etc.), dog taxes, etc.

Except that rent and house taxes and food duties have for the most part been abolished, the broad principles of local taxation continue as laid down sixty years ago.

The latest statutory statement of these principles is contained in the Communal Taxation Act of July 14, 1893, which needs to be considered in conjunction with a law of the same date repealing certain direct State taxes, and with the Income Tax Act and the Trade Tax Act of June 24, 1891, which remodelled the State taxes to which these laws refer. Before 1893 the communes had been allowed to supplement their other revenues by levying percentages of the four State taxes on income, land, buildings, and trade pursuits (including mining dues). Now the State handed over altogether to the communes the old land and building and trade taxes—known as "real" taxes—and gave them still the right to levy percentages upon the income tax as before, while it continued to assess all four taxes on their behalf. With a view to compensating itself for the revenue thus renounced the State revised and increased the income tax and supplemented it by a differential tax on funded income. The amount which was ceded to the communes and which the State had to obtain in other ways was about £5,000,000, made up as follows: Land Tax, £1,995,000; Building Tax, £1,754,000; Trade Tax, £990,000; mining dues, £346,000; making a total of £5,085,000.

It was essential from the standpoint of national revenue, however, that in assigning to the local authorities sources of taxation which had hitherto been reserved by the State for its own use, the State should determine the place which these taxes should in future occupy in relation to the income tax. The Prussian Treasury contended that inasmuch as it had voluntarily fallen back upon the income tax, local authorities must no longer look to this tax for revenue to the same extent as before. Hence the new legislation proceeded from the following principles :—

(1) Direct local taxation was to be restricted as much as possible, and to this end communal enterprises were to be worked as remuneratively as might be ; the practice of imposing dues for the use of communal services was to be developed ; special contributions were to be levied upon those persons who specially benefited by public works of various kinds ; and attention was to be given to suitable indirect taxes in so far as Imperial legislation permitted.

(2) Such revenue as might be needed after these sources of taxation had been exhausted was to be obtained by " real " and income taxes duly proportioned, real estate and commercial undertakings being taxed more heavily for local purposes than hitherto, in view of the fact that the State no longer taxed them specially. While a local income tax might be levied, local supplements to the special tax on funded income were forbidden.

The memorandum in which the Government of the day explained its proposals stated : " The real taxes should require from immovable property and commercial undertakings payments proportionate to the expenditure specially incurred for their benefit, on the principle of reciprocity, while the expenditure on behalf of general public purposes should be a charge on all inhabitants and should be borne by them in proportion to individual capacity in the form of taxation of income."

(3) While the communal income tax was still to form a certain proportion of the State income tax and was not to be levied in any other way, the communes were to be allowed to develop the real estate and trade taxes on such new lines as local circumstances might suggest. " In this direction," said the same memorandum, " a new and fruitful field is opened up to local administrative activity. So long, however, as special taxes on real estate or trade undertakings are not introduced the ' real ' taxation of the communes must take the form of the land, building, and trade taxes as assessed by the State, even though it has renounced these taxes. The

gradual transition to another organisation of their systems of taxation will thus be made much easier for the communes."

PRINCIPLES GOVERNING THE CHOICE OF TAXES.—The degree in which the expenditure of a commune is met by taxes of the kinds named is not supposed to be determined arbitrarily, but must pay due regard to the purposes served by such expenditure. The regulations and directions issued by the Government at various times mention as specially suitable to be charged to the income tax such expenditure as is incurred for the benefit of all inhabitants in common, and particularly on account of elementary schools, poor relief, public health and security, the general costs of administration, and the costs of the civil registry and burials. Expenditure which should be charged by preference to the real estate and trade taxes includes outlay upon purposes which specially benefit the property owning and trading classes, such as street and road construction, sewerage works, continuation schools, courts of industry and commerce, outlay incidental to the acquisition of public institutions (e.g. lunatic asylums) or of a garrison, and standing costs entailed thereby, with expenditure in the special interest of agriculture. As illustrations of expenditure suitable to be charged to the income, real estate, and trade taxes jointly, may be mentioned the cost of maintaining, cleaning, and lighting the streets, parks, bridges, and other public places, the upkeep of sewerage and water works, fire brigades, and higher schools, also taxation levied on the communes by the provinces and "circles."

In budgeting yearly the communal authorities are expected to classify their estimated expenditure on these general principles and to regulate their taxes accordingly, but in charging expenditure to the several kinds of taxes the revenue received in respect of the institutions or works concerned is first deducted.

Other rules of procedure are provided by the Communal Taxation Law itself. The law emphasises the distinction between the "real" taxes and the income tax, and this distinction is important because of its bearing on the ratio in which communes may derive revenue from those two sources. Until the land and building and trade taxes exceed 100 per cent. of the State assessment the income tax may, without any formality, be levied at any rate up to 100 per cent., or not at all. If more than 150 per cent. of the " real " taxes is levied, and the income tax rate has reached 150 per cent., 2 per cent. additional income tax may be levied for every 1 per cent. of " real " taxes. The maximum levy in the case of the real taxes, however, is fixed at 250 per cent. under ordinary circumstances. In particular, the Government reserved the right to sanction or refuse at will permission to levy more than 100 per cent. of the State income tax by way of local supertax. This was done, first, in order to safeguard the income tax against undue local raiding ; yet also from apprehension that excessive taxation of income would lead to under-declaration. It was the more necessary that the Government should have a voice in fixing the amount of this tax since the legal provisions securing to house-owners at least one-half of the seats upon all town councils made it possible for this class of citizens to resist the taxation of real estate.

Subject to these general conditions, the law empowers communes to raise direct and indirect taxes, as well as to require services in kind[1] in lieu thereof, in order to meet their expenditure. Such direct taxes are the income, land and building, and trade taxes ; and the indirect taxes comprise consumption or excise taxes, taxes on the sale and transfer of real estate—answering to the conveyance duty in this country —unearned increment (called in Germany " increased value ") taxes, taxes on amusements, concessions, dogs, etc.

The power to levy taxes, however, may be exercised only to the extent that their other revenues, and particularly those from public property, fees, dues, contributions, etc., prove insufficient ; though this provision does not apply to

[1] These " services in kind " (*Naturaldienste*) consist of the old " Hand- und Spanndienste," implying the obligation to perform night-watchman or messenger service, or place horses or oxen at the disposal of the commune, in lieu of paying money taxes, a substitution provided for in the early Town Ordinances, and still practised occasionally in poor rural districts. In the little town of Jesuborn, in the principality of Schwarzburg-Sondershausen, the night-watchmen not long ago (1910) applied for a small increase in wages. Instead of granting it, the communal council abolished the office of paid night-watchmen and resolved that each adult male citizen should undertake the duties in turn, parading the streets with a horn half the night through. The Government of the principality duly sanctioned this odd arrangement.

amusement and dog taxes, and similar taxes adopted owing to special reasons. Further, direct taxes may only be imposed when indirect taxes prove inadequate. The fees and dues implied here are chiefly payments made in respect of the "public utility" services and institutions provided by the commune, while the "contributions" contemplated are "betterment" contributions towards the cost of public works and improvements, such as street extensions, paving, open spaces, public parks and gardens, etc., where these increase the value of adjoining property.

As to the incidence of the taxes, it is required that the direct taxes shall be apportioned amongst all persons liable to taxation according to fixed and uniform principles. Where, however, institutions of special benefit to a portion of the communal district or a class of the citizens are provided, the commune may tax such district or class of citizens towards their cost in proportion to the benefit derived. The income tax may be replaced in part by "expenditure" taxes—that is, taxes based on or measured by outgoings of various kinds—but taxes of this order may not fall disproportionately on small relatively to larger incomes, and no new taxes on rents (*Anglice*, rates upon rental value) may be introduced.

Indirect taxes may be levied within the limits laid down by Imperial legislation. The law forbids the introduction of new, or the increase of existing, entrance dues on meat, corn, flour, baked goods, potatoes, and fuel of all kinds, but allows dues on game and poultry. The Imperial Customs Law of December 25, 1902, however, provided for the abolition of all local taxes on corn, legumes, flour and other milled goods, baked goods, cattle, meat, meat preparations, and fat, as from April 1, 1910, and these dues have now disappeared throughout Germany. Other indirect taxes which have been introduced in various communes are a wine duty (in wine-producing districts only), a beer duty, taxes on amusements, the sale of real estate, and concessions for licensed premises. Taxes on spirits, petroleum, fire insurance policies, auctions, pianos, cycles, equipages, horses, and the keeping of poultry have been proposed, but have been declared unpermissible.

All new communal taxes, and alterations of existing ones,

in so far as they do not consist of percentage proportions of taxes assessed by the State (i.e., the income, land, building, and trade taxes), need to be introduced in the form of Tax Ordinances, and these ordinances, as has been explained, require the approval of the Ministers of Finance and the Interior or the supervisory authorities.

Persons become liable to local income tax the moment they are assessed to the State tax; in the case of other local taxes three months' grace is allowed. A commune may, however, for a period of three years at the most, exempt from income tax, or tax on a lower scale, foreigners and subjects of other federal States who reside therein without following an occupation for gain.

VARIATIONS IN OTHER STATES.—The local taxation systems of the other States do not differ in fundamental principles. Thus in Bavaria the communes are entitled to levy supplements to the State taxes on land, buildings, trades, and income, but in a given commune these supplements must be uniform in rate and may not vary as in Prussia; as between different communes uniformity is not necessary.

In Saxony, where the communes have long enjoyed an exceptional degree of autonomy in taxation, local supplements to the State income and land taxes, and to the trade tax assessed but no longer levied by the State are allowed, though since the State renounced the trade tax most communes have followed its example. As in Prussia the communes may choose their own taxes within the limits laid down by legislation. Thus in 1910 of the taxes—other than the income and land taxes—most commonly selected, the tax on the sale or exchange of real estate was levied in 2563 communes, the poll tax in 1613, the amusement tax in 2342, the dog tax in 3126, the unearned increment tax in 54, a "rent" tax in 22, and general consumption taxes in only five communes. On the whole Saxon towns rely principally upon the income tax and tax real estate very leniently. In sympathy with this tendency the new Communal Taxation Law (1913) allows communes to raise as much as 85 per cent. of the total amount of revenue to be derived from taxation by the local income tax. Where a local income tax is not levied, at least 30 per cent. of the taxation must take the form of a land and building tax, and every commune which levies direct taxes at all must introduce this tax.

In Saxony it is a peculiarity of local taxation that in most communes special taxes are levied for poor relief, schools, and church administration respectively; though, as a rule, these taxes are collected with the general communal taxes and are then assigned to the purposes for which they are intended. The taxes earmarked for poor relief are those on the sale of real estate, on amusements, dogs, and nightingales, though the last-named tax is now almost extinct.

In Würtemberg local supplements may be levied to the State taxes on lands, buildings, trades, general income, interest on invested capital, and sales and transfers of real estate. The supplements to the last three taxes are limited, but there is no limit to the others except that the rate must be uniform for all.

In all these States the subsidiary taxes and contributions are practically the same in character, though not in productiveness, as in Prussia.

In the following detailed explanation of the local taxes most commonly levied, Prussian communes have again been specially considered, but peculiarities of other States will be noted where of sufficient importance.

The dues and fees leviable by the communes need not be further mentioned, inasmuch as they have been dealt with in the chapters on "Trading Enterprises" and "Finance," and, moreover, they are of the nature of special payments for special services and benefits rather than taxes, though regarded as such by some German writers.

THE LOCAL INCOME TAX.—The local income tax in Prussia, as in the other German States, is levied in the form of a percentage supplement to the State income tax. To the State tax all persons in receipt of income are liable, subject to the exemptions stated below, and its collection is regulated by a general law, passed in 1891, with amendments of 1893, 1906, and 1909, the main provisions of which are as follows: The tax is levied on all persons in receipt of income exceeding £45 a year, the exemption limit, but the incomes of husband and wife, and of children under age living in the household (unless in the latter case derived from employment or bequest), are taken together in order to determine the rate of taxation which applies. The tax is now assessed as a rule by State officers, corresponding to our surveyors of inland revenue, appointed for urban and rural "circles," assisted by civil assessors, also answering broadly to our local commissioners of inland revenue, an arrangement preferred to the old method of assessment by the Landrats. Appeal against an assessment is allowed.

The law of 1891 relieved small incomes and taxed large incomes more highly than heretofore. Before that time incomes not exceeding £45 were exempt from taxation for national purposes, and those between £45 and £150 paid a tax of about 3 per cent. The new law continued the old limit of exemption, but graduated the rate of taxation from a mean of 0·62 per cent. on incomes from £45 to £75, to 1½ per cent. on incomes from £75 to £150, 2 per cent. on incomes from £150 to £500, and 3 per cent. on incomes from £500 to £1525, the rate then rising gradually to 4 per cent. for incomes of £5000, while on incomes in excess of £5250 the increase was fixed at £10 (4 per cent.) for every additional £250 of income. The tax is graduated with great minuteness, the assessment rising first by income increments of £7 10s., then in succession by increments of £15, £25, £50, £75, £100, and finally £250. Somewhat higher rates apply to companies.

Exemption from income tax is enjoyed by certain persons, and deductions from income are allowed before the taxable amount is arrived at, as, for example, the sum of the direct communal taxes paid in respect of land, buildings, and commercial undertakings up to the amount of the State assessment only, statutory insurance contributions, life insurance premiums to the amount of £30, sickness, unemployment, and strike pay, interest on debts, etc. Further, persons with incomes not exceeding £325, who have children or others dependent on them, can claim to be assessed in an income class one, two, or three steps below that which would otherwise apply, according as they have two, three or four, and five or six such dependants respectively, and for every two additional dependants one further fall in the schedule of rates is allowed. Persons with incomes between

£325 and £475 are assessed one class lower than would otherwise apply if they have three children or dependants to maintain, two classes lower if they have four or five dependants, and one further class lower for every two additional dependants. Above £475 no abatement of the kind is allowed. These abatements apply equally to the local supertax. Incomes under £150 are estimated by the taxing authority, but incomes above that amount have to be declared on the English principle. House-owners are required to report to the taxing authority all persons living in dwellings belonging to them, and employers must on demand report the earnings of persons in their employ with an income not exceeding £150.

Upon the amount of State income tax depends the amount of communal income tax levied, since the latter is fixed always at a certain percentage of the former. Hence a "supplement" of 100 per cent. means that the citizen must pay exactly the same sum in local income tax which he pays in the same tax to the State. As has been explained, Prussian communes are allowed to levy up to 100 per cent. at their discretion, but they cannot go beyond this amount without the sanction of the State supervisory authority.

PRINCIPLE OF ASSESSMENT.—The principle of assessment to local income tax is that a person pays the tax in the commune of residence, and that all his income, whatever and wherever its source, is liable, subject to the condition that taxation in respect of real estate and commercial undertakings situated in a commune other than that of residence goes to that other commune. Should the owner of land, a house, a factory, or a shop remove from the commune in which it is situated into another place, the income which he derives from either of these sources will continue liable to taxation in the first commune, as before. On the other hand, if a professional man, an official, or an employee of any grade change his residence, though not his place of occupation, the right to tax his income from such occupation is forfeited by the first commune in favour of his new place of abode. The State pays tax in respect of its income from railways and other trading enterprises, domains, and forests, every enterprise being treated as a separate unit for the purpose of taxation. There are special provisions to prevent the double taxation of individuals, and to provide for the division of taxation between different communes where undertakings operate in two or more communes.

As a rule, the local taxes must be paid at a central office or branches, but in some towns they are still collected, though the fact that the taxes are mostly levied once a quarter makes the cost of collection disproportionately high. Cheques are accepted as in this country. The local authority collects the State tax with the supertax, charging a small commission for so doing.

In some of the States, Crown and State officials, including military officers, clergymen, and teachers in public schools, and certain other persons with official status, have hitherto been exempted from local income tax or have been assessed on a lower scale than others in respect of official income and pensions. This privilege has been justified on the ground that officials are required constantly to change their place of residence, and that the great inequality of this taxation as between one town and another would expose them to unfair fluctuations of effective income. Thus an official might be living in a lightly taxed town one year, and the next year, without higher salary, he might be transferred to one in which the taxation was very onerous; extremes in the local income tax of 100 and 300 per cent. of the State assessment are possible always. On the other hand, it is no less true that while an official may change one time from good to bad, the next removal may more than compensate, and the opponents of the privilege contend that in the long run his risks balance. On the whole public opinion would appear to recognise the existence in the case of officials of special circumstances which justify special treatment, and those who take this attitude, while still opposed to total exemption, agree that a limit might fairly be set to the scale of local income tax which should apply to officials, yet hold that the State should make up the deficiency.

That the communes have an equal right to consideration is clearly incontestable. It is estimated that the privilege of officials costs Königsberg £20,000 and Cassel over £10,000 a year in forfeited taxation. An extreme illustration of the injury suffered by towns from this cause is that of Rostock, a town of 65,000 inhabitants, in Mecklenburg-Schwerin, where all the officials in the service of the Grand Duke, the judicial officials, the university staff, the pensioned military officers, and others are exempt from communal taxation, entailing upon the local treasury a loss of £6500 a year, which has to be made up by classes of the population less favourably situated.

In Prussia, State and Court officials, elementary school teachers, and minor church employees appointed since March 31, 1909, have been liable to pay on their official income a local income tax not exceeding 125 per cent. of the State income tax, and on non-official income the full amount of the local tax, whatever the rate may be. Military persons still enjoy relief in respect of official income, and the clergy also enjoy their old immunity. Similarly the Communal Taxation Law of Saxony stipulates that the official incomes of Imperial, State, and communal officials appointed before 1909 shall only be taxed to the extent of four-fifths.

The following table shows the rates of local income tax now payable by individuals on income in excess of £45 in Prussia where that tax is equal to the State tax :—

Income—						Local Tax at 100 per cent of State Tax.
	£ s.		£ s.			£ s. d.
Above	45 0	to	52 10	inclusive		0 6 0
,,	52 10	,,	60 0	,,		0 9 0
,,	60 0	,,	67 10	,,		0 12 0
,,	67 10	,,	75 0	,,		0 16 0
,,	75 0	,,	82 10	,,		1 1 0
,,	82 10	,,	90 0	,,		1 6 0
,,	90 0	,,	105 0	,,		1 11 0
,,	105 0	,,	120 0	,,		1 16 0
,,	120 0	,,	135 0	,,		2 4 0
,,	135 0	,,	150 0	,,		2 12 0
,,	150 0	,,	165 0	,,		3 0 0
,,	165 0	,,	180 0	,,		3 10 0
,,	180 0	,,	195 0	,,		4 0 0
,,	195 0	,,	210 0	,,		4 12 0
,,	210 0	,,	225 0	,,		5 4 0
,,	225 0	,,	250 0	,,		5 18 0
,,	250 0	,,	275 0	,,		6 12 0
,,	275 0	,,	300 0	,,		7 6 0
,,	300 0	,,	325 0	,,		8 0 0
,,	325 0	,,	350 0	,,		8 16 0
,,	350 0	,,	375 0	,,		9 12 0
,,	375 0	,,	400 0	,,		10 12 0
,,	400 0	,,	425 0	,,		11 12 0
,,	425 0	,,	450 0	,,		12 12 0
,,	450 0	,,	475 0	,,		13 16 0
,,	475 0	,,	525 0	,,		15 0 0

From £525 the schedule rises to £1525 by sums of £50, and the tax is increased by £1 10s. for every additional £50, so that the tax on incomes from £1475 to £1525 is £45. The "steps" or stages are then: incomes of £1525 to £1600, £3 for each additional £75 of income; £1600 to £3900, £4 for each additional £100 of income; £3900 to £5000, £5 for each additional £100, so that a tax of £200 is reached for incomes from £5000 to £5250, after which there is an increase of £10 for every additional £250 of income. The rates for incomes of from £500 to £1000 in multiples of £100 are:—

£	£	s.	d.
500	15	0	0
600	16	0	0
700	21	0	0
800	24	0	0
900	27	0	0
1000	30	0	0

As, however, a local supertax of only 100 per cent. is rare—in 1911 only 6½ per cent. of the urban communes of Prussia levied so low a rate—the foregoing figures afford no adequate idea of the actual taxation paid. Rates from 50 to 100 per cent. higher than the above may be regarded as normal in Prussian towns. A law of April 1, 1909, introduced additions (intended to be temporary only) to the State tax on incomes from £60 upward, rising from 5 per cent., but these additions do not apply to the local percentages, which continue leviable on the normal rates.

RELIEF TO SMALL INCOMES.—Communes are given the option of exempting altogether from taxation for local purposes all incomes below £45 or any smaller sum, or of reducing the rate of taxation in respect of these incomes. One reason for taxing these smaller incomes is the fact that the right to take part in local elections is in Prussia, as in most other States, dependent upon the payment of taxes. To meet the cases where exemption is not granted on incomes freed from the State tax, the law fixes fictitious (*fingierte*) tax rates of 2s. 4·8d. for incomes from £21 to £33, and 4s. for incomes from £33 to £45. For local purposes, therefore, these sums would represent 100 per cent. of the State assessment. Incomes under £21 may be taxed only to the extent of two-fifths, and to a maximum of 1s. 2·4d.

Many towns exercise their full exemption powers, and tax only incomes in excess of £45, among them Berlin and the adjacent communes, Cologne, Düsseldorf, Essen, Duisburg, Aix-la-Chapelle, and other towns in the industrial west. A larger number of towns exempt from taxation incomes below £33, and a still larger number begin to tax incomes at £21. Where the supertax is high it is common to apply a reduced rate to small incomes, and persons in receipt of poor relief must, in any event, be exempted from taxation. Thus in Frankfort-on-Main the tax upon incomes from £45 to £150 is 70 per cent. of the State income tax rate, on incomes from £150 to £300 it is 80 per cent., on incomes from £300 to £525, 90 per cent., and after £525 the full supertax rate, as varied from time to time, applies. On the other hand, Altona has been allowed to retain an old arrangement by which smaller incomes bear higher relative rates, the object being to discourage the immigration into the town of working-class population from Hamburg.

LOCAL INCOME TAXES IN THE OTHER STATES.—Local income taxes based on the State income tax tariffs are levied in the other States, but in most States the exemption limit for the State tax is lower than in Prussia. Thus in Bavaria the limit is nominally £30, though in reality £15, since every male Bavarian citizen has to pay a tax of 1s. in order to be qualified to vote in parliamentary elections; in Saxony the limit is £20, in Würtemberg and Hesse it is £25, but the Prussian limit of £45 applies in Baden and also in the City States of Hamburg and Bremen. On the other hand, lower rates of taxation are levied on small incomes in some States, which means that these incomes are proportionately relieved from taxation for local purposes. The following are the rates of State income tax on small incomes in Saxony :—

			s.	d.				s.	d.
Above £20	to £25	..	1	0	Above £55	to £62 10s.	..	13	0
,, £25	,, £30	..	2	0	,, £62 10s.	,, £70	..	16	0
,, £30	,, £35	..	3	0	,, £70	,, £80	..	20	0
,, £35	,, £40	..	4	0	,, £80	,, £95	..	26	0
,, £40	,, £47 10s.	..	7	0	,, £95	,, £100	..	36	0
,, £47 10s.	,, £55	..	10	0					

MUNICIPAL TAXATION—LOCAL INCOME TAX

The tax may also be levied on incomes between £10 and £20 except in the case of persons with dependants, but, on the other hand, relief may be afforded to small incomes either by exempting all incomes up to £20 inclusive or by reducing the rates of tax chargeable in the lower income classes.

The rates of State income tax in Bavaria for incomes within the same range are as follows :—

	s.	d.		s.	d.
Above £15 to £30	1	0	Above £70 to £75	13	0
„ £30 „ £35	1	0	„ £75 „ £80	15	0
„ £35 „ £40	2	0	„ £80 „ £85	17	0
„ £40 „ £45	3	0	„ £85 „ £90	19	0
„ £45 „ £50	4	6	„ £90 „ £95	21	0
„ £50 „ £55	6	0	„ £95 „ £100	23	0
„ £55 „ £60	7	6	„ £100 „ £105	25	6
„ £60 „ £65	9	0	„ £105 „ £150	28	0
„ £65 „ £70	11	0			

In the case of the Würtemberg State income tax the normal tax (i.e., 100 per cent.) is given below, as the actual rate levied for national purposes is determined by the Diet from year to year, and 105 per cent. of the normal tariff has been levied since 1909:—

	s.	d.		s.	d.
£25 to £32 10s.	2	0	£70 to £77 10s.	11	0
£32 10s. „ £40	3	0	£77 10s. „ £85	13	0
£40 „ £47 10s.	4	0	£85 „ £92 10s.	16	0
£47 10s. „ £55	5	0	£92 10s. „ £100	18	0
£55 „ £62 10s.	7	0	£100 „ £107 10s.	21	0
£62 10s. „ £70	9	0			

It would not be correct to assume that the working classes object to the payment of this tax. On the contrary, they regard it as natural and right, though they are probably as little fond of taxation of any kind as normal men and women of other classes of society. Their attitude is fairly reflected by a remark made by the principal German labour newspaper, the *Vorwärts* (October, 1909) : " No working-man regards the income tax as unjust if the assessment is equal all round ; for that reason we have always been in favour of declaration of incomes, even in the case of small incomes."

As in Prussia the communes in all these States levy local percentages to meet their needs. In Würtemberg the percentage may not exceed 50 per cent. of the State levy, but there is a movement in favour of increasing the limit to 75 per cent. or more.

An unusual arrangement exists in some of the towns of Alsace-Lorraine. By the law of that State every person receiving £35 yearly in wages, salary, or emoluments is liable to State income tax, and according to the amount of the State tax is the subsidiary income tax levied by the communes for local purposes. Towns which levy *octroi* are, however, allowed to exempt incomes up to £65 from the payment of income tax, and to make the deficit claimable by the State a charge on the *octroi* dues. Strassburg carries the exemption to £50; Mülhausen began with £50, but now goes to the maximum figure and pays the State £3500 a year in place of some 9500 persons—nearly all working-people—who would otherwise have been liable for income tax.

It will be interesting to show by actual examples the local income tax payable on small incomes at the present time in large towns of Prussia :—

Income Class.	Berlin, 110 per cent. of State Tax.	Essen, 200 per cent. of State Tax.	Frankfort-on-Main.	Hagen, 275 per cent. of State Tax.
	s. d.	s. d.	s. d.	s. d.
Above £21 0s. to £33 0s. inclusive	Exempt.	Exempt.	Exempt.	6 7¼
,, 33 0 ,, 45 0 ,,	,,	,,	,,	11 0
,, 45 0 ,, 52 10 ,,	6 7	12 0	4 2½	12 0
,, 52 10 ,, 60 0 ,,	9 11	18 0	6 4¾	24 9
,, 60 0 ,, 67 10 ,,	13 2	24 0	8 4¾	33 0
,, 67 10 ,, 75 0 ,,	17 7	32 0	11 2	44 0
,, 75 0 ,, 82 10 ,,	23 1	42 0	14 9	44 0
,, 82 10 ,, 90 0 ,,	28 7	52 0	18 3	76 0
,, 90 0 ,, 105 0 ,,	34 1	62 0	21 9	85 3

In proof of the diversity of rates of local income tax levied in Prussian towns it may be stated that in 1911, 22 of the 280 towns with a population exceeding 10,000 levied from 125 to 150 per cent. of the State tax, 52 levied between 150 and 175 per cent., 77 levied between 175 and 200 per cent., 98 levied between 200 and 250 per cent., and 59 levied more than 250 per cent., the highest percentage being 300. Even within limited and homogeneous areas surprising disparities often prevail. Thus, the rates levied in 10 large industrial towns in the province of Rhineland in 1910 varied from 145 per cent. in Düsseldorf to 177 per cent. in Aix-la-Chapelle, 190 per cent. in Crefeld, 200 per cent. in Duisburg, Essen, and Mülheim, 220 per cent. in Solingen, and 230 per cent. in Barmen, Remscheid, and Saarbrücken. Often small communes have the highest rates of tax. There are rural communes in the provinces of Rhineland and Westphalia with rates of 250, 300, 350, and 400 per cent.

CHAPTER XV

MUNICIPAL TAXATION (*continued*). II.—THE REAL ESTATE TAXES

The land and building taxes—Property transfer tax—Unearned increment tax—" Betterment " taxes or special assessments.

THE Prussian Government's principal object in passing the Communal Taxation Act of 1893, and so making over to the communes the land and building and trade taxes, was to put communal finance in a healthier condition and to open out to the communes new sources of revenue, leaving them to work out details for themselves. The *exposé des motifs* which accompanied the Government's proposals stated : " The full significance for the communes of the transference by the State of these sources of taxation lies in the fact that the communes will not be restricted to the existing forms, but will be in a position to develop their systems of taxation according to their special circumstances."

The law itself particularly encourages the communes to look to taxes on real estate for revenue. It provides that " a commune may introduce special taxes on real estate. Such taxes may be levied—(*a*) on the net yield or usufruct (*Nutzungswert*) as determined each year or on an average of years ; (*b*) on the leasehold or rental value of the common [i.e., sale or market] value of the lands or buildings ; (*c*) according to the classes into which land may be divided in the commune ; or (*d*) on a combination of several of these methods." This provision was intended as a plain suggestion to reform the old land and building taxes as now made over to the communes, and in general to develop the real estate side of local taxation, and as such many towns received and promptly acted upon it.[1]

[1] The taxes on unearned increment and sales of property are here classified with the other taxes falling on real estate, although in the official German classification of taxation they rank as " traffic " (*Verkehr*) taxes in the same group with the pavement dues which are still levied in some places.

A statement of the principles upon which the land tax had hitherto been levied will explain why the Government itself regarded this tax in particular as inadequate in its existing form.

THE LAND AND BUILDING TAXES.—The land tax as regulated by law of May 21, 1861, falls upon all land not built upon with the exception of gardens adjoining houses, if their area does not exceed a Prussian *morgen* or about five-eighths of an English acre, subject to certain exemptions, of which the principal are lands belonging to the Prussian State, lands used for public purposes by provinces, circles, communes, and independent manors; railways, roads, and navigable canals belonging to private persons or to companies but constructed for public use; lands and graveyards attached to churches and chapels, and, finally, lands of such a character that they permanently yield no revenue. The tax is paid by the owner. The basis of assessment suggests the original valuation for and apportionment of the English land tax, with which the tax has perhaps a lineal connection. The proceeds of the tax are the fixed sum of about £2,000,000 for the entire State. The valuation of land is made by areas; the properties in each area are first divided into classes according to the method of cultivation, and these classes are again divided into *bonity* or quality classes. A mean presumptive net yield after deducting the costs of cultivation is then ascertained for typical properties in the various quality classes, and the sum so arrived at forms the basis for the taxation of all the properties in these classes, the tax being fixed once for all and entered in the cadaster or land survey register. The Prussian cadaster dates from over half a century ago. Nevertheless, the land valuations and the taxes calculated upon them to a large extent continue unaltered, though the modes of cultivation and use have undergone great change; thus much agricultural land has become building land, and yet it is still taxed at the old value.

The fatal defect of the tax is, of course, that it is levied on a fallacious and obsolete principle of valuation, for which not even an approximation to equity is claimed. Dr. Adickes, the late chief mayor of Frankfort-on-Main, writes : " According to the existing basis of the land tax, not the actual yield of lands but a potential yield, determined by purely objective considerations, forms the basis and measure of taxation, and the land tax levies so fixed are unalterable."

But the basis of the building tax is only little less open to objection. This tax, which is likewise paid by the owner, falls upon all permanent buildings with the adjacent courtyards and gardens, not exceeding five-eighths of an acre in extent, subject again to certain exemptions, such as royal and official buildings, public schools, libraries and museums, churches, chapels, and other buildings dedicated to religious purposes, including the buildings belonging to the religious houses possessing corporate rights (but this exemption extends only to the State Protestant and Roman Catholic Churches), poor-houses, orphanages, public hospitals, prisons, and the like. In the form prescribed by the existing law (May 21, 1861) the tax is levied on the value of the usufruct of buildings as ascertained by a general valuation made only once in every fifteen years, and based on the average rents of the preceding ten years. In arriving at the value of any property no account is taken of privileges attaching to it, as pharmacy licences, or of its contents, as machinery. A tax of 4 per cent. of this usufruct is levied in the case of dwelling-houses and theatres, ball rooms, public baths, hotels, and similar buildings used for habitable purposes ; while the tax is 2 per cent. in the case of factories, distilleries, breweries, corn-mills, and similar buildings used for commercial purposes.

As already stated, the proceeds of these taxes, though still assessed by the State, go to the local authorities. A peculiarity of the land tax as levied in some of the rural districts, especially in the eastern provinces, is deserving of mention. This tax is assessed and levied in the rural communes and manorial districts for the purposes of these areas, just as in the case of towns, and as in many places a single proprietor owns the entire area it follows that he is both assessed to the tax and is credited with the proceeds, so that in effect he pays nothing.

The Communal Taxation Law of 1893 gave to communes a very large discretion as to the form in which they might levy these two taxes. It empowered them either to change the mode of assessment altogether or to tax certain kinds of land in the old way and the rest on other principles. Where, however, the communes did not modify the taxes, taxation was to take the form of percentages of the assessment fixed by the State, yet no longer used for its purposes. In general the larger communes which so tax land and buildings levy from 200 to 300 per cent. of the State assessment, and seldom less than 150 per cent., though up to 100 per cent. the amount of the tax may be deducted from income declared for income tax purposes.

The basis of taxation which the Government preferred was that of " common " or sale value.[1] This was put forward in the law as a suggestion only, but in later rescripts it was strongly urged upon the communes as a way of redressing the admitted inadequacy of the old methods of assessment. Most of the larger towns followed the Government's advice, and the example of Prussia has spread to all parts of the Empire.

It is important to point out, however, that the introduction of the method of taxation according to common or sale value does not necessarily yield to the commune introducing it a higher revenue from real estate taxation ; the original intention was rather to distribute the burden upon various kinds of property in a fairer manner. A commune still estimates the amount of taxation required from real estate from year to year in the form of a percentage of the old land and building tax assessment as made by the State and estimated on yield, as above explained, and converts this amount into the equivalent proportion (reckoned for convenience per thousand) of the sale value of the property so assessed. If it is desired to tax real estate more heavily, it can always be done by increasing the percentage levy based on the State assessment. Although the tendency is constantly in this direction, the motive of the Government in inviting the communes to tax real estate on the basis of sale value was a more equitable incidence rather than a higher aggregate yield of this taxation. The effect of

[1] This " common value " has been defined by the Prussian Supreme Administrative Court as " not the capitalised value of the annual rent, but the price which could be obtained by sale under ordinary circumstance."

taxation on usufruct or rent was that much valuable but undeveloped land was either exempted altogether from taxation or was taxed in no fair proportion to its value, while blocks of highly rented dwellings inhabited by the poorer classes were taxed with undue harshness. " That a State land tax," writes Dr. W. Boldt, " which taxes a *morgen* (⅝-acre) of urban building land, with a value of £5000, at the same rate as a *morgen* of potato land in a village, with a value of £15, is not a tax suited to the taxation of urban land unbuilt on, the value of which has been increased enormously owing to public works, is self-evident."[1] With the adoption of the sale value basis of taxation this anomaly has been removed. This value is determined by a local assessment committee, and the rate of taxation is fixed yearly.

Frankfort-on-Main was one of the first towns to modify the land and building taxes, and, indeed, to give a lead to Prussian communes in the reformed taxation of real estate. Land not built upon is there divided into classes according to its locality, each class being assessed at a different rate, and each property is taxed at 0·3 per cent. of the average sale value of land in the class to which it belongs, as shown by the prices obtained at sales during the preceding three years when that standard is applicable; but this rate increases to 0·5 per cent. when the land changes ownership, and in all cases it will increase to 0·4 per cent. after April 1, 1915, and to 0·5 per cent. after April, 1920, unless the land continues to be used as agricultural or garden land by its owners. Houses with the land belonging thereto, and also other buildings, not assessed to the trade tax, with assembly halls and rooms, conservatories, stables, etc., are taxed at the rate of 4s. for every £5 (or portion of £5 being more than £2 10s.) of the gross rental in the preceding year, with an addition in the case of buildings rented above £25, ranging from 4s. where the gross rental is from £25 1s. to £30 to one of 30s. where it is from £67 11s. to £75, after which the increase continues at the rate of 10s. for every additional £7 10s. of gross rent up to a rent of £135 (when the addition is £5 10s.), while 4 per cent. is added in the case of rents exceeding £135. Both taxes are paid by the owners.

[1] "Gemeinde Finanzen," Band 1, p. 92 (Verein für Sozialpolitik)'

In other towns the tax upon real estate assessed on the basis of sale value varies from one-fifth to one-half per cent. when the rate is uniform for all kinds of property. Some towns, however, tax land that is not built upon at a higher rate than land with buildings; the tax in the former case is commonly one-half per cent. and in the latter one-quarter. In other towns, again, only from one-half to three-quarters of the value is taxed in the case of houses containing small dwellings.

Berlin began to tax real estate according to sale value in 1908, and the immediate result was that building sites, beer gardens, and other valuable properties, which hitherto had been subjected to little taxation or none at all, yielded a considerable revenue. The rate of taxation is 3 per 1000 of such value, as fixed every year by a committee of the Municipal Taxation Board; property owners have a right to be heard before a valuation is fixed. In 1910 Berlin derived from its land and building tax £1,320,000, or 12s. 9d. a head of the total population.

In a statement published some time ago by the Prussian Minister of the Interior the financial advantage to towns of adopting the "common value" basis of valuation, in preference to the basis of yield or rent, was shown by some striking illustrations relating to building sites in Berlin and its suburbs. Sites which on assessment by rental value would have paid 1d. and 3d. respectively paid when taxed according to sale value £6 15s. and £11; in other cases the difference was between 15s. 8d. and £138, £9 8s. and £210, and in one case £13 18s. and £5700. Some towns which have not adopted the sale value basis of taxation have changed the basis of assessment to rent as ascertained yearly. Altogether 198 Prussian towns with a population exceeding 10,000, including all but one of the towns with a population exceeding 100,000, had up to 1911 modified the basis of the land and building taxes. Perhaps the highest taxation of real estate is that of Altona, where a tax of 12 per cent. of the rental value is levied on buildings used wholly or mainly for business purposes and one of 16 per cent. on other buildings. By this tax alone Altona raises no less than £1 2s. per inhabitant out of a total taxation *per capita* of £2.

In the other States there are State land and building taxes which are similarly liable to be used for local purposes, though the rates and methods of assessment differ. In Bavaria the lowness of the land tax leads to a large amount of land in and around towns being left undeveloped, for it pays the owners to hold it indefinitely in the certain expectation of a steady increase in value. Ten years ago the Government introduced a Bill intended to empower certain communes to levy a tax of one per 1000 on the sale value of land not built upon, but the first Chamber of the Legislature rejected it.

In Saxony supplements to the State land tax are almost universally levied in the communes, though there are a few notable exceptions even amongst the larger towns. In many of the agricultural communes, however, from a quarter to three-quarters of all revenue from local taxation comes from this one tax. Some of the larger towns levy the tax according to the sale value as in Prussia, a reform urged on them by the Government.

PROPERTY TRANSFER TAX (CONVEYANCE DUTY).—Another tax which has been introduced on a large scale in Prussia and several of the other States is the tax on the value of real estate which changes hands by sale or otherwise—the *Umsatzsteuer*. It is a tax which the Governments have persistently pressed upon the communes, and with such success that hardly any large town in Germany has failed to adopt it. In Prussia nearly all towns with over 10,000 inhabitants have introduced it. The tax, which is usually paid by the purchaser, forms a percentage—varying in different towns—of the actual price when property changes hands by sale or of the market value where money does not pass; but transfers due to bequest are, as a rule, exempted.

It is worthy of note that since 1777 Danzig has levied a local tax of 1 per cent. *ad valorem* on sales and exchanges of property within the old fortifications, though in course of time transactions between near relatives and sales to charitable foundations became exempted. In 1899 the tax was extended to transfers of property in the other parts of the modern administrative area, subject to the old exemptions in the case of relatives. Both seller and buyer are jointly liable for the tax, but if one of the two can claim exemption under the Prussian Stamp Duty Acts the other pays one-half only. Frankfort-on-Main has had a similar tax since 1820.

When other Prussian towns introduced this tax some twenty years ago they began with ½ per cent. upon properties of all kinds, or ½ per cent. on land built upon (the tax falling on the building as well) and 1 per cent. on land not built upon; but rates of 1 and 2 per cent. respectively are now usual, though higher rates are not uncommon. Cologne, like a number of other Rhenish towns, levies 2 per cent. all round, and the tax falls on all properties which change hands by gift, exchange, or any legal transaction between living persons; where two properties are merely exchanged the tax is assessed on the one which declares the higher value. No tax is levied on forced sales, consolidations of properties, gifts between near relatives, and in several other cases. The tax falls on the buyer, and the value taxed is that fixed between the contracting parties as the price, but where the price has not been fixed, it is based on a special valuation, and the tax must be paid within four weeks of the demand.

At Frankfort-on-Main the tax is levied in conjunction with a tax on " increased value " (*Anglice*, unearned increment). There a tax on all exchanges of real estate, otherwise than by direct inheritance, is levied to the extent of 2 per cent. of the price or value, as the case may be. This tax is, however, increased in the case of land built upon to 3 per cent. where the property has not changed hands save by inheritance for between twenty and thirty years, to 3½ per cent. where it has not changed hands for between thirty and forty years, and to 4 per cent. where there has been no change of ownership for a longer period; and in the case of land not built upon it is increased to 3 per cent. where it has not changed hands for between ten and twenty years, and by another 1 per cent. for every additional ten years during which it has not been in the market, to the maximum of 6 per cent., making a tax of 8 per cent. on the value in such a case. If the property has not changed hands during the preceding five years in the case of land built upon, or ten years in the case of land not built upon, and the value has increased at least 30 per cent., the normal tax of 2 per cent. is increased by 5 per cent. of the increased value when this is between 30 and 35 per cent., and by 1 per cent. more, to a maximum of 25 per cent., for each additional 5 per cent. of increased value.

Berlin has levied this tax since 1895. It began at the rate of ½ per cent. of the purchase price or market value, but this was raised in 1897 to 1 per cent. for land not built upon, and a further increase took place in 1904 to 1 per cent. on land built upon and 2 per cent. on land not built upon. Gardens and courts are taxed at 2 per cent. when their size and situation show them to be eligible for building purposes. When properties are exchanged both are taxed.

In Bavaria the State itself levies a tax of 2 per cent. *ad valorem* on properties changing hands, and since 1898 the communes have been entitled to levy one of ½ per cent. for their own purposes. More than a thousand communes have made use of this power. In Würtemberg, Baden, and Hesse also the communes levy a local supplement to a State tax, in the first two States to the extent of 1 and ½ per cent. *ad valorem* respectively.

In Saxony taxes on sales and exchanges of real estate are of great age, and during recent years they have become general in the towns and even in the rural communes. The rate ranges in general from 1 per cent. *ad valorem* downwards to as low as one-twelfth per cent. The new Saxon Communal Taxation Law (1913) stipulates that the levy for all purposes may not exceed 2 per cent.

From this tax seventy-five of the larger towns of Germany had in 1910 a revenue of £1,289,000.

UNEARNED INCREMENT TAX.—This is the latest of the local property taxes introduced in Germany, where it is known as the "increased value" tax. The Prussian Government was directly responsible for the introduction of this tax, since in the Communal Taxation Law of 1893 it expressly directed the attention of local authorities to the tax as a legitimate source of local revenue, and as an effective means of checking unhealthy speculation in land values, and so of relieving, prospectively at least, the pressure of the housing problem. The way had been prepared long before, however, by a Prussian law of 1875 containing a provision for a special tax on urban sites which increased in value owing to the regulation of street building lines. Nevertheless, the tax first appeared in the protectorate of Kiau-Chau in 1898. In Germany it was first introduced by the municipality of Frankfort-on-Main in 1904 in the form already explained. Cologne adopted it in 1905, and since then nearly all the large towns of Prussia have adopted it. The tax has also been adopted in many towns, both small and large, in other States, but it is not popular in Saxony.

What is specially noteworthy about this sudden and widespread recognition of the taxation of unearned increment as a natural supplement to existing sources of local revenue in Germany is the fact that the new tax has been introduced without any of those fierce conflicts of interest which accompanied its introduction in this country. The tax having been adopted in one town, its adoption in others followed as a matter of course. Here, again, are seen the simplicity and expedition of German methods of local administration, even when new and large questions of policy have to be decided. Like any petty tax on game, dogs, or cinematograph shows, this far-reaching impost can be introduced without appeal to legislature or Government, and simply on the strength of local by-laws. A municipal authority having affirmed its approval, all that remains to be done is to obtain the ratification of the supervisory authorities, and the tax can be introduced without delay.

The unearned increment tax, as known in German towns, differs in various details—such as the rates charged, the proportions of increased value exempted, the periods of respite, and the like—but the broad principles are everywhere the same. The taxable increment is held to be the excess of the price or value on re-sale or transfer over the price or value at the previous change of ownership. The seller, however, is allowed to deduct all expenditure on permanent improvements, inclusive of the cost of street-making and sewage connections, though expenditure on new buildings and rebuilding cannot be deducted when covered by the proceeds of fire, water, or other insurances. It is also usual to tax land built upon from one-third to one-half less than land that is still free, and as a rule an increment which does not exceed 10 per cent. (or more) of the earlier value is exempted altogether from taxation. In the case of ground not built upon, if not used by the owner for agricultural or industrial purposes, loss of interest up to 4 per cent. and expenditure incurred in keeping it in good condition may be added to the former purchase money, but any receipts derived from the land must, on the other hand, be deducted. While the tax on the sale of property is paid by the purchaser of the property, the unearned increment tax is paid by the seller.

The tax as levied at Breslau may be taken as a fair example of the graduation usually adopted. There the first 10 per cent. of increased value is exempt from taxation, and afterwards the following rates apply:—

Increased value—	Tax.
10 to 20 per cent. inclusive	6 per cent.
20 ,, 30 ,, ,,	8 ,,
30 ,, 40 ,, ,,	10 ,,
40 ,, 50 ,, ,,	12 ,,
50 ,, 60 ,, ,,	14 ,,
60 ,, 70 ,, ,,	16 ,,
70 ,, 80 ,, ,,	18 ,,
80 ,, 90 ,, ,,	20 ,,
90 ,, 100 ,, ,,	22 ,,
100 per cent. and over	25 ,,

In Saxony, where the communes, on the whole, tax real estate with exceptional leniency, the unearned increment tax has not made great progress. With a view to encouraging its adoption on a wider scale the Minister of the Interior has issued a set of model regulations applicable to this tax where introduced, and they have been adopted in a number of communes. The tax begins with an increased value of 10 per cent., and the rates of taxation prescribed are from 2 to 20 per cent., the lowest rate beginning with an increased value of from 10 to 20 per cent., and the highest applying to one exceeding 500 per cent., where such increases have accrued within the space of one year; from 1 to 15 per cent. respectively where the increases have accrued within the space of from one to five years; and from ½ to 10 per cent. respectively where the period exceeds five years; with a further degression in the case of the maximum rate to 4 per cent. where the increased value has accrued within longer periods. The tax may not be levied in the case of transfer of property by inheritance or gift during life, and values due to the natural properties of the land—e.g., the discovery of coal, stone, ore, and springs, etc.—may not be taxed.

The tax quickly proved a source of considerable revenue in towns where speculation in urban land is carried on to an excessive degree, and where as a consequence property frequently changes hands.[1]

The proceeds of the tax in some of the large towns of Germany in 1910 were as follows:—

	£		£
Berlin	61,600	Leipzig	47,300
Charlottenburg	29,000	Neukölln	26,200
Chemnitz	21,200	Schöneberg	40,900
Cologne	11,500	Dortmund	18,600
Essen	46,900	Hanover	13,700
Frankfort-on-Main	18,800		

In 1910 fifty-eight towns with a population exceeding 50,000 received £503,000 from this source.

Impressed by the apparent productiveness of the tax, the Imperial Government, in its search for new sources of revenue, passed a law in 1911 appropriating the tax for its own purposes, while recognising existing rights to some extent. This law taxes at 10 per cent. all increased value up to 10 per cent. of the amount at which the property was acquired, after additions and deductions as prescribed, and afterwards the tax is progressive as follows:—

Increase—							Tax.	
Over	10 per cent.	to	30 per cent.	inclusive	..	..	11	per cent.
,,	30 ,,	,,	50 ,,	,,	..	..	12	,,
,,	50 ,,	,,	70 ,,	,,	..	..	13	,,
,,	70 ,,	,,	90 ,,	,,	..	..	14	,,
,,	90 ,,	,,	110 ,,	,,	..	..	15	,,
,,	110 ,,	,,	130 ,,	,,	..	..	16	,,
,,	130 ,,	,,	150 ,,	,,	..	..	17	,,
,,	150 ,,	,,	170 ,,	,,	..	..	18	,,
,,	170 ,,	,,	190 ,,	,,	..	..	19	,,
,,	190 ,,	,,	200 ,,	,,	..	..	20	,,

[1] In this respect the suburbs of Berlin are notorious. In 1910, 7 per cent. of the entire area of Neukölln, near that city, and 13 per cent. of the land not built upon changed hands. The corresponding proportions for Wilmersdorf were 11 and 5 per cent.; for Spandau, 5 and 6 per cent.; and for Charlottenburg, 3 and 8 per cent.

And henceforward to an increase of 290 per cent. an extra 1 per cent. for every increase of 10 per cent.; where the increase exceeds 290 per cent., 30 per cent. The tax is abated by 1 per cent. for every complete year of the period for which the tax is calculated, and increases of value which would yield less than £1 are exempted. The legal holder of the property before its disposal is liable for the tax, but if the tax cannot be obtained from him, the new owner becomes liable to the extent of 2 per cent. of the purchase price. There are some important exemptions from the tax, viz., the Sovereigns of States and their consorts, the Emperor, the federal States and communes or communal unions in whose areas the property is located, and certain societies of a " public utility " or philanthropic character not carried on for private gain.

The tax is collected and administered by the various States, and the law provides that 50 per cent. of the proceeds shall go to the Imperial Treasury, 40 per cent. to the commune or communal union in whose district the taxed property is located, and the remaining 10 per cent. to the federal States to cover the cost of collection ; in practice the States transfer this duty to the communes and divide with them this 10 per cent. The communes are allowed, however, with the sanction of the State authorities, to levy on their own account supplements to the Imperial tax to a maximum of 100 per cent. of the share (40 per cent.) which falls to them, but the Imperial and communal taxes together may not exceed 30 per cent. of the increased value in any one case. Vested interests were further recognised by the provision that in the case of communes which had decided to levy this tax before April, 1909, and levied it before January 1, 1911, any deficit as between the past average annual yield and the revenue yielded under the new method of distribution should be made up until April 1, 1915, out of the share falling to the Empire, while any excess should go as to five-sixths to the Empire and one-sixth to the Treasury of the State affected, but instead of this method of compensation a commune might be allowed to levy its own tax as before until the above date, paying to the Empire all excess beyond the past average annual yield. The towns which had already adopted the tax

MUNICIPAL TAXATION—REAL ESTATE TAXES

have retained it subject to the restrictions provided by the law, and others have used their option to introduce local supplements to the tax.

The Imperial unearned increment tax produced a total revenue of £2,350,000 in 1912, of which the Empire, after paying all compensation, received nearly one-half. Nevertheless, yielding to pressure from the landed interest, the Government in July, 1913, unwillingly accepted an amendment renouncing the Imperial share of 50 per cent. as from the beginning of that month, and handing it over until April 1, 1915, to the communes entitled to compensation. The question remains, therefore, in an interesting state. The tax itself remains law of the land; it must be collected by the State Governments, and the communes at present have a right to 90 per cent. of its yield. If the Empire persists in refusing to accept its share it is possible that the States may appropriate all or part of the revenue which the Imperial Treasury does not want.

It is certain that the tax will rather be developed than otherwise in the communes. Naturally, the speculative land buyers and house builders do not approve of this method of tapping a source of wealth by which many of them have hitherto made an easy and a profitable livelihood, but public opinion generally heartily favours it. Before the city council of Berlin decided to introduce the tax, the Chief Mayor addressed to it an appeal which well states the public mind of Germany on the question. " Don't deceive yourselves," he said, " the tax will assuredly be introduced whether rejected to-day or not. You will be unable to withstand this movement of the times, for it is right to the core. Remember that the higher administrative authorities not only pointed us the way to this tax, but pressed us to adopt it. If we should later have to adopt other taxes instead, the question would at once be asked, Why have you not made use of this? The great majority of the representatives of economic science are also enthusiastically in favour of the tax, and the movement has spread to the widest circles of society."[1]

[1] At the end of April, 1914, the Prussian Government published a Bill restoring to the communes the right to introduce this tax which was taken

"BETTERMENT" TAXES OR SPECIAL ASSESSMENTS.—A final form of property taxation common in Germany is that based on the "betterment" principle. Power to impose a special tax on building sites on that principle is given to communes by the Prussian Communal Taxation Law of 1893, as it is by the corresponding Würtemberg law of 1903. The Prussian law provides that building sites which increase in value owing to the laying out of alignments may be taxed on a higher scale than others, which bear the simple land tax.[1] A number of towns early introduced special assessments on building sites, but this form of taxation has proved difficult of application owing to the impossibility in many cases of determining satisfactorily the extent to which the value of sites had been increased owing to the alignment adopted—a hypothetical question in the solution of which the defective valuation adopted for land tax purposes offers no assistance whatever. Hence most of the towns which had experimented with the tax abandoned it in despair, and looked for compensation in other directions. In the Würtemberg law of 1903 an attempt was made to overcome the difficulty by applying the "betterment" principle in the form of a differential land tax, but few of the towns in the kingdom appear to have used their powers.

A more definite form of "betterment" taxation, and one widely adopted, is provided for by the Prussian Communal Taxation Law in the power given to communes to require property owners and business people to contribute towards "the cost of executing and maintaining works necessary in the public interest from which they derive special economic advantage, such contributions being proportionate to the advantages enjoyed." Such works comprise clearances of old property, bridge building, the laying out of parks and recreation grounds, and the like, and illustrations of the

from them when the Imperial tax was enacted. The right is to be exercised by towns, by rural communes which have over 5000 inhabitants or had introduced the tax before January 1, 1911, and by the circles. In Prussia, therefore, the proceeds of the tax, in their entirety, are to return to the local authorities.

[1] This provision is independent of the power given to communes by the law of July 2, 1875, relating to the planning and alteration of streets, to require adjacent owners to contribute towards the cost of such works.

application of this form of taxation have already been given in the chapter on the planning of towns. No estimate exists as to the proceeds of " betterment " contributions, since they are from their nature of casual and intermittent occurrence.

A further liability of property owners, differentiating their treatment from the practice followed in this country, is that in respect to sewerage connections, scavenging, and house refuse removal, the cost of which almost invariably falls on them. In 1910 seventy-five of the larger towns raised revenue from dues on account of these services to the amount of £1,804,800, equivalent to 2s. 5d. a head of their aggregate population.

Sufficient has been said to show the remarkable openness of mind with which the German Governments and local communities have approached the thorny question of property taxation. Real estate has been taxed directly for local purposes ever since communal government was organised on the existing lines. For some years, however, the tendency of legislation and of administrative policy, both central and local, has been to increase still further the local burdens falling on this kind of property. The fact that this can be done with such comparative ease, in spite of the predominant position which in some States is secured to house-owners upon communal bodies by statute, might seem to indicate the ready acceptance by the property-owning class of the principle, lying at the basis of all German local taxation, that the burden of this taxation should be distributed according to ability to bear it.

How far the various taxes on real estate affect house rents—in other words, how far the property owners recoup themselves by transferring the taxes to the occupiers—is a question which admits of no definite answer, and upon which speculation would be futile. It may be true that the price of house room, like the price of most articles which are not of a monopolist character, is largely determined by the relation of supply to demand, yet the level of rents under any given conditions is affected by other considerations also, and no cautious theorist would venture to assign to any factor its precise value. German writers on the housing question are prone to assume that when the supply of dwellings is " normal " —a condition which is regarded as being fulfilled when there is a 3 per cent. surplus—it is, as a rule, difficult or impossible to transfer the property taxes to the tenants. Certainly the general rule cannot be established that rents are highest in towns which have most developed the real estate taxes.

CHAPTER XVI

MUNICIPAL TAXATION (*continued*). III.—TRADE, CONSUMPTION, AMUSEMENT, AND OTHER TAXES

The trade tax—Tax on large stores—Consumption taxes (entrance dues and excise duties)—Amusement taxes—Miscellaneous local taxes—Church taxes.

THE TRADE TAX.—The trade tax, as common to Prussia and all the other important States, is at once a tax on business profits and on the capital requisite to carry on any business undertaking. It falls on the trading and manufacturing classes generally, and professional men and the working classes are on principle exempt. Bremen, however, is an exception to this rule, for there professional men of certain classes, e.g., doctors, lawyers, architects, engineers, etc., are equally liable. Payment of this tax does not exempt from liability to pay local income tax in the ordinary way.

The trade tax is assessed on three principal methods, though there are variations in each case, viz., (*a*) taxable undertakings are divided into classes according to their size as determined by the turnover, the amount of working capital, the number of employees, the size of the premises, etc., and separate rates of taxation are fixed for all the classes so formed ; (*b*) the tax is assessed on the ascertained profits, as defined by the special laws on the subject ; or (*c*) the profits which a given capital should yield are estimated on different and arbitrary principles and the tax is based on these. In its crude form the first of these methods of assessment is no longer common ; Prussia is an illustration of the second method, though it is applied in that State with many modifications ; Bavaria now follows both the foregoing methods ; while the third method is specially characteristic of Alsace-Lorraine.

As the Prussian system represents a combination of the methods of trade taxation most favoured, an explanation of its operation will suffice. The Prussian Government itself has always recommended the assessment of this tax on a combination of principles, e.g., the amount of working capital, the number of persons employed, and the assessment of the premises as ascertained for the purposes of the land and building taxes.

The Prussian Trade Tax Law of 1891 and the Communal Taxation Law of 1893, taken in conjunction, specify the following classes of undertakings as liable to the tax :—

1. Industrial, manufacturing, and commercial undertakings in general (including shops), as embraced by the first of these laws, subject to the exemptions specified.
2. Agricultural brandy distilleries.
3. Mining undertakings.
4. The commercial production of amber, the working of peat, sand, gravel, marl and clay pits, and of stone, slate, lime, chalk, and other quarries.
5. The trading enterprises of communal and other public authorities.
6. The trading enterprises of the State and the Imperial Bank.

Amongst trading undertakings exempted from the tax are the State railways, savings banks, certain land and credit banks of a public utility character, sewerage and waterworks (the latter, in as far as they are restricted to the area of the commune owning them), abattoirs and stockyards, market halls, people's baths, and public pawnshops. Further, persons engaged in itinerant trading enterprises do not come under the Trade Tax Law, but pay a licence duty of variable amount.

The trade tax is assessed on the gross proceeds or profits. In ascertaining these, all costs of working and a due allowance for depreciation are first deducted from revenue, but no deduction is allowed on account of expenditure on improvements and extensions made out of revenue, family expenses, and interest on capital. If a tradesman owns the building he occupies the trade tax must include the estimated rental, although this is already assessed to the income and property taxes. The tax may not exceed 1 per cent. of the yield so ascertained.

All undertakings which yield less than £75 a year in profits so determined, or are worked with less than £150 of capital, are exempted from taxation. Other undertakings are divided into four classes, according to the amount of their gross proceeds or working capital, and are taxed within the following limits :—

Class 1.—Undertakings with a profit of £2500 or over, or a capital of £50,000 or over, pay 1 per cent. of the profit, subject to the condition that £26 4s. is paid on profits from £2500 to £2740, and £2 8s. for every £240 of additional profit.

The rates of taxation upon undertakings falling in each of the other three classes are graduated by steps of 4s. up to a tax of £2 ; then by steps of 8s. up to £4 16s. ; then by steps of 12s. up to £9 12s. ; and finally by steps of 36s. up to the maximum tax of £24. But the persons liable to taxation must in each assessment district pay on average the mean rate of taxation fixed by law for the class to which they belong. Subject to this graduation the rates of taxation upon these undertakings are :—

Class 2.—Undertakings with a profit of from £1000 to £2500, or a capital of from £7500 to £50,000, pay from £7 16s. to £24, so that the average amount of taxation for all persons in the class is £15.

Class 3.—Undertakings with a profit of from £200 to £1000, or a capital of from £1500 to £7500, pay from £1 12s. to £9 12s., the mean yield being £4.

Class 4.—Undertakings with a profit of from £75 to £200, or a capital of from £150 to £1500, pay from 4s. to £1 16s., the mean yield being 16s.

Undertakings included in the first, second, and third classes, owing to the amount of their working capital, may be removed into classes corresponding to their gross profits, if such profits have for two years fallen below £1500, £750, or £150 respectively.

Assessment is made under State control by districts, which are the provinces in the case of undertakings in class 1, the Government districts in class 2, and the circles for classes 3 and 4, but Berlin forms an independent district. For each district an assessment committee is formed consisting of a Government commissary and other members, chosen, as a rule, from and by the persons liable to taxation, and appointed for three years at a time; in Berlin, however, the municipal executive and council nominate two-thirds of the members.

The tax payable by every person liable is fixed separately by the local assessment committee appointed for the class to which he belongs. The procedure observed is somewhat cumbrous. The enterprises falling in the second, third, and fourth classes form within the various assessment districts what are called "tax communities" (*Steuergesellschaften*) for each class The amount of taxation to be raised by each of these "tax communities" is found by multiplying the number of the members in the class by the mean rate of taxation as prescribed by the law, and the aggregate sum of taxation so obtained is then divided amongst the individual enterprises in accordance with their importance yet within the minimum and maximum rates, as above stated.

All persons in trade and industry are required to report to the assessment committee at the date of beginning or discontinuing an enterprise, and they are liable to furnish all information necessary to their assessment.

Communes are empowered to levy the tax as assessed by the State, or to raise either a lower or a higher proportion on the percentage basis which applies to the income, land, and building taxes. The rate actually levied is often as high as 200 per cent., but the amount up to 100 per cent. may be deducted from the income declared for income tax purposes. The tax is levied in quarterly instalments, in the first half of the second month of each quarter, but the whole may be paid in advance in one sum at option.

A special tax on licensed houses and businesses in which beer, brandy, and spirits are sold by retail is levied under the same law. The amounts are—(*a*) if the licensee is exempted from the trade tax owing to the smallness of his profits or capital, 10s. a year; (*b*) if he is assessed to the trade tax, £5, £2 10s., £1 5s., and 15s., according as the licensee is assessed to the trade tax in classes 1 to 4 respectively. Every place of business is taxed separately. This tax likewise may be levied at 100 per cent. of the State assessment or otherwise at discretion. As a rule, it ranges from 50 to 100 per cent., but some towns levy a rate of 200 or even 300 per cent.

Though the law prescribes a general basis of taxation, the trade tax, like the land and building taxes, may be assessed in other ways if by-laws approved by the State authority are adopted for that purpose, and this option is largely used. Local authorities are in general opposed to the assessment of the trade tax on profits, the effect of which is to create undesirable fluctuations of revenue from this source and to reduce this revenue seriously in times of bad trade, when the expenditure of the communes in poor relief may be specially high. In introducing special trade taxes, therefore, the communes wherever possible adopt such criteria as will secure a steady revenue by making the tax independent of the ebb and flow of commercial prosperity.

Among the various criteria commonly applied, sometimes in combination, are the number of workpeople, the amount of wages and salaries paid, the rent of premises, the area of premises, and the gross turnover. One advantage of combining the bases of profits and number of workpeople is that it enables the authorities to tax more equally both undertakings which make high profits with few workpeople and those which make relatively small profits with a relatively large personnel. Where the tax is proportionate to the number of workpeople employed, 2s. 6d., 5s., 10s., a head or more may be levied, as the case may be, small undertakings being, as a rule, exempted.

Some of the semi-rural communes in the colliery districts have exercised the power to levy the trade tax in a special form. In 1893 the State renounced the old dues which had been payable to it by mining undertakings, and then yielding nearly £350,000 a year, for the purpose of enabling the communes to tax these undertakings more heavily. There are Westphalian communes which levy upon large colliery and iron and steel companies in trade tax as much as 20s., 25s., and even 30s. a head of all the workpeople employed.[1]

[1] Paul Steller, " Erhöhung der Gestehungskosten der deutschen Industrie durch die sozialen Lasten," p. 28 (Cologne, 1911).

In one form or another the trade tax is levied in all the other important States, but with the exception that, as formerly in Prussia, it is primarily a State tax, except in Saxony. In Bavaria the tax falls on commerce and industry in general, including mining and quarrying, but excluding agriculture and forestry. The tax is levied on the working capital of a business and on the profits. Concerns yielding no profit or a profit less than £75, or carried on with a capital below £200, are exempted from the tax. In Würtemberg the trade tax is levied on the proceeds of businesses as estimated at 5 per cent. of a certain proportion of the working capital, variable from 80 to 40 per cent., according as the undertakings are large or small.

TAX ON LARGE STORES.—In Prussia and the other larger States the department stores are specially taxed, in the form either of a tax supplementary to the ordinary trade tax or of a higher rating under this tax. In so taxing the stores the Governments have been actuated primarily by a desire to protect the small shopkeepers, though the larger revenue which has resulted has not been despised. In Prussia the tax falls on stores dealing in four specified groups of commodities, it applies only when the turnover exceeds £20,000 a year, and the rate begins at 1 per cent. and increases to 2 per cent. of the turnover in the following progression :—For a turnover above £20,000, £200; above £25,000, £375; above £30,000, £475; above £35,000, £575; above £40,000, £675; above £45,000, £800; above £50,000, £1000; above £55,000, £1100; and £100 more for every additional £5000 of turnover. The proceeds must be used in lessening the taxation of persons assessed in the lower classes of the trade tax schedule. In 1910 thirty-six of the larger Prussian towns raised a revenue of £169,600 by the stores tax; of this amount £100,250 was raised in Berlin alone, £8600 in Charlottenburg, £5200 in Cologne, and £4450 in Saarbrücken. A variant of this tax, which is becoming common in Prussian towns, is a special tax on local branches of multiple businesses. The tax is assessed on the threefold basis of estimated profits, number of persons employed, and rental value of premises. The Government has so far insisted that the proceeds of this tax shall not in any individual case exceed 2 per cent. of the annual profits of the branch business.

In Bavaria the stores are specially taxed both for State and local purposes, the State making a levy of between ½ and 3 per cent. of the turnover, and this levy being subject to a local supplement. In Saxony and Würtemberg the communes may levy a special tax on stores at their option ; in Würtemberg the rate varies according to the amount of working capital employed.

In some States the stores tax applies only to undertakings with a certain turnover—in Prussia the tax begins with a turnover of £20,000, in Würtemberg with one from £4000 to £10,000 according to the size of the town, in Baden with one of £10,000, and in Hesse with one varying from £4000 to £7500, but in Bavaria there is no limit of the kind.

The towns may also levy special taxes on itinerant traders— auctioneers and the like—but the proceeds of such taxes are unimportant ; the total yield in 52 of the larger towns in 1910 was only £4500.

CONSUMPTION TAXES (ENTRANCE DUES AND EXCISE DUTIES). —Entrance dues (*octroi*) and excise duties have immemorially existed in German towns, particularly in the south and west. In Prussia the former have gradually ceased to be a large or general source of revenue, though some towns retain them to the present day. They are levied upon certain articles of food, on building materials, cattle, forage, fuel, etc. Excise duties are very common, and are usually charged on beer consumed, or take the form of charges in respect of licences for the sale of spirituous liquors. Saxony is virtually without these local consumption taxes with the exception of a tax on beer.

When the present Communal Taxation Law for Prussia was passed in 1893, the Government made it clear that it was not indisposed towards consumption taxes altogether. While dues on some articles were expressly forbidden, dues on others were allowed and even recommended. " It cannot be the object of this measure," said the *exposé des motifs*, " to regulate the levy of consumption taxes so generally and so positively as has been done by the Hessian Town Ordinance. On the other hand, it cannot be overlooked that the importance of indirect taxes for a communal budget has, in many cases, been unduly subordinated to direct taxes, and in the projected reorganisation of local taxation regard must be paid to the fact that the introduction of suitable indirect taxes is advisable as a means of alleviating the excessive pressure of direct taxes."

Among the articles upon which dues might not be newly introduced were meat, corn, flour, baked goods, potatoes, and fuel of all kinds. New dues on poultry and game might be introduced, and other food dues were made subject to the Imperial laws as passed from time to time. Hence a severe blow was administered to local finance in nearly all the States by the passing of the Customs Tariff Law of 1902, which enacted the abolition after April, 1910, of all *octroi* dues on corn, legumes, flour and other milled products, baked goods, cattle, meat, meat products, and fat. The exemption of these articles took away from many communes a large part of their revenue from entrance dues, while leaving them with almost the same costs of collection, which even before had often amounted in small towns to from one-fifth to one-fourth of the entire proceeds. The Prussian town of Breslau lost by the abolition of the *octroi* on meat £90,000, equal to 3s. 7d. a head of the population. In the south the loss was even more grievous. Over 1000 communes in Bavaria were affected, many to such an extent as to throw their finances temporarily into confusion ; the total loss of revenue was estimated at £200,000 a year. The thirty-two communes entitled to levy entrance dues in Alsace-Lorraine lost over £100,000 a year ; one commune lost all its revenue from these duties, and others from 10 per cent. to 60 per cent.; the loss for Strassburg alone was nearly £40,000 a year, and for Mülhausen £16,500. In the hope of curtailing their deficits some of the large towns in different States set up the plea that game, poultry, and fish were not "meat" in the received meaning of the word, and hence were not covered by the Imperial law. Wherever the matter went to the Courts, however, whether in Bavaria, Baden, or Würtemberg, the contention of the communes was rejected.

The loss caused to the communes by the abolition of entrance dues on articles of food has been met in a variety of ways: in many towns by increasing the slaughter-house charges or the remaining entrance dues, e.g., those on building materials, furniture, etc., or by adding to the list of dutiable articles; in others by increasing the income tax; while in yet others it became a pretext for introducing amusement taxes. Nevertheless, even now the communes of Alsace-Lorraine, owing to the French tradition, still derive a large part of their revenue from entrance dues of various kinds—Mülhausen one-third, Strassburg nearly one-half, and Metz over two-thirds; while in many Bavarian communes the proportion of revenue so raised still exceeds 10 per cent. In the larger Prussian towns, however, the consumption taxes only yield in general from 1 per cent. to 3 per cent. of the total revenue from taxation.

It was a common experience that the abolition of the entrance dues did not usually or permanently lead to a corresponding reduction in the prices of the articles freed from taxation. Prior to the date fixed for their repeal the Bavarian Government, in a circular letter to the communal authorities, pointed out that it was the intention of the Imperial Government that the abolition of the *octroi* should be accompanied by a reduction in prices or an increase in weight (as in the case of bread), and it added:—

" It is desirable to direct public attention to this aspect of the question. If public opinion emphatically insists that the abolition of the duties shall bring advantage to the community at large and not merely to the traders, a corresponding degree of success may be expected. It is in any case expedient that the State and communal authorities should support all endeavours to this end to the extent of their powers. Existing police regulations as to the weight of bread or meat will need to be altered where necessary."

Many of the communal authorities acted as advised, and secured concessions in prices simultaneously with the repeal of the dues, but these, as a rule, proved only temporary.

The Prussian communes are brought into intimate contact with the drink traffic, to use the convenient English phrase, in several ways, viz.: (a) By the statutory right given to the local authority to be consulted before concessions or licences are granted; (b) the right to tax such concessions; and (c) the right to tax the beer consumed.

In general, concessions to carry on inns and hotels, restaurants, or the retail sale of brandy and spirit are granted by the State administrative authorities, conditionally upon proof of public need in places with a population under 15,000, and in other places if local by-laws are adopted for the purpose. Further, before any licence is granted the communal authority and the local police authority must be heard. By-laws introducing the principle of licensing according to the requirements of the population have existed for many years in many of the large towns, and the result has, in general, been satisfactory; the ratio of licensed houses to population has been reduced and the character of the houses is said to have improved.

Power to levy a licence fee on the first granting of these concessions is given to towns and to rural circles by the Circle and Provincial Taxation Law of April 23, 1906. The maximum rates are fixed as follows :—

1. Licence holders who are exempt from the payment of the trade tax on account of the smallness of their profits (£75) or capital, £30 ;
2. Licence holders who are assessed in the fourth class for the purpose of that tax, £60 ;
3. Licence holders in the third class, £120 ;
4. Licence holders in the second class, £180 ; and
5. Licence holders in the first class, £250.

The privilege of thus taxing concessions was originally intended to apply only to rural districts, but it was soon extended to the towns, which have made free use of it. Some towns differentiate the rates of taxation in accordance with the character of the licensed premises, and non-alcoholic restaurants are sometimes exempted from taxation. Where licences are transferred, a reduced fee, at times falling to one-sixth, is charged.

The annual tax upon licensed premises takes the form either of a beer duty charged on all beer produced and consumed in the commune, or imported therein, or of a supplement to the Imperial brewing duty. Where the former method is followed the Prussian Government has fixed the maximum duty at 65 pfennige per hectolitre (equivalent to about 3s. per 100 gallons) for ordinary beer, and 30 pfennige per hectolitre (equivalent to about 1s. 4½d. per 100 gallons) for inferior and harvest beer, containing not more than 1¾ per cent. of alcohol. Many towns raise a large revenue by the beer duty, e.g., Munich £131,500, Nuremberg £26,700, Augsburg £25,500, Strassburg £47,600, Dresden £20,200, Stuttgart £22,000, as estimated in 1911; but the costs of controlling the beer consumed, especially that imported into the town, and of collecting the duty, is said to be heavy. Some towns raise large sums by similarly taxing wine and spirits.

AMUSEMENT TAXES.—Taxes on amusements are of comparatively recent origin, but the communes have been quick to adopt them, and they are now becoming general in the towns, except in Würtemberg, Baden, and Hesse. The Prussian Communal Taxation Act of 1893 directed communes to this source of revenue in the provision: " The taxation of amusements, including musical and dramatic recitals, and of the exhibitions of itinerant artists, is permitted to the communes." Although the law is silent on the point, the power so given is intended to extend only to amusements of a public character in which the element of gain is present; in any case, harsh and arbitrary action is impossible owing to the necessity of obtaining sanction from the supervisory authority to taxes of this kind.

The extent to which amusements are taxed differs greatly. In some places only public dances are taxed, but in general a very wide range of indoor and outdoor entertainment, provided admission be by payment, is covered by the tax, though amusements held for philanthropic purposes and public lectures of a purely scientific character are generally exempted. The tax first took the form of an addition to the price of tickets of admission, which was either paid with the price of the ticket or charged separately on entrance. Other forms have since been adopted, e.g., a lump sum payable by the *entrepreneur*, either per performance or according to the size of room or the character of the entertainment. In Frankfort-on-Main the ticket tax for theatrical, music hall, and circus performances is 0·6d. for tickets from 6·6d. to 1s. 9d.; 1·2d. for tickets from 1s. 9d. to 3s. ; 2·4d. from 3s. to 4s. 6d. ; 3·6d. from 4s. 6d. to 6s. ; and 1·2d. extra for every further increase of 1s. in the price. Tickets at and below 6d. are not taxed.

Schöneberg (Berlin) in 1913 introduced a tax upon indoor and outdoor amusements of many kinds on the following scale: On admission tickets from 1·2d. to 6d., 1 pfennige (⅛d.) for every 1·2d. charged ; on tickets costing 6d. to 9d., 1·2d. ; 9d. to 1s., 1·8d. ; 1s. to 1s. 6d., 2·4d. ; 1s. 6d. to 2s., 3d. ; 2s. to 2s. 6d., 3·6d. ; 2s. 6d. to 3s., 4·8d. ; 3s. to 3s. 6d., 6d. ; and 1·2d. for every increase of 6d. or less. Where a lump sum is paid the tax is proportionate to the number of seats, and is as follows :—100 seats and under, 7s. ; 100 to 150 seats, 10s. ; 150 to 200, 15s. ; 200 to 250, 25s. ; 250 to 300, 30s. ; 300 to 350, 35s. ; 350 to 400, 40s. ; 400 to 450, 45s. ; 450 to 500, 60s. ; 500 to 550, 70s. ; and 15s. for every additional 50 seats. In Berlin the ticket tax on cinematograph shows begins with 0·6d. on tickets of 3·6d., and is then 1·2d. on tickets of 6d., 1·8d. on those of 9d., 3d. on those of 1s., and so on in the same proportion ; while lower rates apply to public dances. At Erfurt a special and very high tax was imposed in 1913 on cinematograph shows with the object of protecting the theatres, the patronage of which had seriously fallen off owing to their competition. While subject to the general amusement tax the cinematograph shows had paid some £350 in taxation, but the new tax is estimated to produce £1500.

In Saxony the amusement tax commonly takes the form of a fixed charge, varying from 1s. to £2 10s. for a performance, and is chiefly levied in the case of dances, concerts, and theatrical performances, and latterly cinematograph shows. Both in this country and in Bavaria the tax is called a " poor relief tax," since the proceeds are in part earmarked for the relief of the poor.

The larger communes are finding the amusement tax a very satisfactory source of revenue. The revenue of Cologne from this source in 1910 was £28,460, that of Munich £19,580, that of Düsseldorf £23,240, that of Breslau £19,680, that of Frankfort-on-Main £15,080, that of Dresden £15,260, while seventy-one German towns with a population exceeding 50,000 raised by amusement taxes in that year no less than £335,640, equal to 7¼d. a head of their aggregate population of 11,000,000.

MISCELLANEOUS LOCAL TAXES.—Of the remaining miscellaneous taxes levied in various towns, the rent and house taxes and the dog tax are the most important. In Prussia, prior to the passing of the Communal Taxation Act of 1893, rent or occupiers' taxes—corresponding broadly to the English "rate"—existed in Berlin, Halle, Danzig, and some other places. They were moderate in amount, and were entirely subsidiary to the main sources of taxation, viz., income, real estate, and trade. They have since been abolished in all the towns named save Danzig. There a tax payable by the occupier is levied on the use of inhabited premises of all kinds, factories and workshops, and even warehouses and cattle sheds, but buildings with a lower rental value than £25 are exempted. The tax is 2½ per cent. of the rental value on property rented at between £25 and £50, and 3 per cent. when the rent exceeds £50. The tax is fixed once in each half-year for each building, and is collected in quarterly instalments in advance. The tax yielded in 1911 £11,750, equal to about 1s. 5d. per inhabitant. Frankfort-on-Main levies a fixed "house tax" of 30s. on houses not used for commercial purposes to counterbalance the trade tax. Bavaria has also a "house tax," which is independent of the building tax, and is, like the latter, paid by the owner.

Out of Prussia the occupiers' tax is most common in Würtemberg, but only as a minor source of revenue. The tax in Stuttgart falls upon all persons who have an independent dwelling, and also upon lodgers who have the sole use of rooms. Male householders pay 2s. a year and female householders 1s., and the municipality raised by this tax in 1912 £7750. Bremen has a rent tax calculated at 7¼d. per £5 for rents up to £10, 9½d. per £5 for those between £10 and £15, 1s. 1¼d. per £5 for those between £15 and £20, 1s. 6d. per £5 for those between £20 and £25, and 1s. per £5 for rents above £25. In Mecklenburg-Schwerin also the rent tax is common; in some towns it forms a fixed percentage of rent, and in others it is progressive, but small rents (up to £2 10s. a year) are commonly exempted.

In most States baths and other health resorts are empowered to levy a *Kur-taxe* on visitors and, usually at a reduced rate, on residents, the proceeds being expended on the development of the baths or on improvement works generally.

A peculiarity of Saxon communal taxation is the poll tax, which in some places is levied on all persons 14 years old and upwards, in others on heads of households, while the amount is dependent upon various circumstances. The Communal Taxation Law of 1913, however, prohibits the introduction of new taxes of the kind and requires the abolition of existing ones by January 1, 1918, at the latest.

The dog tax is universal and everywhere yields a large revenue. In most States this tax is made over to the communes, and the rate varies in Prussia from 10s. to £2. Watchdogs and draught dogs are often exempted. Hamburg has fourteen different rates determined by the size and purpose of the dogs, the number kept by the same owner, etc. In Bavaria the dog tax is a State tax, ranging from 9s. to 15s. according to the size of the communes, which receive one-half of the proceeds. In Würtemberg the dog tax is now made over entirely to the communes and may be as high as 20s. Taxes on cats are levied in some Saxon towns, and in 1912 the Prussian Government sanctioned such a tax in principle.

Pavement and bridge tolls are still common in Bavarian towns, including Munich and Nuremberg. These tolls are usually levied on vehicles and on draught animals entering the town, the former being charged from 1d. to 6d. and the latter from ½d. to 2d., and also on animals used by residents for commercial and other purposes, a common charge for these being 30s. a year.

Other local taxes and contributions are the taxes on automatic machines, horses, and passports, fees for freemanship, a tax on gas and electricity (in Stuttgart and other Würtemberg towns), and hunting and fishing licences in some towns of Saxony and Alsace-Lorraine and elsewhere. Yet all these taxes are subsidiary to the main sources of revenue, which are everywhere the income tax, falling on the community generally, the real property taxes, and the trade taxes.

CHURCH TAXES.—Another class of taxes to which the inhabitants of German towns are liable, though altogether independent of communal taxation and affecting the municipal authorities only to the extent that in some towns they collect them with the local taxes, are the church taxes, corresponding to the old English church rates. Taxes for the support of their religious organisations and work are levied in Prussia and most other States by the churches recognised by law, viz., the Evangelical and Roman Catholic. The taxes are levied on residents only, and companies are exempted. In Prussia the tax forms a small percentage of the State income or land and building taxes, and may be levied on all incomes from £21 upwards; but in some towns it is a fixed poll tax of 1s. In Berlin the Protestant Church levies the tax on incomes of £75 and upwards, and the Roman Catholic Church levies it on incomes of £60 and upwards. In the case of a mixed marriage, husband and wife are each relieved of one-half of the tax levied in support of their respective Churches. Members of the Nonconformist Churches, and others who have formally withdrawn from the State Evangelical Church, do not pay this tax. The tax is a reminder that the established Churches are not above using the secular arm for their own purposes, and is a source of much embitterment; in the case of the working classes it is more responsible than any other cause for the continuous and widespread movement out of the Prussian State Church. Many thousands of persons secede every year in Berlin alone, and the reason assigned in most cases is a desire to escape the church tax.

In Bavaria likewise both the State Roman Catholic Church and the Protestant Church levy a tax in the form of a percentage of the State income tax; it is collected by the State inland revenue officers and handed to the Church authorities.

In Würtemberg the ecclesiastical communes have the right

to levy independently a certain percentage of all the State taxes (i.e., on income, trade, land and buildings) on all persons liable to these taxes. The rate varies from year to year. In Stuttgart 8¼ per cent. of the State taxes is levied by the Protestant and 8½ per cent. by the Roman Catholic Church, except on persons who pay less than 15s. in State taxes, who are exempted. The Jewish communities tax their adherents on the same method, or in the form of a small tax on funded income ; part of the proceeds is devoted to the general purpose of the Israelitish community throughout the State and part to the needs of the local synagogues.

CHAPTER XVII

MUNICIPAL TAXATION (*continued*). IV.—CORRELATION AND YIELD OF LOCAL TAXES

Disparity in local taxation—Relative yield of local taxes—Taxation of real estate in Prussia—Relative local taxation in Germany and England.

IN an exposition whose primary purpose it is to show the German system of municipal government in operation, detailed criticism even of major questions will hardly be expected, yet it seems pertinent to call attention to drawbacks incidental to some of the methods of taxation reviewed in the preceding pages.

DISPARITY IN LOCAL TAXATION.—One obvious effect of the practice of levying the principal local taxes—the income, land, building, and trade taxes—in the form of variable percentages of rates or "norms" fixed by the State is that great disparity often exists as between different towns, even contiguous and similar in character of population and pursuit. This disparity is, of course, most glaring in a congeries of communities like Greater Berlin, where over fifty urban and rural communes, all independent for purposes of administration and taxation, are able to adopt not only different measures of taxation but different taxes. In the rural communes surrounding the city the income tax rate (1911) ranges from 64 per cent. to 180 per cent. of the State tax, and only twenty of these districts levy the rate of 100 per cent., which is normal in the large towns of Greater Berlin. There is the same disparity in the rates of the land and building taxes. As calculated on the rental value, the rates vary from 156 per cent. of the State assessment in Schöneberg and 165 per cent. in Berlin to 210 per cent. in Neukölln, while the assessment on the basis of sale value varies from 1 and 2 per 1000 for land built upon and land not built upon respectively in Nickolassee to 4 and 7 per 1000 respectively in Weissensee. So, again, while the trade tax is 165 per cent. of the State assessment in Berlin, in the surrounding districts it ranges from 200 to 300 per cent. The property sale and transfer tax is variously 1½ and 2 per cent. in contiguous communes, and there is the same diversity in the unearned increment tax.

The most serious disparity is that in the income tax, however, for in so far as local taxation is concerned this is the tax which chiefly determines the question whether a town is a cheap or a dear one to live in. Several years ago one of the villa colony suburbs of Berlin covered its expenditure with an income tax of 15 per cent. of the State assessment, with the result that a wealthy resident of Berlin, paying, for example, £250 in local income tax, had only to remove a few miles out in order to effect the substantial saving of £212 10s. yearly. Even now one of the suburbs of Berlin is able to restrict its income tax to 50 per cent. and another to 60 per cent. Berlin has, in fact, suffered seriously in taxing resources owing to the migration of rich inhabitants to the suburbs, some of which offer, with equally or more amenable surroundings, lower rates of taxation. In 1909, 4 persons with incomes of from £975 to £1275 removed from Charlottenburg to Berlin and 39 from Berlin to Charlottenburg; while of persons with incomes exceeding £2500, 3 changed Charlottenburg for Berlin and 28 changed Berlin for Charlottenburg. The migration of wealth to the villa suburbs is still more ominous. A large portion of these migrants come into Berlin daily for official, professional, and business purposes, and make full use of the manifold conveniences there offered; but while they benefit freely by the city's expenditure they make no contribution to its revenue.

Eventually, either through the operation of the statutory Joint Board for Traffic and Town Building formed for Greater Berlin in 1911, or under pressure of public opinion, it is probable that this entire area will become a unit, if not for taxation purposes altogether, at least for such objects of common interest as poor relief and education; but in the meantime

Berlin's interest lies in agreement upon a policy of equal rates of taxation applicable to a wide area, a large part of which is equally eligible for residential purposes, and to this policy it is addressing itself. Accordingly, when in 1910 the municipal executive found it impossible to carry on the affairs of the city with the old income tax rate of 100 per cent., even with the help of a new tax on amusements, an arrangement was arrived at with several of the neighbouring towns for a simultaneous uniform increase to 110 per cent., while the Chief President of the province, who acted the part of conciliator, undertook to bring pressure to bear upon the surrounding rural communes in the same sense. In the end the increase was staved off, but it can only be for a time.[1]

It was not the first time or the first place in which the State supervisory authority had intervened in the interest of harmonious relationships between adjacent communes.

Where the adjustment of local taxation is desirable in the case of poor communes of limited resources, another procedure has to be resorted to. Some of the rural communes of Rhineland and Westphalia have been allowed in course of time to saddle themselves with local income taxes two, three, and four times as high as the State tax. Owing to this excessive taxation of income, the Ministers of the Interior and Finance called upon the District Presidents to investigate all cases of the kind in their districts with a view to a revision of the existing forms of taxation. The measures of relief adopted were—(*a*) the extension of the system of dues, contributions, and indirect taxes (gas, water, and sewerage dues, dog, beer, amusement, land sale taxes, etc.); (*b*) the combination of unions for special purposes where legislation allowed of it; and (*c*) the absorption of poor by wealthy communes. Another method of relieving poor and overburdened communes, which is advocated more and more by writers on self-government, is the formation by the State of an equalisation fund in their behalf derived from the proceeds of the income tax.

The disparity is not in general so serious in the other States, especially where the local tax supplements may not exceed

[1] Since this paragraph was written several towns in Greater Berlin have increased the local income tax to 110 per cent. of the State assessment.

a fixed figure. In Würtemberg, where no more than 50 per cent. of the State tax may be raised locally, all the towns with one exception levy the maximum rate.

Lest the conclusion should be drawn, however, that the great inequalities in the local income tax rate which exist in practice are an argument against the tax in itself, it may be well to recall the fact that such inequality is due solely to the autonomy of the communes in local taxation. Every commune decides for itself the rate it will levy, and no commune is obliged to levy a higher rate than its neighbour. So far as the State's influence goes, it is all on the side of moderation and uniformity, since it insists that local supertaxes beyond 100 per cent. of the State tax shall receive the sanction of its officials, and that in all cases a proper balance shall be preserved as between personal taxes and those on realty. As applied to this country, no objection to an income tax, at least as an auxiliary source of local revenue, based only on the danger of unequal rates, would hold good if it were limited to a low percentage of the State tax, which for this purpose would need to be extended in a revised form to a larger section of the population than now, and if rates were required to be uniform within wide areas, say, geographical counties, with or without an arrangement for earmarking the proceeds for application to certain objects which are more and more being recognised as matters of national rather than purely local concern, e.g., poor relief, education, road maintenance, etc.

RELATIVE YIELD OF LOCAL TAXES.—It remains to follow the communal taxes into actual operation, and to show the relation they bear to each other and to local finance generally. Throughout Germany—except in Bavaria and Alsace-Lorraine, where the trade taxes and the system of entrance and excise dues have been highly developed—the income tax is still the backbone of local finance. The taxes upon real estate come next in importance, and present tendencies point to the likelihood of these taxes retaining their present prominence. At the same time it is recognised that the real estate taxes are not all in an equal degree reliable as sources of revenue. The taxes on the turnover of property and on unearned increment

MUNICIPAL TAXATION—YIELD OF LOCAL TAXES

are subject to sudden and unforeseen influences which disqualify them from ranking with the land and building taxes in the communal budget.

The relative importance of the several groups of taxes will be seen from the following table, showing for 84 towns with a population exceeding 50,000 the proportions in which local taxation was divided in 1910 and 1911 between five groups of taxes, viz., real estate, trade, income, consumption, and miscellaneous taxes. In this classification the real estate taxes comprise the land and building taxes and the taxes on the sale of land and on unearned increment ("increased value"); the trade taxes comprise the general tax on commercial and industrial undertakings, the special tax on stores, and the special tax on licensed premises and concessions for the same; with the income tax are grouped the capital rent tax (15 towns), poll, rent, or occupiers' taxes (two towns), and citizenship dues (two towns); while the group of miscellaneous taxes includes the amusement and dog taxes, pavement tolls (six towns), and certain minor taxes.

The figures are given separately for (a) towns with 200,000 inhabitants and over; (b) towns with from 100,000 to 200,000 inhabitants; and (c) towns with from 50,000 to 100,000 inhabitants. The figures for 1910 represent actual revenue and those for 1911 budgeted revenue:—

Population in 1910.	(a) 21 towns (8,928,200).		(b) 24 towns (3,423,000).		(c) 39 towns (2,679,400).		All the 84 towns (15,030,600).	
	1910 %	1911 %	1910 %	1911 %	1910 %	1911 %	1910 %	1911 %
Real estate taxes	31·3	29·6	29·6	28·7	26·6	25·7	30·2	28·8
Trade ,,	12·4	13·2	12·7	12·6	14·6	14·8	12·8	13·3
Income ,,	51·9	52·3	50·7	51·5	50·5	50·9	51·4	51·9
Consumption ,,	1·8	2·0	4·7	5·1	6·3	6·6	3·1	3·4
Miscellaneous ,,	2·6	2·9	2·2	2·1	2·1	2·0	2·4	2·6

It will be seen that the mean figures for 1911 for all these towns together were 28·8 per cent. of taxation from real estate, 13·3 per cent. from trade, and 51·9 per cent. from income taxes. Hamburg, Bremen, and Lübeck are excluded from the foregoing calculations as being City States. If to the taxes properly so called be added the dues levied on property owners in respect of sewerage connections, street scavenging, and house refuse removal, where the cost of these services is not charged to the house and building taxes (since in German towns these services are paid for by the adjacent owners), the distribution of taxation in these towns fell in that year as follows :—Real estate taxes, 33·1 per cent.; income taxes, 48·8 per cent.; and trade taxes, 12·5 per cent.; the remaining 5·6 per cent. being accounted for by consumption, amusement, and miscellaneous taxes.

These figures relate to the larger towns, yet they may be accepted as representative of the towns as a whole. An enumeration made by the Imperial Government in 1907, relating to all communes with over 10,000 inhabitants, showed that of a total revenue from local taxes of all kinds of £33,190,000, 49·6 per cent. was derived from income taxes, 26·9 per cent. from land and other real estate taxes, 12·7 per cent. from trade taxes, 5·9 per cent. from consumption taxes, 1·7 per cent. from luxury taxes, and 3·2 per cent. from other taxes.

The taxation per head of the aggregate population of these 84 towns was as follows in the two years named :—

	1910 s. d.	1911 s. d.
Real estate taxes	11 5¾	11 2
Trade ,,	4 10½	5 2
Income ,,	19 7	20 1¼
Consumption ,,	1 2½	1 3¼
Miscellaneous ,,	11	11¾
Total	38 0¾	38 8¾

In addition the dues levied on property owners on account of sewerage connections, street scavenging, and house refuse removal amounted in each year to 2s. 5d. a head of the population, making the taxes falling on real estate 13s. 10¾d. a head in 1910 and 13s. 7d. in 1911.

The correlation of local taxation may be shown in a still more concrete manner by the following comparative figures relating to 1910 for the more important towns of the principal States. In the cases of Danzig and Stuttgart the "house" or "rent" tax paid by occupiers is classed with the income taxes,

MUNICIPAL TAXATION—YIELD OF LOCAL TAXES

while in the cases of Augsburg, Munich, and Nuremberg the real estate taxes include the proceeds of pavement dues.

Percentage of Taxation Falling to Different Taxes in the Larger Towns

Towns.	Total taxation per head.	Real estate taxes.	Trade taxes.	Income taxes.	Luxury and expenditure taxes.	Consumption taxes.
	s. d.	%	%	%	%	%
Prussia—						
Aix-la-Chapelle	41 3	23·4	13·4	57·2	2·4	3·6
Altona	40 8	59·4	5·4	33·3	1·9	—
Barmen	42 2	23·1	12·5	61·5	2·1	0·8
Berlin	41 10	36·9	14·5	46·8	1·0	0·8
Breslau	38 7	31·1	10·6	54·2	2·7	1·4
Cassel	33 2	28·9	11·0	53·9	2·0	4·2
Charlottenburg	54 4	43·4	5·9	49·5	1·2	—
Cologne	42 8	28·3	13·5	53·4	3·6	1·2
Crefeld	36 10	23·2	14·5	57·0	3·4	1·9
Danzig	31 5	33·7	8·9	53·7	2·8	0·9
Dortmund	42 5	32·3	12·1	53·0	2·6	—
Düsseldorf	40 6	31·0	9·2	54·5	4·2	1·1
Duisburg	35 4	23·8	16·6	56·1	2·0	1·5
Elberfeld	47 0	21·5	12·2	61·5	3·1	1·7
Essen	44 4	29·1	13·5	53·4	2·8	1·2
Frankfort-on-Main	59 6	27·4	10·3	60·0	2·0	0·3
Hanover	34 0	33·7	11·9	49·6	2·9	2·4
Kiel	38 5	37·2	9·8	49·0	4·0	—
Königsberg	38 1	37·1	9·6	49·3	2·7	1·3
Magdeburg	38 1	27·1	10·6	57·8	2·9	1·6
Schöneberg	43 2	48·9	5·0	44·4	1·7	—
Stettin	34 7	32·8	10·0	54·4	1·8	1·0
Wiesbaden	49 5	35·3	7·3	48·2	1·9	7·3
Mean of rates	—	32·5	10·8	52·7	2·5	1·5
Bavaria—						
Augsburg	25 10	10·7	26·6	45·7	3·3	13·7
Ludwigshafen	33 4	23·9	47·6	24·5	0·5	3·5
Munich	39 11	36·9	23·8	30·2	2·1	7·0
Nuremberg	29 4	30·9	34·5	26·9	1·4	6·3
Mean of rates	—	25·6	33·1	31·8	1·8	7·6
Saxony—						
Chemnitz	32 4	22·3	0·1	74·1	1·6	1·9
Dresden	32 11	12·1	0·1	80·1	2·6	5·1
Leipzig	37 10	24·6	0·2	73·3	1·9	—
Plauen	25 9	5·6	0·01	88·5	2·4	3·5
Zwickau	21 1	—	6·0	90·8	3·2	—
Mean of rates	—	12·9	1·3	81·4	2·3	2·1

Percentage of Taxation Falling to Different Taxes in the Larger Towns—continued

Towns.	Total taxation per head.		Real estate taxes.	Trade taxes.	Income taxes.	Luxury and expenditure taxes.	Consumption taxes.
	s.	d.	%	%	%	%	%
Würtemberg—							
Stuttgart	44	10	25·2	32·1	35·6	1·2	5·9
Baden..							
Heidelberg	37	1	38·0	11·6	44·9	1·0	4·5
Karlsruhe	31	8	36·3	16·8	42·0	1·1	3·8
Mannheim	43	0	33·0	29·2	34·0	0·5	3·3
Mean of rates	—		35·8	19·2	40·3	0·9	3·9
Other States							
Mayence (Hesse)	35	8	20·5	15·1	56·0	0·5	7·9
Metz (Alsace-Lorraine)	38	4	—	2·5	27·8	2·5	67·2
Mülhausen (Alsace-Lorraine)	42	9	18·2	24·8	21·4	2·3	33·3
Rostock (Mecklenburg-Schwerin)	28	0	41·9	1·7	54·7	1·7	—
Strassburg (Alsace-Lorraine)	35	1	14·7	18·0	17·6	1·6	48·1
Mean of rates	—		19·1	12·4	35·5	1·7	31·3

TAXATION OF REAL ESTATE IN PRUSSIA.—It has been pointed out that one principal object professed by the Prussian Government in passing the Communal Taxation Law of 1893 was to relieve personalty at the expense of realty, and this object has been attained. The extent to which the burden of local taxation has been shifted from personal (income) taxes to real estate and in a less degree trade taxes may be illustrated by the following table showing for a number of Prussian towns the comparative percentages of local taxation which fell at different periods during the past twenty years to various classes of taxes. No account is taken in these figures of the dues levied on property owners on account of sewerage connections, scavenging, and house refuse removal.

Taxation of Real Estate at Various Periods

Towns.		Real estate taxes.	Trade taxes.	Income taxes.	Consumption taxes.	Miscellaneous taxes.
		per cent.	per cent.	per cent.	per cent.	per cent.
Altona	1894–5	55·4	—	42·3	—	2·4
	1902–3	58·2	4·5	35·1	—	2·2
	1910	59·4	5·4	33·3	—	1·9
Cassel	1894–5	13·8	—	53·3	32·3	0·6
	1902–3	27·5	9·7	40·9	20·9	1·0
	1910	28·9	11·0	53·9	4·2	2·0
Cologne	1894–5	11·3	3·5	80·3	2·5	2·4
	1902–3	29·6	15·7	49·0	3·3	2·4
	1910	28·3	13·5	53·4	1·2	3·6
Crefeld	1894–5	3·9	8·5	86·2	—	1·4
	1902–3	21·2	14·2	60·4	1·6	2·6
	1910	23·2	14·5	57·0	1·9	3·4
Düsseldorf	1894–5	12·9	6·2	74·7	4·2	2·1
	1902–3	28·7	9·7	56·8	2·7	2·1
	1910	31·0	9·2	54·5	4·2	1·1
Elberfeld	1894–5	2·2	1·8	92·1	3·1	0·9
	1902–3	27·4	10·5	57·5	2·4	2·2
	1910	21·5	12·2	61·5	1·7	3·6
Essen	1894–5	8·1	6·9	80·4	3·4	1·1
	1902–3	20·7	12·1	63·6	2·1	1·4
	1910	29·1	13·5	53·4	1·2	2·8
Frankfort-on-Main	1894–5	6·8	—	90·4	—	2·8
	1902–3	25·8	8·2	63·6	0·4	2·0
	1910	27·4	10·3	60·0	0·3	2·0
Hanover	1894–5	19·6	—	72·9	6·3	1·3
	1902–3	35·1	10·4	49·6	3·9	1·1
	1910	33·2	11·9	49·6	2·4	2·9

Of late years a slight reaction in favour of real estate, at least to the extent of not increasing its relative burdens, appears to have set in here and there, and even amongst practical municipal administrators there are those who believe that the taxation of realty has gone as far as is consistent with equity and safety. One of these, now the chief mayor of Charlottenburg, writes: "It may, in general, be affirmed that the effects of the law (of 1893) have in practice fulfilled the expectations of the legislature. The tendency of the law, which aims at the development of fees, contributions, and indirect taxes, and at laying greater stress on the 'real' taxes in comparison with the income tax, is primarily directed at the owners of property and in a secondary degree at the commercial classes. All contributions, most of the fees, and the most productive indirect taxes fall on them, and for the most part sufficient regard is not paid to this undeniable fact in apportioning the revenue needs between the real taxes and the income tax. On the other hand, it must be remembered that in the last resort all the expenditure of a commune is more or less for the benefit of those who pay the 'real' taxes, and that the domination guaranteed by statute to the house and land owners in the communal administration counterbalances the somewhat excessive disposition of recent legislation to overload the real taxes."[1]

Since these words were written the relative taxation of real estate has remained on the whole stationary, though absolutely it has increased with the other forms of taxation. The proposal of the Prussian Government to amend the existing communal taxation legislation, however, has everywhere put the property owners and their powerful associations on the defensive, and it is hardly likely that the outcome of the measure now before the legislature will seriously affect the present incidence of local taxation.

RELATIVE LOCAL TAXATION IN GERMANY AND ENGLAND.— One of the questions that will before now have occurred to the reader will be: How does individual taxation in English and German towns compare? Who pays more—the "taxed" German citizen or the "rated" English citizen? Statistical comparisons have always a fascinating interest for many minds, and the more difficult the comparison the greater usually is the fascination. If comparison of crude figures showing annual taxation per head of the population and nothing more would suffice, the matter would be easy enough, but an answer of that kind would be entirely misleading. The question is, in fact, complicated by a number of considerations, not all of which are apparent on the surface.

It is obvious that any fair estimate of relative local taxation would need to take account of the services purchased in the two countries by the taxation paid. Here difficulties of an almost insuperable kind at once present themselves, and principally the impossibility of finding a satisfactory

[1] Dr. E. Scholz, "Die heutigen Gemeindebesteuerungsysteme in Preussen," in "Gemeinde-Finanzen," 1ster Band, pp. 300–301 (Verein für Sozialpolitik).

money equation for some services which may be similar in kind but not in extent and efficiency. For example, it would not be sufficient to say that in both of two towns compared certain public services are in municipal hands; it would be necessary to know the relative prices paid for these services, e.g., water, light and power, means of communication, education, etc., for in one town lower prices may be counterbalanced by higher taxation, or *vice versâ*.

As between German towns, for example, a substantial yearly saving may be effected in tramway transit where, as in Berlin, passengers are carried any distance for the uniform charge of 1¼d., as compared with towns in which the zone or sectional system of charges is in force. Similarly in regard to education: the primary schools are free in one town and not free or only partially free in another, while in the fees charged in the higher schools there is great diversity. In the case of the drama and music loving public also, it is important to know whether, owing to municipal ownership of theatres and concert halls or municipal subsidies to lessee-managers, the prices of admission are kept at a relatively low level. It is clear that what a household pays in taxes in aid of schools and theatres it may save many times over in a diminished budget for education and pleasure.

If considerations like these are important in the case of German comparisons they are doubly important if comparisons are instituted between German and English towns. To complicate matters still further, the system of Government grants-in-aid is much more developed in this country than in Germany, with the result that the English ratepayer bears a proportionately larger part of the cost of local administration in the form of national taxes.

There can be little doubt that taxation for local purposes is higher in German towns than in English, but, on the other hand, German taxpayers unquestionably receive more for their money. The principal explanation of this fact is that the German citizen is willing that the municipality shall perform for him many services which in this country are left to private effort or are not performed at all. In proof of this it is only necessary to instance the larger expenditure of

German towns on higher education, on the furtherance of culture generally (including the drama), the hospital service, and the large range of activities which have been grouped under the name " Social Welfare."

As an indication of the cost of local government, in so far as it can be measured by taxation, the following data are not without interest. The average amount of taxation raised in 1910 in 45 German towns with a population in excess of 100,000 (in the aggregate 12,351,200 inhabitants) was £1 19s. 4d. a head, to which must be added 2s. 7d. a head of the population levied on property owners in the form of sewerage, scavenging, and house refuse removal charges, giving a total of £2 1s. 11d. The average amount of taxation raised in 39 towns with a population between 50,000 and 100,000 (in the aggregate 2,679,400) was £1 12s. 6d. a head, increased by 1s. 9d. on account of the sewerage, etc., charges, or together £1 14s. 3d. The taxation of all these 84 towns, with a population of 15,030,600, was £1 18s. 1d. a head, increased by 2s. 5d. on account of the sewerage, etc., charges, giving a total of £2 0s. 6d.

It may be noted in passing that about one-half of this taxation was of a special kind, e.g., taxation of real estate, trading enterprises, amusements, etc. Taking only the taxes which fell upon the whole community, i.e., the income and consumption taxes, the average for all towns was just over £1.

On the other hand, the amount raised by rates in the administrative year 1911–12 in 40 towns in England and Wales with a population in excess of 100,000 (in the aggregate 9,122,200) was £1 17s. 3d. a head; the amount raised in 48 towns with a population between 50,000 and 100,000 (in the aggregate 3,226,800) was £1 14s. 10d. a head; and the average for all these 88 towns (with a population of 12,349,000) was £1 16s. 7d. a head.

In Germany as in England there are expensive and less expensive towns, though it is probable that the extremes are far greater there than with us. The reason of this is the wide latitude allowed to the towns in determining the extent to which local needs shall be covered by the income tax, the source, as has been shown, of more than one-half of local taxation. Where the local supplement to the State income tax does not exceed, or only slightly exceeds, the amount of that tax, a relatively low level of taxation may be said to exist. So low a rate of supertax as 100 per cent. is exceptional, however, and the mean of the rates levied in 1912 by 56 Prussian towns with a population exceeding 50,000 was 180 per cent. That rate would make incomes of the following amounts liable to the payments stated :—

Income. £	Local income tax at 180 per cent. £ s. d.
100	2 15 9
200	8 5 7
300	13 2 9
400	19 1 7
500	27 0 0
600	28 16 0
700	37 16 0
800	43 4 0
900	48 12 0
1000	54 0 0
1500	81 0 0
2000	117 0 0

This table may usefully be supplemented by another showing the State income tax tariffs of all the four German Kingdoms for incomes from £100 upwards. The reader is reminded that in Würtemberg only 50 per cent. of the State levy can be raised for local purposes and that in the other States the normal rates levied in the towns range from 150 to 200 per cent. of the following amounts :—

Income. £	Prussia.[1] £ s.	Bavaria. £ s.	Saxony. £ s.	Würtemberg. £ s.
100	1 11	1 3	1 16	1 1
200	4 12	3 18	5 5	4 1
300	7 6	7 3	10 0	8 8
400	10 12	10 10	14 5	12 14
500	15 0	14 0	17 14	17 19
600	18 0	17 10	21 0	21 0
700	21 0	21 0	25 0	26 7
800	24 0	24 12	29 0	31 1
900	27 0	28 4	33 0	35 3
1000	30 0	31 16	37 0	39 6
1500	45 0	51 6	59 10	60 0
2000	64 0	72 6	83 10	82 0
2500	84 0	94 6	108 10	105 0
3000	104 0	117 6	133 10	129 0
4000	145 0	166 16	187 0	176 0
5000	195 0	222 6	247 0	225 0

[1] Without the supplementary tax, rising from 5 to 25 per cent. in excess of these rates, levied for State purposes under the law of April, 1909.

With the foregoing tables before him the reader can make for himself comparisons of local taxation on the basis of any desired scale of income taxation in German towns or rental value taxation in English towns. Comparisons so made, however, will be subject to an important adjustment. For in addition to paying income tax persons carrying on commercial and industrial undertakings, e.g., factories, workshops, shops, banks, etc., pay a special tax assessed on their income from that source as calculated upon the method prescribed by law. Owners of real estate are further liable to a tax assessed on the rental or sale value of their property ; in most towns amusement taxes are levied ; and there are other minor taxes of general or partial incidence. The amount of this supplementary taxation differs greatly both as between States and towns, and no figures of value for comparative purposes can be given.

In spite of the somewhat negative results to which all inquiries into comparative taxation must lead, two general statements may be made with safety. One is that local taxation is much heavier in Germany than in this country in the case of persons with large incomes (inasmuch as the income tax is progressive), the industrial and trading classes (owing to the double taxation of income from commercial enterprise), and owners of real estate (who are likewise assessed in two capacities).

Of these three classes the industrialists and traders fare least favourably. Individuals, firms, and companies falling into this class pay two local taxes at least—the income and trade taxes; in the case of companies the former tax is levied in Prussia at a higher rate than applies generally, while, if they happen to own the premises in which their business is carried on, they have to face a further tax on land and buildings. The consequence is that this class of taxpayers bears burdens of a weight unknown in this country. In general it may be said that their local taxes amount to between two and three times the amount of the State income tax. Thus, to cite actual cases, seven large Westphalian companies in the steel and colliery industries in a recent year paid State and municipal taxes of the following amounts respectively : £10,260 and

£28,000; £2010 and £6750; £5700 and £13,170; £6220 and £12,880; £3450 and £9110; £2460 and £5180; and £1010 and £6750. Local taxes equal to £6 19s., £5, £4 4s., and £3 6s. a head of all workmen employed, and to from 1½d. to 5½d. per ton of the output, are paid by certain Westphalian colliery companies, and these taxes are increased to the extent of from 25 to 40 per cent. by the State income tax. Not long ago the Press organ of the Rhenish-Westphalian industry stated that "the factory chimney has to smoke two months in the year in order to pay the local taxes alone." In spite of their heavy burdens, however, these firms are still able, by reducing the technical costs of production to the lowest possible point, to compete successfully in foreign markets and to distribute high dividends.

The other safe generalisation is that in German towns without an abnormally high rate of income tax persons in receipt of very small incomes are proportionately taxed more leniently than with us. Without giving the details of the calculations involved, it may be stated that while in 32 out of 56 Prussian towns with a population in excess of 50,000, for which data are available, incomes up to £33 a year and in 14 towns incomes up to £45 a year (both inclusive) were in 1911 exempted from any direct share in either local or national burdens, the mean rates of income tax, where levied, represented the following annual calls upon small incomes :—

Incomes of	Local income tax. £ s. d.
Above £21 to £33	4 5
,, £33 to £45	8 9
,, £45 to £52 10s.	10 10
,, £52 10s. to £60	16 2
,, £60 to £67 10s.	1 1 7
,, £67 10s. to £75	1 8 10
,, £75 to £82 10s.	1 17 10
,, £82 10s. to £90	2 6 10
,, £90 to £105	2 15 10

If these amounts of taxation are compared with the rates on small occupiers in English towns of the same size, estimated, according to returns obtained from a number of such towns for the purposes of this book, at an average of 25 per cent. of the rent where the compounding system applies, it will be found that English working-class householders are on the whole much worse off. For on the foregoing ratio the rates included in rents of 4s., 5s., 6s., and 7s. 6d. a week, as the case may be, would amount to £2 12s., £3 5s., £3 18s., and £4 17s. 6d. a year respectively. The inequity of the system of taxing on rental value hardly needs a severer condemnation than is contained in these figures.

CHAPTER XVIII

SURVEY AND COMPARISON

Modern reform movements—Constitution of local authorities—Derivation of duties and powers—Scope of administration—Systems of local taxation—External supervision and control—Concluding remarks.

THE field of German municipal government having now been surveyed, it will be useful to bring together some of the conclusions, and comparisons with English conditions, which our review seems to justify. The idea has largely prevailed in this country in the past, and possibly exists still, that here only is local government real as well as popular, liberal in substance as well as in spirit; that here only are communities able to make their will prevail effectually within the entire province of organised civic life. How does this bold assumption square with the facts? The answer to this question will enable us to do greater justice to the legislative genius and administrative capacity of another nation, and may not be entirely without profit to ourselves.

Not until the municipal systems of the two countries are thus regarded side by side is it possible to appreciate fully how marked are their dissimilarities, how few and unimportant are the features they possess in common. Just as, at the beginning of the nineteenth century, Stein, the Prussian statesman, with all his sympathy with England and his admiration for its political institutions, found little or nothing in our system of municipal government which he was willing to translate to the country of his adoption, so the great reform of the English corporations in 1835 showed no trace whatever of Prussian influence.[1]

[1] The principles underlying the municipal systems of the two countries decide this question. Professor Seeley points out, however, in his " Life and Times of Stein " (Vol. II, p. 229), that in the debates and blue-books in

The remarks pertinent to this concluding chapter may be conveniently given under the five headings: constitution of local authorities, derivation of duties and powers, scope of administration, systems of local taxation, and methods of supervision and control, it being understood that now as hitherto comparison is made with the conditions applying to English boroughs and urban districts, as these correspond most nearly to German " towns."

MODERN REFORM MOVEMENTS.—One fact of special significance in the history of German municipal government cannot be too strongly emphasised at this point: the singular facility with which the system of Stein, introduced in Prussia over a century ago, has proved adaptable to the conditions of a period of unexampled change and expansion. Twice the Municipal Ordinance of 1808 has undergone revision—the last time just sixty years ago—yet in these revisions its basal principles were not departed from, and, remembering how Stein's ideas have influenced the municipal systems of the other States, it is literally true that German towns are to-day being governed, and governed with complete success, under laws devised to meet the conditions of an epoch when large communities did not exist, when local administration, fallen into disrepute and decay, had almost to be built up again from the ground, when one-half of the tasks which fall to the modern municipality were not so much as contemplated, when none of the great enterprises upon which the convenience of local communities so largely depends and from which the local authorities draw so large a part of their revenue—gas, water, and electricity works, tramway enterprises, and the like—existed; when, in a word, the scope of

which the history of the Municipal Corporations Act of 1835 is contained he found but one slight reference to Stein's reform, and that proceeding from a private member. He writes with delicate satire : " It has been sometimes hinted by German writers that the Municipal Corporations Act of our own Reform Ministry was borrowed from Stein's measure; and assuredly it would have been no disgrace, but rather natural and praiseworthy, that our reformers should examine and profit by such a successful experiment tried in Prussia. Yet every Englishman feels instinctively convinced that our reformers did no such thing. What English statesman of that age would have dreamed of going to Prussia for lessons in self-government ? What English statesman of that age knew anything of Stein's legislation ? "

local administration bore just such a relationship, in character and magnitude, to the great tasks that were coming, as the obligations of an absolute German prince of the eighteenth century bore to those of a constitutional Government of the twentieth.[1]

It would be wrong to ignore the fact that reforms are desired and are necessary, yet the changes called for do not, as a rule, relate to organic matters, and some of them might be made at once in virtue of administrative action, or rather inaction.

The principal claim of local authorities is that they shall be allowed to control in their own right, and not merely in the person of the mayor, the police arrangements in relation to such questions as public health, building regulations, traffic, and the like, with a view to ending the existing division of jurisdiction. A wider control over the administration of education—which makes so large an inroad on local finance—is also claimed, and the obligation to obtain the Government's consent in Prussia before the local income tax can be raised beyond the State income tax rates is felt to be a grievance.[2] Many towns also chafe against the legal obligation to seek Crown or other sanction to appointments of mayors and members of executives, and most towns would like to see the interference of the Government and its supervisory agents in general reduced to a minimum or abolished altogether.

For it must be remembered that the conception of self-government held by German towns is far wider than that which appears to satisfy English municipal administrations, for the old idea of the town as an independent republic is still vigorous, and animates all endeavours for further liberty. The aims underlying these endeavours are the clear demarcation of the competence of local government and, most of all, absolute autonomy within that sphere.

[1] "For the best and most useful parts of the Municipal Ordinance in its present form we must still go back to the original Ordinance of 1808," writes Dr. H. Preuss, and though these words refer to Prussia, they are equally applicable to the rest of the country.
[2] A Government Bill for the amendment of the Prussian Communal Taxation Law now before the Prussian Diet (March, 1914) proposes to allow the communes to levy a local income tax up to 150 per cent. of the State tax without Government sanction.

Yet even in regard to the matters in regard to which reform is desired, it must be understood that the need is more pressing in Prussia than in the rest of the country; in some States police powers are already vested in the local authorities and appointments to the mayoralty and executive are subject to only formal confirmation, if to any at all. In general it may be stated with confidence that the oversight exercised by Government causes little inconvenience in practice and that in some of the States its influence upon the action of the local authorities is quite negligible.[1]

CONSTITUTION OF LOCAL AUTHORITIES.—It has been shown that in the constitution of the municipal authority the theory of the two countries and the practice built upon it are entirely different. While the English borough or urban district is governed on the unicameral principle by a body which unites deliberative with administrative—legislative with executive—functions, in Germany the two sets of functions are kept separate and are assigned to different bodies.

At the head of the English town or urban council is a mayor or chairman respectively, holding no special administrative powers in virtue of his office, which is honorary,[2] though as the civic head of the town he is responsible for the general direction of local affairs, and in certain emergencies he may have to perform important functions in the name of the Crown. All the various departments of town government are nominally controlled by committees of voluntary workers, who may or may not have special knowledge of the duties they are elected to discharge, and who are responsible to the council for every single act they perform.

In spite or because of the fact that the most attractive programme that can be placed before the ratepayers of an

[1] This assertion is made on the strength of replies to questions on the subject issued for the purpose of this book to the chief mayors of important towns. The statements made were unequivocal.

[2] Under the Municipal Corporations Act of 1882 (sect. 15 [4]) mayors " may receive such remuneration as the council think reasonable," but such payment is not regarded as payment for services rendered, and it has been held (in the case Attorney-General *v.* the Mayor of Cardiff) that the power to pay a salary must not be used in order to meet payments which would otherwise be illegal.

average English town is one of a single clause—a promise to keep down the rates at all costs—the elections to the councils evoke much public spirit of a more or less indifferent moral value, and, as a rule, the towns probably secure as local administrators men at least as good as they deserve. The chairmen and members of the various committees often bring to their work a capacity and skill which have won success and distinction in their professional and commercial vocations, and in general they show a degree of devotion to civic service which seldom receives due public recognition; yet the system affords no guarantee of technical knowledge and thorough oversight, and it is seldom possible for even the most ardent of these honorary servants to give to the work of his special department the close and detailed attention which it may or ought to need.

The practical work of administration is done by able salaried officers, forming in the greater towns a large and powerful hierarchy, with the town clerk at the head, but each one of them is theoretically dependent upon the council or the several committees for direction in every matter, and he can only act independently within the limits expressly laid down for him.

From first to last, therefore, the council as a whole is omnipotent in local government; for good or ill, its will—whether expressed directly or through the administrative committees—must prevail; and where public opinion is strong enough to award praise for success or blame for failure in administration it is apportioned to the representative body and not to the officials who work behind the scenes. But because the independence and responsibility of the permanent officials are limited, and the constitution of the town councils continually changes, it is difficult to carry out, on any question whatever, large policies needing foresight and steady, continuous action, uninfluenced by the wavering favour of a fickle electorate.

Such a system may be admirably suited to small and rudimentary organisations, but more and more it is proving inadequate to the government of modern municipalities, with their unlimited needs, far-reaching interests, and large and ever multiplying enterprises.

On the other hand, we have seen that the German municipal governments are organised on the bicameral principle. While the representative assembly, or lower house, is theoretically supreme in its general control over policy, and actually supreme in its control over finance, the collateral body is a permanent executive, composed—sometimes altogether and always in part—of salaried, professional officers, who are chosen as experts in their several capacities. Although elected by the town council, this executive, equally under the "magisterial" system of East Prussia and parts of South Germany, and the "mayoral" system of West Prussia and those districts which have been specially subjected to French influence, is for practical purposes independent and is at least as much so as the Government in relation to the British Parliament. At the head of this executive is the mayor, who is likewise a permanent official, chosen indeed at first for a limited period (twelve years) but on re-election usually appointed for life.

The operation of this system implies government by experts. It is a guarantee that every department of local administration is in the hands of men who are specialists in their own work. It is the business of these men to make administration efficient, without waiting for impetus from outside, and no weakness, ineptitude, or lack of public spirit on the part of the representative assembly, and no indifference or want of enlightenment on the part of the citizens, can exonerate them from this obligation as one inherent in their office. It is the right of the town council to debate to its heart's content and of the citizens to grumble, but upon the mayor and his colleagues rests the more important duty of showing their masters what ought to be done and of doing it.

There is a growing belief on the part of municipal workers in this country who have seen the German system in practice that we shall before long be driven by the force of circumstances to adopt some such arrangement as that of the permanent mayor and executive. The limits of municipal enterprise have of late years extended so widely and so rapidly that the system of honorary service already shows signs of breaking down. It cannot be expected that the busy professional and business men who fill our town councils can continue indefinitely adding one responsibility after another to their administrative work, as chairmen and members of committees. At present they must give prodigally of their time on pain of a fatal sacrifice of efficiency, and the question has already arisen—How soon will the point of exhaustion be reached? If municipal enterprise and responsibilities continue to grow, as they are bound to do, the alternatives on present lines are that the work must suffer or that it must be more and more handed over to the salaried officials, who, with their greater power, would still be without administrative responsibility.

To these alternatives Germany adds a third choice—the institution of executive bodies answering to its administrative magistracies, composed of proved experts, each one having charge of some special municipal task. It may be the commercial work of gas-making or tramway running, it may be the work of education or Poor Law administration, the control of municipal finance, the ordering of taxation, or the care of the municipal charities. Whatever the work is, the German citizen has the satisfaction of knowing that it is under the headship of some one individual who is responsible for its efficient oversight from beginning to end, who is a perfect master of every one of its details, and who knows more about it than anyone else. The institution which creates and the efficiency which justifies such a satisfaction are invaluable municipal assets.

Whatever arguments may be advanced from the standpoint of expediency against the introduction of such a bureaucratic element into local government, they will derive little strength from the common objection that it is contrary to the principle of free self-government. Underlying much of the vague prejudice against the German institutions of a paid mayor and executive, is the curious assumption that self-government which is not carried on directly by honorary service cannot be genuine. Such a theory, if tenable, would convict the most democratic systems of political government in existence. For we no longer pass our laws in assemblies of the people convened on hill-tops or in the market-place. On the contrary, without any suspicion that the democratic principle is being violated, we elect legislatures which, though possessing unlimited power, are nevertheless quite content to allow their wishes to be executed by paid Ministers and civil servants, over whose executive action they exercise only the most superficial and shadowy control and the nation at large none at all.

But what, after all, is the essence of free self-government? Not necessarily direct government by the people in all details, for such an arrangement is in practice impossible. The essential thing is that the will of the people shall be done, with its knowledge or at least with its acquiescence, that it shall be free to say how and by whom its will shall be executed, and hence to give or withhold administrative powers at its option. If these conditions are fulfilled all the essentials of " free " and " genuine " self-government exist, and a system of administration, whether national or local, established on these principles will be more rather than less efficient if it calls in the aid of experts who have made a life's study of the special work which they are required to do.

DERIVATION OF DUTIES AND POWERS.—Different alike in origin, character, and extent are the powers exercised by the local authorities of the two countries. The English system is self-government by statutory delegation, the German system might be called self-government by prescriptive right, modified by administrative sanction.

The principal powers of English urban authorities are derived from general statutes of three kinds: (a) the Acts under which they are constituted, i.e., in the case of boroughs, their Charters and Local Acts and the Municipal Corporations Act of 1882, and in the case of unincorporated towns the Local Government Act of 1894; (b) Acts assigning to them special administrative duties, as in regard to public health (principally the Public Health Act, 1875), education, housing, etc.; and (c) a series of permissive or adoptive Acts relating likewise to specific matters, e.g., public libraries, baths, housing, etc., which may be applied at their option. Any powers which a town wishes to exercise beyond those sanctioned by laws of these kinds must be acquired on their own initiative and at their own cost by Private Acts (application for which is subject to the assent of the ratepayers as ascertained by town's meeting or by general poll) applying only to the authorities seeking them, or as regards certain questions by Provisional Orders granted and by-laws sanctioned by Government Departments (i.e., the Local Government Board and the Board of Trade) after inquiry, and subject to Parliamentary approval. An English local authority can exercise no powers whatever without sanction so derived, in each case of a statutory or quasi-statutory character.

In contrast to this rigid system of reglementation we see the local authorities in Germany possessed of autonomy to an extent unknown in this country. While our borough and urban councils can only exercise such powers as have been delegated to or conferred upon them, German town councils can do anything that seems necessary to the good government of their areas and populations, and acts and measures only become *ultra vires* when they are expressly forbidden or are in conflict with the general law. Certain general duties and powers are assigned to the councils by statute, but probably the greater part of the work done by German municipal bodies is of a permissive character, and is done either in virtue of local statutes or by-laws obtained expeditiously by administrative sanction (i.e., the approval of the supervisory authority, and without legislative procedure at any stage), or without outside sanction of any kind. It has been shown that no cost is incurred in obtaining these local by-laws—though often conferring powers corresponding to those obtained by our local Acts of Parliament—where long and tedious legal and legislative procedure, attended by the expenditure of thousands of pounds, may be necessary in this country.

One effect of the English method of imposing duties upon local authorities from without is that independent initiative on a large scale is impossible. Perhaps its greatest condemnation lies in the fact that it dooms to inaction the progressive authorities which would be only too ready to act vigorously upon a multitude of questions if they were allowed, yet are bound hand and foot by the paralysing doctrine that nothing can be done that is not expressly authorised by the law. If English local authorities have lagged behind those of Germany in such matters as town planning, Poor Law reform, the medical inspection of schools, and the feeding of necessitous children, it is not their fault, but the fault of the system under which they work. It is not complimentary to our national sense of capacity that our local education authorities could not institute a system of medical examination of children or even provide play-centres and other means of recreation for scholars during the holidays until special legislation had been passed to empower them so to do.[1] In these and other matters German local authorities could and did act on their own initiative, without the need of statutory powers, and hence they were able to anticipate us.

SCOPE OF ADMINISTRATION.—Most of the powers and functions exercised by the local authorities are naturally the same in both countries. There are, however, important exceptions to this rule. On the one hand, the English local authorities have full responsibility for a group of important duties, relating specially to public health, the regulation of buildings, traffic, etc., which in some German States are reserved to the province of the police authority, and hence of the central executive. The inconvenience of this arrangement is lessened, however, owing to the fact that the State usually delegates local police functions to the mayor personally. With this exception municipal jurisdiction in Germany covers the entire range of local affairs, where with us the Poor Law and to a large extent education are administered by different bodies. The result is that in all his civil relationships the German citizen has to do with one local authority.

Perhaps the greatest correspondence is found in the domain of trading and other enterprises and undertakings carried on in the interest of public convenience and of revenue, though Germany has advanced much further in the direction of what is commonly known as municipal communism. In the larger towns gas and water are now almost generally owned

[1] Education (Administrative Provisions) Act, 1907, operative from January 1, 1908.

by the municipalities; electric power and light works and tramways to a less though to a rapidly increasing extent; the stock markets and abattoirs are invariably in public hands; the sea and river port towns generally have a large share in the local harbours and docks; and other public enterprises common to most large towns are market halls, theatres and concert halls, land and mortgage banks, people's savings banks, and pawnshops. In Germany, however, private enterprise in some of these matters is subject to restrictions which often go a long way towards reconciling the municipal socialist to a tolerant policy of live-and-let-live. For example, where a local authority hands over valuable tramway, light, and power monopolies to private corporations it not only regulates the prices of supply and other conditions of working, but secures a substantial share of the profits.

In several directions German local government exceeds the limits recognised in this country. This is particularly the case in regard to the planning of towns, public ownership of and trading in land, the " social welfare " work of the municipalities, and the general measures adopted by them for the promotion of culture outside the provision and support of schools.

In regard to town development German towns are still at an advantage over our own, in spite of the reforms introduced by the Housing and Town Planning Act of 1909 applying to Great Britain. One of the principal merits of the German system is that inasmuch as the local authority lays out the streets and determines the directions in which the towns shall extend, town building is not fortuitous but follows a regular scheme, often prepared a generation in advance, and in this way land speculation is to some extent checked. Yet the advantages of systematic growth would not be obtained, or obtained in the same degree, but for the bold policy of land purchase pursued by all progressive municipalities. It has been shown that many German towns own from one-third to two-thirds of their areas, and that few towns, large or small, are without a large reserve of land available in part for building purposes. Often the estate held within the administrative district is supplemented by still larger possessions on the periphery or in the immediate suburbs. As a consequence of their land policies it generally happens that when sites are needed for public buildings or works there is no necessity to buy from private owners at exorbitant panic prices. Further, a municipal authority is often able by its competition in the land market to use its influence in favour of healthy investment in place of blind speculation. It follows also that to the extent that municipalities own eligible land in and around their areas they share in the increased value caused by growth of population and public enterprise. The policy of landowning on a large scale more than any other cause has enabled German municipalities to lay out their towns on large lines and to provide for the needs of the remote future.

We are beginning to copy German example in town planning, but we are at a great disadvantage in so doing, for the mischief resulting from the past unsystematic and haphazard development of our urban areas is to a large extent irreparable. Even so, we are running no risks of precipitate action. For under the Act of 1909, admirable as are its objects and great though its superiority to earlier housing legislation, local authorities are left in the old condition of dependence even on so immediate a matter as the planning of their areas. Town planning schemes can have effect only if approved by order of the Local Government Board, which has power to alter any scheme and can make its sanction conditional on such modifications and conditions as it may think fit to impose. Before the Local Government Board itself can approve a scheme, however, notice of its intention to do so must be published in the *Gazette*, and if any person or authority interested objects, the draft order must be laid before each House of Parliament for a period of not less than thirty days during the session of Parliament. If during this period either House presents an address to the King against the draft, or any part of it, the scheme will fall to the ground, though a new scheme may be prepared. And this piece of legislation—otherwise so excellent in purpose—belongs to a time when all political parties are agreed as to the necessity of a large devolution of Parliamentary powers.

In the planning of their towns German local authorities need no special powers, except in the event of expropriation being necessary, and in some States even this extreme measure is expeditiously carried through without legislative procedure. For the rest, the local authority, in the exercise of its ordinary powers, fixes the building lines, constructs the streets at the expense of the adjacent owners, requires builders to erect their houses on the streets so prepared, and in some States pools awkwardly situated properties and redistributes the land amongst the several owners with a view to its more advantageous use from the standpoint of public convenience and interest. If any dispute arises between the authority and the property owners it is decided by the supervisory authority. No Ministry of State interferes from first to last, and if all the municipalities in a State were to prepare new " town plans " at once the legislature would never hear of it.

In regard to land ownership in particular English legislation is curiously distrustful of local authorities. Normally municipal corporations may not purchase and hold, otherwise than for immediate use for the purpose for which it was purchased, more than five acres of land either within or without the borough, and a larger holding is only possible when special powers have been obtained, while they may not sell land without the sanction of the Local Government Board.[1] Further, land not used for the purpose for which its purchase was authorised must be sold unless the Local Government Board directs otherwise. On the other hand, there is no limit, save its financial resources, to the amount of land which a German town may own; it may both buy and sell without permission, unless borrowing powers are necessary; and the Governments have for years urged the towns to invest freely

[1] While section 105 of the Municipal Corporations Act empowers a municipal corporation to acquire only five acres, the corporations have, of course, powers under other general Acts to acquire an unlimited amount of land so long as it is required for the purposes of the Acts in question. For example, under section 175 of the Public Health Act, 1875, they can purchase any lands within or without their district for the purposes of that Act. That section, however, contains a provision which seems to indicate the desire on the part of Parliament that Local Authorities shall not be large landowners, because it provides that any lands acquired under that Act and not required shall be sold unless the Local Government Board otherwise directs.

in the purchase of land and to retain as much as possible in their own possession.

The activities of German towns in the domain of " social welfare " and in the advancement of culture, as described in previous chapters, if not foreign to the English conception of local government, are at least not contemplated by any existing powers.

SYSTEMS OF LOCAL TAXATION.—Divergencies even more fundamental differentiate the English rating system from the German system of local taxation and give to it a position well-nigh unique in singularity, and also in inequity. The English local authorities raise the principal part of their revenue in the form of rates assessed on what is approximately the rental value of the property within their administrative areas and payable entirely by the occupiers and not by the citizens as such. As with the administrative powers of local authorities in general, so with their taxing powers in particular, the law of rating is inflexible, and no local deviation from the principle of meeting public needs by a single tax on occupiers measured by rent is permissible. The local authorities are allowed to share in the proceeds of certain State taxes and duties, e.g., the estate duty, dog and gun licences, customs and excise duties, etc., but these revenues are in the nature of grants-in-aid or subventions.

A method of taxation which is automatic and mechanical is either a masterpiece of constructive statesmanship or a masterpiece of ineptitude. No one has ever claimed that the English rating system is the former, and it is hardly surprising that no countries outside the British Empire[1] have paid it the flattery of imitation. Apart from injustices done to individuals and classes of individuals, some of its least defensible features are that (a) it is in effect a tax on living space, and in consequence sets a premium upon a low standard of housing ; (b) small incomes are taxed with undue severity and owing to the high ratio of rate to rent a disproportionate share of the cost of relieving poverty ultimately

[1] The principle of local rating on rental value has been adopted in some of the Australian and South African colonies.

falls on the poor themselves; (c) the occupiers pay for a large amount of expenditure which directly increases the value of land, with the result of enhancing the cost of houses and rents; and (d) the accident of their not being householders secures to a large section of the inhabitants exemption from direct local taxation, although it benefits by local expenditure with the taxed portion of the community. Such a privileged class of non-taxpayers is unknown elsewhere in Europe.

In contrast to this mechanical system of local taxation, the German towns enjoy a very wide measure of autonomy. Certain taxes have statutory sanction, though their imposition is theoretically optional, but beyond these each local authority can adopt other taxes in accordance with its special conditions and needs. Moreover, new taxes can be introduced with singular facility. No special law or legal procedure of any kind is required; all that is necessary is that the local authority shall prepare a scheme and obtain the approval of the State supervisory authorities. While the English rating system is based on no other principle save that of raising money with the least possible trouble, the German system is deliberately devised so as to give expression to two clear and complementary principles, viz., taxation according to ability and taxation according to reciprocal benefit. The application of these principles necessitates taxation in a variety of ways, and hence the English student may at first sight be disposed to regard the German system as excessively cumbrous. When its principles are understood, however, much of the apparent complexity disappears and the impression left is that of a system elaborate indeed and possibly costly to administer yet singularly well-balanced and equitable.

The backbone of German local finance is the income tax, levied in the form of a supplement to the State income tax, and falling lightly on small incomes but progressive up to a certain maximum rate. To this tax all persons, whether householders or not, in receipt of income above a specified minimum, are liable. In German towns more than one-third of the entire population pay this tax, while the proportion of residents of an English town who are assessed to rates, as occupiers, is barely a quarter. The local taxes next in importance are those on real estate, viz., the direct taxes on land and buildings and the indirect taxes on sales of property and on unearned increment. There are also taxes on commercial undertakings, luxury and amusement taxes, and sundry others.

It has been shown that taking the mean rates of 84 of the larger towns of Germany, no less than 51·9 per cent. of all the revenue from taxation for local purposes is derived from income taxes and taxes allied to them (poll taxes and rent taxes), 28·8 per cent. from real estate taxes of various kinds, 13·3 per cent. from taxes on commercial undertakings, and 6 per cent. from consumption, amusement, and other minor taxes. Further, special contributions are levied on the owners where the value of their property is increased owing to public expenditure, and the owners almost invariably bear the costs of sewage removal, scavenging, and the removal of house refuse.

Many as the local taxes are in Germany, they are not imposed in an arbitrary manner. As regards the principal taxes, e.g., those on income, real estate, and commercial occupations, the general rule is followed of charging to them such expenditure as may fairly be regarded as incurred for the special advantage of those who pay these several taxes. For example, outlay upon the construction of streets, upon sewerage works, upon the acquisition of State and provincial institutions and garrisons (since all German towns are ambitious to have State institutions in their midst and to be garrison towns), and continuation schools is regarded as specially beneficial to property owners and the trading classes, and hence as proper to be charged to the real estate and trade taxes. On the other hand, expenditure on account of elementary schools, poor relief, public health, and security (i.e., police), and the general administration is regarded as for the benefit of the inhabitants in common and as proper to be covered by the local income tax, which falls upon every inhabitant, whether a householder or not, in receipt of income above a specified amount, variable according to the State, and again according to the towns within each State. Certain other expenditure is regarded as suitable to be charged to all these taxes jointly, e.g., expenditure on the maintenance, cleaning, and lighting of the streets and public places, the upkeep of sewerage works, fire brigades, and higher schools.

That this method of apportioning expenditure on the principle of reciprocal benefit is perfectly practicable is proved by the fact that it is universally adopted ; and that the principle of taxing real estate in particular proportionately to the advantages conferred upon it by public expenditure is regarded as equitable by the property owners themselves may fairly be concluded from the facts that the town councils control the budget absolutely and must sanction every tax, and that in the larger States house-owners are by statute secured a representation upon the councils of at least one-half, while in practice their representation ranges from over one-half to as much as five-sixths.

The growing expenditure incumbent on our local authorities, due not merely to the liabilities assumed by them voluntarily in pursuance of progressive administration, but to the increasing obligations imposed upon them by Acts of Parliament, is bound before long to reach a point when house rent will cease to be regarded as a fair test and measure of ability to bear local burdens, and when other sources of taxation, falling upon sections of the population now exempted, will become necessary. Here German practice may afford us useful suggestions.

Apart from the strength of tradition, the deep-rooted dislike of fundamental changes characteristic of English people in general, and the resistance to be expected from those who have a vested interest in the present system of charging the whole cost of local government to the occupiers —an entire departure from and perversion of the principle of " rating " as originally introduced and understood—the most obvious difficulty in the way of a fairer incidence of local taxation is the absence in this country of the institution of a local income tax. Nevertheless, even without such a tax much might be done to alleviate the inequities of the rating system, following the German principle of taxing for local purposes according to benefit received. Thus expenditure deemed to be for the special advantage of real estate might be charged wholly or partly to the owners on the basis either of a rental or a sale value assessment of their properties. An incidental effect of such a measure would be that the cost of local government would henceforth be shared by part at least of the large class of non-occupying residents which in every town evades local taxation altogether, though enjoying on equal terms with householders the benefits of local expenditure. Only by the introduction of some form of local income tax, however, would it be possible to require this class of persons as a whole to bear its rightful share of the burden of local taxation.

EXTERNAL SUPERVISION AND CONTROL.—The differences in the external control exercised over local authorities in the two countries will be shown by comparison to relate rather to its form than its extent. Owing to the elaborate legal and administrative provision made for supervising the action of German town councils in various matters, it would be natural to assume that these bodies are in a quite special degree subject to Government interference and check. It is possible to overlook the fact that the control exercised by the central authority in the United Kingdom, particularly through the three Local Government Boards, is surprisingly thorough, and in some directions exceeds anything known in Germany.

The theory of control from above in each country is that the State bears ultimate responsibility for the public welfare, and hence is entitled to satisfy itself that all the duties and functions which it delegates to local authorities are efficiently discharged. In this country supervision is further justified on the ground that as the State makes liberal grants in aid of local taxation for certain purposes it is both its right and its duty to see that the money so given is properly expended—a reasonable claim, which must not, however, be allowed to obscure the fact that the strictest control is that exercised over a department of local government to the cost of which the State makes a comparatively small contribution, i.e., the administration of the Poor Law.

The fundamental difference between the two systems is that in this country supervision is centralised and is exercised directly and bureaucratically by the State through different Ministries, i.e., the Local Government Board in relation to local government generally, the Board of Trade in relation to electrical undertakings and tramways, the Home Office in relation to police matters, and the Board of Agriculture in relation to veterinary matters.

In Germany, on the other hand, the central authority delegates the duty of supervision to local administrative officials and bodies, the former being part of the State bureaucracy and the latter containing a lay and even a representative element.

Advantages may no doubt be claimed for both systems; *ceteris paribus*, the exercise of control from the centre may be assumed to ensure completer impartiality and a greater regard for general interests where these seem to conflict with local interests, while under the decentralised German system full weight can be given to local knowledge and circumstances, there is not the same disposition to subordinate commonsense considerations to a slavish regard for forms and precedents, the official is balanced by the lay view, and proceedings are in general marked by greater promptitude and expedition.

The extent to which supervision is exercised by the State in this country differs greatly according to the standing of the local government authority; it is greatest in the case of the urban and rural district councils and the boards of guardians, allied to them in constitution, and least in the case of the municipal corporations. In general the appointment and dismissal of medical officers, sanitary inspectors, and Poor Law officers must be approved by the Local Government Board in virtue of the fact that their salaries are partly paid by Government; the appointment of public analysts must be approved by the same Board and that of chief constables by the Home Office. Except in the case of the police administration, public officers in Germany are appointed by the municipal authority without consultation with either Ministry or supervisory authority.

Further, in this country there is a large range of powers which can only be exercised by local authorities subject to the sanction of one of the central departments of State. Thus the Local Government Board must make all Provisional Orders and confirm all by-laws adopted by local authorities under the Public Health, Housing, and other Acts; the Board of Trade does the same in relation to electrical and tramway undertakings; and the Home Office must confirm by-laws relating to the police. The Local Government Board's sanction must be obtained before authorities can carry out town planning and housing schemes of any kind, and also water and sewerage schemes (*a*) if objection is taken to proposed sewerage works or water mains outside the authority's district; (*b*) if objection is taken to the construction of a reservoir; (*c*) if compulsory powers are required; or (*d*) if a loan is required, which is almost invariably the case. Provisional Orders are required for water or sewerage schemes when compulsory powers are needed for the acquisition of lands. A borough council may neither promote nor oppose a Bill in Parliament without the Local Government Board's assent, and rural authorities may not even plant trees or erect monuments in their streets unless the Board first authorises them so to do.

In Poor Law matters the Local Government Board exercises control in every direction, not merely imposing upon the local bodies the general policies they shall adopt, but laying down rules for their action in every detail of internal administration; so that boards of guardians are in reality merely so many local committees through which the will of the central authority is enforced. In the administration of education the influence of the central authority in the person of the Board of Education is equally intimate and decisive. And all these forms of supervision and control are enforced by means of inspectorates, covering the whole country, while in the background there is a coercive weapon for use against contumelious authorities in the form of the judicial *mandamus*.

As to financial matters in particular the general rule applies that local authorities cannot borrow for any object whatever without direct sanction in each individual case, unless they have obtained special borrowing powers in virtue of local

Acts of Parliament, which powers, again, must be specific as to purpose, though there is an exception in the case of loans obtained on security of lands, works, or other property acquired for the purpose of sewage disposal. If a local council needs money for permanent works, not only must it obtain the assent of the Local Government Board (or the Board of Trade if it is required for a tramway), but it must go through the elaborate form of a local inquiry held by the Board's officers. The assent of the Local Government Board must also be obtained to a loan required for an electrical undertaking, though the department to authorise such an undertaking, to approve the scheme, and to make the regulations is the Board of Trade. Moreover, the finance of urban and rural district councils and boards of guardians, and also the education accounts of borough councils which are the education authorities for their areas, are subject to audit by Government officials.

In contrast to this highly centralised system of control over local authorities, the full range of which is not covered by the foregoing summary, Germany has instituted a system of control by district supervisory officers and bodies, the latter partly elected, forming part of the higher administrative organisation of the country, whose powers are limited to specific acts and departments of local government. Education is, for obvious reasons, as much controlled from the centre in Germany as in this country. Poor Law administration, on the other hand, is regarded as a local concern, and there is no outside interference even on large questions of policy. New powers can, as a rule, be acquired by the simple process of adopting by-laws which become operative directly the supervisory authority has signified approval, without appeal to Parliament or Ministry; and with the assent of the Ministry of Finance new taxes can be introduced. While in this country the works which may be executed and (in the case of some local authorities) even the buildings which may be erected are specified in Acts of Parliament, and unless expressly authorised by private Acts must be sanctioned by the central authority in addition if loans are involved, German local authorities are, in general, free to undertake projects of any kind which fall within the province of municipal government without any limitation, and it is only when loans have to be contracted in relation thereto that the question of sanction comes in, and then the assent of the local supervisory authority is sufficient. As a rule, appeal is allowed from the lower to the higher supervisory authorities, but in some matters final decision rests with one of the Ministries of State. The last measure of coercion open to the Government in the event of a local administration proving refractory is the dissolution of the town council and the transaction of its duties in commission pending the election of another body—a measure seldom resorted to.

There is no institution in Germany corresponding to the Government audit, and in regard to accounting the position of a municipal authority there corresponds closely to that of the English corporations, for while the accounts of the latter are audited by three auditors, one appointed by the mayor from amongst the members of the town council and the other two by the burgesses—none of whom, however, need know anything about finance or accountancy—those of German town councils are audited under the supervision of the permanent mayor and the chairman of the council. Where the strict letter of the statute is observed, the two systems of audit are equally defective and unsatisfactory, and it is not surprising that the larger municipalities in both countries are more and more recognising the wisdom of having their accounts examined and certified by professional accountants.

In Germany the public is protected to some extent owing to the obligation of every local council to supply to the supervisory authority a copy of its budget immediately on preparation and before it has been discussed by the council, not in order that it may be sanctioned—for that is unnecessary—but that it may be scrutinised. That authority is thus able to call attention to any expenditure which it may be proposed to make improperly or to the absence of provision for expenditure which ought to be incurred. The English system of Local Government Board audit, where required by statute, leads at the most to the surcharge or disallowance of illegal expenditure after the event, though, numerous as are such surcharges and disallowances, the general practice of the Board amounts to no more than a pious protest, for in the great majority of cases appeals against the decision of the official auditors are gracefully allowed. It may be noted here that there is no provision in German legislation for limiting expenditure upon certain objects, as in this country to the proceeds of a certain rate unit, e.g., in the case of public libraries, higher education, etc.

It is evident from what has been said that State supervision is very real in both countries, yet on the whole active interference of the kind in Germany relates to minor matters; when it comes to large measures and undertakings the German authorities enjoy a degree of independence which with us is unknown. Certainly bureaucratic Germany knows no such concretion of administrative power as our many-sided Local Government Board. When one remembers that this department possesses the right to direct, control, and override the action of local authorities at so many points, to give or withhold assent not only to their acquisition of special powers but to their use of powers created by general statutes, to determine whether they shall be allowed to borrow and what they shall borrow for, to surcharge expenditure which has not been objected to beforehand, to force upon them its imperatives by means of the deprivation of grants of public money due, and in the last resort by the process of *mandamus*, and, added to all this, to scrutinise their doings by means of its corps of inspectors and auditors, one may well wonder if anywhere else in the world bureaucracy exists in so powerful and so highly concentrated a form.

CONCLUDING REMARKS.—It is not necessary to carry comparison into minor details of local government, though in every direction interesting points of difference occur, and few of them are without some special significance. Nor are the comparisons which have been made intended to convey the idea that either system of administration in its entirety is the superior of the other, or to suggest the expediency of wholesale imitation. The institutions of every country are the outcome of its peculiar conditions, they follow certain more or less definite lines of development, and inevitably express with varying fidelity the traditions and mental habit of its people.

Both in England and Germany the spirit and forms of local government have been largely determined by the course of their political history and the character of their political institutions. In both countries local government stands in intimate relationship to the central authority—the State, but with the fundamental difference that in one country the State represents not merely in theory but in fact the nation's collective life and will, while in the other it incorporates even to-day a personal sovereignty, whose prerogatives have indeed been limited by national constitutions and legislatures, yet because of that very fact, have become within their constitutional limits more definite, more real, perhaps more enduring than before.

German intellects have been sharpened and learned German books have been written by the hundred upon the subtle differences between State supremacy in a collective and a personal sense as applied to local administration. Such questions are irrelevant to an exposition which is not one of theories of jurisprudence but of practical questions, and they have been passed over. What is profoundly interesting and significant for us is the fact that there have sprung out of a soil apparently so little favourable to the growth of free and independent institutions systems of local government offering in some respects far larger opportunities for civic activity and ambition, and embracing a far wider range of duties and responsibilities, than can be claimed by the corresponding institutions in our own country.

Happily for Germany, the authors of its systems of municipal administration did not limit their functions and powers by inflexible statutes, but, treating them as organic institutions, left them room for indefinite growth and development. We have built up our system of local government throughout upon the doctrine of delegation—of legislative and Ministerial sanctions—and to every type of local authority we have assigned fixed limits of action which it may not transgress. The elaborate provisions for keeping local authorities, even of the highest status, in perpetual tutelage are inspired by a profound spirit of distrust, a spirit singularly out of harmony with the prevailing tendencies in other spheres of government, yet so deeply rooted in tradition and custom that even to-day every new devolution or extension of administrative duties is accompanied by all the old harassing reservations, checks, and safeguards, devised for utterly different conditions.

It is not the only department of our national life which is being governed by the traditions and spirit, the precedents and preconceptions, of times with which the present has little or nothing in common. Every age has its special tasks to perform, and their due discharge is a paramount duty to the future, which only thus can come into its certain heritage of responsibility untrammelled by arrears of neglected work and unencumbered by the debts of past inefficient stewardship. Why, then, should the present at every turn be impeded by the dead hand of tradition, and be doomed to lethargy and inaction by a spurious veneration for forms and conventions which, though they have served their day, are now ineffectual and effete?

Sociologists, surveying their peculiar domain, agree that no tendency of present-day social movement is more persistent, more impressive, more distinctively "modern" than the prevailing eagerness for new powers of expansion—the power to act freely, to attempt and achieve, the power to realise and develop personality, the power to translate into fact the seductive theory, the haunting vision, the impelling conviction. In every part of the social organism this instinct of self-expression may be seen attaining a new vigour and directing itself towards large, ambitious, and often daring ends— in the hurly-burly of political rivalries, in the undisciplined struggles of industry and commerce, in the orderly advance of science, in the awakening of labour to a new consciousness and a vague yet intensely real craving for wider opportunities, a better chance, and a fuller life. It is inconceivable that our municipal organisations should be expected to remain outside this modern stream of development, indifferent to its profound significance, giving no clear response to the clamant challenge of a new age and a changed order.

It is for municipal workers in this country themselves to consider whether our existing system of local government, with its grudging recognition of responsibility, its jealous withholding of powers which elsewhere are exercised without permit or restriction, and its highly centralised system of supervision and reglementation, satisfies the aspirations of the present or is likely to meet the needs of the coming time.

APPENDICES

I.—ORGANISATION FOR PURPOSES OF LOCAL GOVERNMENT IN GERMANY

(TO CHAPTER I)

(i)—PRUSSIA

IN stating the principles underlying organisation for local government in Germany it is only needful to refer at length to Prussia, since the corresponding organisations of the other larger States agree in broad outlines, in spite of much variety in nomenclature.

The Kingdom of Prussia is organised for the purposes of local government, and also of State supervision, into provinces, Governments (or Government Districts), circles (*Kreise*), and communes (both urban and rural) and manors; while for certain police purposes rural communes and manors are formed into police districts (*Amtsbezirke*). These several divisions were introduced into some of the provinces at different times, and subject to various modifications in matters of detail, but in main features the local government authorities are the same throughout the kingdom. The organisation of the provinces, districts, and circles of the six eastern provinces was from 1872 forward modified in the direction of greater decentralisation and the extension of the civil as distinguished from the bureaucratic element in local administration.

THE PROVINCE: THE CHIEF PRESIDENT.—The administrative head of the province is the Chief President (*Oberpresident*) who is appointed by the Crown. Inasmuch as he is the highest representative of the Crown and the State within his administrative area, his nearest counterpart in this country might seem to be the Lord-Lieutenant of a county. The Prussian Chief President, however, combines with equal rank wider jurisdiction and greater authority than a Lord-Lieutenant. As an administrative official he has points of similarity to the prefect of a French Department—not least in his identification with the Government and its policy—but again with the difference that his powers and functions are wider and more responsible. He is the State in miniature in the civil life of the province; he superintends matters and institutions extending beyond the jurisdiction of a district " government " or relating to the entire province, he directs the affairs of the Provincial Diet, and he exercises general control over all the " governments " within the province, granting or withholding sanctions on the Executive's behalf where prescribed by law, and in many matters acting as a final court of appeal ; and he is responsible for certain military functions and in time of war or civil commotion exercises far-going prerogatives in this capacity.

PROVINCIAL COUNCIL.—The Chief President is assisted by the Provincial Council (*Rat*) and a number of auxiliary officials, who act on his directions. The council consists of the Chief President (or his deputy), acting as chairman, a higher administrative official accredited to his department (or a deputy), nominated by the Minister of the Interior, and five other members chosen by the Provincial Committee (*Ausschuss*) from amongst those residents of the province who are eligible to election to the Provincial Diet, each of these having also a deputy. The lay members of the council are as a rule appointed for six years. All ordinances issued by the Chief President need to be approved by the Council.

PROVINCIAL DIET.—The Provincial Assembly or Diet is constituted of deputies elected by the rural and urban circles, in the normal ratio of two per circle, with one more where the population reaches a certain number, varying from 40,000 to 80,000 according to the province, and then one further member for every additional 50,000 inhabitants. The deputies of the rural circles are chosen by the Circle Diets, and those of the urban circles by the executives and town councils in joint sitting, and election is for six years. The Provincial Diet is convened at least once in two years by the Chief President in the name of the Crown, and at such other times as business may require. The Diet elects its own chairman, but the Chief President has a right to be present at its meetings, which are public. Apart from the representatives sent by the towns the lay members of the Diet are for the most part large landowners.

The Provincial Diet appoints (subject to approval by the Crown) a provincial director (*Landeshauptmann* or *Landesdirektor*), whose duty it is to look after current business, but the executive organ is the Provincial Committee, consisting of a chairman and from seven to thirteen other members chosen by the Diet, either from its midst or from outside, with the director as an *ex officio* member.

Committees may be appointed for the transaction of special business or the oversight of special institutions.

Among the matters for which the Provincial Diets are responsible are education, roads, reclamation schemes, agricultural improvements, institutions for lunatics, epileptics, and the blind, deaf and dumb, forced labour houses for convicted vagrants and certain other offenders, and the relief of poor persons without settlement. The Diet also controls the budget of the provincial administration and taxation for provincial purposes. The provinces are authorised to raise the necessary revenue, in so far as Government grants, the proceeds of provincial undertakings and institutions, and miscellaneous contributions and fees are inadequate, in the form of precepts on the communes leviable in respect of the direct taxes, viz., those on land, buildings, trading enterprises, and income, these taxes being collected by the communes on their behalf.

DISTRICT GOVERNMENTS: THE DISTRICT PRESIDENT.—The District Governments are organised for the purposes of the central executive, and are not corporate bodies, and at the head of each is the Government or District President. The "Government" is composed altogether of State officials, and at least one of its members must be qualified for the office of judge. The questions referred to the "Government" include State taxation, domains, forests, and primary education, but the President has independent jurisdiction in regard to some others. A "Government" is divided into two or more departments, each with a divisional director, and each section decides as a whole all the more important questions with which it has to deal, but the Government President exercises general supervision and has a suspensive veto.

DISTRICT COMMITTEE.—The "Government" shares power and responsibility with the District Committee (*Bezirksausschuss*), which consists of the District President as chairman and six other members, of whom two (who must be qualified for the office of judge or for higher administrative rank respectively) are nominated for life by the Crown, while the other four (with four deputies) are chosen by the Provincial Committee for six years at once. Members of the Provincial Council may not simultaneously be members of the District Committee. This body exercises very important powers; all police ordinances issued by the District President require its endorsement, it exercises supervision over the lower local government authorities, and it acts as a court of appeal as against the Circle Committees and also as a court of first instance for the hearing of administrative disputes.

THE CIRCLES: THE LANDRAT.—The Circle as an administrative area corresponds broadly to the French *arrondissement*. Circles usually comprise a combination of urban and rural communes, with manors, but the larger towns are detached and form separate circles. The head of the Circle is the Landrat, who wields not only great administrative powers, but much political influence. He comes into contact with the communal authorities, other than those of the larger towns, more directly and more frequently than any other State administrative officials. Excluding the towns which have been detached from his Circle in virtue of population, he exercises supervision over the communes and self-governing manors within that area, while the Government President is the higher instance in cases of reference and appeal. Only persons who possess the qualifications for the higher branches of the State administrative or the judicial service and have served for a probationary period of four years in one of these services may hold the office. Although the Circle Diet pays his salary the Landrat is appointed by the Government and can be dismissed by it; he is, in fact, expected to represent the Government's policy unwaveringly, even in political matters.

THE CIRCLE DIET.—This body consists of twenty-five members in Circles with a civil population not exceeding 25,000, with one member more for every 5000 additional inhabitants in Circles with a population between 25,000 and 100,000, and afterwards one more for every additional 10,000 inhabitants in Circles with a population exceeding 100,000. The members are chosen by a cumbrous method intended to secure equal representation of urban and rural districts and of large and small proprietors and business people respectively within the latter districts. Election is for six years. The Landrat acts as chairman.

The Circle Diet represents the Circle organisation in corporate matters, discusses and decides on matters referred to it by the law or by Royal Ordinances, and in particular authorises all taxation necessary for the purposes of Circle government, and controls the budget and finance generally, including the contracting of loans. Special committees are appointed according to need. The Circle Diet usually issues an official gazette (*Kreisblatt*) in which all its orders, decisions, and announcements are published.

Questions to which the Circle governments give special and increasing attention are the construction of main roads, light railways, and waterworks, the promotion of continuation and technical schools for rural communes, and the provision of libraries, hospitals, and sanatoria; while in some districts rural housing schemes have been carried out by these bodies. The necessary revenues of the Circles are derived from Government grants, the proceeds of their trading undertakings and other institutions, fees, indirect taxes on transfers of property and land value increment, upon concessions in respect of the sale of alcoholic liquors, and dogs; and when these resources are insufficient, from direct taxes, i.e., on land and buildings, trading enterprises, and income, these being collected by the communes together with their own taxes.

THE CIRCLE COMMITTEE.—The executive body is the Circle Committee, which consists of six members chosen by the Circle Diet for six years, with the Landrat as chairman *ex officio*. This Committee prepares and executes the resolutions of the Diet, manages the affairs of the Circle in accordance with the law and the Diet's decisions, appoints Circle officials, and exercises control over them. The Landrat convenes the meetings of the Committee, and directs the business delegated to it.

Besides being an executive body the Circle Committee exercises supervision over the rural communal authorities and acts as an administrative court of first instance.

It will be seen that in Provincial, District, and Circle administrations alike the State preserves a dominant position in virtue of the fact that a Government official is at the head and of the influence reserved to the bureaucratic element in the executive bodies. The special importance of the directing heads and executives of these three administrative divisions for the purposes of communal government lies in the fact that they act as the supervisory authorities in the name of the State; their sanction is necessary to certain acts done or proposed to be done by the communal authorities, while the District and Circle Committees act as administrative courts of first instance in many matters, subject to a right of appeal to the higher instances.[1]

RELATION OF TOWNS TO THE CIRCLES.—Towns with a civil population varying from 25,000 to 40,000, according to the province, may claim to be detached for administrative purposes from the Circle to which they belong geographically and to be constituted independent Circles; and the same privilege may be conferred on smaller towns by Royal Decree where special circumstances exist. A somewhat similar arrangement exists in Bavaria, where towns are described as " immediate " (*unmittelbar*) or " mediate " (*mittelbar*) in relation to the " Districts." Withdrawal from a Circle is subject to financial adjustments, which in practice means that a town that wishes to go its own way has often to pay dearly in the first instance for its freedom.

The desire of the towns to be emancipated from the Circles is natural, however, since while included they pay for meagre benefits received a disproportionately heavy amount of taxation as compared with the rural communes in the Circle. Not only so, but their influence in and upon the Circle Government is insignificant, while on the other hand they are subject to a large measure of control at the hands of the Provincial Council and the District Committee, whose constitution the Circle Diets are able indirectly to influence, for, as has been shown, while these bodies elect the Provincial Diet the latter in turn elects the Provincial Committee, and this nominates the honorary members of the Provincial Council and of the District Committee.

[1] The question of Prussian administrative law, which lies beyond the scope of this book, is dealt with in Percy Ashley's "Local and Central Government" (in England, France, Prussia, and the United States), 1906.

The effect of this population limit qualifying for detachment from a Circle is that a Circle may comprise, together with the distinctively rural communes, many towns, inasmuch as the urban status is to a large extent independent of the number of inhabitants. Although, therefore, the larger towns are, as a rule, detached from the Circles to which they belong geographically it would be incorrect to conclude that Circles other than the distinctively urban Circles (*Stadtkreise*) are strictly rural in character. At the census of 1910, of 1276 towns in Prussia only 99 formed independent (" Circle-free ") urban districts. These districts would correspond to the 43 " immediate towns " of Bavaria.

A town which is excluded from the Circle passes from the jurisdiction of the Landrat into that of the District President, while the functions of the Circle Diet and Committee in relation to communal matters are transferred to the municipal authorities, and the functions of the Circle Committee in relation to general administration to a special Town Committee consisting of the mayor (or a deputy) as chairman and four members of the municipal executive, chosen by the latter, but either the chairman or one of the other members must be qualified for judicial or higher administrative office.

SPECIAL ARRANGEMENTS IN BERLIN.—Special arrangements apply to Berlin, which for administrative purposes is detached from the province to which it belongs (Brandenburg). There the Chief President of the province of Brandenburg acts also as Chief President of Berlin, and exercises oversight over the communal government in place of the District President, while the place of the latter in many other matters is taken by a President of Police. Berlin has also its own District Committee, with a president nominated by the Crown, while the four elective members are chosen by the municipal executive and town council in joint sitting, though none of the members of these bodies may be appointed. This Committee acts as a court of reference in the case of certain administrative disputes.

RURAL SELF-GOVERNMENT.—It would be departing from the purpose of this book to digress further into a consideration of the system of local government in the rural communes. Two fundamental characteristics, distinguishing the government of the urban from that of the rural communes, may be mentioned. One is that while the towns are usually governed by town council, executive, and mayor, the rural communes are governed by a representative council and a mayor or president, the latter alone exercising executive powers. Furthermore, as the rural communes fall directly under the control of the Circle government and its head the Landrat, their independence is far less complete than that of the towns. With the rural communes may be ranked the manors (*Gutsbezirke*) common to Prussia, Bavaria, and other States. These are self-governed areas which were created out of the estates of the large proprietors when the peasants became the free owners of their farms and formed themselves into independent village communes. In these manors, which are specially numerous in the east of Prussia, and everywhere represent social conditions in a somewhat primitive state of development, the large proprietors possess all the rights and are subject to the duties and liabilities of self-governing bodies. In Prussia, as in most other German States, their administration is regulated by special laws applying to them alone.

(ii)—THE OTHER STATES

Bavaria has no provincial organisation, but is divided for purposes of administration into eight Circles, and these again are divided into administrative districts, over which are District Boards (*Bezirksämter*). Each Circle forms a separate Government, of which the administrative organ is the Circle Council, while the administrative districts are similarly represented by District Councils. The District Councils are composed of large proprietors and delegates of the communes, with whom a State official confers in financial matters, while the Circle Councils consist of representatives of the District Councils, the larger towns, the large proprietors, the clergy, and the universities. Both councils elect executive committees of six members which direct their business.

Saxony and Würtemberg are similarly divided into Government districts (called in Saxony Circles) corresponding broadly to the Prussian " Governments " in that they are State administrative divisions, while in Bavaria they are organised for purposes of self-government like the Prussian Circles. Between these higher districts and the communes come intermediate divisions as in Prussia, having their representative assemblies and executives.

The system of Baden approximates to that of Bavaria, while the organisation of the grand duchy of Hesse adopts the Prussian divisions of Provinces and Circles, each with a State official as its administrative head, a Diet, and an executive committee.

II.—REGULATIONS OF MUNICIPAL LAND FUNDS

(TO CHAPTER V)

(i)—DÜSSELDORF

A. FORMATION OF REAL ESTATE FUND.—1. The lands and buildings set forth in the register of October 3, 1901, the moneys at present remaining in the "Fund realised by the sale of real estate," in amount £7274, the mortgage claims credited to this fund, in amount £17,107, and such lands, buildings, sums of money, and claims as may in future be assigned by resolution of the Town Council or in virtue of these regulations shall form a separate and independently administered municipal fund, to be kept at the original amount, bearing the name "Real Estate Fund."

2. The current revenue of the Real Estate Fund, the receipts from the sale or leasing of properties assigned or falling to the Fund, the claims realised and other reversions, including any loans that may be assigned to the Fund for the purpose of carrying out the objects in view, may be used only in meeting the current expenditure of the Fund, in acquiring properties or rights in respect of the same, the erection of profitable buildings, the payment of interest, and the formation of sinking funds in respect of loans contracted, and in defraying the costs which have been incurred in acquiring any of the properties assigned to the Fund in accordance with Article 1.

3. Properties which are exclusively intended to fulfil a definite municipal purpose shall not be acquired for the Real Estate Fund but for the said purpose. On the other hand, lands which are only in part intended for a definite purpose may be acquired for the Fund in the first instance.

4. Should properties assigned to the Real Estate Fund be applied later to municipal purposes the full value of the properties so used shall be paid to the Fund out of the votes assigned for the objects in view. Should the property, however, be used for any statutory object obligatory on the municipality, the compensation may be based on the value as set forth in the register of October 3, 1901, and in the case of properties acquired later may consist of the cost price increased by $3\frac{1}{2}$ per cent. interest for every year which has expired since its purchase.

5. Should the expenditure of the Fund in any year exceed the receipts the deficit shall be carried forward to the coming year.

6. The state of the Fund shall be shown every year in the form of a trading account and a balance sheet. The principles to be followed in preparing the latter shall be prescribed by the Deputation administering the Fund.

7. The Real Estate Fund shall be so administered that the outstanding debt, in the form of the loans approved by the State supervisory authority, less the amount of outstanding claims, shall not at any time exceed £1 5s. a head of the population of Düsseldorf at such time. In ascertaining the debt the value of the lands and buildings belonging to the Fund shall be disregarded.

8. The administration of the current business of the Fund and the preparation of proposals for submission to the Town Council shall rest with the " Deputation for the administration of the municipal real estate."

B. REGULATIONS RELATING TO THE ADMINISTRATION OF THE REAL ESTATE BELONGING TO THE MUNICIPALITY OF DÜSSELDORF.—

1. In the management of the municipal real estate (lands and buildings), in so far as the same is not used directly for the purposes of specific branches of the municipal administration, the Chief Mayor shall be assisted by a Deputation, formed in accordance with section 54 of the Rhenish Municipal Ordinance, bearing the name " Deputation for the administration of the municipal real estate." The Deputation shall exercise the rights vested in the Town Council under the Rhenish Municipal Ordinance, and in particular the right to empower the Chief Mayor to make proposals to public authorities for the protection of the rights and interests of the town, to institute proceedings in the ordinary and administrative Courts, to appear against the same, to come to agreements in legal cases, and to renounce legal claims.

2. The Deputation shall be appointed by the Town Council and shall consist of six citizens entitled to vote in municipal elections, of whom four must be town councillors. The Chief Mayor shall decide whether and which technical officers of the municipality or other expert persons shall be summoned to the meetings of the Deputation.

3. The Deputation shall prepare proposals for (a) all purchases and sales of properties on behalf of the municipality, even when these properties are intended to fulfil or do actually fulfil the purposes of any branches of the municipal administration, but in the latter event the Committee in charge of the department concerned shall make recommendations to the Deputation ; (b) the erection of municipal dwellings ; (c) the letting and leasing of municipal properties, both built on and not built on, in so far as

the yearly rent or interest exceeds £100, yet with the exception of the leasing of wharfage space and warehouse room at the docks.

It shall, however, decide independently in regard to (a) the letting and leasing of municipal properties, both built on and not built on, where the yearly rent or interest does not exceed £100, with the exception of the letting and leasing of wharfage space and warehouse room at the docks ; and (b) the conditions upon which municipal properties shall be assigned to specific public purposes.

(ii)—MUNICH

1. The Committee shall bear the name " Committee for Municipal Traffic in Land." The members of the Committee and their deputies shall be elected by the Magistracy for the duration of an administrative period and, in so far as they are not already bound to official secrecy by oath of office, they shall pledge their word of honour to observe secrecy regarding all the Committee's negotiations and announcements. They shall be bound by the instructions of the Magistracy.

2. It shall be the duty of the Committee to confer upon—

(a) all proposed purchases and sales of land of any considerable extent and of special importance which shall be referred to it by the Magistracy for this purpose ;

(b) general questions of municipal land policy and matters appertaining thereto. It is entitled to make proposals to the Magistracy in regard to such questions and is bound to give opinions in regard to questions addressed to it by the Magistracy.

The Committee shall examine all vouchers regarding the position of the land purchase fund and the street building fund, as well as the regular reports on municipal finance.

The Committee shall decide regarding properties the purchase or sale of which is referred to it by the Town Council and Magistracy with full power to act. It shall in such cases execute the commission of the Town Council and Magistracy and give an account of its proceedings.

In important cases falling within its competence the Committee can conclude provisional agreements in accordance with Article 181 of the Law regarding Fees. It is further authorised to make proposals to the Magistracy regarding the manner in which the municipal properties are being used, and in important cases regarding the letting or leasing of those properties, both built upon and not built upon.

3. The office of a member of the Committee is honorary ; but members receive repayment of actual outlay and, in the event of their having to travel or to undertake inspections, the prescribed **allowances.**

4. The Chief Mayor presides over the Committee and convenes the meetings, notifying the agenda. There shall be summoned to each meeting the four permanent legal reporters belonging to the Committee, as well as the ordinary members (not, however, their deputies) in such time that in the event of the inability of a member to attend it may be possible to invite a deputy. Should an ordinary member be prevented from attending his deputy shall be summoned. Deputies have the same rights as ordinary members of the Committee. Deputies to take the place of the legal members of the Committee shall be nominated by the Chief Mayor.

5. A quorum of the Committee shall exist when in addition to the reporter one legal member of the Magistracy, two civil members of the Magistracy, and three members of the Town Council are present, and decision shall be by simple majority of votes.

6. The Committee is empowered to take the opinion of experts or municipal officials and if necessary to summon the same to the meetings or to consider their written opinions.

7. The Committee shall keep a continuous record of the matters dealt with at its meetings, which record shall be certified by the acting chairman. The Committee may authorise a secretary, summoned to the meeting for the purpose, to make this record.

(iii)—CREFELD

1. A special account of the Land Fund shall be kept, and every year a report upon the Fund, containing a capital account, shall be issued.

2. Those municipal properties which are not intended for definite public purposes shall be transferred to the Fund. In future all properties to be acquired shall be paid for out of the moneys of the Fund, and, on the other hand, properties the use of which for a definite purpose is certain shall be paid for out of the credit specially provided therefore.

3. A register, with plans, shall be kept of the properties transferred to the Fund, and it shall contain an exact drawing of every property not built upon.

4. Should any properties transferred to the Fund be wholly or partly used for definite public purposes, the values of the same shall be charged to the credit referred to in Article 2, and shall appear in the account of the Fund as receipts. The value of such a property shall consist of the purchase price with interest to the end of the month preceding its transfer to the Fund, less receipts derived from the use of the property. For every single property, therefore, a balance sheet shall be prepared at the end of the year, compound interest being reckoned. Interest shall throughout be reckoned at 4 per cent. In the case of buildings depreciation shall be deducted at a minimum rate of 1 per cent.

5. The costs of acquiring properties shall be shown in the capital account, such costs including the purchase price, stamp duties, property transfer duty, and other costs, such as commission, incurred in the transaction.

6. Interest in respect of the period between the date of purchase and the actual payment of the purchase money shall always be shown under the heading " interest " in the trading account.

7. The yearly statement shall show the total costs of acquiring a property. Where the payment of the purchase price is spread over two or more years, the total amount paid up to the end of the past year must be stated. On the completion of every transaction the total expenditure shall be shown, and balances remaining on mortgage loans shall be noted.

III.—BY-LAWS RELATING TO BETTERMENT CONTRIBUTIONS

(TO CHAPTER VI)

(i)—KÖNIGSBERG

IN virtue of section 9 of the Communal Taxation Law of July 14, 1893, and of the resolutions of the Town Council of April 5, 1910, and April 19, 1910, the following Local By-law is issued :—

1. Towards the costs of the following works executed in the public interest special contributions shall be levied on those owners of property who enjoy economic advantages owing to the execution of the said works, viz. :—
    (a) The widening of streets or portions of streets.
    (b) Clearances of property.
    (c) Open spaces.
    (d) Parks.
    (e) Bridges.
    (f) Street overhead ways or subways together with all the works belonging thereto (ramps, entrances, etc.).

2. The same provision shall apply equally to the first construction of footways, by the laying down of kerbstones, tiles, artificial stone slabs, or other stone paving in place of inferior material.

3. There shall be no liability to further contribution under this by-law in so far as the costs have to be borne by adjacent owners in virtue of section 15 of the law of July 2, 1875, and the by-law issued under that law (i.e., the law relating to the repayment of the costs of street construction).

4. The contributions shall be proportioned according to the advantages which accrue to those liable owing to the execution of the works. The portion of the total cost to be covered by such contributions, the list of the owners to be assessed, and the amount of the contributions of those liable shall be fixed separately by resolution of the Town Council in every individual case, subject to the following conditions.

5. In the case of street widening works and clearances and the creation of open spaces and parks [section 1 (a) to (d)] liability to assessment may be cancelled if the land required for the works is given to the town free of cost.

If such land is made over to the town only partly free of cost or at a reduced price, the full value of the land shall be set against the total cost of the works, but the amount due from each of the persons interested in the transfer of the land to the town shall be reduced by the value of the land he has so made over to the town.

6. In the construction of footways (section 2) the contributions shall amount to one-half of the costs and shall be divided amongst the adjacent owners in proportion to the length of their respective street frontages.

Towards the costs of constructing or renewing the approaches from the strect channels over the footways to adjacent properties contributions shall be levied on the property owners interested to the extent of 90 per cent. of such costs.

7. Where the Town Council does not decide otherwise in individual cases the contributions shall be paid :—

(*a*) In the cases specified in section 1, as soon as new buildings are executed, or existing erections are rebuilt on the land liable, or the properties change hands, yet at the latest within two years after the costs have been apportioned ;

(*b*) in the case specified in section 2, within four weeks of the apportionment being made.

The municipal executive can defer payment or accept instalments on account in special cases provided adequate security is given.

8. For the rest the procedure prescribed in section 9 [(3) to (6)] of the Communal Taxation Law shall apply.

9. This local by-law shall come into force from the date of promulgation, but it shall also apply to all works the costs of which have not been fully and definitively met at the time of its coming into operation.

(ii)—POTSDAM

1. In respect of the following works required in the public interest, contributions shall be levied on the owners of property deriving special economic advantages therefrom, according to the measure of such advantages :—

(*a*) The widening of streets, squares, and any parts of the same, including works of the kind carried out on existing alignments.

(*b*) The new pavement of streets and street corners with a specially costly material.

(*c*) The construction, removal, raising or sinking of railway lines, stations, or other railway works, in so far as the foregoing are carried out either altogether by the town or with the aid of a municipal subsidy.

2. This by-law shall not relieve adjacent owners of any liability to costs leviable under existing by-laws in virtue of section 15 of the Alignment Law of July 2, 1875.

3. The following conditions shall apply to works connected with the widening of streets :—

(a) Contributions shall as a rule cover the costs which are incurred by the commune in the acquisition of land ;

(b) No liability to pay contributions shall exist if the whole of the land needed for such works is transferred to the commune free of cost by all the owners.

(c) If only part of the land is transferred free of cost, the value of the land so given shall be taken into account in fixing the total cost of widening the street and the contributions shall be reduced accordingly, but such reduction shall be in favour of the properties from which the land needed for street purposes has been taken, even though the land was given by the previous owners.

In fixing the value of the land given, the executive (Magistracy) shall have regard to the price of the land which had to be bought.

4. In the case of new paving works, contributions in respect of rammed asphalte shall, as a rule, only be levied to a maximum amount of 3s. per square metre (10½ square feet) of asphalted surface. Where such new paving works are carried out in virtue of an agreement with the persons interested, those persons who have already made a payment towards the cost shall be exempt from further liability and the other interested parties shall be assessed to the amount of the average payment so made. Adjacent owners shall not be assessed to the cost of paving works in respect of more than one-half of the street, and if the street is wider than 26 metres (84½ feet) not more than 13 metres (42¼ feet).

5. The liability to pay these contributions shall be a charge on the building plots, and that person shall be liable to pay it in the first instance who owns the land at the time the obligation arises. In the case of several owners all are jointly liable.

6. The contributions shall be paid within three months after the assessment has been made by the executive (Magistracy), but the executive is empowered to sanction postponement or to receive payment by instalments.

7. Such further provisions as may be necessary shall be decided by special resolution in every individual case.

IV.—TOWN PLANNING AND EXPROPRIATION LEGISLATION OF GERMANY

(TO CHAPTER VI)

THE following notes summarise the existing German legislation on the subject of compulsory expropriation in the interest of public improvements and of Town Planning. No general law applicable to the whole Empire exists upon this subject. The question of expropriation is, indeed, dealt with in the Imperial constitution, but only in relation to the construction of railways which may be deemed to be necessary for national defence or in the interest of the whole Empire, and even here expropriation must be legalised by special statute in each individual case. Most of the federal States have Expropriation Acts, some of them going back to the first half of the nineteenth century. Two methods are followed :—

(a) either the principle of expropriation for reasons of public interest is laid down in general terms, without specialising permissible objects of expropriation ; or

(b) the cases and the circumstances in which expropriation is permissible are particularised.

The law of Baden of August 28, 1835, and the law of Prussia of June 11, 1874, are illustrations of the first method ; the Bavarian law of November 17, 1837, is an illustration of the second. In general, however, the application of expropriation in any given case is authorised by Royal Ordinance or Ministerial Decree and no special or local statute is necessary to put the law in operation. The State of Hamburg is, however, an exception to this rule.

EXPROPRIATION UNDER THE BAVARIAN LAW.—The cases in which expropriation is declared by the Bavarian law to be permissible are :—

(a) the building of fortresses and other works for national defence, including military establishments of all kinds ;
(b) the building and enlargement of churches, public schools, hospitals, and lunatic asylums ;
(c) the laying out or extension of graveyards ;
(d) the rectification and deepening of rivers and streams ;

(e) the construction of new, or the extension, curtailment, or levelling of existing State, Circle (*Kreis*), and District roads;
(f) the construction of public water conduits ;
(g) the draining of noxious swamps in the neighbourhood of towns ;
(h) protection against floods ;
(i) the construction of public canals, locks, and bridges ;
(j) the construction of public docks or the extension of existing ones ;
(k) the construction of railways ;
(l) the construction of telegraphs for the State service ;
(m) measures required by the public health and safety ; and
(n) measures to protect against fire and other danger the State's artistic treasures and scientific collections.

EXPROPRIATION UNDER THE HAMBURG LAW.—In the case of Hamburg, the State (i.e., the Senate and House of Burgesses) is, by law of May 5, 1886, amended September 27, 1899, empowered to pass a decree of expropriation for the purpose of executing works of public interest, and particularly the building and rectification of streets and canals, the construction of public buildings, railways, docks, dykes, and river improvements, in return for full compensation both for value taken and loss inflicted. Whether the proposal to expropriate emanates from a State authority, from a commune, or from a private person, the decision as to its permissibility rests with the two Houses of Legislature. After a decree of expropriation has been passed, if no agreement has been arrived at as to the compensation to be paid, the matter is carried before an Assessment Commission consisting of one Judge as President, and two Assessors. Experts are heard and either party can appeal against the Court's first decision, but only to a second Court consisting this time of two Judges and three Assessors, none of whom can have taken part in the first proceedings. Resort to the ordinary Courts of Law is not allowed.

EXPROPRIATION FOR THE PURPOSE OF TOWN PLANNING.— During recent years a strong tendency to embody the principle of compulsory expropriation in State Building Acts, and through them in local statutes, has asserted itself in Germany, the object being to ensure the development and extension of towns on rational and healthy lines. Legislation of this kind, however, is not new in Germany. As early as 1845 the Duchy of Saxe-Meiningen passed an Expropriation Law providing that " the compulsory cession of landed property can be required for the . . . advantageous extension of towns and the necessary enlargement of villages, the construction of a straight or new street in towns, the laying out and extension of market places, churches, schools, hospitals, and other public buildings, and the re-erection of public or private buildings that have been destroyed in so far as the general building plan shows an alteration of the earlier site to be necessary," etc.

The modern State laws on Town Planning go beyond this, however, for, as a rule, they provide for the compulsory laying together or " pooling " of areas of undeveloped urban land with a view to the re-distribution of this land amongst the various owners, in the old proportions either as to area or value, in such a way as will best promote the opening up of the ground, the laying out of public streets, roads, and spaces, and the advantageous use of building plots. These laws apply to large and small townships equally, whatever their form of local government, and not merely to such towns as would correspond to the large English municipalities.

THE POOLING OF PROPERTIES UNDER THE LAW OF BADEN.—The best known German law on the subject of Town Planning is the Township Street Law of Baden, dated July 6, 1896. As the title indicates, the law applies to township streets as distinguished from main highways. It provides (section 2) that—" In order to the laying out of township streets plans shall be prepared in a form corresponding to the needs to be contemplated." Precautions are taken against dilatoriness on the part of towns in preparing such plans, and the Act (section 10) gives power to prohibit persons from building outside the area already enclosed by a town, and where Town Building Plans exist outside the area covered by these plans, if there should be reason to apprehend " obstacles in the way of the suitable continuation of the Town Building Plan." Further (section 11) : " Where a Building Plan has been prepared but the suitable building of the land embraced by the plan would be obstructed by the position, form, or area of the properties a re-division of the properties for the purpose of securing more advantageous sites, either by pooling or the alteration of boundaries, may take place on the application to the Communal Council, even against the will of the owners, so far as such re-division is in the public interest, and the land necessary for the laying out of the streets has either been obtained for this purpose or will be obtained before the re-division is effected."

The procedure prescribed is as follows : The whole of the properties to be redistributed, including such public roads as will be superfluous, are pooled. Before the re-distribution takes place the land required for the new streets and places is set apart and apportioned to the commune. The rest of the area is divided amongst the various owners in the proportions in which they were originally interested. For every single piece of land which in point of size was suitable for building one or more building sites adjoining a street are to be returned to the owners, as far as practicable in the same situations as before. Properties so small that they would have to be exchanged for plots unsuited for building purposes may be thrown together to other properties belonging to the same owners, so as to make suitable building plots, and failing this they must be ceded in return for compensation to the commune, which will apportion them amongst the other owners. Unavoidable differences in value, both under and over the apportionment due, are to be rectified by money payments, the commune receiving the excess value from those owners who receive too much and paying the deficit to those who are allotted too little. The commune must also compensate the owners for the land which it takes for public streets and places over and above the amount of its own land which it pooled, and this compensation may take the form of land which the commune may own within the area pooled or which may fall to it by the re-division. So far as compensation is given in money the provisions of the Baden law of August 28, 1835, on compulsory expropriation shall apply.

When a communal authority proposes to re-divide the properties within a given area it must prepare a plan showing the existing and the proposed apportionment of land, and opportunity must be given to all persons concerned to protect their interests. The preparatory work completed, the plan must be deposited with the District Board (*Bezirksamt*) with full details of the scheme proposed, and this Board refers the plan with all objections raised against it to the District Council, building operations being in the meantime prohibited within the scheduled area.

Should the District Council be of opinion that the plan is not in the public interest, or that the objections raised against it are well-founded, it may reject it. Within a month the communal authority may appeal to the Ministry of the Interior against such decision, but should the Ministry endorse the opinion of the District Council its decision is final and the matter is determined. Should the District Council approve the plan it notifies the Ministry of the Interior to that effect, but this Ministry may still either approve or reject the plan, and in the latter case the communal authority may appeal to the full Ministry of State. A plan having been definitively approved, it rests with the communal authority to execute it, and while it must do this in the first instance at its own costs, it may later, with the consent of the Ministry of State, charge all its expenditure under a plan of pooling to the owners, proportionately to the benefit which they derive from the redistribution of the properties.

On the strength of this law the Municipal Council of Mannheim adopted, on March 11, 1889, a series of " general principles relating to the return of the costs of street construction," as follows :—

" Besides the value of the land used for new or existing town streets yet unbuilt upon (which shall be the current value or original cost), the expenditure incurred in the first construction of the streets in a manner corresponding to the needs of traffic, including the over-ground channels serving for the conveyance of water, shall be entirely refunded to the town by the adjacent owners, according to the length of their several frontages, as soon as they shall execute buildings upon their properties, and so far as owing to the existence of these buildings with their appurtenances, such as courts, entrances, gardens, business and warehouse places, etc., the plots may be regarded as built upon. Nevertheless, the owners can only be required to bear the cost of street making to the extent of a width of 29¼ feet on either side.

" The owners of existing buildings adjoining such streets shall be required to refund a proportion of the costs referred to, such proportion to be fixed in each case by resolution of the Municipal Council, when the streets offer them conspicuous advantage.

" The costs of constructing all subterranean conduits of the town passing before the properties shall fall upon the municipality in so far as such works are executed by the municipality in the public interest."

TOWN PLANNING UNDER THE LAW OF SAXONY.—A similar Law exists in Saxony (July 1, 1900). This Law provides for the issue of local statutes regulating buildings, the adoption of building plans for undeveloped areas, and the pooling of properties in different ownership, with a view to the more advantageous laying out of particular areas. These local statutes do not require the sanction of the national Parliament, but, after being elaborated by the communal authorities (whether urban or rural), only require the approval of the Minister of the Interior.

In case of " urgent need " communal authorities may be required by the higher State administrative authorities to adopt local statutes or to amend existing statutes on the lines of the present law, and in default the Minister of the Interior may step in and act in their stead.

Sections 15 and 16 set forth that where it is desired to open up for building purposes an area which is " in the main not built upon," a building plan taking the form of a local statute shall, as a rule, be adopted. Such plans shall regulate the building lines, the method of building, the situation, height, and purpose of the buildings to be permitted, the rectification of watercourses, the draining of the area planned, and the subways and overhead ways of streets.

In the preparation of a building plan (section 18) due allowance is to be made for the requirements of the public traffic to be anticipated, for the development of the town or district, the need for dwellings that is likely to arise, and the requirements of public health and safety, and the following, among other points, have to be borne in mind :—

(a) The width of the streets and footways must depend upon the needs of local traffic, and be graduated according as a street is intended to be a main street, a secondary street, or only a residential street. Streets with busy traffic must be at least 55¼ feet wide.
(b) Gradients must, as far as possible, be equalised; steep gradients and straight building lines of excessive length must be avoided.
(c) In fixing the direction of streets provision must be made for short and convenient connections between one street and another, and between these streets and the principal traffic centres.
(d) Open spaces and planted areas should be provided, conformable in size, position, and number to the needs of traffic and the public welfare. Sites for churches and schools, and for playgrounds and recreation grounds are to be provided in sufficient number.
(e) In laying down rules as to the method of building to be allowed, and as to the permissibility of factories and industrial works, the past character of the town or district and the existing need should be considered.

Should no objections be taken to a building plan which has been formulated it passes direct to the Minister of the Interior for sanction.

The provisions (sections 54, etc.) as to the pooling of land and its subsequent redistribution are much the same as those in the law of Baden. This procedure may be set in operation by the Building Police Authority acting on a resolution of a Communal Council, or on application by more than one-half of the owners of the area affected, provided they also own more than half the land.

The Act also provides (sections 68 to 71) :—" Should the demolition of buildings or groups of buildings be indispensable in the interest of traffic or of the public health, and should the building plan for an area whose buildings have been destroyed by fire, water, or other natural forces, be incapable of execution otherwise in such a way as to avert similar dangers, the Minister of the Interior may, on the application of the communal authority, confer powers of expropriation in respect of the entire area necessary to the advantageous carrying out of the undertaking. . . . Before the application is served on the Ministry of the Interior the Building Police Authority shall endeavour to effect an amicable agreement amongst the persons interested.

" After the granting of the right of expropriation it shall be competent for the property owners under section 68 themselves to execute the new buildings contemplated in the building or expropriation plan on their own property within a period to be fixed by the Minister of the Interior. On the expiration of this period those properties or portions of property which have not by that time been built upon according to plans are forthwith expropriated."

TOWN PLANNING AT FRANKFORT.—One of the best known local Acts dealing with town planning is that which was obtained by the town of Frankfort-on-Main in 1903. It provides for an extensive use of the power to pool and redistribute inconvenient building plots within scheduled areas. Before the law can be set in motion, it is required that the Municipal Executive shall prepare a complete plan of the properties to be pooled, together with a register of the owners, and both plan and register must be deposited for public inspection, objections being invited within a period of four weeks. These objections are, as far as possible, to be adjusted by friendly means, and the time of grace having expired, the proposal goes forward to the District Committee, which pronounces a definite decision, after hearing the Police Authority, on the question whether legal conditions and requirements have been complied with, and after considering unsettled objections.

Properties can be pooled and redistributed on the application of the municipal authority, or of more than half the owners interested if these own more than half of the land concerned.

The laying together and pooling of properties having been authorised, the Government President nominates a commission to carry out the measure, two of whose members shall represent the President, and shall be the chairman and vice-chairman of the commission respectively, while the other members shall include at least one building expert, one legal expert, one certificated surveyor, and a land valuer. Members of the Municipal Executive may not sit on the commission, but in the appointment of its members both the Executive and the property owners shall be heard.

The costs incurred by the municipality under this procedure are to be apportioned amongst the several owners according to the advantage accruing to them if that method be practicable, or failing it, according to (*a*) the frontage, area, and position, or (*b*) the value of the properties allotted, but an owner has the option of paying interest on the capital sum of his share of costs at the rate of $3\frac{1}{2}$ per cent. until his property is sold or built on. Should an owner be dissatisfied with compensation payable in money, he may go to law within two months of the laying together of the land, but the execution of the plan of redistribution is not delayed thereby. Should the costs of the municipality be increased owing to legal proceedings, the Municipal Executive may charge the excess to the owners.

In its original form the Frankfort Local Act provided that where land was pooled and redistributed on the application of the owners 35 per cent. of the total surface might be allotted to street purposes and where compulsory procedure was adopted 30 per cent. This limitation was at once found untenable, and an amendment of 1907 increased the proportions to 40 and 35 per cent. respectively.

STREET IMPROVEMENTS IN HAMBURG.—The State of Hamburg, by a law of June 23, 1882, entitled the Building Police Law for the City of Hamburg, the Township of St. Paul's, and the Suburbs, assumed far-reaching powers in regard to street planning. It was stipulated that immediately on the publication of a resolution of the Senate and House of Burgesses signifying their intention to lay out a street, no land in the neighbourhood of that street might be built upon, and the town could claim the right to acquire a certain portion of such land for public purposes. In fixing the price the additional value to be expected from the construction of the street should not be considered. The law provided for the laying out into streets of eligible building areas in the outskirts, but stipulated that a building plan of this kind must join on to the principal traffic roads of the district, and must not create obstacles in the way of the opening out of main arteries which might in the future be necessary for the development of other outer districts. In such a building plan also provision should be made for a sufficiency of streets and open spaces. Permission is only given in exceptional cases to private persons to lay out streets within undeveloped areas, and even then only on condition that such streets shall not stand in the way of the later development of the land on rational lines, and that the owners concerned give an undertaking to cede to the town such land as may be necessary for additional cross-streets and public places.

WÜRTEMBERG MODEL TOWN PLANNING REGULATIONS.—Reference may also be made to Article 16 in the series of Model Town Planning Regulations drawn up by the Würtemberg Minister of the Interior, which runs :—

" If in crowded parts of a town the demolition of buildings appears desirable in the interest of traffic or the public welfare, compulsory expropriation shall be permissible on the application of the municipal authority in respect to the properties and the rights appertaining to them needed for the satisfactory execution of the undertaking, according to the provisions of the law on compulsory expropriation of December 20, 1888. . . . The expropriating authority is the Ministry of the Interior."

V.—AGREEMENT FOR THE ERECTION AND SALE OF WORKING-CLASS DWELLINGS BY THE MUNICIPALITY OF JENA

(TO CHAPTER VII)

THE municipality of Jena began in 1912 to build on town land small dwellings for sale to working-people and others on the instalment principle as first adopted at Ulm in Würtemberg. The special feature of its scheme is the reservation by the municipality of the right of ultimate repurchase. Six types of dwellings, each with a garden, are built, and the municipality retains a general supervision over the houses in virtue of its interest in the freehold. The following is the copy of the agreement concluded with purchasers :—

The following agreement has been concluded between the municipality of Jena, represented by the town council and the municipal executive, and . . .

The municipality of Jena sells to . . . the site indicated on the annexed plan at the price of 1·90 marks per square metre [=1s. 7d. per square yard], being . . . marks for the whole, subject to the following conditions :—

1. The municipality of Jena shall build a workman's house, at the expense of the purchaser, on the land so sold according to plans approved by the Building Police.

2. The person ordering the house (the purchaser of the site) shall repay to the municipality of Jena the cost so incurred in building the house according to estimates prepared by the municipal board of works, as well as 2·60 marks per square metre [= 2s. 2d. per square yard] of the land sold by way of recompense for the cost of making the street.

3. A payment of £50 shall be made to the municipal treasury on account of the purchase price of the land, of the cost of building the house, and of the cost of street works prior to the judicial declaration of the sale. The balance shall bear interest at the rate of 3½ per cent., and shall be repaid at the rate of one per cent. per annum. The purchaser may if he chooses make a larger payment on account than £50.

4. As security for the balance of the debt the purchaser shall give to the municipality of Jena a first mortgage on the property to the amount of £350, which shall be entered in the mortgage register.

5. The interest and instalments in repayment of the debt shall be paid in quarterly amounts at the beginning of the quarter, and a debtor in arrear with such payments shall pay one per cent. additional for the preceding quarter, making $4\frac{1}{2}$ per cent. interest instead of $3\frac{1}{2}$ per cent., but delay not exceeding one week following the date for payment shall not be counted so long as payment is made within the said week. In case of illness or other extraordinary circumstances payment may be temporarily postponed by the municipal executive.

6. The purchaser shall receive a debt repayment scale and an account book, from which he will be in a position to ascertain at any time the amount of his debt.

7. The municipality of Jena reserves the right to increase the rate of interest in case it should itself have to pay a higher rate of interest than $3\frac{1}{2}$ per cent. on its loans for the building of workmen's dwellings.

8. As soon as one-half of the total debt for purchase money, costs of building, and costs of street works has been repaid, the municipality of Jena shall be entitled to require the repayment of the remaining moiety within a period of six months on giving notice to that effect. Should the owner of the property be compelled on this account to take a new mortgage to the amount of the remaining debt the municipality of Jena shall permit this to be done on condition of its mortgage being first cancelled.

9. In the event of the debt only amounting to 50 per cent. of the valuation placed on the property by the municipal board of works the debtor may suspend repayments. The municipality of Jena is entitled in this event to increase the rate of interest to the current market rate, to a maximum of 5 per cent.

10. The new building shall be given over to the purchaser when it is entirely completed, and if possible by . . . but no claim for damages shall be made against the municipality of Jena in the event of delay occurring. The transfer shall be delayed until the purchaser has discharged the liabilities incurred by him up to the date of the transfer.

11. All costs incidental to purchase and transfer and all taxes incidental to the sale of real estate shall be paid by the purchaser.

12. The fencing in of the gardens attached to the houses shall be done at the expense of the new proprietors on the order of the municipality.

13. The parti-walls between double (semi-detached) houses shall be owned in common, and neither of the proprietors shall alter the same without the permission of his neighbour and the written consent of the municipal board of works.

14. The owner shall maintain the buildings upon the site in good condition, shall promptly and without objection make all necessary repairs and other works which may be deemed requisite

to the proper upkeep of the same, in accordance with the orders of the municipal government, to whose supervision the owner shall be subject. No important alteration to the building shall be undertaken nor may the building be pulled down without the permission of the municipal executive. The executive shall have the right to have the building inspected on its behalf at any time.

15. The municipality of Jena as the seller shall have a right of repurchase, in accordance with sections 497 of the Civil Code, in respect of the land and building, which right it may exercise :—

(a) after the expiration of one hundred years;
(b) as soon as the debtor or his heirs shall have been in arrear with one of the stipulated payments for a longer period than half a year without such delay having been sanctioned by the municipal executive;
(c) in case and as often as the owner or his legal successors (particularly the heirs) shall desire to sell the property within a period of one hundred years dating from the present. This shall also apply if joint heirs to whom the property has come by inheritance transfer the same either to one or several of their number;
(d) in case the owner of the dwelling-house, in spite of written warning on a single occasion, lets dwellings at rents in excess of the maximum fixed by the municipal executive;
(e) if the owner takes a further mortgage on the property without the consent of the municipal executive;
(f) if the owner fails to inhabit the house himself, in spite of being repeatedly called upon to do so;
(g) if the owner refuses to fulfil the conditions set forth in section 14;
(h) if the owner intentionally or owing to gross negligence damages the house and reduces its value;
(i) if distraint is proposed in respect of the property, or proceedings in bankruptcy are taken in respect of the owner;
(k) in the cases named in 18 and 19 below.

The right of repurchase specified in cases (b) to (k) shall be claimed within six months of the circumstances establishing the right coming to light.

The right of repurchase can be exercised in the cases (d) to (k) within one hundred years of to-day and not only within the period specified in section 503 of the Civil Code.

The purchaser shall apply for the registration of the right of sale in the mortgage register.

16. The sum to be paid in the contingency of repurchase shall be fixed by a valuation committee in such manner that the exact price which was fixed for the land and building at the time of the erection of the house shall be taken as a basis ; but this original

price shall be increased by the amount by which the value of the building has been increased owing to improvements, in so far as this increased value is still in existence at the time of repurchase, while, on the other hand, there shall be deducted the sum by which the value of the property has been decreased by use.

From the sum thus fixed as to be paid at repurchase shall be deducted the amount of the debt still due by the owner to the municipality of Jena, and the balance shall be paid by the municipality in cash at the completion of the transaction.

17. The valuation committee shall be composed of (*a*) an expert to be nominated by the municipal executive ; (*b*) an expert to be nominated by the owner, and (*c*) an arbitrator to be nominated by the supervisory judge of the District Court of Jena, who shall also act as chairman of the committee.

Should the owner nominate no expert within the prescribed time the town council shall be entitled to nominate one in his stead.

The municipal executive shall call upon the owner to appoint an expert for the day fixed for the valuation and to notify to it the appointment, giving the name and address of the expert, by the sixth day before the date fixed for the valuation at the latest. The summons shall contain the warning that in the event of an expert not being nominated or of failure to notify nomination within due time the valuation will nevertheless take place, another expert being nominated by the town council.

The result of the valuation, whether it shall have been effected by the proper committee or without participation by an expert nominated by the owner, and hence with the aid of one appointed by the municipality in his stead, shall be binding both upon the municipality and the owner.

The owner and the municipality of Jena waive the right of legal redress against the valuation and the repurchase sum fixed in accordance therewith, and in particular the right to resort to judicial proceedings, and agree to accept the result of the valuation as binding without protest.

18. The owner of the house shall not take in lodgers except with the sanction of the municipal executive. The keeping of lodgers of any kind in rooms which are not from the beginning intended for habitation is prohibited.

Should the owner without permission take lodgers, or more lodgers than are allowed to him, or should he act in contravention of the last provision of the preceding paragraph, the municipal authority, after prior written warning on one occasion, shall be empowered to make use of its right of repurchase in accordance with the provisions of sections 15 to 17.

19. The use of the whole property, or of any parts thereof, for industrial purposes, whether by the owner himself so using his

property or by his letting the same or parts thereof for industrial purposes to third persons, shall only be permissible with the express sanction of the municipal executive and subject to conditions to be laid down by the same.

The owner shall give an undertaking that neither he nor his legal successors shall carry on in his property an industry or trade with goods of any kind, nor let any portions of the same to third parties for this purpose.

Should the owner be guilty of a breach of this undertaking the municipality shall be entitled to exercise the right of repurchase in accordance with the provisions contained in sections 15 to 17, which shall be extended to the foregoing case.

Should the municipality not make use of this right it is provided that the owner, in the event of failure to observe the conditions relating to the use made of workmen's dwellings set forth in the first paragraph of this section, shall be liable to pay a penalty of £100 to the municipal treasury; but the town council reserves the right to reduce this penalty according to circumstances.

The contractual penalty shall be secured by a bond for £100 in the form of a mortgage on the property ranking after the purchase and building money.

20. If the street and building alignments do not coincide the municipality of Jena reserves a right of repurchase within the meaning of section 497 of the Civil Code in respect of the land lying before the dwelling-house in so far as the municipality may have to re-acquire such land for the purpose of any widening of the street that may be necessary. It is provided that :—

(a) the land shall be repurchased at the price of 1·90 marks per square metre;
(b) in the event of such repurchase the owner shall not be able to require any compensation for any expenditure which he may have incurred in respect of the area so sold, but, on the other hand, he shall be entitled to remove any works which he may have carried out.

21. The municipality shall have the right in the event of the disposal of the property by the debtor or his heirs, either with or without payment, and also in the event of the occurrence of one of the cases (d) to (k) specified in section 15, to require the immediate payment in cash of the debt still due instead of the exercise of the right of repurchase.

22. No buildings shall be placed upon the land sold without the prior sanction of the municipal board of works. The keeping of pigs and cattle is forbidden. In the event of any infraction of the provisions of this section the legal consequences provided in paragraphs 3 and 4 of section 19 shall take effect.

VI.—RULES OF THE MUNICIPAL LEGAL ADVICE OFFICE AT NUREMBERG

(TO CHAPTER XI)

1. THE Legal Advice Office established by the municipality shall be under the supervision of the Magistracy (municipal executive), which shall assign to it a reporter and an administrative committee. The Office shall be directed by a municipal officer appointed by the Magistracy and such assistants shall be allotted to him as may be necessary.

2. The Legal Advice Office shall on request give advice and information on all questions of public and civil law, and in particular questions arising out of Sickness, Accident, Invalidity, and Old Age Insurance, the legislation relating to handicrafts and the protection of labour, the law of association and public meeting, the penal law, and in police, school, military, taxation, poor relief and settlement matters, etc. The Legal Advice Office shall serve simultaneously as a municipal agency for the settlement of private slander disputes.

3. Information shall be given without respect of person and gratuitously. It shall as a rule be given orally, but in exceptional cases it may be given in writing and in workmen's insurance matters documents may be prepared.

4. No information shall be given—

(a) in regard to matters which the applicant has placed in legal hands ;
(b) in cases which relate to breach of morals or which give rise to the suspicion that the applicant desires to evade a legal or moral duty ; and
(c) in matters regarding which complaint has been made against the municipality of Nuremberg or resolutions of the Magistracy.

5. The Legal Advice Office shall be open during the usual official hours.

6. The director of the Office is authorised in suitable cases to attempt a non-judicial mediation between contending parties.

7. An officer of the Legal Advice Office may not undertake to legally represent any party seeking advice.

8. The municipality of Nuremberg assumes liability for the

consequences of legal advice given only within the limits of the existing legal provisions.

9. For the administration of the Legal Advice Office a special committee shall be appointed consisting of the chief mayor of Nuremberg or his deputy, the reporter of the Magistracy, four members each of the Magistracy and the town council (one member of the Magistracy being nominated as warden), and the director of the Office.

VII.—MUNICIPAL THEATRE REGULATIONS OF HALLE
(THE SUBSIDY SYSTEM)
(TO CHAPTER XII)

THE municipal theatre of Halle was built at a cost of £62,500, and has hitherto been leased to an actor-manager for £1750. The amount of the yearly subsidy, chiefly in the form of a reduced rent and of the performance of certain services (e.g., supply of light, power, and water, etc.) has been about £5000. The latest agreement with the lessee converts the rent into a nominal payment, fixes the subsidy at £3000, and gives the municipality a share in the profits. The conditions of the lease are as follows :—

1. The municipality of Halle leases to the director . . . (*a*) the theatre and store-rooms (with the exception of certain portions of the building and seats reserved for the Theatre Committee), and (*b*) the stage properties, consisting of wardrobe, with weapons and armour, decorations, stage furniture and requisites, and the theatre and concert library.

2. The municipality undertakes, at its own cost, responsibility for the maintenance of the building, the maintenance and increase of the stage properties, on which it shall incur expenditure to a maximum amount of £750 yearly, the electric lighting and all lights, and the supply of current to a maximum amount of 50,000 kilowatt-hours yearly free of cost ; the lessee paying for all current beyond that amount at the rate of 3d. per kilowatt-hour, for the emergency lights, fire brigade service at all performances, heating and ventilation, the supply of water, and the supply of the steam necessary for stage effects.

3. The municipality provides at its own cost the following *personnel* : the inspector of stage properties, the master mechanic, the book-keeper, the stage mechanic, three assistant mechanics, one fitter, and one boiler tenter, and five charwomen. The lessee shall provide the rest of the *personnel* at his own cost.

The employees, with the exception of the book-keeper, shall comply with the orders of the lessee in accordance with service rules issued by the municipal executive. In the event of disputes between them and the lessee the Theatre Committee shall decide. It shall be the duty of the book-keeper to audit all books and accounts, and the lessee shall place before him all the documents necessary for this purpose.

The lessee undertakes to exercise due supervision (or to co-operate in supervision) over the above-named employees in the theatre during performances and at other times on the request of the Theatre Committee.

The lessee shall refund the costs incurred by the municipality by reason of special work, night work, and holiday work done by the municipal employees during performances and rehearsals.

4. The lessee shall pay a yearly rent of £5 on the first day of October. The municipality shall pay the lessee for every year of the contract a subsidy of £3000. The lessee shall pay to the municipality one-half of the net profit beyond £750 which he realises in each year of the contract, the municipal subsidy being reckoned to such profit, but of all net profit in excess of £1250 he shall pay to the municipality two-thirds. One-half of the subsidy shall be paid on October 1, and the rest at the close of the theatre season, but payments on account may be made at the discretion of the municipal executive. The lessee shall not be entitled to set up counter-claims against claims made by the municipality.

5. The lessee acknowledges that all the rooms and properties leased to him have been handed over in good condition. He shall properly and carefully use them, shall prevent damage to and the wrongful use of them, and shall take the measures necessary to prevent their being injured by cold, sun, dust, moths, damp, etc., being responsible alike for his own negligence and that of his *personnel*. Losses and damages for which he may be found to be responsible shall be made good at his cost. Within 14 days after the expiration of every theatre season the Theatre Committee shall inspect the rooms and properties, the lessee being invited to be present, and a written report shall be made upon the defects for which the lessee or his *personnel* may be found to be responsible. Before new properties are acquired or repairs executed as a consequence, the Theatre Committee shall notify the lessee, stating the approximate cost, but the lessee shall not be entitled to object to the cost.

No liability shall be incurred by the lessee in respect of the proper use of any objects covered by the lease. The lessee shall be entitled to compensation for repairs made by himself only in the event of the same having been promised by the municipal executive in writing.

6. The auditorium may only be occupied according to the division of seats prescribed by the lessors. The approaches to the seats may not be occupied by chairs or be used as standing space.

7. The lessee shall not undertake the management of another theatre, give performances elsewhere than in the municipal theatre, or be concerned in any way in other undertakings or performances of the kind, nor lend any properties leased to him, without the written consent of the municipal executive.

8. The theatre season shall last each year from September 1 to May 15. During the period May 16 to August 31 the municipality shall have free disposal of the properties leased, and in particular may execute structural alterations, repairs, and enlargements at its discretion, but the lessee shall not thereby be inconvenienced in his preparations and rehearsals during the 14 days preceding the opening of the theatre season.

The lessee shall give a performance on each evening during the theatre season unless the same is prohibited by legal or police regulations ; and he shall be entitled to give performances on the afternoons of Sundays and festivals. He may not, however, give performances on weekday afternoons or Sunday mornings except with the written sanction of the municipal executive and on payment to the municipality of £3 15s. for each such performance.

The lessee shall not give or allow other people to give performances of any kind in the municipal theatre out of the season except with the written consent of the municipal executive.

Should the lessee omit to give a performance on any evening on which he is liable so to do, without the express acquiescence of the municipal executive, he shall pay a fine of £15.

9. The chief mayor, a member of the executive, a member of the Theatre Committee, the fire brigade superintendent, a delegate of the building police department, and such special representatives as the municipal authority may depute have the right to inspect all rooms of the theatre at all times, even during performances and rehearsals. The members of the Theatre Committee have the same right except during performances.

10. The lessee is required (*a*) to take steps to preserve order and to maintain good behaviour in the theatre; (*b*) to prohibit persons whose presence is not needed for the carrying on and the supervision of the theatre—particularly relatives of employees—from remaining on the stage, the stage galleries, or within the wings and the dressing-rooms; (*c*) to keep the iron door between the auditorium and the stage room closed during performances and intervals, and (*d*) to adopt all possible precautions against fire and to insure himself against personal liability and accidents. The receipts for premiums shall be produced for the inspection of the Theatre Committee.

11. The lessee shall not cede any rights under this agreement without the written permission of the municipal executive.

12. The lessee shall before the commencement of every season, and as early as possible, place before the Theatre Committee a list of the new and newly studied works which it is proposed to present, and shall further send in semi-monthly lists (a week in advance) of the pieces to be performed, with the pieces held in reserve, and also every Friday the programme for the following week. In the case of first performances and all performances of special importance the Theatre Committee shall have a preferential right to buy such seats as they desire. On being requested in writing the lessee shall attend meetings of the Theatre Committee and give such information as may be required.

13. In the month of June the lessee shall hand in to the municipal executive his complete budget for the coming year (September 1 to August 31). Each month he shall present a return, with vouchers, of all receipts and expenditure, and a register of subscribers or a list of alterations to the same. He shall further lay before the Theatre Committee, as soon as possible, and at the latest a fortnight before the commencement of the season, a list of the entire theatre *personnel*, with actual names and professional names, salaries, and addresses. This list shall be correctly kept at all times.

The lessee shall keep an account in proper business form of all receipts and expenditure. The municipal executive, the Theatre Committee, and the agents of the same shall have the right to inspect the lessee's books and vouchers at all times, and the lessee shall give all required information. No charges shall be allowed on account of the personal activity of the lessee and members of his family, as in the nature of salary for management. The lessee and the members of his family shall not appear on the stage of the municipal theatre, nor the lessee on any other stage, without the written consent of the municipal executive. Benefit performances are not allowed.

14. The lessee shall engage an efficient force of dramatic and operatic talent, including ballet and orchestra. Unless otherwise prescribed in this agreement, engagements shall be concluded for the period September 1 to May 15, and in the case of the opera *personnel* from September 1 to April 30.

The lessee shall insert in the engagement contracts the following provision: " The municipality of Halle reserves the right to take the place of the director . . . in the engagement contract should the agreement of lease between the municipality and the director . . . for any reason terminate before the expiration of such contract. The municipality shall then within a week state whether it wishes to make use of its right, and in default of such statement the right lapses. This right of the municipality is independent of the question whether the municipality decides to carry on the theatre itself or to transfer it to another lessee."

The lessee shall supply to the Theatre Committee copies of all contracts concluded with the theatre *personnel* immediately after the conclusion of the same. In the case of leading artists it shall be stated at which theatres they have been engaged during recent years, and during the last preceding season.

15. The salary account for the drama and opera *personnel* (inclusive of chorus and ballet) and the two opera orchestra directors shall amount to at least £1125 a month during the season and shall be so divided that about £325 a month shall be paid on account of dramas, £475 on account of operas, and £325 on account of choruses and ballet. Double honoraria, remuneration for overtime, for supernumeraries, chorus school, extra chorus, office, technical staff, visiting artists (" stars "), etc., may not be included in these estimates. The minimum monthly salary for men and women (including chorus) shall be £6, and in the case of the ballet £5. Rehearsals required before the season shall be paid for at the rate of half a day's salary for each day of rehearsal.

The men's and women's choruses shall each consist of at least 20 members engaged for the year, sustenance fees of £3 a month being paid for the summer months when the theatre is closed.

16. [Relates to historical costumes supplied to *personnel*.]

17. The orchestra shall consist of at least a conductor and 52 instrumentalists, all engaged by the year. The lessee undertakes to pay the members of the orchestra minimum monthly salaries on the following scale—[The rates range from £15, paid to the conductor, downwards to £7 5s.]

18. The lessee may not use the orchestra outside the municipal theatre except with the written permission of the municipal executive. The Theatre Committee reserves the right to determine at any time the maximum amount of service that may be required of individual instrumentalists. The lessee is required to give the members of the orchestra a summer holiday of at least two weeks without deduction of salary.

19. The lessee shall give at least four popular concerts yearly with the full orchestra, the charge of admission being 2½d. with programme. The times and places of these concerts shall be sanctioned by the municipal executive.

20. The lessee shall during each theatre season give at least twelve popular performances at approximately equal intervals. The Theatre Committee may fix the days for these performances at the commencement of the season, and choose pieces for presentation out of the dramas, operas, and operettas to be given during the season. Every popular performance, with the name of the piece, shall be publicly announced by the lessee at least a week beforehand.

21. During the season at least 232 subscription performances shall be given. Subscription shall be for the entire season, and the conditions shall receive the written sanction of the municipal executive.

22. The box prices shall be as follows:—[Operas and operettas, 4s. 10d. to 6d.; all other performances, 3s. 6d. to 5d.; subscription prices, 2s. 6d. to 1s.; popular performances, 7d. to 2½d.]

23 and 24. [Relate to the obligation of the lessee to pay taxes in respect of the theatre, to adopt precautions in the interest of public safety, and to deposit security.]

25. On the expiration of the agreement the lessee shall deliver the properties leased in good condition, and shall replace all missing articles, in so far as their disappearance is not attributable to normal usage.

26. Should the lessee die before the expiration of the agreement, his heirs shall, on the demand of the municipal executive, carry out the agreement to the close of the current season, but the municipal executive reserves the right to terminate the agreement without notice.

VIII.—MUNICIPAL REFORM PROGRAMMES

(TO CHAPTER XVIII)

IF the party of Social Democracy be disregarded, German municipal parties are not, as a rule, divided greatly by their programmes, and almost the only questions upon which acute political feeling can be said to exist are the questions of land taxation and the privileged position secured to the property owners on the town councils. Of various programmes of municipal policy in circulation possibly the one which has behind it the weightiest body of considered opinion is that put forward by the German Progressive People's Party (now the German People's Party) and it is reproduced below :—

1. SELF-GOVERNMENT. — The realisation of free self-government is one of the fundamental demands of the democracy. The right of the communes to self-government must be developed and be legally protected by independent administrative courts against attacks and tutelage by the State authorities. The supervisory rights of the State must be legally defined, circumscribed, and graded according to the size and character of the communes. The right of the communal assemblies, whether acting individually or in combination (as, for example, in municipal congresses) publicly to assert their opinions in relation to all questions affecting their interests shall not be curtailed.

2. REPRESENTATION.—The representatives of the communes and the executive bodies shall be elected by universal, equal, direct, and secret franchise for definite periods on the principle of proportional representation. All privileges based on ownership of property shall be repealed. The right of the State to confirm representatives and officers of the commune shall be abolished. So long as the question of women's suffrage has not been settled by legislation the communes shall have the right to elect women in a deliberative capacity as members of administrative committees, as, for example, the committees dealing with poor relief, education, and family care. The proceedings of the communal bodies shall in general be public and the cases in which publicity may be withheld shall be legally specified.

3. TAXATION.—The revenue necessary for the communal budget shall in the main be derived from " real " taxes (i.e., taxes on real

estate and commercial undertakings), taxes on income and interest on capital, and probate duties. The income tax shall be progressive, the smallest incomes being exempted and small incomes taxed only at low rates. The land tax shall be assessed not on the yield but on the sale value of the property, abatements being made in favour of small proprietors who derive their livelihood from the use of their property. Together with this tax there shall be levied taxes on the sale and transfer of property, a tax being levied on the purchase price and in addition upon any unearned increment realised by the sale of the property. Excise duties on necessary articles of food, fuel, and building materials may not be introduced even within the limits which Imperial legislation may in future allow, and where they exist an attempt shall be made to secure their repeal.

4. TRADING ENTERPRISES.—Economic enterprises of a monopolist character, such as tramways, suburban railways, gasworks, electricity works, water supply, refuse removal, and abattoirs, shall systematically be carried on by the commune. The management of such works, even when carried on with a view to profit and to the relief of local taxation, shall not be determined by purely fiscal considerations, but the public interests which the undertakings are intended to serve shall be considered.

5. EDUCATION.—The communes shall take an active part, together with the State, in the work of popular education. The uncertain relationships between State and commune in this domain shall be clearly defined. The primary schools shall be organised as common schools for all classes; special preparatory schools for the higher schools shall not be supported out of the communal funds. The church shall not have a right to co-operate in conjunction with the State in public education, and in any case the principles of the inter-confessional school and of secular instruction shall be applied throughout the entire educational system. In no case may compulsion to attend religious instruction be applied. State supervision shall be exercised by teachers trained for the purpose. The maximum number of scholars in the various classes shall be fixed with due regard to considerations of health. Special classes shall be provided for defective children. Instruction in household management shall be given to girls. Obligatory continuation schools, with an adequate period of instruction, without Sunday and evening instruction, shall be provided for boys and girls. For scholars employed in industries, trade, and agriculture, continuation schools offering special training shall be provided. The State shall make contributions towards the support of the primary schools and particularly the continuation schools. School fees shall not be charged, and school materials shall be supplied free. The larger communes shall appoint school doctors, and the smaller

communes shall make provision for the periodical examination of the health of scholars. The communes shall also promote popular education by establishing or supporting public libraries, reading rooms, and lectures, and by making all educational institutions, and particularly the theatres, as accessible as possible to the masses of the people.

6. POOR RELIEF.—The care of orphans and the poor must be based on individual treatment; as far as possible the bodies necessary for this purpose shall be honorary, the co-operation of women being sought. Attention shall be given to the care of foster-children, and if necessary institutions for their reception shall be established.

7. LABOUR POLICY.—The communes shall co-operate in the amelioration of the condition of the wage-earning classes, particularly by the establishment of labour boards, labour registries, managed jointly by employers and employed, and the promotion of unemployment insurance. In the giving of public contracts care shall be taken that the contractors maintain the wages rates and other conditions of labour usual in their trades. Where these are regulated by wages agreements between workmen and employers public works and other contracts shall only be given to employers who agree to observe the said agreements; should such contracts contain a "strike" clause it shall only provide for an extension of time provided the contractor accepts the arbitration of the Industrial Court in its capacity as a Board of Conciliation, and this Court decides in his favour, or in the event of the workpeople refusing to carry the dispute to the said Industrial Court in its capacity as a Board of Conciliation.

The communal undertakings shall be carried on as model institutions, particularly in regard to the following matters: The conditions of employment shall be laid down in general works regulations, workpeople's committees shall be set up, wages shall increase with the duration of service, the right to pensions shall be conceded, provision shall be made for widows and orphans, and holidays shall be granted without deduction of wages. An unconditional right of coalition shall be given to communal workpeople.

8. ENCOURAGEMENT OF TRADE AND INDUSTRY.—The economic life of the communes shall be promoted by attracting vigorous industries by the offer of special inducements (e.g., the offer of suitable land at low prices, and abatements of taxes or other charges); by the provision of motive power, special regard being paid to the needs of the small traders; by the establishment and support of measures for the improvement of technical instruction; by the regulation of contract arrangements, with a view to preventing, as far as possible, arbitrary proceedings in the giving of public

works and favouritism towards individuals, and, on the other hand, to cutting out all underbidding arising from business ignorance, thoughtlessness, dishonesty, or the exploitation of employees and apprentices, and conversely to the encouragement of honourable and efficient trading ; and by the giving out of works of minor consequence according to rota. In rural communes, land improvements, particularly in the way of reclamation, drainage, and irrigation works, shall be supported.

9. HOUSING QUESTION.—Housing boards shall be established, whose duty it shall be to inspect dwellings and carry on house registries in the interest of healthy and cheap housing. Suitable regulations shall be issued to prevent the building of unhealthy dwellings. Building enterprise shall be promoted, particularly as regards small dwellings, in so far as a social need exists, by the support of public utility building societies and by the leasing of town land in suitable cases. The communes shall be given a right of expropriation with a view to the opening up of eligible building land. Municipal estate shall be preserved, and additions shall be made to it where this can be done without increasing the price of land generally.

10. PUBLIC HEALTH.—Due concern for the public health and the proper feeding of the population requires the adoption of the following measures: Adequate water supply and drainage with very moderate fees in respect of the same, proper street sanitation, the taking over of refuse removal by the larger communes, the provision for recreation grounds and gymnasiums, bathing establishments, public parks, shelters, and food depots, an efficient control of articles of food, the establishment and working by the communes of markets and abattoirs, the promotion of cheap food supplies, the combating of monopolies and rings in food, systematic inspection of dwellings, the promotion of cheap nursing for the sick and for women in child-birth independently of the Poor Law, the establishment or support of free cribs and homes for children, free maternity help, the establishment in the larger towns of milk depots for the supply of good milk for infants, the appointment of school doctors, the provision or support of holiday colonies for sick children, the establishment of municipal pharmacies in the larger towns, and the free disinfection of dwellings in the case of infectious diseases. The entire burial system shall be taken over by the communal authority. No fees shall be charged for mortuaries or interments. Crematoria shall be established by the communes.

INDEX

Abattoirs, public, 218, 243, 244.
Absolute government, era of, 6–14.
Adickes, Chief Mayor of Frankfort-on-Main (quoted), 127, 153, 387.
Administrative powers of municipal authorities, 31–57, 81–122, 442–448.
Administrative areas, municipal, 156–160.
Administrative Court, Prussian Supreme, 36, 41, 48.
Administrative staffs, 113, 114.
Advertising German towns, 35.
Agrarian reforms of Stein and Hardenberg, 15.
Aldermen or magistrates, 20, 22, 81–97, 438–442.
Alignment Law of 1875, Prussian, 45, 146–148, 151.
Amusement taxes, local, 413–415.
Apprentices, training of, 310, 322.
Architecture, public, 311, 312.
Art galleries, 312.
Art and science, public expenditure on, 313.
Assets of German and British municipalities, 359–361.
Autonomy in taxation, 43, 362–366, 449.
Autonomy of towns in Middle Ages, 2–6.

Balance sheets of German and British municipalities, 358–361.
Barthold (quoted), 3 (note), 10 (note).
Baths, public, 201, 202.
Berlin, government of, 10–13, 117–119, 131, 145, 160, 466.

Betterment contributions, 148–150, 400, 401, 473–475.
Bill-posting pillars, municipal, 253, 254.
Boldt, Dr. W. (quoted), 390.
Borrowing powers, municipal, 345–355, 456.
Brand and Stein, 18.
Budget, municipal, 85, 342–345, 456.
Building laws and regulations, 45, 142–155, 164.
Building societies, encouragement of, 176–180.
Buildings, local taxes on, 42, 43, 148–150, 386–402, 426–428.
Bureaucratic influence in local government, 50–57, 440–442, 452–457.
Burgess fees, 62, 63.
Burgesses and burghers, the earlier, 20, 60; in modern times, 61–64.
By-law powers, 38, 39, 443.

Cemeteries, municipal, 205, 206.
Chief Presidents of provinces, 51, 93, 119, 121, 364, 365, 461–466.
Child-care movement and centres, 292–296.
Church taxes, local, 417, 418.
Circles and circle government, 119–122, 364, 463–466.
Clauswitz, Dr. (quoted), 18.
Commissions and Committees, municipal, 107–113.
Common Law, Prussian, 12, 44, 153.
Comparison of German local taxes and British local rates, 428–434.
Composition of town councils, 112, 438.

INDEX

Concession system in regard to public utility enterprises, 212, 213; electric light, 226; tramways, 234–237; licensed premises, 411, 412.
Consumption. See Tuberculosis.
Consumption taxes, local, 409–413.
Continuation schools, 322–324.
Convalescent homes, 299, 300.
Co-ordination of charities, 273.
Correlation and proceeds of local taxes, 419–433.
Cost of police administration, 47; of poor relief, 276, 277; of obtaining by-laws, 39; of obtaining Local Acts of Parliament in England, 39 (note), 443.
Credit facilities, municipal, 356–358.
Crefeld Municipal Land Fund, 471, 472.
Crematoria, 53, 206, 207.

Dahlmann, F. C. (quoted), 14.
Deputations, municipal, 107–109.
Disfigurement, protecting the streets against, 153, 154.
Dispensaries for infants, 195, 287, 288; for consumptives, 296–298; for dipsomaniacs, 280.
Disqualification from membership of town councils, 61; of executives, 91.
District Committee, 39, 46, 51, 93, 99, 119–122, 364, 365, 463–466.
District (Government) President, 46, 51, 93, 99, 119–121, 463, 464, 466.
District superintendents (*Bezirksvorsteher*), 112.
Docks and quays, 240–242.
Drainage, 198–201.
Drama, municipal support of the, 328–336.
Düsseldorf, town planning scheme, 144; Municipal Land Fund, 468–470.

Educational movements, working-class, 315.
Education, administration and cost of, 37, 48, 49, 316–328.

Elberfeld poor relief system and its variations, 265–273.
Elections to town councils, 73–76.
Elector, the Great, 8, 10 (note).
Electric light and power works, 226–229.
Emperor Henry I., the " town builder," 2, 18.
England, Stein and, 17, 19, 20, 435.
Essen, housing policy of, 136, 137.
Executive, municipal, 20–22, 26; functions and power, 94–97, 104–107, 440–442.
Expropriation, powers of, 150–153, 169, 476–483; Empire, 150; Saxony, 150, 481; Baden, 150, 478–480; Prussia, 150–152; Bavaria, 150, 476, 477; Hamburg, 151, 477, 483; Frankfort-on-Main, 152, 482.

Families, influence of patrician, 5, 6.
Federations of cities and towns in early times, 4, 5; in modern times, 115, 116.
Finance, municipal, 85, 337–361.
Food supply, municipal enterprise in, 245–247.
Foods and drinks, regulation of, 197, 198, 244.
Forest in municipal ownership, 130–132.
Franchise, municipal, 20, 21, 24, 25, 59–70; disqualifications, 70.
Frankfort-on-Main, power to pool building sites at, 152, 153, 482, 483.
Free cities, 5.
Freemanship fees, 62, 63.
Frederick I. of Prussia, 9; Frederick William I., 9–11; Frederick II., 9; Frederick William III., 15–18; Frederick William IV., 11 (note).
Freiburg, housing policy of, 174, 175.
French municipal system, 13, 20–23.
French Revolution, 13, 20, 21, (1830) 23, (1848) 25.
Freund, Government Councillor (quoted), 170.

INDEX

Frey, Police Director, and Stein, 12, 18, 19.
Freytag, Gustav (quoted), 8.

Gas supply, 224–226.
Geusen, Herr (quoted), 171.
Government Districts and Presidents, 46, 51, 93, 99, 119–121, 463, 464, 466.
Government, scope of local, 31–57.
Guardianship of illegitimate children, municipal, 290–292.
Guilds, influence of trade and handicraft, 5, 6, 20, 25.

Halle municipal theatre regulations, 491–495.
Handicraft guilds, influence of, 5, 6.
Hanseatic League, 5.
Hardenberg, 15, 16.
Health administration, public, 189–207.
Honorary service in local government, 111–113.
Hospital system, public, 193–195.
House speculation, 165–167.
House-owners, privilege of, 21, 25, 54, 71–73, 167, 428.
Housing and Town Planning Act of 1909, 445, 446.
Housing question in the towns, 161–188.
Housing schemes, municipal, 137–142, 161–188.
Humboldt, Wilhelm von, 24.

Illegitimate children, mortality amongst, 290; municipal guardianship of, 290–292.
Income taxes, local, 376–385, 419–434.
Incorporation movement and procedure, 35, 157–160.
Increased value taxation. See Unearned increment taxation.
Indirect (consumption) taxes, local, 409–413.
Industry, furtherance of, 134, 135, 241–243.

Infant mortality, crusade against, 286–289.
Infectious disease, measures against, 196, 197.
Insurance, assisted unemployment, 303–305.
Insurance enterprises, municipal, 252, 253.
Intellectual life, provision for, 311–336.
Isolation hospitals, 196.

Jena, battle of, 12, 15.
Jena, regulations for municipal house building and selling at, 484–488.
Joachim I., Elector, 9.
Joint Administrative Boards, 116–119.
July Revolution of 1830, 23.
Juvenile care movement, 292–296.

Kant, 18.
Kappelmann, H. (quoted), 37, 159 (note).
Königsberg by-law relative to betterment contributions, 473, 474.

Laboratories, municipal, 198.
Labour houses for the workshy, 275, 276.
Labour registries, 301–303.
Landmann, Dr. (quoted), 168.
Land-purchase policy, municipal, 123–140, 241, 445, 468–472.
Landrat, 46, 120, 463–466.
Land speculation, 140, 146, 147, 165–167, 397.
Land taxation, 42, 43, 148–150, 386–402, 426–428, 473–475.
" Large " towns, 20, 31.
Leagues of towns in Middle Ages, 4, 5.
Legal advice agencies, 307, 308, 489, 490.
Liabilities of municipalities, 349–352 ; German and British compared, 359–361.
Libraries and reading-rooms, 314, 315.

INDEX

Licensed premises, taxes on, 412.
Lindemann, Dr. H. (quoted), 54 (note).
Loans, municipal, 345–355, 456; for trading enterprises (German and British), 352.
Local administration, principles of, 31–57; organisation of, 58–113, 461–467.
Local Government Act of 1894, 27, 442.
Local Government Boards, British, 34, 35, 124, 262 (note), 443–448, 452–457.
Local taxation, 37, 42, 43, 362–434, 448–452.
Lodging-houses for single men, 300, 301.
Luneville, Peace of, 14 (note).

Magisterial and mayoral systems of executive compared, 104–107.
Magistracy and magistrates (aldermen), 20, 22, 81–97, 438–442.
Mannheim, municipal development policy of, 134–136, 142, 241; housing policy, 177, 178.
Markets and market halls, 244.
Marriage dowries for working-girls, 310.
Maternity insurance, 288, 289.
Mayor, position and powers, 98–107, 440.
Meat supply, inspection of, 197; municipal enterprise, 246.
" Medium " towns, 20, 31.
Middle Ages, municipal government in, 1–6.
Milk supply, inspection of, 198.
Mortality rate, general, 189; infant, 266, 289; illegitimate infant, 290.
Mortgage and rent-charge banks, 250–252.
Most, Dr. O. (quoted), 29 (note), 170.
Munich Municipal Land Committee, 470, 471.
Municipal Corporations Acts, 27, 435, 436 (note), 447 (note).
Municipal estate, extent of, 123–140.

Municipal executive, 20–22, 26, 82, 86–97, 104–107, 440–442.
Municipal finance, 85, 337–361.
Municipal government in the Middle Ages, 1–6; under the absolutistic system, 6–12; at the beginning of the nineteenth century, 12–23; under Stein's Ordinance, 17–26; at the present day, 29–122 and *passim;* in Prussia, 13–27, 31–58, 61–122, 369; in Bavaria, 23, 25, 27, 42, 48, 58, 61–64, 73–75, 86, 87, 91, 93, 98, 104, 369, 375, 382, 383, 392, 394, 408–411, 413–416; in Württemberg, 23, 25, 27, 58, 61–64, 74, 87, 92, 98, 376, 382, 383, 394, 400, 408–410; in Saxony, 25, 27, 48, 58, 62, 64, 67, 68, 71, 73, 74, 92, 98, 369, 375, 376, 382, 392, 394, 408, 409, 414–416; in Baden, 27, 58, 61, 62, 73, 85, 88, 92, 394, 409, 413; in Alsace-Lorraine, 58, 62, 64, 73–75, 86, 384, 410, 411.
Municipal hospitals, 193–195.
Municipal land boards and funds, 133, 468–472.
Municipal leagues and congresses, 115, 116.
Municipal Ordinance of 1808, Stein's, 1, 13–23, 44; revisions of, 23–26.
Municipal taxation, 37, 42, 43, 85, 362–434, 448–452, 473–475.
Municipal theatres, 328–336, 491–495.
Municipal trading enterprises, 208–259. See " Trading enterprises."
Municipal workpeople, 256–259.
Music, municipal support of, 328–336.

Napoleon I., 2, 12–14, 17, 23.
Newspapers, municipal, 110.
Nuremberg, regulations of the municipal legal advice office at, 489, 490.
Nurses, public, 287, 297.

Octroi dues, 409–411.

INDEX

Officials, 113-115.
Orphans, care of, 269, 272.
Out-relief, 270, 271.

Parks, public, 202-205.
Pawnshops, municipal, 308, 309.
Pension management for officials, 21, 103, 104.
Pharmacies, municipal, 253.
Planning of towns, 141-160, 445-447, 476-483.
Playgrounds for children, 204, 205.
Police powers reserved by the State, 22, 43-48, 437.
Politics in town councils, prohibition of, 41.
Poll taxes, 416.
Pooling of properties for the purpose of town planning, 152, 153, 478-483.
Poor-law systems compared, German and English, 34, 261, 278.
Poor man's lawyer, municipal, 307, 308, 489, 490.
Poor relief, administration of, 34, 37, 122, 260-278.
Population, ratio of municipal estate to, 125, 126; ratio of administrative areas to, 156, 157.
Potsdam by-law relative to betterment contributions, 474, 475.
Powers of municipal authorities, administrative, 29-57, 81-122, 442-448.
Preuss, Dr. H. (quoted), 2, 4, 11, 93 (note), 163, 437 (note).
Privilege of officials in relation to taxation, 379, 380.
Profits from municipal estate, 132, 133; from trading enterprises, 217-224.
Programme, municipal reform, 496-499.
Property owners, privilege of, 21, 25, 54, 71-73, 167, 428.
Property (real) taxation, 42, 43, 148-150, 386-402, 426-428, 473-475; property transfer taxation, 392-394.

Provincial Government, Diet, Council, 119-121, 364, 462-466.
Prussia, municipal government in, 13-27, 31-57, 58, 61-122, 369-434.
Prussian Common Law, 12, 44, 153.
Public health administration, 189-207.
Public health authorities, Imperial, State, and municipal, 190-193.
Public works, execution of, *régie* versus contract, 254-256.

Rating system, British, 367-369, 415, 432, 448-452.
Real estate, local taxation of, 42, 43, 148-150, 386-402, 426-428; land and building taxes, 387-392; tax on sale of property, 392-394; unearned increment tax, 394-399; "betterment" taxation, 148-150, 400, 401, 473-475.
Recreation grounds, public, 202-205.
Reform movements, modern, 436-438, 496-499.
Refuse removal, 200, 201.
Relief works for the unemployed, 305-307.
Rent taxes, 369, 415, 416.
Revenue from communal estate, 132-134.
Rönne, L. von (quoted), 10 (note), 14.

Salaries of mayors, 103.
Sanitation (public). See Health.
Savings banks, 247-250.
Scavenging, 200.
School dentists and dental clinics, 294, 295.
School doctors and school hygiene, 34, 40, 293, 294.
School for housewifery, 310.
Schools for communal government, 115, 155.
Schools, primary, 316-320, 326-328; higher, 321, 322; continuation, 322-324; technical, 324.
Schön, Theodor, 17, 22.
Seeley, J. R. (quoted), 10 (note), 13, 435 (note).

INDEX

Services in kind, 373.
Sewerage, 197–201.
Shelters for the homeless, 301.
Site value taxation. See Land taxation.
Slaughter-houses, public, 218, 243, 244.
Small houses, reaction in favour of, 169–172.
" Small " towns, 20, 30.
Social welfare work, municipal, 279–310.
State influence in local government, 7–12, 22, 24, 43–55, 50–56, 452–457.
Statistical Offices, municipal, 110.
Status of towns, 29–31.
Stein, Baron von, 1, 2, 13–26, 29, 82, 435, 436.
Stein's Municipal Ordinance, 1, 15–26, 29, 44, 436.
Stores, local tax on, 408, 409.
Streets, protection against disfigurement of, 153, 154.
Stübben, Dr. (quoted), 161, 170 (note).
Supervision of local authorities, State, 50–56, 452–457, 465.
Swabian League, 4.
Swimming baths, public, 201, 202.

Taxation, municipal, 37, 42, 43, 362–434, 448–452; real estate taxes, 42, 43, 148–150, 386–402, 426–428, 437–475; income taxes, 376–385, 419–434; trade taxes, 403–409; department stores taxes, 408, 409; amusement taxes, 413–415; licensed premises, 412; indirect (consumption) taxes, 374, 409–415; church taxes, 417, 418; poll taxes, 416; rent taxes, 369, 415, 416; dog taxes, 416.
Technical schools, 322–324.
Theatre, municipal support of the, 328–336, 491–495.
Thirty Years' War, 5, 7, 8.
Three-class system of voting, 26, 64–70.

Tilsit, Peace of, 15, 16.
Town councils, first institution, 4; constitution, 20, 24, 25, 58–80; powers and duties, 81–86; Labour representation, 70, 76–80; composition, 112.
Town halls, 110, 111.
Town planning, 141–160, 445–447, 476–483; legislation — Prussia, 151, 152; Bavaria, 150, 476, 477; Baden, 150, 478–480; Saxony, 150, 481–483; Hamburg, 477, 483; Frankfort-on-Main, 152, 153, 482; Würtemberg, 483.
Trade and handicraft guilds, influence of, 5, 6, 20, 25.
Trade and industry, furtherance of, 242, 243.
Towns, rise in Middle Ages, 2–5; decay in era of absolutism, 6–12; influence of Thirty Years' War, 7, 8; federations and leagues, 4, 5.
Trade taxes, local, 403–409.
Trading enterprises, municipal—the old German tradition, 208–210; the modern revival, 210–212; concessions and royalties, 212, 213; scope, 213–217; revenue and profits, 217–224; gas supply, 224–226; electric light and power works, 226–229; water supply, 229–232; tramways and transport, 232–240; docks and quays, 240–242; furtherance of trade and industry, 242, 243; public abattoirs, market halls, and food supply, 243–247; municipal savings banks, 248–250; mortgage and rent-charge banks, 250–252; insurance enterprises, 252, 253; miscellaneous trading enterprises, 253, 254; execution of public works, régie versus contract, 254–256; municipal workpeople, conditions of employment, 256–259.
Tramways and transport, 232–240.
Treitschke (quoted), 14 (note).

INDEX

Tuberculosis, measures against, 197, 296–299.

Ulm, housing policy of, 175, 176.
Unearned increment taxation, 43, 364, 365, 394–399.
Unemployment, measures against, 274, 275, 303–307.

Vienna, Congress of, 23.
Vogt, Professor (quoted), 171.

Water supply, 229–232.
Wolff, Dr. H. (quoted), 166.
Women in local government, 113, 268, 269.
Working classes, taxation of, 381–384.
Working-men on town councils, 70, 76–80.
Workpeople, municipal, conditions of employment, 256–259.

Titles in This Series

Edwin Hodder, ed. **Cities of the World: Their Origin, Progress, and Present Aspect, Vol. IV: Great Britain and Ireland.** London, 1889.

Robert Vaughan. **The Age of Great Cities: or, Modern Society Viewed in Its Relation to Intelligence, Morals, and Religion.** London, 1843.

Thomas Archer. **The Pauper, the Thief, and the Convict; Sketches of Some of Their Homes, Haunts, and Habits.** London, 1865.

Walter Besant. **London in the Nineteenth Century.** London, 1909.

John Garwood. **The Million-Peopled City: or One Half the People of London Made Known to the Other Half.** London, 1853.

James Grant. **The Great Metropolis.** London, 1837.

James Greenwood. **The Wilds of London.** London, 1874.

John Hollingshead. **Ragged London in 1861.** London, 1861.

James Cantlie. **Degeneration Amongst Londoners.** London, 1885.
bound with J. Milner Fothergill. **The Town Dweller: His Needs and Wants.** London, 1889
bound with John Edward Morgan. **The Danger of Deterioration of Race from the Too Rapid Increase of Great Cities.** London, 1866.

Hector Gavin. **Unhealthiness of London and the Necessity of Remedial Measures.** London, 1847.
bound with Gavin Hector. **The Habitations of the Industrial Classes: Their Influence on the Physical and on the Social and Moral Condition of These Classes: Showing the Necessity for Legislative Enactments.** London, 1851.

John Hogg. **London as It Is; Being a Series of Observations on the Health, Habits, and Amusements of the People.** London, 1837.

George Godwin. **London Shadows; A Glance at the "Homes" of the Thousands.** London, 1854.

James Hole. **The Homes of the Working Classes, with Suggestions for Their Improvement.** London, 1866.

S. D. Adshead and Patrick Abercrombie, eds. **Liverpool Town Planning and Housing Exhibition. Transactions of the Conference, March 9–13, 1914.** Liverpool, 1914.

James Budgett Meakin. **Model Factories and Villages: Ideal Conditions of Labour and Housing.** London, 1905.

Robert Pemberton. **The Happy Colony.** London, 1854.
bound with Benjamin Ward Richardson. **Hygeia: A City of Health.** London, 1876.

C. B. Purdom. **The Garden City: A Study in the Development of a Modern Town.** London, 1913.

Robert Williams. **London Rookeries and Colliers Slums: A Plea for More Breathing Room.** London, 1883.

Helen Dendy Bosanquet. **Social Conditions in Provincial Towns.** London, 1912.

John M. Knapp. **The Universities and the Social Problem: An Account of the University Settlements in East London.** London, 1895.

John Shaw. **Travels in England: A Ramble with the City and Town Missionaries.** London, 1861.

Hugh Shimmin. **Liverpool Life: Its Pleasures, Practices, and Pastimes. First Series.** Liverpool, 1857.
bound with Hugh Shimmin. **The Courts and Alleys of Liverpool, Described from Personal Inspection.** London, 1864.

Robert Slaney. **Reports of the House of Commons on the Education (1838) and on the Health (1840) of the Poorer Classes in Large Towns, with Some Suggestions for their Improvement.** London, 1840.
bound with Robert A. Slaney. **A Plea to Power and Parliament for the Working Class.** London, 1847.

Arnold White. **The Problems of a Great City.** London, 1886.

William Harbutt Dawson. **Municipal Life and Government in Germany.** London, 1914.

Frederick Dolman. **Municipalities at Work: The Municipal Policy of Six Great Towns and Its Influence on Their Social Welfare.** London, 1895.

J. H. Muirhead, ed. **Birmingham Institutions: Lectures Given at the University.** Birmingham, 1911.

Glasgow City Corporation. **Municipal Glasgow: Its Evolution and Enterprises.** Glasgow, 1914.

J. R. Somers Vine. **English Municipal Institutions; Their Growth and Development from 1835 to 1879, Statistically Illustrated.** London, 1879.